101 859 092 7

ONE WEEK LOAN

D1422516

This is an exciting and innovative exploration of the Victorians' attitudes towards sight. Tantalised by physiologists who proved the unre-
liability of the eye, intrigued by the role of subjectivity within vision,
and provoked by new technologies of spectatorship, the Victorians
were also imaginatively stirred by the sense of a world which lay just
out of human sight. This ground-breaking, interdisciplinary study
draws on writers as diverse as George Eliot, Elizabeth Barrett
Browning and Rudyard Kipling as well as Pre-Raphaelite and realist
painters, and a host of Victorian scientists, cultural commentators
and art critics. Its topics include blindness, the location of memory,
hallucination, dust and the importance of the horizon – a dazzlingly
eclectic range of subjects linked together by the operations of the eye
and brain. This richly illustrated work of cultural history will make us
look freshly at how Victorians saw and interpreted their world.

KATE FLINT is Reader in Victorian and Modern English Literature at
the University of Oxford and fellow of Linacre College, Oxford. She is
author of *Dickens* (1986), *The Woman Reader 1837–1914* (1993) and editor
of *Impressionists in England: The Critical Reception* (1984). She has published numerous articles on Victorian and twentieth-century fiction,
painting and cultural history and contributes regularly to pro-
grammes on BBC Radio 3 and 4.

Henry Garland, *Looking for the Mail Packet*, 1861. Oil on canvas, 52 × 41.9 cms.

The Victorians and the
Visual Imagination

Kate Flint

CAMBRIDGE
UNIVERSITY PRESS

PUBLISHED BY THE PRESS SYNDICATE OF THE UNIVERSITY OF CAMBRIDGE
The Pitt Building, Trumpington Street, Cambridge, United Kingdom

CAMBRIDGE UNIVERSITY PRESS
The Edinburgh Building, Cambridge CB2 2RU, UK
40 West 20th Street, New York, NY 10011-4211, USA
477 Williamstown Road, Port Melbourne, VIC 3207, Australia
Ruiz de Alarcón 13, 28014 Madrid, Spain
Dock House, The Waterfront, Cape Town 8001, South Africa
http://www.cambridge.org

First published 2000
Reprinted 2002

Printed in the United Kingdom at the University Press, Cambridge

Typeface Monotype Dante 11.5/15 pt.   *System* QuarkXPress™   [SE]

A catalogue record for this book is available from the British Library

Library of Congress Cataloguing in Publication data
Flint, Kate.
The Victorians and the visual imagination / Kate Flint.
    p.   cm.
Includes bibliographical references and index.
ISBN 0 521 77026 2
1. Visual perception.   2. Art, Victorian – Psychological aspects.   3. Aesthetics,
British – History – 19th century.   I. Title.
N6767.F58   2000
701'.15'094109034–dc21   99-042110

ISBN 0 521 77026 2 hardback

TO NIGEL

Contents

Illustrations

Preface

Henry Garland's *Looking for the Mail Packet* (1861: frontispiece) dramatises different ways of looking. The central male figure peers out towards the horizon with his telescope, a symbol of the Victorian delight in technologies of vision. But his companions do not follow his line of sight. The woman on the right raises her eyes towards him, her expression a combination of affection and inquisitiveness. On the left, a younger woman – the couple's daughter? – looks down at a dog with a letter in its mouth. This network of gazes within the main group is made into an enclosing circle by the warily hostile glares that the two dogs exchange. But the circle is challenged by a further observer: the man who sits on the rocks behind the young woman's right shoulder. Is he, too, waiting for the mail? Or, rather, is he, via the letter-bearing dog, the sender of this missive (thus adding a punning resonance to the word 'mail'), his communication avoiding the amplified eye of paternal authority? Is he, too, an artist? For this picture is not just about looking, and deciphering, but about depicting. A paintbox and brushes lie at the foot of a painter's stool in the left foreground. Although we do not see the work in progress, we can guess, from the fact that it is the girl's oriental shawl that is draped over the stool, and from the small, tidy box of watercolours, that they belong to her. What she has produced, however, is invisible: it is left to our imaginations to call it into being.

To describe Garland's painting in this way is not to wander too far from conventional Victorian modes of reading pictures, translating visual language into narrative form. A Victorian critic might have produced some suitably homiletic comments about family values, or imposed a glib moral about the nature of hopefulness, or speculated about what was going to happen next. However, he or she probably would not have paid too much attention to the canvas's margins, and to that slippery, intriguing borderline between the seen and the unseen – that which lies out of sight on the horizon, the disruption that may be introduced by the almost-obscure male figure. Nor, despite the widespread Victorian fascination with the act of seeing, the workings of that imperfect instrument, the eye, and the power of seeing in the mind's eye – or imagining – would this hypothetical critic have been likely to comment on the activity of looking itself. This, one might say, was the blind spot of Victorian writing about art. It is, however, placed at the very centre of this book.

The Victorians and the Visual Imagination has been a long time in its gestation and writing. It has its origins in my D.Phil. thesis, on 'The English Critical Reaction to Contemporary Painting, 1878–1910', and ghostly remnants of this thesis linger on in a couple of the chapters. My warm thanks are due to Christopher Butler, my main supervisor; to Alan Bowness, who first suggested that I write on late nineteenth-century art criticism; and to Francis Haskell and Bernard Richards, for the work that they, too, put into its supervision. From this thesis work grew my interest not just in the function played by art criticism in the nineteenth century, but in its intersection with the Victorian interest in that which was not readily visible to the eye – and, indeed, in the eye itself. Very early versions of some of the chapters which follow – sometimes in considerably different form – can be found in the *Journal of Victorian Culture* (chapter 3); *Nineteenth-Century Literature* (chapter 4); *Textus* (chapter 5); *After the Pre-Raphaelites*, ed. Elizabeth Prettejohn (chapter 9); '*Lost Worlds & Mad Elephants*'. *Literature, Science and Technology 1700–1990*, ed. Elmar Schenkel and Stefan Welz (chapter 10); and the *Australasian Victorian Studies Journal* (conclusion). I am extremely grateful to the editors concerned for letting me re-use and re-work my material. I owe a good deal, too, to all of those people who have invited me to speak on various occasions, invariably providing audiences whose questions and knowledge have stimulated me and helped the progress of this book enormously. A special thank-you for this, and for much more besides, to David Amigoni, Karen Armstrong, John Bowen, Maria Teresa Chialant, Helen Groth, Ellen Harding, Margaret Harris, Juliet John, Sally Ledger, Judy McKenzie, Tim Morton, Sarah Nuttall, Elizabeth Prettejohn, Elinor Schaffer, Elmar Schenckel, Sally Shuttleworth, Helen Small and Tiffany Urwin.

The Humanities Research Centre of the Australian National University were generous enough to give me a Visiting Fellowship, which allowed me to write and revise a considerable portion of this book in surroundings which were simultaneously restful and stimulating. I would like to thank everyone there who made my stay such a happy and profitable one. I would like to thank, too, the staff of the following libraries and institutions for their assistance: the Bodleian Library, the British Library (especially the Newspaper Division at Colindale), the English Faculty Library of Oxford University, Cambridge University Library, the London Library, the Witt Library, and the Library of the Courtauld Institute of Art, the National Library of Australia and the libraries of the Australian National University and the University of New South Wales. I am very grateful to the News International Fund of the University of Oxford for financial assistance in reproducing the pictures in this volume. The personnel in the English Faculty Office of the University of Oxford have been unfailingly helpful and patient: Sarah Barker, Jenny Houlsby and Jackie Scott-Mandeville.

Other friends, colleagues and students have helped in all kinds of ways, in allowing me to discuss my ideas with them, in providing conversational spaces in which I've hesitatingly outlined my arguments, in providing me with examples and suggestions, and in expanding my own intellectual and visual horizons. This book could not have been written without the input, stimulus and friendship of Bill Ashcroft, Matthew Beaumont, Gillian Beer, Lucy Bending, Sarah Bilston, Dinah Birch, Rachel Bowlby, Jo Griffiths, Louise Hudd, the late Don McKenzie, Martin Meisel, Francis O'Gorman, Sally Powell, Julia Reid, Nick Shrimpton, Michael Slater, Matthew Sweet, Katie-Louise Thomas, Jenny Uglow,

Tilly Warnock, Hertha Wong and Mark Wormald. Steven Connor was an invaluable reader of the final drafts, and helped me find the courage to give the book its final shape. Josie Dixon has been an exemplary editor and friend, knowing exactly when to be patient, and exactly when to apply pressure: her trust and encouragement have been crucial to my writing. Linda Bree has admirably over-seen the final phase of production. John House has known this book well in its various mutations, and has continually and profitably made me think about visuality and language: I am grateful for his support in very many ways. Clare Pettitt has been the best of friends both to this book and to me, knowing exactly when my wails about its lack of progress would benefit more from the Bodleian or from a margarita.

I would like to thank my parents, Joy and Ray Flint, for their love and affirmation, and for first introducing me – before I can even properly remember – to the pleasures and challenges of Victorian visual culture. Finally, my deepest debt is to Nigel Smith, who has lived with this book for as long as I have. His energy, intellectual incisiveness and enthusiasm have continually inspired me, and this book is dedicated to him.

CHAPTER I

The visible and the unseen

In 1849, Henry Mayhew set out to inquire into the conditions of the labouring population of London. As part of his investigation of specialist trades, he visited a dolls'-eye maker. This manufacturer told Mayhew about those factors which determined whether trade was slack or busy, and then revealed:

> 'I also make human eyes. These are two cases; in the one I have black and hazel, and in the other blue and grey.' [Here the man took the lids off a couple of boxes, about as big as binnacles, that stood on the table: they each contained 190 different eyes, and so like nature, that the effect produced upon a person unaccustomed to the sight was most peculiar, and far from pleasant. The whole of the 380 optics all seemed to be staring directly at the spectator, and occasioned a feeling somewhat similar to the bewilderment one experiences on suddenly becoming an object of general notice; as if the eyes, indeed, of a whole lecture-room were crammed into a few square inches, and all turned full upon you. The eyes of the whole world, as we say, literally appeared to be fixed upon one, and it was almost impossible at first to look at them without instinctively averting the head. The hundred eyes of Argus were positively insignificant in comparison to the 380 belonging to the human eye-maker.][1]

This book is about eyes, and about sight. The Victorians were fascinated with the act of seeing, with the question of the reliability – or otherwise – of the human eye, and with the problems of interpreting what they saw. These problems extended from the observation

I

of the natural world and the urban environment, to the more specialist interpretation demanded by actual works of art. In each case, the act of seeing was something performed by individuals, each with their particular subjectivities, and their own ocular physiology. Simultaneously, what was seen was necessarily selected, stressed, described and filtered through many cultural conventions. The interplay between these differing factors was increasingly recognised and explored as the century went on. Victorian commentators on the visual, however, were concerned with matters which went beyond the dialogue of subjectivity and the social. For the topic becomes yet more complicated and controversial when one recognises the tension that existed between the different valuations given to outward and inward seeing; to observation, on the one hand, and the life of the imagination on the other. Seeing in the mind's eye was linked to scrutinising the world around one, but it was not an identical process. The slipperiness of the borderline between the visible and the invisible, and the questions which it throws up about subjectivity, perception and point of view, lie at the heart of this study.

Mayhew's uncomfortable experience can be read as a near-hallucinatory realisation on his part of the power of the specular within mid-Victorian society. This society was characterised not just by the accelerated expansion of diverse opportunities for differing sorts of spectatorship, but by a growing concern with the very practice of looking, and with the problematisation of that crucial instrument, the human eye. Mayhew's own contributions to the *Morning Chronicle*, brought together in volume form as *London Labour and the London Poor*, are testimony to the value of the observing eye in assembling a thick description of the urban life of the metropolis, however much his nose, his ears and his statistic-recording pencil were also at work. Such collection of detail, in different forms, crowds the painting and fiction of the period, establishing a materiality, a circumstantiality which in turn becomes imbricated with interpretive resonances for both contemporary and subsequent commentators who acknowledge the degree to which the representation of objects entails the encoding of values.

This preoccupation with the visible, recordable world on the part of many Victorians has been continually remarked upon in recent years. 'The second half of the nineteenth century lives in a sort of frenzy of the visible', wrote Jean-Louis Comolli, basing his assertion on 'the social multiplication of images'. He specifically had in mind the access to visual information which the invention and growth of the illustrated press and photography brought with them, providing information about one's own nation and culture, and, more particularly, about the unfamiliar. The period witnessed, as he put it, 'something of a geographical extension of the field of the visible and the representable: by journies, explorations, colonisations, the whole world becomes visible at the same time that it becomes appropriable'.[2] David Spurr, too, writing about the part the gaze comes to play in colonial discourse generally, pertinently reminds one that 'The gaze is never innocent or pure, never free of mediation by motives which may be judged noble or otherwise. The writer's eye is always in some sense colonizing the landscape, mastering and portioning, fixing zones and poles, arranging and deepening the scene as the object of desire.'[3] Whilst Comolli and Spurr both suggest the hegemonic power of Western scopic techniques in capturing and representing other cultures, a power which may also be turned on one's more immediate society, the same mechanical apparatuses can be remarked on as affecting domestic understandings of selfhood.[4] Mayhew, again, visits a photographer's studio, and the tradesman claims that it is quite possible to palm off customers with portraits of sitters other than themselves: 'The fact is, people don't know their own faces. Half of 'em have never looked in a glass half a dozen times in their life, and directly they see a pair of eyes and a nose, they fancy they are their own.'[5] Even if Mayhew, just possibly, was also being duped by this photographer, who, judging by his testimony, took pride in his role as a trickster preying upon the credulous, the claim conveys the novelty which could be involved in obtaining visual knowledge, of fixing and objectifying an image of the self.

The dissemination of images, whether photographic or engraved, was made possible by the development of the press and the diminishing costs of newsprint and printing technologies.[6] Such periodicals as the *Illustrated London News* (founded 1841) and the *Graphic* (founded 1869) relied as much, if not more, on images as on words in their representation of the world: they had numerous imitators, some successful, some short-lived, such as the *Pictorial Times*, the *Illustrated Times*, *Pen and Pencil*, the *Penny Illustrated Paper* and *Quiver*.[7] The editor of the *Strand* magazine (founded 1891) insisted on a picture on every page. *Punch* (founded 1841) provided a running commentary on Victorian social trends and political issues through its combination of cartoons and captions.[8] In both periodical and volume form, fiction's appeal to the imagination could find itself circumscribed or supplemented by the provision of illustrations: illustrations which – most notably in the case of Thackeray and Dickens – could provide an interpretive gloss on the written word.[9] Knowledge could also be acquired through other forms of visual display: from such crowd-pulling phenomena as the Exhibitions which celebrated the commerce and art of particular nations;[10] through panoramas, in which the spectator perambulated in front of a huge image, and dioramas, when the representation of landscapes or events moved in front of the audience; to displays of racial types which mingled anthropological curiosity with elements of the freak show, and the countless human 'curiosities' displayed by showmen.[11] More permanent display of material artifacts was provided by the increasing quantities of museums in the capital and in the provinces, particularly after the 1845 Museums Act, and the Museums and Libraries Act of 1850, allowed local boroughs to allocate a proportion of the rates for the establishment of such public amenities. The Royal Academy Summer Exhibition (founded 1769) – the 'great annual commercial advertisement of all the art of the day'[12] – sustained its domination over the London art scene throughout the nineteenth century, joined by the growing number of art exhibitions which were mounted both in this city and in other metropolitan centres. The Old Water-Colour Society had been holding exhibitions since 1804; the British Institution put on shows between 1806 and 1867; the Society of British Artists was founded in 1824. Notably pioneering both in the art it promoted and in exhibition staging was the Grosvenor Gallery (1877–90), its relatively avant-garde mantle passing to the New Gallery in 1888.[13] Responses to all these shows, and to paintings exhibited in private salerooms and venues, combined with the proliferation of the press itself to see the establishment in turn of certain dominant modes of writing about art, translating the visual into the verbal for the non-specialist spectator.[14]

Other optical inventions brought the excitement of looking differently into the domestic environment itself: the magic lantern, the kaleidoscope, the stereoscope, the pseudoscope, the zoetrope. As Isobel Armstrong has eloquently put it, such gadgets meant 'a sensory experience without a sensory, tactile image, an image that was more spectral the more reproducible it became, so that the gazing subject played a risky game with materiality and phantasmagoria . . . Possibly the intense allure of these gadgets was their capacity to suggest experiments with different subject positions, control, displacement, obliteration, power, centrality, powerlessness.'[15] These instruments, together with the marvels of visual scale produced by the telescope and the increasingly domesticated microscope, served to challenge, at the level of popular perception, the quality of observations made by the unaided human eye. Outside the home, distinctions between the public and the domestic were collapsed by the burgeoning amount of imagery which advertised and boosted consumer culture – on hoardings, in the press, in the form of window displays and spectacular promotions. Mass production used visual means to circulate ideals, to stimulate desire. 'Spectacle and capitalism', to quote Thomas Richards, 'became indivisible'.[16] The co-presence of iconography and letterpress in advertisement form turned the streets quite literally into environments to be read, a practice carried mimetically into paintings of modern life and thence turned to interpretive ends. Thus in the third painting in Augustus Egg's triptych *Past and Present* (1858), the woman huddled under the Adelphi arches by the side of the Thames is given an ironic chorus of posters on the wall behind her (figure 1). A playbill turns emotions into entertainment ('Victims'; 'A Cure for Love'); an advertisement for 'Pleasure Excursions to Paris' in this context suggests the short-sightedness of hedonism, or at the very least the lures of the world which have led this woman to adultery, disgrace and – given that she is now sitting in a notorious suicide haunt – presumably death.[17] In Luke Fildes's painting of a queue waiting to enter the workhouse, *Applicants for Admission to a Casual Ward* (1874), a sharp commentary on the social evaluation of the homeless poor is given by the backdrop of advertisements,

1 Augustus Leopold Egg, 'August the 4th. Have just heard that B— — has been dead
more than a fortnight, so his poor children have now lost both parents. I hear she was seen
on Friday last near the Strand, evidently without a place to lay her head. What a fall hers
has been!' (known as Past and Present), no. 3, 1858. Oil on canvas, 63.5×76.2 cms.

where £2 reward is offered for a missing child, £20 for a missing dog,
£50 for a murderer and £100 for a runaway (figure 2).

Tracing this undeniable 'culte des images'[18] across a range of
contexts is not enough in itself, however, to establish the visual as
the dominant mode of the Victorian period. More recent methodological approaches have been crucial here. The publication of
Michel Foucault's *Discipline and Punish* in 1975 famously drew
attention to the power of the gaze within Victorian social formations. Foucault postulated the notion of the 'carceral archipelago',
a network of supervisory surveillance that derives its model from
the Benthamite panoptic scheme of a prison where the occupants

2 Luke Fildes,
*Applicants for
Admission to a Casual
Ward*, 1874. Oil on
canvas,
142.24×247.65 cms.

would be visible, in their lighted cells, from a central tower. He uses the language of staged formalised display to describe how this system reverses the principle of the prison, where the inmate is enclosed, hidden in darkness:

> By the effect of backlighting, one can observe from the tower, standing out precisely against the light, the small captive shadows in the cells of the periphery. They are like so many cages, so many small theatres, in which each actor is alone, perfectly individualised and constantly visible. The panoptic mechanism arranges spatial unities that make it possible to see constantly and to recognise immediately . . . Visibility is a trap.[19]

This 'axial visibility', Foucault goes on to argue, may in fact be traced through 'all the disciplinary mechanisms that function throughout society'. If the Panopticon induces in the inmate 'a state of conscious and permanent visibility that assures the automatic functioning of power', this same anxiety of observation permeates the 'panoptic society' of the nineteenth century.[20]

Foucault's theories have proved to be enormously influential with interpreters of Victorian culture since the mid-1980s, many of whom have followed his line that to make something visible is to gain not just understanding of it, but control over it. This process has been repeatedly located within Victorian practices themselves – practices both material and linguistic – with their presumed drive towards exposure, towards bringing things to the surface, towards making things available to the eye and hence ready for interpretation. The drive to exposure in a literal sense conjoins with the visual bias within Western culture so eloquently described by Martin Jay in *Downcast Eyes*, where he describes how our language is infused with visual metaphors, the visual manifesting its dominance not merely in terms of perceptual experience, but also as a cultural trope. Victorian ways of seeing, in broad terms, were both modelled upon, and effectively legitimated by, certain dominant strands within contemporary science, especially the work of physiologists, and of natural scientists, whose work with the microscope in particular provided an endless source of comments filtering into popular culture about how the invisible could be brought to view, and how knowledge and control over the natural world could thus be obtained.

Other technologies permitted new positions of spectatorship which afforded an overview, an altered mode of vision. 'The railroad', to quote Dolf Sternberger, transformed the world 'into a panorama that could be experienced . . . it turned the travelers' eyes outward and offered them the opulent nourishment of ever changing images that were the only possible thing that could be experienced during the journey'.[21] This quantitative increase of visual stimuli could, however, be figured as exhausting, through the physical and mental strain it allegedly adduced. The Report of the Commission into the influence of railway travelling on public health (1862) commented anxiously on the bodily effects of this new mode of looking:

> The rapidity and variety of the impressions necessarily fatigue both the eye and the brain. The constantly varying distance at which the objects are placed involves an incessant shifting of the adaptive apparatus by which they are focused upon the retina; and the mental effort by which the brain takes cognizance of them is scarcely less productive of cerebral wear because it is unconscious.[22]

Whilst the themes of almost all Dante Gabriel Rossetti's painted canvases are marked by nostalgia, archaism or the mystical, 'A Trip to Paris and Belgium' – based on his travels on the continent with Holman Hunt in 1850 – dramatises the visual disruption of modern railway travel, the 'floating at our eyes', that is the product of 'Strong extreme speed, that the brain hurries with'. The passengers move between brick walls, 'passed so at once / That for the suddenness I cannot know / Or what, or where begun, or where at end'. 'The country swims with motion', he writes, as he records shifting effects of sky and light as he journeys through the landscapes of poplar trees, the countryside slanted with sunlight and shadows, that the Impressionists were to explore in their paintings: 'Time itself / Is consciously beside us, and perceived.'[23]

Moving skyward, the balloon allowed its passengers to shift their perspective on the urban scene in the most literal of terms.[24] Henry Mayhew and John Binny's *The Criminal Prisons of London* (1862) introduces their survey of actual forms of incarceration with a sustained commentary on how 'it is an exquisite treat to all minds to find that they have the power, by their mere vision, of extending their consciousness to scenes and objects that are miles away', with the intellect experiencing 'a special delight in being able to comprehend all the minute particulars of a subject under one associate whole', bringing, for example, 'the intricate network of the many thoroughfares . . . into the compass of one large web'. Such a viewpoint may be achieved from the balloon's basket. Yet aerial flight can change perspective still further. At first, in language which has become clichéd through descriptions of subsequent air travel, each object is distinct: houses looking 'like the tiny wooden things out of a child's box of toys', barges like summer insects, factory chimneys like pins.[25] Then, however, the description shifts the locus of perspective from the visible to the metaphysical, hence emphasising what will become one of the concerns underpinning my own study, the constant slippage from concern with viewing the material world to inner forms of vision. The chapter draws heavily on an account written by Mayhew of the ascent he made in the last flight of the famous balloon

'Nassau', in which the transition from outer to inward perception
is even more sharply delineated:

> I had seen the world of London below the surface, as it were, and
> I had a craving to contemplate it far above it – to behold the
> immense mass of vice and avarice and cunning, of noble aspira-
> tions and humble heroism, blent into one black spot; to take, as it
> were, an angel's view of that huge city where, perhaps, there is
> more virtue and more iniquity, more wealth and more want
> huddled together in one vast heap than in any other part of the
> earth; to look down upon the strange, incongruous clump of
> palaces and workhouses, of factory chimneys and church stee-
> ples, of banks and prisons, of docks and hospitals, of parks and
> squares, of courts and alleys – to look down upon these as the
> birds of the air look down upon them, and see the whole dwindle
> into a heap of rubbish on the green sward, a human ant-hill, as it
> were; to hear the hubbub of the restless sea of life below, and hear
> it like the ocean in a shell, whispering to you of the incessant
> strugglings and chafings of the distant tide – to swing in the air far
> above all the petty jealousies and heart-burnings, and small ambi-
> tions and vain parades, and feel for once tranquil as a babe in a cot
> – that you were hardly of the earth earthy; and to find, as you
> drank in the pure thin air above you, the blood dancing and tin-
> gling joyously through your veins, and your whole spirit becom-
> ing etherealised as, Jacob-like, you mounted the aërial ladder, and
> beheld the world beneath you fade and fade from your sight like a
> mirage in the desert; to feel yourself really, as you had ideally in
> your dreams, floating through the endless realms of space, sailing
> among the stars free as 'the lark at heaven's gate'; and to enjoy for
> a brief half-hour at least a foretaste of that elysian destiny which is
> the hope of all.[26]

Specific panoptic awareness may readily be located across a
range of writing. In Charlotte Brontë's *Villette* (1853), a novel dominated by images and actions of scrutiny and surveillance, M. Paul
takes a room in one of the college boarding-houses, 'nominally for
a study – virtually for a post of observation', from which he looks
down and inspects 'female human nature' as displayed in the *pen-*

sionnat garden.[27] Famously, in Dickens's *Bleak House* (1853) the detective Bucket 'mounts a high tower in his mind' to survey, in his imagination, the haunts of social outcasts in order to try and locate Lady Dedlock: a power displaced in this novel from individual human agency to the superior vantage point available to the mobile narrative voice.[28] It is logical, therefore, that when looking at urban topographies in Dickens, Jonathan Arac can conjoin Foucauldian method with Dickens's own desire, in chapter 47 of *Dombey and Son*, for 'a good spirit who would take the house-tops off' and expose the social and moral corruption within contemporary London;[29] something which is partially enacted when Dombey's railway journey enables him to see into the 'wretched rooms . . . where want and fever hide themselves in many wretched shapes' in those slums through which the railway has sliced, letting 'the light of day in on these things'.[30] Dickens's commitment to the concept of a literal overview had already been signalled by Cruikshank's incorporation of a rising balloon in the frontispiece to *Sketches by Boz* (figure 3). This desire for disclosure is recapitulated in Conan Doyle's 'A Case of Identity' (1891), when Sherlock Holmes observes to Watson:

> 'If we could fly out of that window hand in hand, hover over this great city, gently remove the roofs, and peep in at the queer things which are going on, the strange coincidences, the plannings, the cross-purposes, the wonderful chains of events, working through generations, and leading to the most *outré* results, it would make all fiction with its conventionalities and foreseen conclusions most stale and unprofitable'.[31]

When this story was first published in the *Strand*, incidentally, it was immediately followed by an article entitled 'London from Aloft', not merely describing a balloon flight over the capital, but illustrating it with pictures taken by a Kodak camera.[32]

Moving indoors, D. A. Miller has extended the concepts of unseen but all-seeing surveillance, working in the service of what Foucault calls 'a regime of the norm' and combining with 'various technologies of the self and its sexuality', from their functioning in a publicly administered arena to 'the private and domestic sphere

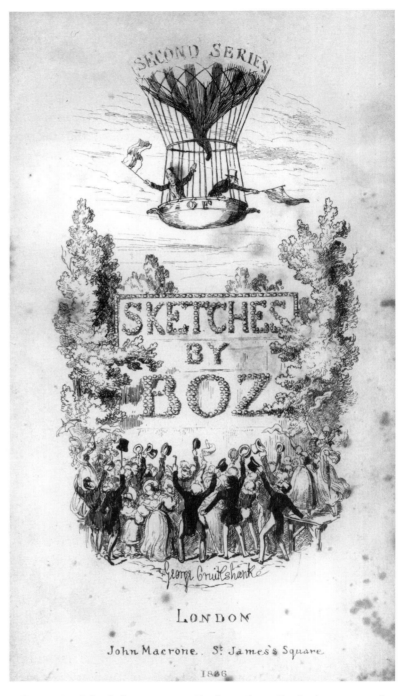

3 George Cruikshank, frontispiece to Charles Dickens, *Sketches by Boz*, second series, 1836.

on which the very identity of the liberal subject depends'.[33] At a less metaphorical level, Anthea Trodd writes how 'In mid-Victorian fictions of domestic crime we see a world of spying servants, conspiring wives, intrusive policemen, in which the home is threatened from within and without, and the irreconcilable claims of the private and public spheres exposed.'[34]

Disciplinary surveillance is not the only aspect of Foucault's fascination with the visible to be built upon. Jeremy Tambling, for example, has drawn not just on *Discipline and Punish*, but on *The Birth of the Clinic* (1963), and in particular on the passage Foucault quotes from Bichat's *Anatomie générale* advising the making visible of that which lies below the human surface: 'Open up a few corpses: you will dissipate at once the darkness that observation alone could not dissipate.'[35] Tambling relates this imagery of illumination both to George Eliot's interest in Bichat himself, as evidenced in chapter 15 of *Middlemarch*, and to the more general imagery that we encounter in this novel. This is a novel permeated, as a number of critics have noted, with optical imagery,[36] imagery which is employed to suggest the importance of throwing light on social anatomy – piercing 'the obscurity of those minute processes which prepare human misery and joy',[37] as one of the phrases which links novelist and physician puts it – moving from an exploration of the body to wider concerns; a thematics of imagery which, as in Holmes's phrase, connects concept with the formal organisation of fiction.

A Foucauldian reading of the nineteenth century emphasises the fact that practices of surveillance, of bringing material to the surface, worked in collaboration with practices of codification and classification. In turn, this was linked to a broader aesthetic drive: what Mark Seltzer has termed the 'realist imperative of making everything, including aesthetic states, visible, legible, and governable'.[38] Many of these classificatory procedures are well known, from the growth in statistical societies to the establishment of the British Museum Catalogue; from cartography to the work of natural historians; from graphology manuals to dictionaries of plants and of dreams. Almost inevitably, the determinants of classification were dependent, to at least some extent, on the recognition of something's, or someone's, material existence or properties, which were subsequently ordered according to certain schemata. Symptomatically, in terms of recent studies of such enterprises, Thomas Richards remarks in *The Imperial Archive: Knowledge and the Fantasy of Empire* (1993): 'The ordering of the world and its knowledges into a unified field was located explicitly in the register of representation.'[39] Numerous recent critics of the Victorian period suggest that if we can understand the laws and associations that governed systems of representation during this period, and the symbolic resonances that are at stake, we can, to all intents and purposes, 'read' the Victorians. Peter Brooks, in *Body Work. Objects of Desire in Modern Narrative* (1993), writes of the 'semioticization' of the body during the nineteenth century:

> Representing the body in modern narrative – . . . seems always to involve viewing the body. The dominant nineteenth-century tradition, that of realism, insistently makes the visual the master relation to the world, for the very premise of realism is that one cannot understand human beings outside the context of the things that surround them, and knowing these things is a matter of viewing them, detailing them, and describing the concrete milieux in which men and women enact their destinies.[40]

Brooks's foregrounding of the body is crucial, because it points us to the central site for debates concerning the relationship between inner and outer, between assumptions concerning surface and essence on the one hand, and the misleading guidance which exteriors can offer about interiority on the other.

The idea was widespread, in the mid-century, that different social types, and different types of character, were physiognomically distinguishable. Not only faces in their entirety offered themselves up to be read, but facial expressions (pathognomy), lines on the forehead (metoposcopy), lines on the hand (chiromancy and chirognomy), and moles (neomancy) were all available for deciphering. This assumption that the appearance of bodies revealed the truth about the person who inhabited it was not confined to ideas concerning individual personality traits. Notoriously, after the mid-century, it became an increasingly consolidated article of faith that racial characteristics were irrevocably inscribed through the measurable size and shape of the human body.[41]

'Nature', asserted Dickens in an article, 'never writes a bad hand. Her writing, as it may be read in the human countenance, is invariably legible, if we come at all trained to the reading of it.'[42] Eliza Lynn, in her 1855 *Household Words* article 'Passing Faces', said that one might expect to discover not just the individual secrets of those we encounter through looking at their physiognomies, but 'their social condition and their histories, stamped on them as legibly as arms are painted on a carriage-panel';[43] Mary Cowling, in *The Artist as Anthropologist* (1989), has valuably shown quite how readily both artists and anthropologists, following in the wake of such physiologists as F. G. Gall, seized on external appearance, particularly the faces of those in modern urban crowds, as providing a quick indication of the character of an individual. This pleasure is linked to a form of understanding and control – however illusory – derived from the belief that it is possible, through observation, to gain knowledge of the mass, to turn faceless anonymity into individuality and hence render it less disturbing and threatening. In turn, Cowling argues, the widespread acceptance of physiognomy as a method of human interpretation, and the notion of the anthropological type, 'help us to understand the kind of interest and pleasure which Victorian modern life art offered'.[44] Such interpretation rested on the assumptions articulated by Lavater in his *Essays on Physiognomy*, first published in Leipzig in 1774–8 and unceasingly in demand until around 1870: 'is not all nature physiognomy; superficies, and contents; body, and spirit; exterior effect, and internal power; invisible beginning, and visible ending?'[45] As Hippolyte Taine observed in his *History of English Literature* (1863): 'When you consider with your eyes the visible man, what do you look for? The man invisible.'[46]

Yet it would be wrong to assume an absolute acceptance by mid-Victorians of these populist tenets. Notwithstanding Dickens's compulsive fascination with personal appearance, it is notable that in *Hard Times* (1854), a novel which protests against classification as a means of dealing with individuals, he rebels, too, against the language of physiognomy. He describes the mill-hand, Stephen Blackpool, thus: 'A rather stooping man, with a knitted brow, a pondering expression of face, and a hard-looking head sufficiently capacious, on which his iron-grey hair lay long and thin, Old Stephen might have passed for a particularly intelligent man in his condition. Yet he was not.'[47] More provocatively, George Eliot pointedly shows us in *Adam Bede* (1859) that appearance may be a less sure guide to character than *assumptions* about appearance are a reflection of the mind and the desires of the perceiver. In turn, this is metonymic of the way in which even Eliot's earliest fiction manifests, as Catherine Gallagher puts it, 'a deep skepticism about the legibility of facts, the apprehendable significance of appearances'.[48] The narrator warningly describes Adam's wishful responses to Hetty's prettiness:

> Every man under such circumstances is conscious of being a great physiognomist. Nature, he knows, has a language of her own, which she uses with strict veracity, and he considers himself an adept in the language. Nature has written out his bride's character for him in those exquisite lines of cheek and lip and chin, in those eyelids delicate as petals, in those long lashes curled like the stamen of a flower, in the dark liquid depths of those wonderful eyes. How she will dote on her children!

We are admonished, however, after what proves a proleptic piece of irony: 'I believe the wisest of us must be beguiled in this way sometimes, and must think both better and worse of people than they deserve. Nature has her language, and she is not unveracious, but we don't know all the intricacies of her syntax just yet, and in a hasty reading we may happen to extract the very opposite of her real meaning.'[49] Later, in *Daniel Deronda* (1876), a novel much more insistently concerned with the problematics of looking, Eliot explicitly extends the untrustworthy principle of the physiognomic scrutiny of faces to more generalised acts of interpretation: 'often the grand meanings of faces as well as of written words may lie chiefly in the impressions of those who look on them'.[50] Outside fiction, others record how their own misreadings served to unsettle their confidence in physiognomy. The art student Anna Mary Howitt, who went to study in Munich in 1853, recounts her experience of the deceptiveness of appearance. On one occasion, she and some fellow students went on an outing to a model penitentiary. Their guide drew their express attention to a group of four women clustered round a washtub, and asked what they could deduce about these inmates from their looks:

> 'Three out of the four', we remarked, 'are the only agreeable faces we have seen in the prison; and, judging from this momentary glance at their countenances, we should say could not be guilty of much crime; perhaps the fat old woman may be so; that tall young girl, however, is not only handsome, but gentle-looking.'
>
> 'That tall young girl', replied our guide, 'was the one who, a year or two ago, murdered her fellow-servant, and cutting up the body, buried it in the garden; the little woman next to her, some two years since, murdered her husband; and the handsome, kind, motherly-looking woman who stood next, destroyed her child of seven years old. The fat old woman is in only for a slight offence. So much for judgment by physiognomy!'
>
> ... As I returned home, all the faces I met in the streets seemed to me, as it were, masks. I saw faces in expression a thousand times more evil than the countenances of those three unhappy women. How was it? Was it alone that some unusually painful and frightful circumstances had aroused passions in them which only slept in the breasts of hundreds of other human beings who wander about free and honourably in the world; or was *expression*, after all, a deception?[51]

Despite this continuing interrogation of the certitude with which the surface of the body rendered character legible, the idea endured the nineteenth century, receiving its updated scientific imprimatur through the absorption, in part, of Cesare Lombroso's typology of criminal degeneracy. In turn, this was challenged in a way that simultaneously called assumptions about representation into question. In Robert Louis Stevenson's *Dr Jekyll and Mr Hyde* (1886), the uncouth Hyde, even if bearing signs of

degeneration, genetic reversion and stuntedness, is more remarkable for the intangible and revulsion-provoking aura which he
emanates than for any identifiable physical marks of evil: a
counter-blast to what Stevenson deplored, in 'A Note on Realism',
as the realist compulsion to make everything 'all charactered and
notable, seizing the eye'.[52]

Innately present character traits were not the only indicators of
individuality which were believed, at least by some, to be decipherable from a body's appearance. Indeed, Dickens's argument in the
article already cited, 'The Demeanour of Murderers', is that
actions come to show their traces on human faces, rather than that
physiological characteristics are invariably indicative of a predis-
position to criminal activity. This is the developmental commonplace on which Oscar Wilde builds when showing that the palm of
Lord Arthur Savile comes to bear the stigmata of a murderer, or,
indeed, when dramatically displacing Dorian Gray's transgres-
sions onto the features of his portrait. Codes of physical legibility
are, however, not confined to moral histories, but operate in far
more materialist contexts. One need only recall Sherlock Holmes's
famous statement that 'By a man's finger-nails, by his coat-sleeve,
by his boots, by his trouser-knees, by the callosities of his
forefinger and thumb, by his expression, by his shirt-cuffs – by each
of these things a man's calling is plainly revealed',[53] such noting of
detail itself being advocated by the master detective as part of necessary training in the capacity to observe and deduce. As Holmes's
own masterful adoption of disguises intimates, and the blurring of
the physical – finger-nails and calluses – with clothing in his procla-
mation to Watson suggests, identity came to be recognised as
something which was not innate, but performative – the type of
performativity recognised by Henry James when he makes
Madame Merle, in *The Portrait of a Lady*, say that 'One's self – for
other people – is one's expression of one's self; and one's house,
one's furniture, one's garments, the books one reads, the company
one keeps – these things are all expressive.'[54] In fact, the whole
Victorian literary fascination with disguise and its capacity to
deceive successfully – from Mayhew's beggars with their carefully
concocted sores, through Isabel Vane, hiding behind her blue-

tinted spectacles in *East Lynne*, to Rudyard Kipling's Kim's capacity (apart from, one presumes, his tell-tale Irish eyes) to pass as a bazaar-boy – may be seen as a counter-current to the belief in the sufficiency of physiognomic encodement.[55] Additionally, and with no performative deliberation on the part of their occupants, one encounters those skins which have been both literally and figuratively inscribed with the marks of toil: Boucher's drowned corpse, in Gaskell's *North and South*, stained with the industrial dye which pollutes the streams of Milton; Tess's arms, in *Tess of the d'Urbervilles*, scratched and torn by field work, which may be read both as a sign of labour, and as a displacement of the way in which sexual activity has lacerated her.[56]

As with the individual body, the understanding of society as a whole relied on the gathering and organisation of information about its parts. This has led to systemic readings of Victorian culture based upon what several commentators have isolated as a significant feature of the period: its dependence, across a variety of fields, on the accumulation and precise recording of detail. The importance of this proliferation of detail has been discussed in relation to a range of contexts. Thus Carol Christ considered the problems of relating details to the whole at a time when the collapse of religious belief, and the co-terminous developments in political and scientific theories, left the individual isolate: 'conceiving of the universe as a mass of particulars led logically to seeing experience as wholly subjective and particular', and she traces the effect this response to detail had on Victorian poets.[57] More common, however, is the linkage of crowded detail with the literary – usually fictional – and artistic practice of realism, with its stress on the solid and the circumstantial, creating the rhetoric whereby the reader or spectator may believe that the world represented is in some way continuous with their own.[58] 'It is almost by now a truism of criticism', remarked Laurie Langbauer in 1990, 'that the classical realism of nineteenth-century novels especially draws on metaphors of sight for its effect',[59] and she went on to cite Mark Seltzer's observation that the techniques of realism, with their emphasis on the particularities of the all-seeing narrator's vision, 'are concerned "with seeing, with a seeing in detail",

. . . to aid our acceptance as subjects not just of one true unified vision but of an invisible supervision'.[60] Some critics, notably Herbert Sussman and George Landow, have pointed to the ways in which particular employment of detail, particularly in Pre-Raphaelite work, stands for spiritual significance made manifest, through systems of typological symbolism, in the material world.[61] Chris Brooks, in *Signs for the Times* (1984), relates such Pre-Raphaelite manipulation of detail to a broader European metaphysical context, taking as his starting point Thomas Carlyle's own individualistic expansion of German transcendentalism in *Sartor Resartus*, and his insistence that in the field of human investigation, there are material objects, which may be seen by the bodily eye, and there are invisible objects, which not only cannot be seen by any eye, but which cannot be pictured or imaged in the mind. In particular, Brooks takes up Carlyle's comment that 'All visible things are emblems; what thou seest is not there on its own account; strictly taken, is not there at all: Matter exists only spiritually, and to represent some Idea, and *body* it forth.'[62] He uses this to explore what he terms 'symbolic realism' at work in Dickens, in Pre-Raphaelite painting and in mid-Victorian architecture.

Such a model of inner and outer representation and signification, however, is a very static one. Carlyle is also notable for his voicing of a sense – later developed into the webs and circulatory systems of Darwin and Herbert Spencer, Eliot and Hardy – that there are hidden 'bonds that unite us one and all'. In their material form, these may be observed as a 'venous-arterial circulation, of Letters, verbal Messages, paper and other Packages, going out from [an individual] and coming in . . . a blood-circulation, visible to the eye'. Such filaments of communication, however, are no more than symbols of 'the finer nervous circulation, by which all things, the minutest that he does, minutely influence all men, and the very look of his face blesses or curses whomso it lights on, and so operates ever new blessing or new cursing: all this you cannot see, but only imagine'.[63]

Yet despite Carlyle's warning, crucial to my own argument, that the unseen may be more powerful than the seen, countless metaphors within Victorian writing substantiate the drive towards specularity to which many critics of the late twentieth century attest. It is such a desire to uncover which led Charlotte Brontë, in the preface to the second edition of *Jane Eyre*, to write that the world has found it 'convenient to make external show pass for sterling worth – to let white-washed walls vouch for clean shrines. It may hate him who dares to scrutinise and expose – to rase the gilding, and show base metal under it – to penetrate the sepulchre, and reveal charnel relics: but, hate as it will, it is indebted to him.'[64] As Brontë makes apparent in Gothically chilling language, to reveal is not always to put on display that which is pleasant, but revelation is informed by a desire to lay bare the truth, whatever the cost to one's peace of mind. Whilst Brontë is primarily concerned with individual morality and hypocrisy, however symptomatic these may be of wider social failings, the language of exposure increasingly resonates through acts of unveiling designed to illuminate areas of ignorance in relation to general social spheres.

The current fascination with the legibility of Victorian surfaces and the apparent transparency of signifying systems has not, of course, gone unchallenged. The very stability of the visible has partly been called into question by those who, like Jonathan Crary, have demonstrated how early nineteenth-century investigations in optical science, involving both optical devices and physiological experiments, led to the growing acceptance that visualisation is itself dependent upon cerebral process, and to the accumulation of knowledge 'about the constitutive role of the body in the apprehension of a visible world'.[65] He describes, in other words, the movement from an eighteenth-century model of the camera obscura, with its implicit postulation of the objective observer, to the admission of subjectivity into vision (whilst noting that, as Victorians themselves readily admitted, the acknowledgement of the role of subjectivity in seeing had taken place long before their own century). However, as W. J. T. Mitchell has effectively, if sympathetically, pointed out, Crary's argument is weakened by the way his 'skepticism about the "single nineteenth century observer" leads him, against all logic, to conclude that there is *no* observer, except in the "dominant model" he has extracted from physiological optics and optical technology'.[66] One of the central aims of my own study is to reinstate what might be thought of as the particularities of spectatorship: considering not just the intense attention which was paid to the mechanics of the eye, and the growing interest in the linked involvement of the unconscious, but, through investigating the terms in which visual acts were discussed and recorded, I shall be considering the ends which looking at art was made to serve. This means going way beyond discussions concerning the immediate operations of the eye, despite their proliferation during the whole period, and considering the act of viewing in the light of other current practices employed in the interpretation of culture, dependent upon, and reinforcing, the hidden, invisible, interwoven threads of ideology.

One should, however, avoid falling into the trap of believing that Victorians necessarily privileged the importance of visibility: as Carlyle's *Sartor Resartus* has already been used to indicate, the unseen could be far more suggestive than the seen. This could hold true not just in a straightforward religious sense, but also in a more Carlylean metaphysical one.[67] For in what follows, I shall be drawing extensively on scientific writing, and emphasising the frequent interpenetration of its concerns with literary and artistic culture. This influence had its limits. In particular, and tellingly – telling, that is, when it comes to assessing how people were actively encouraged to look at works of art – it was – as we shall see in chapter 7 – rarely drawn upon by those whose professional task it was to describe and encourage the act of seeing and interpretation.[68] Aside from this, however, the insistence by numerous scientists on the importance of the imagination drew together differing fields of speculative activity.[69] Yet the most far-thinking of scientists were quick to express reservations about the extent of their vision and powers. Thomas Huxley, for example, wrote in 'Science and Morals' that 'Nobody, I imagine, will credit me with a desire to limit the empire of physical science, but I really feel bound to confess that a great many very familiar and, at the same time, extremely important phenomena lie quite beyond its legitimate limits.'[70] John Tyndall remarked in 1860 that 'The territory of physics is wide, but it has its limits from which we look with vacant gaze into the region beyond.'[71] Not everything, in other words, may be explained by science; not everything can be read according to attending to what is visible, however alertly. 'Once at the sacred heat that opens regions beyond ordinary vision', Forster wrote of Dickens's power in creating individualised characters, 'imagination has its own laws.'[72]

Not to be able to see with the physical eye is to call into play the powerful forces of imagination and memory. Such an idea was one of the most powerful legacies of the early Romantic writers on Victorian sensibilities. As Akenside put it in his 1772 version of *Pleasures of Imagination*, in which he considers the importance not so much of perception, but of the memory of perception:

> **To man alone**
> Of sublunary beings was it given
> Each fleeting impulse on the sensual powers
> At leisure to review; with equal eye
> To scan the passion of the stricken nerve
> Or the vague object striking; to conduct
> From sense, the portal turbulent and loud,
> Into the mind's wide palace one by one
> The frequent, pressing, fluctuating forms,
> And question and compare them.[73]

Memory may certainly prove preferable to an image which, through its function as simulacrum, signifies loss more powerfully than presence. After the death of George Lewes, George Eliot wrote to Elma Stuart that she had no regret whatsoever that she possessed no portrait or bust of him. Indeed, she was bitterly repentant that she had been led into buying an enlarged copy of his photographic portrait: 'It is smoothed down and altered, and each time I look at it I feel its *unlikeness* more. *Himself as he was* is what I see inwardly, and I am afraid of outward images lest they should corrupt the inward.'[74] This anecdote suggests a personal enactment of the belief put into Will Ladislaw's mouth in *Middlemarch*, that 'Language gives a fuller image, which is all the better for being vague. After all, the true seeing is within.'[75] The connection of this belief with the language of contemporary scientific investigation – indeed, with those processes which aided the operations of the human eye through optical enhancement – is brought home by the passage in the same novel when, commenting on the actions of the imagination, the narrative voice remarks how Lydgate values that particular form of imagination 'that reveals subtle actions inaccessible by any sort of lens, but tracked in that outer darkness through long pathways of necessary sequence by the inward light which is the last refinement of Energy, capable of bathing even the ethereal atoms in its ideally illuminated space'.[76]

In more recent critical terms, a considerable challenge to the assumption that easy legibility is desirable has necessarily come from those whose attention has focussed on questions of language. In particular, critics writing on Victorian poetry – a form less closely associated with realism than either the novel or painting during this period – point to the fact that while optical metaphors abound in poetical works, this mode of writing, with its capacity to cut away narrative links, and to revel in a play of formal elements, including elusive symbols, evades that analysis which looks to readily decipherable systems of representation.[77] Jerome McGann's *Towards a Literature of Knowledge* (1989) – spanning writing from Blake to Pound – argues against the Kantian tradition that insists on the value of empirical experience in acquiring knowledge, and claims that the 'truth-functions' of poetry 'have grown to seem increasingly displaced from actuality',[78] or, in other words, that poetry's referential quality matters far less than its emotive or metaphysical potential: it is a domain in which knowledge is a form of activity, rather than involving the possession of an idea. Isobel Armstrong's *Victorian Poetry* (1993) in many places supports McGann's argument from within the Victorian period, tracing the history of those nineteenth-century commentators on poetic language, both critics and practitioners, who drew repeated attention to the tantalising, frustrating, but suggestive gap between word and thing, and who exploited the potential of this. W. David Shaw, in *Victorians and Mystery. Crises of Representation* (1990), explores a whole range of topoi – in fiction as well as in poetry – which proved resistant to representation, grouping his examples around the unconscious (including attempts to fill agnostic voids with meaningful signs, and the problem of showing God's hiddenness); around mysteries of identity, including self-knowledge and interiority; and around the kind of problems of historical reconstruction that were faced by Browning, and the inadequacies of fictional detectives when it came to grasping the minds of their criminal suspects. More generally, and with useful reference to psychoanalytic theory, Peggy Phelan has attempted, in *Unmarked. The Politics of Performance* (1993), to 'revalue a belief in subjectivity and identity which is not visibly representable',[79] arguing that there may be power in remaining invisible – since visibility summons surveillance and the law, provokes fetishism, stimulates colonial appetites for possession. The invisible, she maintains, is 'representation's supplemental excess and its failure to be totalizing'.[80]

This challenge to the adequacy of representation, to the sufficiency of the visible, was expressed in a range of ways by the Victorians, and it is this challenge which I seek to explore. I am not so much concerned to examine debates which specifically centre on the limitations of language as I am to investigate some of those challenges which erupt *through* literary and artistic acts of representation themselves. I wish to call into question, in other words, some prevalent beliefs about the Victorians' assumed drive towards specularity. In sum, this study sets out to show that though the visual was, indeed, of paramount importance to the Victorians, it was a heavily problematised category. The terms of this problematisation in fact tell us a good deal not just about how Victorians 'saw' and interpreted the world, but about how they understood, accepted or interrogated the relationship between language and its objects.

It is very readily apparent that, whilst fascinated by the operations of the eye, both scientific thinkers and, to a lesser degree, writers who concentrated on aesthetic issues drew attention to its physiological instability, and also its limitations. In popular scientific writing, whether oriented towards medical matters, or towards the importance of observing the natural world, the wonderful, miraculous properties of vision were endlessly stressed, by scientific specialists and journalistic generalists alike. The natural philosopher Sir David Brewster, whose own works relate chiefly to optical investigations, reviewing a range of recent books about ocular science in 1856, summarised the qualities of touch and taste and smell and hearing, before celebrating sight for being able both to study the vastness and minutiae of the natural world, and to penetrate into the heart of life itself. 'The sight alone', he asserts, 'lays open the prolific cells of vegetable and animal organization, and displays to the astonished inquirer the structure of those wonderful tissues which cover the fountains of intellectual and animal life.'[81] Writing the same year, the popularising writer Joseph Turnley brought out *The Language of the Eye*, in which, after some broad remarks about how 'the life of the eye . . . cannot be imitated, nor its absence compensated',[82] he first describes, with a very fanciful grasp of biology, how the physiological structure of the eye works as a miniature version of the whole body ('this little organ repeats in itself the whole of man, which is the highest and most complete organisation').[83] He proceeds to praise the eye's beauty as well as its manifold functions, and then discusses the different ways in which the expressions of the eye may be read, for 'it is certain that the eye gives the promptest and surest indication of mental motion'.[84] Health, moral condition and intellectual cultivation will all show themselves in the eye, and plates illustrating different ocular expressions are included (figures 4 and 5). Thus 'Love wears a flowing, full eye . . . the iris glistens, as though beaming in humid pearls; confidence sits gallantly enthroned in the enlarged pupil';[85] 'the eye of Imagination seems to look through all presence, and calmly regards that which others see not'.[86] This practice of interpreting the expression of the eye does not just apply to ascertaining the condition of the individual, for we are exhorted to 'look on the nations under slavery; how dull, sullen, dissatisfied, is the expression of the eye, as though rapture and real temperament were put back for want of exercise of independence'.[87] Gender difference is indicated through the eye ('the eye of man is the most firm; woman's the most flexible . . . Man's surveys and observes; woman's glances').[88] Eyes are everywhere;

4 Illustration, 'Love', Joseph Turnley, *The Language of the Eye*, 1856.

5 Illustration, 'Imagination', Joseph Turnley, *The Language of the Eye*, 1856.

'nature is full of eyes; the past, the present, and the future are full of eyes', and looking over all of these, in turn, is God's 'kind eye . . . the externality of sight of the searching One'.[89]

The eye was traditionally the window to the soul, and this, combined with the implications raised by the continual presence of a divine, unseen watcher, was in part responsible for the fascination of the interplay between the seen and the unseen. Thomas Bull, himself blind, elaborated on this idea as making the human organ superior to that of other creatures: 'The human eye is more beautiful in its construction than that of any other of God's handiworks. In the eagle and the hawk, in the gazelle and the feline tribe, the perfection of the eye is admirable; but in the human eye there is a glory which excelleth these. The spirit speaketh through the eye'.[90] The popular naturalist, Joseph Wood, was even more explicit about this duality, claiming that

> The sight of the eye, the most precious of all a man's physical gifts, is only a parable of that truer sight of the world which makes a man a poet, an artist, a lover, a spiritual creature. To 'see the unseen' is the paradox of religion as it is the crowning glory of man . . . Properly speaking, Sight and Insight are not two antagonistic tendencies, but opposite poles of one and the same magnet.[91]

Other writers, however, temper and mediate their praise, when it comes to considering the human physiological faculty on its own, operating independently of spiritual influence. 'A long list of indictments might indeed be brought against the eye', announced Tyndall, in a lecture on light: '– its opacity, its want of symmetry, its lack of achromatism, its absolute blindness, in part. All these taken together caused Helmholtz to say that if any optician sent him an instrument so full of defects, he would be justified in sending it back with the severest censure.' Notwithstanding the theoretical problems with the eye, however, Tyndall concluded that 'as a practical instrument . . . it must ever remain a marvel to the reflecting mind'.[92] Moreover, what emerges with this fascination with the physiology of seeing is an acknowledgement of the individuality of each eye, each exercise of vision. Additionally, emphasis was laid on the importance of training the eye. Observation, however careful, is – and this came to be well recognised by Victorians – never removed from the exercise of subjectivity, and of personal investment in the act of looking. Nothing showed up the limitations of the eye so much as technological developments: not just the shifts in visual scale made possible by more sophisticated microscopes and telescopes, but also what George Eliot, in *The Impressions of Theophrastus Such*, termed the 'micrometers and thermopiles and tasimeters which deal physically with the invisible, the impalpable, and the unimaginable'.[93] The invention around 1840 of various forms of specula which enabled one to dilate and view the body's orifices, attempts to introduce solar or artificial light to allow the body's cavities to be explored further, the invention of the ophthalmoscope and the laryngoscope (introduced into London in 1862), all permitted the investigation of the most intimate of interiors,[94] and enhanced the authority of the visual within medical science. 'There is an old and trite saying that "seeing is believing";' wrote Alfred Meadows in the *Lancet* in 1870, 'and, in a realistic age like the present, it might almost be said that not seeing is not believing.'[95]

Photography promised an enhanced role for ocular proof in modern society, and certain recent theorists of nineteenth-century photography, notably John Tagg, have emphasised its links with practices of surveillance. Yet also, as Lindsay Smith has shown, its practices had the power to unsettle expectations concerning sight and representation, particularly with regards to demystifying geometrical or Cartesian perspective,[96] and to exposing what Walter Benjamin famously termed the 'optical unconscious', offering the opportunity to make us realise what we see without realising that we have seen it.[97] Moreover, the camera lens could render visible that which the human eye could not see at all. Thomas Huxley, writing of 'The Progress of Science' in 1887, drew attention, for example, to the camera's capacity to record spectroscopic phenomena, and reveal 'the existence of rays having powerful chemical energy, or beyond the visible limits of either end of the spectrum'.[98] The most significant development in this respect was Wilhelm Roentgen's invention of the X-ray. He took the first X-ray of the human body – his wife's hand – and the concept passed swiftly into the popular cultural imagination. An advertisement of mid-1896, for example, shows a beam of strong light illuminating a cheerful-looking woman in a dentist's chair, whilst a serious-looking, older professional man examines what appears to be a photographic plate. The legend reads: 'Dr Van Buskirk applies the Röntgen Rays in his Dental Practice and finds that those habitually using SOZODONT have perfect Teeth, hard Gums, and sweet Breath' (figure 6).

Richard Proctor's article 'The Photographic Eyes of Science' elaborated further on the eye's limitations in the context of recent experiments in recording observations. The eye requires a certain time to receive and dispose of an impression, which means that it cannot take in, say, all the visual information that reaches one from a swiftly moving body – in the case of something moving as fast as a cannon-ball leaves a cannon, it may not see at all; or it may respond to rapid motion by seeing what is not, as in the case of the apparent stillness of a spinning top. An eye's power does not increase by gazing at an object for a long time – we can stare for ten minutes or an hour at a faint nebula, and never see it more clearly than we do at first. Indeed, our attention is likely to waver. Even when we believe that we have seen clearly, fully, accurately, the memory would have to be perfect to recall all that we have seen. However, in all the points where 'the eye of man is defective, an eye provided by science is practically free from fault . . . instead of the retina, with all its defects, physical and physiological, the photographic plate, wet or dry according to circumstances, is employed for scientific vision'.[99] He demonstrates how Galton's photographs of a galloping horse or swiftly flying bird, Henry Draper's long-exposed views of the great nebula of Orion, taken through a telescope, and the use of ultra-violet in recording the stars have enabled the photographic eye to achieve what the human eye could not. 'With its three eyes – the eye of keenness, the eye of patient watchfulness, and the eye of artistic truth, photography

6 Advertisement for Sozodont, *Illustrated London News*, 1896

promises', Proctor claims, 'to be a Cerberus to the science of the future . . . indeed, with photography, spectroscopy, polariscopy, and other aids, science promises soon to be Argus-eyed.'[100]

I begin this study with a consideration of the limits of visibility: the fascination with the simultaneous presence of the seen and the unseen. The opening chapter looks at dust, a paradoxical phenomenon for many Victorians: paradoxical because it was a transmitter of disease and also productive of beauty; a possible source of life, and the base condition to which we will return; waste product, and crucial to the climatic conditions which sustain life. In its minuteness, it forms one end of the Victorian fascination with the suggestivity of the infinite, a suggestivity which was continually being pointed up by the revelations offered and promised by those optical instruments which help humans to extend their vision. The next chapter shows how, even in the 1850s, artists themselves could suggest the limitations of physical sight. In reading John Everett Millais's *The Blind Girl*, I propose that it functions as a paradigm through which we may understand Victorian awareness of the inadequacy of the eye, and, through linking its topos of blindness to the language and themes of Elizabeth Barrett Browning's *Aurora Leigh* (1856), the terms in which inner vision could be privileged over physical vision are examined. This leads me to address questions raised by the relationship between science and the domain of the visible, questions which are continued in the third and fourth chapters. First, the relationship between matter and mind interrogated by George Eliot's *The Lifted Veil* (1859) is considered and linked back to George Lewes's views on the role of the imagination in art and science. What may be seen to be at stake is the relationship between empirical, quantifiable data, and 'the mind's eye'. From this, I move to examine the ways in which scientists used metaphor in order to make invisible forces – in this case, the imperceptible movement of the glacier – visible to the imagination of the non-scientific reader.

The functioning of the metaphor to explain the operations of the invisible was necessarily crucial to the figuration and popularisation of many further developments in Victorian science, particularly those concerning molecular laws, the workings of electricity, magnetism and wave theory. The invisible means of transmission which enabled the new technologies of communication – the telegraph and the telephone in particular – further served to collapse the boundaries between the material and immaterial modes of circulation about which Carlyle had been able to write with such confidence.[101]

Yet it is impossible to ignore the fact that for many Victorians, that which was not visible did not so much inspire as frighten. Nowhere was this more apparent than in the city, where both the metaphoric and the mephitic threatened eruption, whether in the form of class unrest or of foetid sewage arrangements. The invisibility of metropolitan life at various levels – something which went hand in hand with the continuing and rapid transformation of the architectural and social spaces of its surfaces – was, I argue, linked with concern about the relationship of the present to history, and the desire to find continuity by exploring the locations of the memory. In this context, I consider the Victorian fascination with what lay under London, the arteries of the city's body. Making these channels visible was not just a matter of scrutinizing the metropolis's healthy or putrid workings, but was a means of writing historical depth onto the site of the modern, just as examining the memory could help ground an individual's sense of identity. It was a means, moreover, of giving stability not just to changing topography but to the onrush of visual impressions that urban life brought with it: what Georg Simmel was to characterise as 'the rapid crowding of changing images, the sharp discontinuity in the grasp of a single glance, and the unexpectedness of changing impressions'.[102]

In the following two chapters, I return to the surface – this time, to the painted surface, and to the language of art criticism during the period. In other words, from looking at both generalised and metaphoric concern with the act of seeing, I consider its employment in a specific cultural field, and the implications of the fact that, as Norman Bryson has put it, 'It is in the interaction of painting with social formation that the semantics of painting is to be found, as a variable term fluctuating according to the fluctuations of discourse.'[103] What becomes instantly apparent is that notwithstanding the problematisation of the visual that I have outlined, the act of looking at a painting is rarely discussed as though the operation of the eye, and the assimilation and comprehension of the sensations it receives, causes any difficulties whatsoever, or prompts any debate. Why should this be the case? Why the slippage between an intellectual interrogation of the act of seeing, and a bland acceptance, by many of those whose job was seeing and the interpretation of the visual, of the apparent ease of the act in which they were engaged?

I begin by enquiring into the role of the art critic during this period, showing how variegated agendas were at stake for them other than educating the public to look at and to form standards of judgement about what they saw – however important they also believed these factors to be. This necessitates examining the relationship between art and language both as it was discussed, and as it was tacitly present, in the work of critics of contemporary painting. Simultaneously, it involves acknowledging the commodity function, as opposed to, or in excess of, the aesthetic function of painting within the Victorian period, whether this commodification is related to the status of art in market terms, or, more broadly, as an element within the circulation of cultural capital.[104] The assumption that one could write about paintings in the same way that one criticised and commented on novels, which is strongly present in the narrativising drive in both art and art criticism, led to the development of a critical vocabulary that rested heavily on ethical and social assumptions.[105] Much populist art criticism privileged paintings where the meaning seems to lie in its narrative content and the concomitant decoding of proffered visual detail – in the 'prose' rather than the 'poetry' of painting, to use a frequently reiterated distinction. This provoked scorn in those who believed that both art, and those who wrote about art, had more valuable tasks to perform, but its dominance as a mode of writing about art indicates the ways in which paintings were so frequently 'read', not so much according to the terms of their innate, formalist attributes, but in relation to a wider social agenda structured according to a range of dominant narratives. This is demonstrated in relation to the contemporary reception of some specific works, centring around those which take gambling as their central theme: Robert Martineau's *The Last Day in the Old Home* (1860), Alfred Elmore's *On the Brink* (1865) and William Powell Frith's series, *The Road to Ruin* (1878) and *The Race for Wealth* (1880), which play both on a spectator's ability to construct a coherent narrative from the encoded visual evidence placed before them, and on his or her wider familiarity with narratives of gambling.

Not all paintings, however, were as easy to read, and carried such a clear didactic message, as these works. In the criticism that seeks to elucidate subject painting, what emerges is that the act of looking is frequently subordinated to an enforcement of dominant social opinions that bear little relation to the self-conscious employment of the eye. Yet the direction taken by art criticism shifted along with the paintings it addressed, and the prevalence of narrativising, moralising criticism became, by the later 1870s, less apparent even within writing aimed at a non-specialist public. In the next chapter, James Sully's essay on 'The Undefinable in Art' (1878)[106] is drawn on as a way into considering both the painting of Whistler and that of English Symbolist artists, including Burne Jones, whose *Mirror of Venus* (1876) is a focal point for Sully's argument. I discuss the ways in which the language of surface and depth comes to feature in later nineteenth-century aesthetic writing, often in conjunction not just with painterly technique, but with the operations of the perceiver's 'dim regions of the sub-conscious'.[107] This involves placing Sully's work on perception in the wider context of the relationship between science and art in the latter half of the nineteenth century, thus returning to the question of what happens in the perceiving mind, behind the gaze, and showing how the developing science of psychology is enlisted in the understanding of the operations of perception. George Eliot's *Daniel Deronda* (1876), and its relationship to G. H. Lewes's final work, *Problems of Life and Mind* – its final two volumes completed and made ready for publication by Eliot – allow one to see these factors intersecting within imaginative writing.

In the penultimate chapter, I return briefly to narrative art, albeit that which took a much more open-ended form, when I consider two 'problem pictures': Frank Dicksee's *A Reverie* (1894), and Millais's *Speak! Speak!* (1895). These particular paintings, showing spectral female figures appearing to men, may fashionably allude to 'a spiritual realm above or beneath the material one'.[108] They also may be related to a further important borderland between the seen and the unseen: the issue of hallucination, and what this phenomenon may be made to say about the act of seeing. The relationship of science and literature in respect to this issue is explored through the rhetoric of ghost stories, and by considering a couple of H. G. Wells's tales which seek to find allegorical form for abstract mathematical concepts.

The angle of vision, the point of perception, whether actual or metaphorical, is never fixed and final. It is with this in mind that my conclusion draws on the concept of the horizon, both as it figured within Victorian writing and painting, and, more particularly, as it has been taken up in a phenomenological sense by thinkers this century. The idea that there may always be another way, or set of ways, of looking at an object; that there may be more to it than 'meets the eye'; that a different subjectivity will ensure that it is seen and interpreted in a different way; that new techniques of viewing will enable a different conceptualisation of the object – all these notions serve to destabilise confidence in the equilibrium of the visual world. It is my aim, in what follows, to show the Victorians' increasing awareness of the instability of the visual, and their problematisation of what they saw. The issue of visuality, in the Victorian period, has as shifting a focus as the curious, inquisitive, roving eye itself.

James Sully remarked in 1876 that:

> There is probably no region of phenomena which has received less illumination from the activities of the modern scientific spirit than the processes of the Fine Arts. This fact is unmistakably betrayed in the associations which still cling to the term *aesthetic*.

> To speak of an aesthetic inquiry is to the ordinary mind to refer to the densest stratum of nebulous thought. To call a subject aesthetic is to claim its exemption from a clear and searching investigation.[109]

But he counters this point of view. In addition to reminding his readers of the number of great artists who have themselves taken part in the discussion of scientific problems, he advances the importance of what he terms 'the psychological method' when it comes to dealing scientifically with aesthetic issues. This would involve 'an appeal not only to the study of mental operations by individual self-reflection but also to the newer inquiries [he doubtless had Herbert Spencer particularly in mind] into the laws of mental development in the race, and of the reciprocal actions of many minds in the social organism.[110] Even by the end of the nineteenth century, however, the fact that art and science might be seen as inter-related was far from securely established, and a countermovement – a desire to separate visual art and science and to assert the autonomy of each – must be recognised. Mary Costelloe commented that 'Art is so much an "extra" in the lives of most people that they can hardly bring themselves to think of it seriously, and the idea of using the two words "art" and "science" in connection seems like a mere paradox.'[111] Yet she, like many others, was committed to breaking down this apparent paradox, and showing the intersections generated by paying attention to the complex processes involved in looking.

In 1879, the mathematician, essayist and popularising scientist William Kingdon Clifford published *Seeing and Thinking*. In this, he claims that the topic of seeing:

> is a sort of Clapham Junction of all the sciences in regard of the number of trains of thought which converge at this point, and which go out from it. In the first place we have a connection with physiology; in the next place we have a connection with physics . . .; and we have a connection with mechanics by means of the mechanical explanation of those actions which go on within us; and we have connection with a subject far more difficult than any of these, namely, the subject of consciousness – what it is that we

see, whether we see rightly, and how it is that we think. And also, it may be observed, as this is a sort of junction of all the lines of the sciences, that there are more trains of thought which go off the line just at this point than at any other.[112]

In what follows, I investigate the fact that seeing, for the Victorians, involved not just the scientific issues which branched off Clifford's railway junction, but intertwined scientific understanding with a whole matrix of cultural and social practices. For us, as for the Victorians, the topic of seeing is one which breaks down disciplinary divisions, and a commitment to the importance of bringing differing disciplines into dialogue with one another informs this work.

CHAPTER 2

'The mote within the eye'

In 1898, the natural historian Alfred Russel Wallace published a retrospective study: *The Wonderful Century. Its Successes and its Failures*. In this, he devotes a whole chapter to 'The Importance of Dust'. Dust in our towns and in our houses, he acknowledges, 'is often not only a nuisance but a serious source of disease'. As it is usually perceived by us, it is, 'like dirt, only matter in the wrong place'. We might look to get rid of it as far as possible, for example by implementing legislation against excess or inefficient combustion of coal. But, Wallace continues:

> though we can thus minimise the dangers and the inconveniences arising from the grosser forms of dust, we cannot wholly abolish it; and it is, indeed, fortunate we cannot do so, since it has now been discovered that it is due to the presence of dust we owe much of the beauty, and perhaps even the very habitability, of the earth we live upon. Few of the fairy tales of science are more marvellous than these recent discoveries as to the varied effects and important uses of dust in the economy of nature.[1]

Dust was a paradoxical substance, its position within Victorian culture perennially unstable. Emotively – and logically – it was associated with disease; its elimination or control with necessary practices of hygiene. As such, its properties are co-terminous with the wider category of dirt, and – to quote Mary Douglas's *Purity and Danger* – 'dirt avoidance for us is a matter of hygiene or aesthetics and is not related to our religion'.[2] As Peter Stallybrass and Allon White have reminded us, the emphasis upon dirt was central to the discourse of the city which mapped divisions between slum and suburb, sewage and 'civilisation'.[3] Dust may be seen as the marker of undesirable class status. Pip, in Dickens's *Great Expectations*, wants to escape from Joe's forge, where he felt 'dusty with the dust of small coal';[4] when Magwitch is transported, dust fuels his ambitions, too, as ' "The blood horses of them colonists might fling up the dust over me as I was walking",'[5] but he determines to become a better gentleman than them. Dust, here, as in much writing of Empire, is the marker of colonised lands; the substance which has to be washed off at the end of the day, or which causes confusion, as in Kipling's story, 'A Strange Ride', where, blowing up in thick storms, it disrupts identities and obscures vision. As we shall see, cleanliness, by contrast, is the marker of imperial power.[6]

Yet once one accepts that not all dust is dirt, its resonances broaden out. Dust is an equaliser, as well as a factor in establishing hierarchies. Its long-standing equation with the most reductive form of matter to which we must all return – 'dust to dust' – ensured that its evocation was full of metaphorical opportunities. At the same time, its indispensable value was also perceived, both in the basic sense of waste reclamation – typified by the material value of the Harmon Mounds in Dickens's *Our Mutual Friend*, with their 'golden dust' – and in the functions that it was seen to perform within nature. Here, again, the potential for moral elaboration is unmistakable, even in the introduction to a scientific article. J.G. McPherson writes in *Longman's Magazine* for 1891:

> Some of the most enchanting phenomena in nature are dependent for their very existence upon singularly unimportant things; and some phenomena that in one form or another daily attract our attention are produced by startlingly overlooked material. What is the agent that magically transforms the leaden heavens into the glorious afterglow of autumn . . . What is the source of the beautiful, brilliant, and varied colouring of the waters of the Mediterranean . . . What produces the awe-inspiring deep blue of the zenith in a clear summer evening, when the eye tries to reach the absolute? Whence comes the gentle refreshing rain, the biting sleet, the stupefying fog, the chilling mist, the virgin snow, the glimmering haze, or the pelting hail? . . . What is the source of

much of the wound putrefaction, and the generation and spread of sickness and disease? What, in fact, is one of the most marvellous agents in producing beauty for the eye's gratification, refreshment to the arid soil, sickness and death to the frame of man and beast? That agent is *dust*.

The paradox does not end here, in the juxtaposition of beauty and utility with disease and decay. It is a paradox crucially interwoven with the Victorian interest in the visible and the unseen. For dust gives rise to atmospheric effects which, as McPherson puts it, 'have a most important influence upon the imagination . . . an aesthetic eye is charmed with their gorgeous transformation effects', since they stretch the mind towards contemplation of the vastness of space, of infinity. One cannot, however, extrapolate simplistically from this and say that if one can see dust, it is to be equated with waste, with excess, with residue, yet if one cannot see it, only the effects to which it gives rise, we can appreciate its value and beauty. Danger, as well as the potential for beauty, may well lie concealed from the human eye: individual dust particles are so tiny that 'a microscope magnifying 1,600 diameters is required to discern them', yet, McPherson writes, 'some are more real emissaries of evil than poet or painter ever conceived'.[7] Even without optical aids, one's ability to see dust may depend on particular material circumstances. 'This very question of visibility is an endless one', remarked John Ruskin, 'wavering between form of substance and action of light'. He was asserting this as a general principle, but turned to a precise example: 'Dust, unperceived in shade, becomes constantly visible in sunbeam.'[8] To think about dust, in other words, is not just to think about aspects of the materiality of Victorian life, but to consider debates concerning the perception of the material world and the conditions of vision that make this perception possible. Dust, both pervasive and evanescent, not only functions as a powerful literary metaphor, but its specks also provide a meeting point for the intersection of science, vision and imagination.

What is dust? Nineteenth-century scientists developed a series of increasingly refined experiments to determine its composition.

Christian Ehrenberg, in 1847, subjected dust that had been deposited on objects to microscopic examination; Schroeber and Dusch, a decade later, filtered air through cotton wool in order to catch even smaller particles. The method was refined by Pasteur, who used gun-cotton or asbestos as a filter and then dissolved these substances in ether, and this proved the most effective method. John Tyndall, in the latter years of the 1860s, conducted a series of experiments by means of this technique which proved, to his surprise, that a considerable proportion of the particles floating in the air of London were of organic, rather than inorganic, origin. Tichborne, in Dublin, quantified the composition of street dust yet more accurately, finding that it contained 54 per cent inorganic matter, and 45 per cent organic.[9] Nobody could deny that Victorian city streets were full of dust, and to remark on it was to underscore the unhealthy hostility of the urban environment. Several times in Tennyson's 'Edwin Morris', for example, it is metonymically associated with 'city life'.[10] It swirls around the spring-time streets of London – 'such a gritty city; such a hopeless city'[11] – at the opening of chapter 12 of *Our Mutual Friend*, a novel notoriously permeated with dust imagery, and for which Dickens considered 'Dust' a possible title; it characterises the bleakness of a sandwich-board man's existence as he treads through W. E. Henley's 'Trafalgar Square' at the end of the century in 'An ill March noon; the flagstones gray with dust; / An all-round east wind volleying straws and grit.'[12] Henry Mayhew, in *London Labour and the London Poor*, remarks that 'In some parts of the suburbs on windy days London is a perfect dust-mill', and records the water-carts that used to go out to damp down the streets.[13] The inorganic dust particles came from the pulverised dried mud of the streets, the wearing down of granite pavements and roadways by feet and by iron-shod horses, and from what Wallace called 'our enormous combustion of fuel pouring into the air volumes of smoke charged with unconsumed particles of carbon' – helping form, on occasion, what Esther Summerson, in *Bleak House*, mistook as 'dense brown smoke' from a 'great fire';[14] what Elizabeth Barrett Browning called in *Aurora Leigh* 'the great tawny weltering fog' that could strangle the city.[15] By the end of the century, it was claimed that 'No less than 350 tons of the products of the combustion of sulphur from the coal are thrown into the atmosphere of London every winter day.'[16] The problem was even worse in some industrial towns, prompting Ruskin's apocalyptic recognition of the 'storm-cloud of the nineteenth century', Manchester's 'sulphurous chimney-pot vomit of blackguardly cloud' spewing out a pall of pollution.[17] The particles might come from further away. Meteoric dust was continually falling on the surface of the earth, and some astronomers, including Norman Lockyer, asserted that both the solar system and the stellar universe grew out of the aggregation of such diffused solid particles.[18] More spectacular in its results, if less disturbing in what it suggested about the ultimate origins of us 'frail children of dust',[19] was the dust blown into the atmosphere by volcanic explosions, sometimes falling as 'showers of red and other coloured rain'.[20] In addition to the inorganic materials, 'particles of every description of decaying animal and vegetable matter. The droppings of horses and other animals, the entrails of fish, the outer leaves of cabbages, the bodies of dead cats, and the miscellaneous contents of dust-bins generally, all contribute their quota to the savoury compound.'[21]

This, however, was only half of the story. For dust was not confined to the outside. Invasively, it quickly built up in the home, a fact given a menacing spin in a curious book by H.P. Malet, *Incidents in the Biography of Dust* (1877), where the dust particles themselves threateningly address the reader: 'At this present moment we see ourselves on the table, the books, and the inkstand; if we were not carefully removed daily, we should soon bury them, as we buried Tyre and Sidon.'[22] 'Few people have any conception of the amount of dirt contained in an ordinary carpet', the physician Robert Brudenell Carter ominously announced in 1884; 'Curtains are even worse.'[23] Stir up a sitting-room carpet with a broom, he suggests; let the dust settle for half an hour, put it under the microscope, and what does one find? Mrs Beeton's comment that 'Nothing annoys a particular mistress so much as to find, when she comes downstairs, different articles of furniture looking as if they had never been dusted'[24] had increasingly more than a fastidious sniff behind it as the understanding of bacterial transmission grew. Even if the only bacterium to be identified with certainty by the 1890s was that which caused suppuration in wounds, hypothetical speculation from the mid-century onwards populated the air with tiny disease-bearing organisms like dangerous insect swarms. Certainly it became recognised that dust settling on food caused the multiplication of bacteria: one commentator of the 1890s went further in his tirade against 'this ever-present enemy, dust', alleging that 'the micro-organisms floating in the air settle on the teeth, set up trouble there, and thence pass to the stomach and intestines'.[25] Moreover, the body created its own dust, through the constant shedding of 'the scales of the epidermis'.[26]

Other dusty dangers lurked within the home. Florence Nightingale, in her *Notes on Nursing*, warns that certain green wall-papers give off arsenic dust:[27] one summer, the Tennyson family went down with whooping-cough-like symptoms from their new wallpaper, which had to be replaced.[28] It follows that those who worked in the manufacture of such papers, and in other dust-producing industries and trades suffered badly. The lungs of 'coal miners and miners in general, knife-grinders, needle-pointers, quarrymen, stonecutters, millers'[29] – to borrow the list of a physician in the mid-1860s – were all subject to injury from dust. Painters suffered from the dust of white lead; the Guards' tendency to lung disease was attributed to the quantity of pipe clay used to clean their jackets.[30] If Mrs Thornton, in Elizabeth Gaskell's *North and South*, covers up her furniture against damage from the dirty Manchester air (Gaskell, incidentally, is credited by the *OED* as the first recorded user of 'dust-sheets'), and gazes with disapproval at the Hale's small drawing room ('The room altogether was full of knick-knacks, which must take a long time to dust; and time to people of limited income was money'),[31] this pragmatic middle-class angst is put into perspective by Bessy Higgins telling of the conditions in the mill, where the air is full of bits of fluff, 'as fly off fro' the cotton, when they're carding it, and fill the air till it looks all fine white dust. They say it winds round the lungs, and tightens them up. Anyhow, there's many a one as works in a carding-room, that falls into a waste, coughing and spitting blood, because they're just poisoned by the fluff.'[32]

If dust was a hazard of the industrial city, it also formed an unfavourable aspect of colonial life. This is brought out well in Emily Eden's *Up the Country*, a collection of letters written in 1837–40 and published in 1866. The dust in India is 'much worse' than a London fog back home.[33] In Cawnpore, which 'we all detest', 'people lose their way on the plains, and everything is full of dust – books, dinner, clothes, everything'.[34] When the dust is stirred up by storms, people 'never stir' from camp, and lock their doors for protection.[35] It is as though the substance of the country is performing a kind of reverse colonisation, its very foreignness being emphasised when the Maharaja Ranjit Singh puts some dust 'on his forehead' as part of an apparently incomprehensible cultural ritual.[36] Anxiety about the insinuating, corrupting qualities of dust was certainly merited in terms of practical hygiene. Flora Annie Steele and Grace Gardiner, in *The Complete Indian Housekeeper and Cook* (1890), warn that 'Dirt, illimitable, inconceivable dirt must be expected, until a generation of mistresses has rooted out the habits of immemorial years', and advise 'Till then look at both sides of your plates, and turn up the spare cups ranged so neatly in order in the pantry. Probably one-half of them are dirty.'[37] They employ a thoroughly practical approach when they recommend that a much larger quantity of dusters will be necessary than in an English household, and when they advocate tan stockings and shoes, 'as they do not hold the dust'.[38] This anxiety concerning hygiene, however, is also a metaphorical lens, as Gail Low has claimed, through which a central problem of Empire – the fear of contamination of national identity – becomes evident.[39]

Mary Douglas maintains that:

> If we can abstract pathogenicity and hygiene from our notion of dirt, we are left with the old definition of dirt as matter out of place. This is a very suggestive approach. It implies two conditions: a set of ordered relations and a contravention of that order. Dirt then, is never a unique, isolated event. Where there is dirt there is system. Dirt is the by-product of a systemic ordering and classification of matter, in so far as ordering involves rejecting inappropriate elements.[40]

Once one moves away from a definition of dust as dirt, its status becomes less stable. Its position as marginal, surplus, unwanted matter may be reversed. 'Rubbish', as has been succinctly stated by Michael Thompson in his book on *Rubbish Theory*, 'is socially defined',[41] and hence one person's discarded waste can be another person's source of wealth. The arguments surrounding precisely what *was* in those mounds which dominate the plot and landscape of *Our Mutual Friend* have been well enough rehearsed, and it has been satisfactorily established that even if these heaps probably did not, after the sanitary measures of 1848, stand in proximity to where human excrement was deposited, the two were likely to have been closely associated in the popular mind. Hence the symbolic relationship of wealth to shit ('dust' had been a colloquial word for money since the early sixteenth century) has been a plausible enough critical extrapolation, and, moreover, one which has received psychoanalytic endorsement through Freud's equation of money with faeces.[42] Readers of *Household Words* would already have been familiar with the idea of the value of dust – taking the word in its broadest sense. John Capper's article 'Important Rubbish' in *Household Words* in 1855 classifies the contents of the mounds, thus bringing system to them and rescuing their constituents from the category of dirt,[43] and a visit to the dust-yards, showing a concomitant fascination with recycling, became something of a mid nineteenth-century journalistic standby. The most valuable of all components – excepting the occasional coins or pieces of jewellery – were coals, coal-dust and half-burned ashes: the 'breeze' that was baked into building blocks, and 'thus', the readers of the *Leisure Hour* were reminded in 1868, 'our houses may be said to arise again from the refuse they have cast out'.[44] Bones went to boiling-houses, to be turned into soap and gelatine, or became toothpicks and knife-handles and toothpowder, or were ground into fertiliser: 'Thus the old bone goes to form and nourish new bones.'[45] Paper becomes papier-maché or reverts to paper; clothes are sent off to make shoddy – torn-up woollen material – and in turn transformed into clothes again. This shoddy was known as 'devils-dust', ostensibly from the name of the machine used to tear up the fabrics, but in fact redolent of the poisonous nature of the greasy, germ-ridden, 'choking clouds of dry pungent dirt and floating fibres', as Mayhew termed them. 'Devilsdust', the double-edged name, signifying both exploitation and sedition, was given by Disraeli to a dark, melancholy, ambitious, discontented ponderer on the rights of labour in *Sybil*, who had started his working life as a nameless orphan manufacturing shoddy.[46] Glass, old shoes, metals: all were re-used. Decaying vegetable matter went to feed pigs; broken crockery made 'excellent foundations for roads'.[47] One late nineteenth-century company tried optimistically to launch a scheme to turn dust into steam power to produce electric lighting, producing energy from the inert.[48] Broken toys and chipped china were frequently appropriated for their own homes by the women who carried out most of the dust-sifting. A philanthropic visitor of the 1880s remarks how one interior she knows 'is beautified throughout with dust-bin trophies, the mantelpiece and side-table shining with showy bits of glass and china and ornaments of various devices. There are cut-glass decanters, flower-vases, wine-glasses, tumblers, and even a delicate little bowl of the lately fashionable iridescent glass.'[49] If dust at its most pernicious is insidious, invisible, here we have dust brought into view and celebrated, commodified.

Andrew Miller, in *Novels behind Glass*, has usefully noted that 'Dickens' final validation of the dust-heap . . . presents the possibility that revolutionary change is unnecessary: if the potential of what we discard is actually used, then a fundamental restructuring of the economy will not be required.'[50] The metaphoric potential of dust, the extraction of value from the abject or the restitution of the discarded was a common trope. At its simplest, excavating a dust-heap for what is lost provides a return to order. In Wilkie Collins's *The Law and the Lady* (1875), the heroine, Valeria Woodville, gains proof that her husband did not in fact murder his former wife when she has a dust-heap excavated in the grounds of the house where they had been staying at the time of her death. This archaeological dig in miniature rummages through layers of ashes and other household refuse in order to turn up morsels of paper, fragments which in turn, when painstakingly restored into the form of the letter they had once been, prove Eustace

Woodville's innocence, reinstate his good name, save his second marriage and bring the complex plot to a resolution. At a more obviously figurative level, Ruskin, in *The Ethics of the Dust*, provides a paradigm which was borrowed by others, and which itself was recycling paragraphs already published in *Modern Painters* v. He invites one to consider 'the dust we tread on', taking, by way of example, 'an ounce or two of the blackest slime of a beaten footpath on a rainy day, near a large manufacturing town'. In this, all kinds of geological elements are at helpless war with one another. Suppose, however, we could separate out and in some wonderful way extract and recombine their atoms, we obtain a clear blue sapphire from the clay, an opal from the sand, a diamond from the soot and a star-shaped drop of dew from the water. This instantly becomes a lesson in politics: 'political economy of competition' is replaced by 'political economy of co-operation'.[51] The distillation of even the most unpromising, basic raw material produces naturally formed beauty combined with material wealth.

Ruskin's lesson here is secular. A different conclusion is drawn at the end of the century when, in *Diamonds from Dust*, a pamphlet extolling the work of the London Female Guardian Society, the reader is invited to visit one of the Society's homes and witness their 'rescue work', their 'Laboratory' manifesting

> a process excelling that of which Ruskin dreamed – human lives which seemed so unlovely and worthless becoming refined under the patient alchemy of loving hearts and tender hands, the dross of the past gradually giving place to the pure grain of gold, or to the glitter of the polished crystal, the result of a renewed heart – gems destined to shine in this world, and in the next to adorn the crown and display the transforming power of our Lord and Saviour Jesus Christ.[52]

A similar, if wider, point is made in Charles Reed's *Diamonds in the Dust* (1866), in which he asks his Sunday School readers to consider, among other things, 'the boyhood of great men, men who have come up from the ranks of poverty': a Smilesian list of self-helpers like Isaac Newton, Humphry Davy, James Watt, Brunel and

Martin Luther: 'Are not all these from the dust of the earth, and are they not diamonds of the first water?'[53]

Other religious appropriations of dust take the reader straight back to the dust-heap. Mabel Mackintosh's children's story *Dust, Ho! or, Rescued from a Rubbish Heap* (1891) tells of a couple of girls sorting the rubbish that their drunken father collects.[54] One day, one of these girls, Janet, comes upon a coloured picture of a seated man who had drawn a little boy close to him; beyond him a group of mothers with children, beyond them a crowd of angry men, and beneath the illustration the text 'Suffer little children to come unto Me . . .', and a hymn. She takes the picture inside as a present to amuse her little crippled brother; a middle-class charitable visitor, who had noticed the beautiful girls in their squalid surroundings, visits their home, explains the message of the pamphlet. The words provide sustenance and hope for the dying cripple; the visiting woman gives Janet the opportunity to become a servant in her own home, and the other girl proves the means of salvation through which her father is weaned off gin and onto the gospel. Providential illumination here is literally found in the dust, where it might least be looked for; similarly, there is a message about human good being redeemable from the least promising surroundings. All these homiletic lessons derive from asking, at least implicitly, the question posed by Eustace R. Conder:

> What can seem of less consequence, or more worthless, than a pinch of dust? You have but to open your fingers and the wind blows it away in a moment and you see it no more. Yet if but one small grain of dust is blown into your eye it will give you a great deal of trouble. One of the terrible plagues of Egypt sprung from a handful of dust, which God commanded Moses to fling into the air. Every little grain scattered into millions and millions of invisible poison-atoms floating through the air

causing boils and ulcers; 'Very great things, you see, may come from very small things – even from dust.'[55] If one picks up on this Biblical reference, incidentally, the heart of the speaker of Tennyson's *Maud* ('My heart is a handful of dust'[56]) is seen not just as dessicated, robbed of loving feeling, but as possessing the

capacity to exude corrosive sentiments. It is not, however, a venge-
ful Old Testament God that is primarily in Conder's mind, but
rather a watchful Christian one, as the reader is reminded that
every one of our actions is watched; that throughout our life, we
constantly leave deposits and pick things up: 'Pray that when your
life-journey comes to an end, the *dust under your feet* may show that
you have been walking in the right road.'[57] God here is turned into
a detective-like figure, just as Sherlock Holmes reads signs of past
movements in the dust in *A Study in Scarlet*:

> 'Patent-leathers and Square-toes came in the same cab, and they
> walked down the pathway together as friendly as possible – arm-
> in-arm, in all probability. When they got inside, they walked up
> and down the room – or rather, Patent-leathers stood still while
> Square-toes walked up and down. I could read all that in the dust;
> and I could read that as he walked he grew more and more
> excited.'[58]

To clear away dust and deposits is to bring the past to light. Harriet
Martineau, visiting Egypt, insists that her choice of a 'fairy gift'
would be 'a great winnowing fan, such as would, without injury to
human eyes and lungs, blow away the sand which buries the monuments . . . What a scene would be laid open then!'[59] To fail to rise
from the dust is to be consigned to the dust-heap of history.[60]
Ouida makes this point strongly, if a little mawkishly, in her short
story 'Street Dust' (1901), in which two orphan children from the
Campagna come into Rome after their mother's death to sell
flowers, are arrested for begging, victimised by what Ouida por-
trays as a corrupt, compassionless bureaucracy, turned helpless
and penniless out of doors, and take shelter in a church portico in a
half-demolished street, down which a keen wind blows 'clouds of
grey dust'. However, in this late Victorian tale, there is no divine
rescuing hand helping these social victims. They are found by scav-
engers the next morning, dead; taken to the mortuary: 'and
thence, none recognizing them, they were carried to the common
ditch in which the poor and nameless lie. / What were they more
than the dust of the street, blown about a little while by the winds,
and then swept away and forgotten?'[61] It is this fear, that dust equals

oblivion, a return to origins which we cannot transcend, that Tennyson seeks to redress in his poetry, most notably in 'In Memoriam'. His dread is that all we will come to is 'Two handfuls of white dust, shut in an urn of brass!' as he puts it in 'The Lotos-Eaters'.[62] 'Dust are our frames', the opening of 'Aylmer's Field' reminds us, drawing on Genesis 2:7: 'God formed man of the dust of the ground.'[63] In the early times after Hallam's death, Tennyson wants to have trust in a notion of immortality, 'Else earth is darkness at the core, / And dust and ashes all that is',[64] but he is vulnerable to the suggestion that it might be possible for a voice from beyond the grave to murmur – from some presumably earthbound afterlife – ' '"The cheeks drop in; the body bows; / Man dies: nor is there hope in dust." '[65] The dread is that human existence, and the memory of it, will be subject to the same process of erosion as hills slowly eaten away by streams to create 'The dust of continents to be';[66] subject to 'Time, a maniac scattering dust';[67] that those who have loved, and suffered, and 'battled for the True, the Just', will at the end of it all 'Be blown about the desert dust',[68] reduced to the elemental fragments that go to make up our physical composition, and deprived of all sense of identity. In the Prologue, however, Tennyson has already set up God's role in all of this. 'Thou wilt not leave us in the dust',[69] he confidently announces, and goes on to piece together the atomised being. Sorrow passes into a sense of 'some strong bond which is to be' as spring comes round for the final time in this poem, offering a conventional promise of renewal with 'the songs, the stirring air, / The life re-orient out of dust'.[70] The final stanza of the poem itself, before Tennyson moves into epithalamium mode, prays, echoing Isaiah, that it may be possible to raise a voice to God to celebrate unprovable truths: 'That we may lift from out of dust / A voice as unto him that hears'.[71]

Tennyson's fear, I suggest, is not just of the certainty and finality of mortality. It chimes with a wider fear of reversion, of history not moving in a confident forwards direction, of contemporary society decaying, or alternatively sinking as a result of catastrophe or degeneration under 'fine ashen dust', to use Bulwer-Lytton's term for that which covered the skeletons found when excavating

Pompeii.[72] The apprehension that haunts Tennyson, and others, is of what might happen both to an individual, and to morally bankrupt society, as apotheosised in the final line of Hopkins's 'The Sea and the Skylark', which expresses the anxiety that we are breaking 'down / To man's last dust, drain fast towards man's first slime'.[73] This dread of reversion provides a dialectical contrast to the prevalent myth of historical progress. It is this property of dust, to remind one that the machines of the industrial age have not supplied the power to drive history forwards, that technological change is not to be equated with social betterment, that history involves the destruction as well as the accumulation of the material aspects of the world, that led to Walter Benjamin's fascination with dust in his vast, incomplete *Passagen-Werk*. He quotes Henri de Pène, writing in 1859 of how he returns from the *Courses de la Marche*: ' "The dust has surpassed all expectations. The elegant people back from the *Marche* are practically buried under it, just as at Pompeii; and they have to be disinterred, if not with pickaxes, then at least with a brush." ' Dust, he goes on to say, 'settles over Paris, stirs, and settles again. It drifts into the Passages and collects in their corners; it catches in the velvet drapes and upholstery of bourgeois parlors; it clings to the historical wax figures in the Musée Gravin. The fashionable trains on women's dresses sweep through dust.'[74] All of this helps suggest to Benjamin that history is, at the very least, standing still: the phenomenon of dust calls the whole idea of progress, of teleology, into question.

Celebrating the beauty of history's meaningless accretions, Marcel Duchamp, as part of the visual notes that he took for the *Large Glass*, fixed dust which had fallen on the surface of a flat pane of glass over a period of months: the result, photographed by Man Ray, was entitled *Elevage de poussière* (*Dust Breeding*) (figure 7). It was not, however, dust itself that was seen as possessing aesthetic potential by the Victorians, with the exception of motes dancing in the sunbeam – and the 'thick-moted sunbeam' which 'lay / Athwart the chambers' in Tennyson's 'Mariana' was above everything else an image of torpor.[75] Even these specks in the air have their demonic opposite, the motes in the moonbeam in *Dracula* which, metamorphosing into vampiric figures, show how Stoker

7 Man Ray, *Elevage de poussière*, 1920, photograph.

has picked up on the poisonous, miasma-like potential of dust in the air. Rather, dust's aesthetic importance, the grounds on which dust is something to be welcomed, rested on its presumed ability to cause certain atmospheric and climatic effects.

The researches and writing of John Tyndall are crucial here. In his essay 'The Scientific Use of the Imagination', first delivered to the British Association in Liverpool in 1870, he presents his fascination with the physical basis of light to a general audience; it is a piece in which, as Gillian Beer has eloquently shown, he places great stress on the scientific importance of the invisible, of oscillating, light-producing waves in the ether.[76] In so doing, he claims that the light of our firmament is not direct solar light, but reflected light. He elaborates on the nature of this reflection by asking why the sky is blue. He rejects the hypothesis that if the sky is blue, the air must also be blue: if this were so, how 'can the light of sunrise and sunset, which travels through vast distances of air, be yellow, orange, or even red?'[77] Rather, the light reflected is blue; the light transmitted orange or red. He asks his audience to imagine that white solar light, as it falls, somehow gets divided, breaking into the colours of the spectrum. What he calls an 'undue fraction' of the smaller light waves are scattered by particles, particles in the air, and the proportions of this scattering ensure the predominance of the colour blue. At this point, Tyndall asks us to consider 'sky-matter':

> Suppose a shell to surround the earth at a height above the surface which would place it beyond the grosser matter that hangs in the lower regions of the air – say at the height of the Matterhorn or Mont Blanc. Outside this shell we have the deep blue firmament. Let the atmospheric space beyond the shell be swept clean, and let the sky-matter be properly gathered up. What is its probable amount? I have sometimes thought that a lady's portmanteau would contain it all. I have thought that even a gentleman's portmanteau – possibly his snuff-box – might take it in. And whether the actual sky be capable of this amount of condensation or not, I entertain no doubt that a sky quite as vast as ours, and as good in appearance, could be formed from a quantity of matter which might be held in the hollow of the hand.[78]

This handful of dust excites not fear, but awe: an awe which Tyndall mediates through Kant's comment that two things fill him with this condition: 'the starry heavens and the sense of moral responsibility in man'.[79] The tiny particles which go to make up 'sky-matter' are responsible for creating our sense of infinity, a sense which A.W. Moore has in turn described as partaking of the paradoxical. Infinity 'is standardly conceived as that which is boundless, endless, unlimited, unsurveyable, immeasurable', yet set against this is our own finitude: 'It is self-conscious awareness of that finitude which gives us our initial, contrastive sense of the infinite and, at the same time, makes us despair of knowing anything about it, or having any kind of grasp of it.'[80] The smallness of dust, in other words, as Tyndall uses it, has the power to create tension between our own sense of equivalent smallness, and the vastness of our physical universe: moreover, the employment of the imagination which is necessary to our comprehension of the operation of 'sky-matter' involves moving beyond our own materiality, the dust of our own bodily composition. 'Breaking contact with the hampering details of earth', Tyndall concludes his piece, the awe felt by the scientist 'associates him with a power which gives fulness and tone to his existence, but which he can neither analyse nor comprehend'.[81]

Not everyone wished to accept Tyndall's theories. Ruskin, in particular, scorned them, and 'rebelled' – in the words of Oliver Lodge, who sent him an article he had published in *Nature* in 1884 on 'Dust' – 'against the idea of dust-motes in the upper regions of the air, and especially resented the idea that the clear blue of the sky could be due to anything so gross and terrestrial as dust'.[82] Tyndall's arguments, however, (although their veracity was being questioned by the end of the century in respect to what *actually* causes the blue of the sky), were rehearsed again by Wallace, who, if anything, was even clearer in explaining that the number of dust particles in ordinary air is so great that they reflect an abundance of light of all wave-lengths; how no dust particles, under experimental conditions, produce darkness; and how a small number of small particles allow blue light to appear, since these are the particles which 'are so minute as to reflect chiefly the more refrangible rays, which are of shorter wave-length'.[83] He goes on to talk about the effect of thicker dust particles in the lower atmosphere, particularly when struck by the slanting rays of the setting sun, producing 'not unfrequent exhibitions of nature's kaleidoscopic colour painting'. The most spectacular effects are produced when the sun has slid below the horizon, and when there are a certain quantity of clouds:

> These, as long as the sun was above the horizon, intercepted much of the light and colour; but, when the great luminary has passed away from our direct vision, his light shines more directly on the under sides of all the clouds and air strata of different densities; a new and more brilliant light flushes the western sky, and a display of gorgeous ever-changing tints occurs which are at once the delight of the beholder and the despair of the artist. And all this unsurpassable glory we owe to – dust![84]

These theories had been confirmed, for Wallace, by the explosion of Krakatoa on 26–27 August 1883 which had released, it was estimated, some 70,000 cubic yards of dust into the atmosphere. These circled the globe several times over the succeeding years, causing the spectacular sunsets of the 1880s. Gerard Manley Hopkins, in one of his rare appearances in print, contributed to a correspondence in the science journal *Nature* recording these recent phenomena, before their cause was ascertained. He notes how they differed from ordinary sunsets, the light being both more intense and yet lacking in lustre, the colours being impure and not of the spectrum. His account of the sunset of 16 December 1883 demonstrates his Ruskin-influenced techniques of precise observation as he notes:

> A bright glow had been round the sun all day and became more remarkable towards sunset. It then had a silvery or steely look, with soft radiating streamers and little colour; its shape was mainly elliptical, the slightly longer axis being vertical; the size about 20° from the sun each way. There was a pale golden colour, brightening and fading by turns for ten minutes as the sun went down. After the sunset the horizon was, by 4.10, lined a long way by a glowing tawny light, not very pure in colour and distinctly textured in hummocks, bodies like shoals of dolphins, or in what are called gadroons, or as the Japanese conventionally represent waves.

So strange are these solar manifestations that he is resorting to similes drawn not from other aspects of nature, but from stylised representation.

> The glowing vapour above this was as yet colourless; then this took a beautiful olive or celadon green, not so vivid as the previous day's, and delicately fluted; the green belt was broader than the orange, and pressed down on and contracted it. Above the green in turn appeared a red glow, broader and burlier in make; it was softly brindled, and in the ribs or bars the colour was rosier, in the channels where the blue of the sky shone through it was a mallow colour. Above this was a vague lilac –

and so it continues.[85] Such sunsets fed directly into Tennyson's 'St Telemachus', into a rather limp and lengthy 'New-Year Ode: to Victor Hugo' by Swinburne, and into *Eros and Psyche*, by Hopkins's friend Bridges:

> Broad and low down, where last the sun had been,
> A wealth of orange gold was thickly shed,
> And touching that a curtain pale of green,
> Like apples are before their rinds grow red:
> Then to the height the variable hue
> Of rose and pink and crimson freaked with blue,
> And olive-bordered clouds o'er lilac led.[86]

Unsurprisingly, as a comparison of Bridges's poem with the entirety of Hopkins's published commentary shows, Hopkins felt somewhat piqued that his own observations seemed to have been appropriated.

The spectacular solar effects were largely seen between October and December 1883, although recurrences were noted throughout 1884. Although the colours described were less strange, apocalyptic hues, probably produced by more localised pollution, continued to characterise *fin-de-siècle* depictions of the London sky, as in Richard le Gallienne's 'Sunset in the City':

> Above the town a monstrous wheel is turning,
> With glowing spokes of red,
> Low in the west its fiery axle burning,

giving back to dust, if indirectly, something of its malevolent quality.[87]

Despite the emphasis which Wallace placed on the aesthetic appeal of dust's effects, he was ready to concede that there might be some who would be willing to sacrifice them if by doing this they would be escaping its disagreeable properties. But dust is not dispensable. He, like other late nineteenth-century commentators on the topic, calls attention to the work of the Scottish scientist, John Aitken, who, through a series of experiments which admitted jets of steam into glass receivers, proved that it is the presence of dust in the higher atmosphere that causes 'the formation of mists, clouds, and gentle beneficial rains, instead of waterspouts and destructive torrents'.[88] The mere cooling of vapour in the air will not condense into such valuable forms of precipitation 'unless *particles of solid matter* are present to form *nuclei* upon which condensation can begin'.[89] Moreover, if there are a lot of particles present – as in the sulphurous atmosphere of a city – particularly dense fogs will form. Aitken's experiments allowed him not only to develop theories about condensation and rainfall, but to perfect an instrument which would count dust particles in specific locations, or produced under specific circumstances (he estimated that 'a cigarette smoker sends forth into the air 4,000,000,000 particles, more or less, with *every puff he makes!*'),[90] and to explain how different atmospheric conditions affect the lungs in different ways. All of this allows Wallace to make a strong case for the rehabilitation of dust's reputation. Despite the fact that it brings dirt, discomfort and even disease, it is 'an essential part of the economy of nature', both helping to render life more enjoyable in aesthetic terms, and being nothing less than essential to our climatic systems. From this, he draws a conclusion very similar to other, more pious commentators: 'The overwhelming importance of the small things, and even of the despised things of our world, has never, perhaps, been so strikingly brought home to us as in these recent investigations into the wide spread and far-reaching beneficial influences of Atmospheric Dust.'[91]

To focus on dust, as I suggested at the beginning of this chapter, raises certain questions about the Victorian fascination with the relationship between the visible and the invisible, and with techniques of seeing, both technological and physiological. Added to this must be concern with the individuality which manifests itself in the act of seeing and the recording of this act: what G. H. Lewes called 'our subjective co-operation in the perception of objects';[92] the fact that 'every single sensation is seen in the light of our Personality'.[93] To recast this through George Eliot's words in *Middlemarch*: 'Will not a tiny speck very close to our vision blot out the glory of the world, and leave only a margin by which we see the blot? I know no speck so troublesome as self.'[94] This analogy, employed to show the impossibility of stable, objective vision, draws on the sense that dust is simultaneously indispensable yet problematic.

The study of dust and its effects, both injurious and beneficial, would have been impossible without the developments which took place in the technology of the microscope, unlocking, as Philip Gosse put it, 'a world of wonder and beauty before invisible'.[95] Once again, the popular literature which developed around the domesticised version of this instrument tended to emphasise the divinely sanctioned social messages to be gleaned from concentrating on the miniature and the obscure. Mary Ward, for example, in *A World of Wonders Revealed by the Microscope* (1858) reminds the 'Emily' to whom this work is ostensibly addressed that one is looking at 'the works of One who judges not as we do of great and small; who "taketh up the isles as a very little thing", and counts the nations as "the small dust of the balance"', yet promises individual salvation to each being from those nations.[96] More generally, the microscope was praised for its ability to train one's powers of careful observation, and for its democracy – a considerable amount of useful work could be performed by the amateur naturalist, it was asserted, with a very cheap instrument; this work could be performed by those living the most cramped of urban existences, taking the raw materials of their science from the world around them, investigating 'the commonest weed or the most familiar insect . . . There is not a mote that dances in the sunbeam, not a particle of dust that we tread heedlessly below our feet, that does not contain within its form mines of knowledge as yet unworked. For if we could only read them rightly, all the records of the animated past are written in the rocks and dust of the present.'[97] Such observation, moreover, may overturn customary categories of judgement. A peacock's feather looks surprisingly boring under a powerful lens,[98] whilst our aesthetic appreciation may be stirred by 'the very beautiful egg of the very horrid Bed-bug'.[99] The plates which Mary Ward includes in her volume suggest the intricate patterns and designs that may be revealed within the most quotidien pieces of detritus (figure 8). We may come to see through '"the world of small"', to use William Carpenter's term, that size is relative, that mass has nothing to do

Specimens of Hair, magnified 200 diameters.   Plate 7.

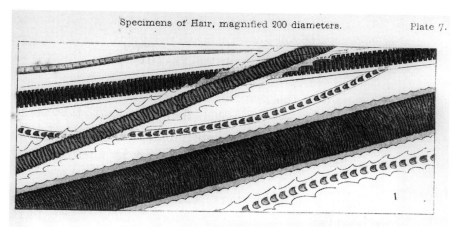

1. Hair of Cat.

2. Hair of Otter.

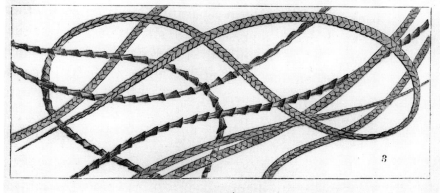

3. Hair of Bat.

8 Illustration to Mary Ward, *A World of Wonders Revealed by the Microscope*, 1858.

with real grandeur. 'There is something', he continues, 'in the extreme of minuteness, which is no less wonderful, – might it not almost be said, no less majestic? – than the extreme of vastness.'[100]

As we have already seen in relation to Tyndall's examination of the heavens, this other extreme also fascinated Victorian scientists, again aided by optical advancements, particularly the development of Herschel's telescope which allowed the galaxy to be penetrated with far greater precision than ever before, with the inevitable result of increasing the individual observer's sense of their own insignificance. In Thomas Hardy's *Two on a Tower* (1882), Swithin, the young astronomer, introduces Lady Constantine to the wonders of astronomy with precisely this outcome:

> At night, when human discords and harmonies are hushed, in a general sense, for the greater part of twelve hours, there is nothing to moderate the blow with which the infinitely great, the stellar universe, strikes down upon the infinitely little, the mind of the beholder; and this was the case now. Having got closer to immensity than their fellow-creatures they saw at once its beauty and its frightfulness. They more and more felt the contrast between their own tiny magnitudes and those among which they had recklessly plunged, till they were oppressed with the presence of a vastness they could not cope with even as an idea, and which hung about them like a nightmare.[101]

This is the vastness into which Tennyson stares in his poem of that name, contemplating the smallness of humanity, the smallness of this earth, whilst out in space 'Many a planet by many a sun may roll with the dust of a vanished race.'[102]

Yet, the more one could see when the natural powers of the eye were augmented by the crafted lens, the more scientists were aware of what lay beyond one's visual reach. It was here that observation of the natural world had to yield place to the importance of the imagination, increasingly recognised as having a central role within scientific inquiry. It took one beyond the part played by the eye – an instrument which, as we saw in the last chapter, in its turn came to be acknowledged as having certain inherent defects. The imagination is the instrument with the true power to open things up. Tyndall invited his reader to:

> Conceive a grain of sand of such a size as just to cover the dot placed over the letter *i* in these pages; there are animals so small that whole millions of them, grouped together, would not be equal in size to such a grain of sand. These are the results of microscopic research; but the microscope merely opens the door to imagination, and leaves us to conjecture forms and sizes which it cannot reveal.[103]

What we are being encouraged to do, in other words, is to learn to see differently, to see with the mind's eye. The powerful lens of the microscope, revealing simultaneously the dangers and the welcome properties of dust, is not enough in itself. Neither is it sufficient to see with the eye of the social recorder, although this may allow one to bring order to the components of dust and hence, in Mary Douglas's terms, to reclaim the properties of the dust-heap from over the borderline of that which has been discarded, and which therefore threatens social order. Dust, as so many commentators on the materiality of this substance pointed out, is a paradoxical substance: a threat, yet, to use a formulation of Wallace once again, 'a source of beauty and essential to life.'[104] Its real fascination to the Victorians lay, however, not so much in the dialectics of this materiality, but in the fact that its insidious physical presence also partook of something far more metaphysical; reached, even, towards the Kantian sublime. As Tyndall acknowledged in 1870, 'beyond the present outposts of microscopic enquiry lies an immense field for the exercise of the speculative power.'[105] The importance of dust to Victorian culture lies precisely in this capacity to suggest the vastness of imaginative conjecture that may lie behind and beyond the most apparently mundane: the invisible behind the visible.

CHAPTER 3

Blindness and insight

In his memoir, *Touching the Rock*, John M. Hull describes the experience of blindness. Partially sighted until his mid-forties, he then lost all vision completely. He recorded a meditative journal on tape, chronicling over a couple of years his adjustment to a sightless world, examining the place of visual memories, the power of dreams, the tension between what he had known and what he now experienced. This tension is one between outward- and inward-looking powers of perception, between ocular and imaginative visualisation. 'Sighted people', Hull remarks, 'live in the world. The blind person lives in consciousness.'[1]

Blindness offers up a central trope for examining the nature and limitations of visual experience. By forcibly reminding one of the fragility of sight ('This sleek and seeing ball / But a prick will make no eye at all'),[2] it presents a challenge to those who assert the dominating nature of the gaze. Moreover, considering blindness dramatises the co-presence of inner and outer vision, and hence problematises the representation of each. Two works of 1856, John Everett Millais's *The Blind Girl* (1856)[3] (figure 9) and Elizabeth Barrett Browning's long poem *Aurora Leigh*, invite their audiences to consider the state and implications of blindness; both demand reading within the many discourses concerning this condition which were in circulation in mid-Victorian England. Whilst in purely practical and material terms, blindness could readily be termed 'one of our greatest calamities. It shuts out from the eye the view of all material objects, and it is accompanied by a train

64

9 John Everett Millais, *The Blind Girl*, 1854–6. Oil on canvas, 82.6 × 62.2 cms.

of mental, physical and pecuniary privations',[4] others were determined to see advantages, even privileges, as attaching to the handicap.

In Millais's painting, the spectator and main subject are unequivocally positioned. The one has the task of interpreting an iconographically charged and crowded representation of a landscape which in its turn bears witness to the power of the visible sign; the other is figured as being in need of an interpreter, a translator of the material world into language, and as being someone who, in her sightlessness, is in a completely passive relation to the artist / spectator. The style of painting, in which each detail is rendered with distinctness and clarity, in itself invites this form of unpacking. As Karl Kroeber puts it, 'We "read" the picture not as a visually coherent object but as a set of self-sufficient details unified by a coherence of affective *significations*.'[5] Yet the blind girl, in her sightlessness, may also be read as a vehicle which reminds the spectator of the importance of a higher, inward vision: a valorisation which interrogates the limits of what a painting may directly be able to show. Thus the dominance of the material and visible world is called into question: moreover, Millais's painting can be seen as a consideration of how one might represent a different sort of vision.

Jacques Derrida, in *Memoirs of the Blind*, a speculative essay considering issues raised by a Louvre exhibition of drawings (largely from the Renaissance) of blindness, provocatively hypothesises that the representation of blindness is nothing less than a representation of the act of drawing itself: 'Every time a draftsman . . . makes the blind a *theme* of his drawing, he projects, dreams, or hallucinates a figure of a draftsman'.[6] All scopic fields, all scenes of drawing are, he argues, organised by means of blind spots: the blind spot, above all, that does not allow oneself to represent the position from which one draws or sees. The spectator's critical role in relation to *The Blind Girl*, therefore, is in part analogous to that which is itself represented in Millais's work, the voice which verbalises and interprets that which the principal subject of the painting cannot see. Our critical practice can profitably go beyond this immediate function, however, in order to clarify that which Millais's medium cannot tell us directly that it knows. In developing this argument, I do not imply that all the meanings extracted here from the painting were necessarily consciously intended by Millais, but rather that they would have been potentially available to a spectator at the time the work was first exhibited, given the contexts in which blindness was discussed. The critical responses to this and other paintings shown in the 1856 Royal Academy exhibition, however, suggest that critics were much more concerned with the implications of colour deployment (were Millais's paintings this year less bright, less vulgar, than previously?) and with accuracy in drawing (are the 'sister's . . . lower limbs . . . out of perspective or out of proportion?'[7]) than with the type of decoding I am employing here. It was in these terms that the *Athenaeum* protested against 'sweetmeat rainbows of lollypop colours, raw green fields, and lace-up boots ostentatiously large' whilst simultaneously condemning Pre-Raphaelite attempts at 'mystical' painting and the absurdities of typological symbolism.[8]

This depiction of a travelling blind girl with a younger figure may be interpreted in a variety of ways. Firstly, one may take it as a work of social commentary, 'a subject full of pathos and very touching in its story', as Millais's wife Effie put it.[9] Depicting a blind, poor woman was an appropriation of a theme more conventionally culturally associated, as Derrida notes, with heroic male suffering. Whilst this particular female is incorporated, as we shall see, into a visual and rhetorical lexicon of blessedness, the incapacitating nature of blindness was, on occasion, compounded with woman's 'natural' constitutional deficiencies:

> Woman without the aid of man is naturally weak, and how incomparably so must they be who are not only debarred from having man's aid, but are also deprived of the inestimable blessing of sight! Weak in body, fearful in mind, utterly without friends and pecuniary resources, and their condition almost rendered hopeless by that greatest of all afflictions, blindness, the position of the greater number of our poor sightless sisters is indeed extremely wretched.[10]

As a representation of powerlessness it serves a different point when, as the Reverend B. G. Johns, one of the mid-Victorian

10 John Everett Millais, *The Blind Man*, 1853. Pen and sepia ink, 20.3×28 cms.

period's foremost commentators on the condition, reminds one, blindness was particularly to be found among the middle and lower classes, 'because smallpox and fever go hand in hand with impure air and scanty food',[11] domestic injuries are more frequent among the poorer members of society and, moreover, outbreaks of epidemic ophthalmia had been especially frequent during and after the Irish potato famine. Certain occupations, such as needlework, notoriously weakened or destroyed the sight of those who practised them.[12]

To read the painting as a social critique would be to develop the theme launched by Millais in his 1853 drawing, *The Blind Man*, where a blind beggar, his begging tin held in his dog's mouth, and bearing the same sign round his neck as the girl in the later painting – "Pity the Blind" – is helped across the street by a charitably minded, respectably dressed young woman (figure 10). This sign was a widely recognised prompt to charity: ' "Pity the poor blind" is an appeal which there is no resisting.'[13] Behind them, the stationers' shop suggests the reading and writing which are denied the

BLIND CHARITY.

11 Cuthbert Bede, 'Pity the Poor Blind!' *Punch* 25, 19 November 1853.

man, an urban counterpart to the visible delights of nature which the blind girl can only appreciate at second hand. The man's companion holds up the horses with her parasol: these horses, significantly, have their own sight restricted by their blinkers, and shy away, like society, from both the blind man and the begging crossing-sweeper. Millais's emphasis on the averted eye can also be found in a *Punch* cartoon by Cuthbert Bede, published the same year: here a portly gentleman drops his pittance, at arm's length, into a hat held out by a ragged man speaking the familiar request: 'Pity the poor blind!' Had he glanced sideways, he would have seen the street child collecting the coin, from a hole cut in the hat's bottom (figure 11).[14] Understood in this context, Millais's painting is a stimulus in the context of the growing concern for those whose

talents are imprisoned by their lack of sight, a manifestation of a
culture of compassion. Increased awareness of the needs of the
blind provided a spur to the founding and support of such institutions as the Institution for Training the Blind in St George's Fields,
London, or Miss Gilbert's Association for Promoting the General
Welfare of the Blind, founded in 1854.[15] This Association, among
other things, supported those who travelled the country – like this
girl with her accordion – retrained and employed workers in their
former or new trades, established a circulating library of Braille
works and, at its centre in Euston Road, had a museum of fossils,
minerals and stuffed animals which could be handled. Such a
touch-oriented collection fostered the sense so important, as
William Michael Rossetti pointed out in the *Spectator*, to the
subject of Millais's painting: of the glorious landscape 'she knows
only what she can *feel*; the mild warmth of the sun, but not its
splendour; she only knows the presence of her sister, who is
turning round to gaze upon the rainbow, by holding her hand, and
the harebells which cluster the bank only by fingering them'.[16]

It was frequently remarked upon that blindness causes the
development of senses other than sight. Annalists of blind achievement adduced, for example, Gough, the blind botanist, who
readily recognised plant specimens with his fingers. This is a belief
explored, in a very tempered way, by Wilkie Collins in *Poor Miss
Finch*, his 1872 novel centring on a girl who has been blind from
early infancy and is faced with the possibility of regaining her
sight. Not only is she a highly competent pianist; much more to the
point of the novel's implausible plot, her fingertips can tell the
difference between the man she loves and his identical twin, who
attempts to usurp his place. Others hypothesised that being blind
involved a reconceptualisation of one's sense of space. John Kitto,
contemplating what the loss of each one of the senses would
mean, suggests that frequently, though blind travellers were often
encountered, their 'progress is less from place to place than from
company to company', conversation taking the place of an actual
change of scene.[17] The aural component of a blind person's life
that was most frequently alluded to, however, was not talk and
communication, but the potentially more interiorised activity of

music-making. Whilst blind musicians had been a commonplace of genre painting from Dutch art through John Wilkie's *The Blind Fiddler* to this accordion player, the presence of the musical instrument in Millais's work is more than a pathos-arousing instrument of her begging. It functions as a reminder of blind people's 'passionate attachment to music':[18] an art form seen as possessing a consolatory quality.

> The great passion . . . in the life of a Blind man once roused to work is Music. 'It is our only enjoyment,' said a blind tramper; 'we all likes it'. Here he thinks he can achieve, if not immortality, at least renown and certain independence. It is to him a source of the highest, purest, pleasure, a solace under all his troubles, almost light in his darkness.[19]

M.F. Halliday's *The Blind Basket-Maker with his First Child*, shown at the Royal Academy in 1858, suggests the uplifting quality of this pleasure through showing the violin and bow of the basket-maker lying on a window-sill in his simple cottage, bathed in the same rays of ennobling light which fall on his wife's face and on their baby's head. In *Mary Barton* (1848), Elizabeth Gaskell appears to grant Margaret her beautiful singing voice, which is also an alternative source of income, as a kind of consolation for blinding her in the interest of the point she is making about the rigours of needlework as a profession.[20] The eyes of many seamstresses suffered from long hours spent working by artificial light: this was particularly true of those who worked entirely on black fabrics.[21] Mayhew records how those who were occupied in sewing soldiers' uniforms had their eyes dazzled and strained by prolonged exposure to scarlet fabric.[22] Exhausted eyes became synonymous with the exploitation of this class of worker, from Thomas Hood's needlewomen with 'eyelids heavy and red . . . eyes . . . heavy and dim',[23] to the speaker of 'The Needlewomen's Farewell', supporting schemes for emigration: 'And so we strove with straining eyes . . . Blear-eyed or blind, we pored and pined'.[24]

We may, however, read *The Blind Girl* according to a different system altogether, one which does not look for direct correlation between its subject matter and the real world which it purports to

12 William Holman
Hunt, *The Scapegoat*,
1854–5. Oil on
canvas, 33.7 × 45.9
cms.

represent. It very readily lends itself to understanding through
typological symbolism, a reading according to the method advocated in Robert Aitken's *The Teaching of the Types* (1854): types
being 'emblems or symbols by which some reality is represented,
or by which something future is prefigured . . . possessing a kind of
living continuity of application, like the actions and words, the
sufferings and death, of our blessed Lord'.[25] Thus the double
rainbow may be read as a symbol of God's covenant of mercy: a
symbol seen also, for example, in the first version of Holman
Hunt's *The Scapegoat* (1854–5), shown at the same exhibition (figure
12).[26] For Ruskin, such a sight appealed to the democracy of sensibility rather than to the demands of systematic scientific investigation: he wrote in *Modern Painters*, III, that 'I much question
whether any one who knows optics, however religious he may be,
can feel in equal degree the pleasure or reverence which an unlet-
tered peasant may feel at the sight of a rainbow.'[27] Simultaneously
with its typological signification, of course, this rainbow stands for
the effects of light which are denied to the blind girl, in the same
way that she cannot take in the delicate beauty of the tortoiseshell

butterfly which perches on her shawl, or see the intense purplish blue of the harebells by her right hand. Nonetheless, it may well be that she would have been thought of as being more acutely sensitive to the touch of the sun on her skin than she would have been had she not lost her sight. With a rather hazy grasp of physics, Thomas Bull, intrigued by the fact that blind people can commonly tell the difference between day and night, surmised that possibly 'the exquisitely sensitive surface of the body, rendered doubly so by the absence of sight, may not only be cognisant of the pulsations of the air, but of modifications of that fluid caused by light itself'.[28]

Light, like the rainbow, was commonly thought of as inseparable from the power of God. This was made abundantly clear by Holman Hunt, again, through *The Light of the World* (1851–3), showing the figure of Christ carrying a lantern (figure 13). Hunt explained the broad significance of this: 'In making it a night scene, lit mainly by the lantern carried by Christ, I had followed metaphorical explanation in the Psalms, "Thy word is a lamp unto my feet, and a light unto my path", with also the accordant allusions by St Paul to the sleeping soul, "The night is far spent, the day is at hand." '[29] Others, notably Ruskin, expanded upon the importance of light in this picture. Ruskin, indeed, detected a two-fold type of light – 'first, the light of conscience, which displays past sin': this is the light carried in the lantern, falling on the closed door, on the weeds which surround it and on the fallen apple, 'thus marking that the entire awakening of the conscience is not merely to committed, but to hereditary guilt'. Second, there is the light springing from the head of the figure, from the crown of thorns: itself 'sad, subdued, and full of softness', this is the light which signifies 'hope of salvation'.[30] The Reverend Richard Glover, in a pamphlet prompted by Gambart's touring exhibition of *The Light of the World* in the autumn of 1861, asks rhetorically: 'What meaneth *that mysterious Lamp* in the Saviour's hand? . . . That lamp symbolizes the Light of His Word – or the truth revealed therein, by which He instructs and teaches His people in all things pertaining to life and godliness.'[31] The prevalence of the idea that light should be equated with God can be demonstrated by looking away from spiritually oriented writing to two contemporary popular scientific

13 William Holman Hunt, *The Light of the World*, 1851–3. Oil on canvas over panel, 125.5 × 59.8 cms.

works. Edwin Sherratt's *A Popular Treatise on the Origin, Nature, and Properties of Light* (1856) cannot be more specific about the *ultimate* origin of light than to quote the originator of the phrase 'LET THERE BE LIGHT';[32] Lieutenant Hardy's *Incidental Remarks on Some Properties of Light*, yet another work of 1856, not only looks to the same luminous source, but, before turning to 'that material light which comes more immediately within the province' of his work, reminds one of the powerful Biblical presence of light, whether in a burning bush, a pillar of fire or embodied in one 'who HIMSELF was that Light which "shineth in darkness, and the dark comprehended it not"'.[33]

The figure of the blind girl's companion can be seen as adding emphasis to the importance of acknowledging the beauties of the natural world. She shelters behind the shawl as a rain shower passes over, but her main function is that of interpreter, the same role which Jane Eyre adopts in relation to the maimed Rochester: 'never did I weary of gazing for his behalf, and of putting into words the effect of field, tree, town, river, cloud, sunbeam – of the landscape before us; of the weather round us – and impressing by sound on his ear what light could no longer stamp on his eye'.[34] A little lower down, the forget-me-nots act as a conventional reminder to the spectator *not* to forget; they perhaps hint that the girl's blindness is doubly cruel since she can remember what she does not now enjoy. The flowers are, in fact, of precisely the same blue as the eyeballs which can just be glimpsed through the gap in the girl's lids. In the middle distance, what the *Morning Chronicle* dismissively termed 'some curious zoological curiosities . . . are scattered about':[35] both the donkey, figuring Christ's passion, and the white horse, from the Book of Revelation, have Biblical overtones, like the flocks grazing on green pastures and the stream of living waters. The black birds certainly count as birds of the field. The hill-top presence of Winchelsea Church, and the fact that the butterfly is a traditional emblem of the soul, underscore the point of God's omnipresent goodness. Moreover, returning to the central figure, the form of her simple headdress, and her expression of rapt attention to an inner vision, are strongly reminiscent of a multitude of representations of the Virgin Mary.

Such a mode of reading is consonant not just with spiritual but with secular modes of signification in Pre-Raphaelite painting of the mid nineteenth century. For example, in another, post-Crimean-War painting exhibited at the Royal Academy in 1856, *Peace Concluded*, Millais has the children, in their play, make what the *Art Journal* termed 'a pointed allusion to the political phase of the time . . . one offering a dove with an olive branch to the father, and on the mother's knee the other typifies the four belligerent powers by a lion, a bear, a cock, and a turkey' (figure 14). One might further note – as contemporary critics did not – the prominent presence in the children's toybox of a tiger and an elephant, as though there were other overseas lands remaining to be played with. Millais's practice of representation on this occasion fell foul of a literal-minded critic – 'These allusions could not be understood by children of such tender years – hence this passage of the composition becomes caricature'[36] – but the general point, the allusive power of symbol, remains clear. Only the difference between the two paintings is a significant one, since *Peace Concluded* draws on symbols which derive their force through a system of signification which has been produced through political and nationalistic associations, whilst to some extent, *The Blind Girl* relies on a far older tradition, the idea that the world is an intelligible text, the 'book of nature'. The slippage between the two – the shift from reading the world to 'looking at it as an observable but meaningless object', to use Martin Jay's terms, and using its contents as a means towards one's own conceptual concretisation – may be read as the shift which Foucault and others have discerned between the old and the modern epistemological orders.[37]

The desire to find compensatory factors, symbolic or otherwise, in blindness leads one to a further, and still more suggestive, set of possibilities. These provoke more generalised exegetical readings than the interpretation prompted by the typological symbolism referred to above. Although they are strongly linked to such interpretation through religious connotations, they can be seen to belong firmly within a less arcane epistemological matrix.[38] For *The Blind Girl* can be understood as alluding to the promise held out by God of inner, rather than external, illumination. This

14 John Everett Millais, *Peace Concluded*, 1856. Oil on canvas, 116.8 × 66 cms.

would be consonant with a repeated Victorian stress on the paradoxical blessings of blindness: a hypothesis with a long history. Calvin had argued that physical blindness was spiritually valuable, because it forces one to listen to the voice of God.[39] Searching for the blessings of blindness, the writer of an article on 'The Blind' in the *National Review* (1860), having cited the philosophers mentioned by Diogenes Laertius, including Democritus, who put out their eyes in order to concentrate their attention on the abstractions on which they were engaged, claimed that 'Vividness of sensation, and clearness of perception, exist always in an inverse relation.'[40] Dinah Mulock Craik wrote that Milton was perhaps able 'all the more through that visual darkness, to see clear into the very heaven of heavens'.[41] Milton, indeed, was continually invoked in the context of the importance of inward vision throughout the Victorian period. He provided the starting point himself when, in *Paradise Lost*, he lamented being cut off 'from the cheerful ways of men',

> Presented with a universal blank
> Of nature's works . . . So much the rather thou celestial Light
> Shine inward, and the mind through all her powers
> Irradiate, there plant eyes, all mist from thence
> Purge and disperse, that I may see and tell
> Of things invisible to mortal sight.[42]

Andrew Marvell took up the theme of compensation for blindness in 'On Paradise Lost', prefixed to the epic's second edition: 'Just Heav'n Thee, like *Tiresias,* to requite / Rewards with *Prophesie* thy loss of sight.'[43] This tradition was readily taken up again in the nineteenth century. William Aytoun, in his poem 'Blind Old Milton' (1841), has the poet soliloquise about how:

> I have had visions in this drear eclipse
> Of outward consciousness, and clom the skies,
>   Striving to utter with my earthly lips
> What the diviner soul had half divined,
>   Even as the Saint in his Apocalypse
> Who saw the inmost glory, where enshrined
>   Sat He who fashion'd glory.[44]

In her *Essays on the Greek Christian Poets*, Elizabeth Barrett Browning celebrated Milton's bravery, 'never reproaching God for his griefs by his despair, . . . praying without ceasing in the security of his sightless eyes; and, because the whole visible universe was swept away from betwixt them and the Creator, contemplating more intently the invisible infinite, and shaping all his thoughts to it in grander proportion'.[45] Earlier in her life, however, she understandably saw the restrictions as well as the inspirational elements attaching to the condition of sightlessness. Her seclusion first in broad social terms as an upper-middle-class woman, and then, after her illness, in the specific location of the sick room, induced ignorance of the world, and put her, she felt, at a disadvantage as a writer. 'Why', she wrote, 'if I live on & yet do not escape from this seclusion, do you not perceive that I labour under signal disadvantages . . . that I am, in a manner, as a *blind poet*?'[46]

But the idea that Milton was aided by his blindness persisted. At the other end of the century, Stephen Phillips published the sonnet 'To Milton, Blind' in 1898:

> He who said suddenly, 'Let there be light!'
> To thee the dark deliberately gave;
> That those full eyes might undistracted be
> By this beguiling show of sky and field,
> This brilliance, that so lures us from the Truth.[47]

More material advantages were seen as accruing from Milton's blindness, too. W. H. Levy hypothesises:

> there is every reason to believe that if he had not lived for the last twenty-two years of his life in a darkened state, the best fruits of his labours would have been lost to mankind. If he had been able to see, it is probable he might not have been pardoned by the king; or his ardent spirit might have induced him to follow the example of so many of his compeers, and seek a home in New England.

If he had remained in England, his love of political life would certainly have been a snare to him; if he had retired from public life, he would have expended much effort on his dictionary and history of England:

As a sighted man, he would not have possessed the powers of concentration necessary to enable him to produce the inimitable 'Paradise Lost' and 'Paradise Regained'. In a word, Milton would never have been what he was unless he had possessed the advantages arising from the possession of sight, and also those which spring from blindness, and it must be generally admitted that the world has only seen one other author at all equal to Milton, viz. Homer; and he, too, was without sight.[48]

Physical blindness may call out compassion in the cultural spectator, as in the case of Oedipus, or Gloucester. Alternatively, it may initially be bestowed like Samson Agonistes', or, more recently, Rochester's blindness in *Jane Eyre*, or the blinding of the over-vengeful hero of Kingsley's *Westward Ho!* as a form of punishment, that ultimately proves to be a means of illuminating the 'inward eye'. Brontë has Jane describe Rochester's pious contrition to us: 'bending his sightless eyes to the earth, he stood in mute devotion. Only the last words of the worship were audible. / "I thank my Maker that in the midst of judgment He has remembered mercy. I humbly entreat my Redeemer to give me strength to lead henceforth a purer life than I have done hitherto!"'[49] In this redemptive guise, blindness functioned as a common trope in sermons and tracts. The author of *Blindness; Its Trials and Blessings* (1863), for example, takes the case of his sightless sister as an example of one who was led by suffering to feel God's mercy: blindness is here taken as a literal manifestation of the way in which the Lord leads humans through bodily darkness to His own marvellous spiritual light. James Smith, in *All Things Preaching Christ* (*c.* 1840), conducts the readers of his pamphlet on an imaginary, but typical, country walk, showing how the simplest things in nature – the sun, a rain shower – may conceal divine meaning, and introduces a blind man into his landscape, to show how dependent he is on trust in his guide: similarly, 'Thy Spirit, thy providence, and thy presence, shall lead me right and bring me through; they shall lead me to fountains of living waters, and I shall feed in green pastures.'[50] The Reverend H. J. Lewis, preaching on 'Human Blindness and Divine Guidance' following the deaths of both a well-loved parishioner and his own son, spoke of the need for trust in God:

the difference between a blind man groping miserably and help-
lessly along the edge of a precipice, over which he may at any
moment fall, and a blind man guided gently and securely home
by the hand of a thoughtful loving friend, that is just the
difference between the condition of a pious and that of a worldly
man, when they are respectively overtaken by overwhelming
calamities.[51]

Notably, blindness was equated with an over-emphasis on the
material world. John Hamilton Thom, holding forth on *Spiritual
Blindness and Social Disruption* in 1849, produced a model for typological readings of nature when he proclaimed that 'there are in
Nature *symbols* of God's character which convey to us many a conviction of the Divine benignity . . . The earliest record of human
feelings tells us that the bow in the cloud was taken for an open
avowal of God's Love.' He goes on to warn his congregation,
however, against placing too much trust in symbols and remaining
blind to the '*real* evidence of God's Goodness to Man',[52] which is to
be found in spiritual experiences: confining one's gaze to what is
before one, he says, prevents one from looking above and beyond.
This, for Thom, is particularly applicable in 'this age of Machinery,
of Great Cities'.[53] In even more sustained fashion, the year after
Millais showed his picture, Christopher Wordsworth, canon of
Westminster, preached 'On Spiritual Blindness'. Many are the vic-
tories, he claimed, which the goodness of God has enabled his contemporaries to achieve in the material universe, but 'whenever the
human mind is absorbed in tracing link by link the sequence of
visible cause and effect – when it moves, as it were, along the rigid
groove of mechanical processes and material results, then it is in
peril of forfeiting its higher and nobler faculty of appreciating the
existence and operation of things invisible'.[54] The redoubtable
High Anglican, Edward Pusey, in *Sinful Blindness Amidst Imagined
Light*, was also to warn against taking too much pride in 'progress
and enlarged knowledge', for we may have 'full light (as men
imagine) as to the material universe in which God has placed us',
and yet be in 'gross moral darkness as to ourselves': 'we are most in
peril of deepest, intensest, absolute blindness, when we imagine
ourselves encompassed, arrayed, penetrated with light. One

might say boldly, since He teaches us, that the completest darkness is where there is the fullest light.'[55]

Read in this manner, *The Blind Girl* becomes more than a work of social commentary, or even of spiritual commentary. It may be seen as a contribution to a developing discourse which set the visibility and epistemological certainties of the material, industrial world, blindly self-regarding in its own pride in its achievements, against the higher worth of divine illumination. In such a context, even such an eminent scientist as the astronomer Richard Proctor could write that 'the man of science who trusts to science alone is too apt to glory in what is known, forgetful how the pride of material knowledge may blind him to far more important truths'.[56] Interpreted within this broader critique of the desirability of utter visibility, the painting may also be understood as forming an interrogation on Millais's part concerning the limitations of his own art. One should probably approach the topic of underlying spiritual solemnity with regards to Millais himself, bearing in mind an anecdote related by his son. During the painting of *The Blind Girl*'s background at Winchelsea, Thackeray joined Millais. An elderly clergyman, one Sunday morning, seeing Millais in front of him as he preached, 'directed his discourse to the comparative beauties of Nature and art. There was no mistaking what he meant for, warming up as he went along, he punctuated his remarks by personal appeals to the artist as to the inferiority of man's work to God's. Leaning over the pulpit with outstretched hands, and eyes fixed on Millais, he cried aloud, "Can you paint that? Can you paint that?" And then, turning to the congregation as he slowly drew himself upright, he added in solemn tones, "No, my brethren, *he cannot paint that*". Again and again this embarrassing scene was repeated, until at last Millais and his friend became almost hysterical in the effort to suppress their laughter.'[57] This tale functions as a double reminder not to read intentionality into available interpretations, and that not all sermonising hit home.

Nonetheless, it is notable that around and after this date, Millais moved away in his painting from compositions crowded with symbolically loaded forms. It was in November 1854 that he is recorded as talking with Tennyson 'as to the limits of realism in painting'.[58]

As Malcolm Warner has very plausibly demonstrated, *Autumn Leaves*, shown the same year as *The Blind Girl*, may usefully be read in a tradition of *vanitas* painting, presenting a message about the inevitable withering of youth and beauty through its incorporation of picked fruit and flowers and rising smoke, and its adoption from the northern poetic tradition of assumptions concerning autumn as a season of decay (figure 15).[59] Unlike the narrative-dependent work of the earlier 1850s – *Mariana* (1851)or *Ophelia* (1852), say – *Autumn Leaves* is, as Warner terms it, 'metaphorical, self-contained and strangely static'.[60] The same adjectives may be applied to *The Blind Girl*.

Millais's critics were not particularly skilled when it came to deciphering these paintings. Whilst a number of newspaper critics were quick to condemn, in the term used by *The Times*, the 'puerility' of the Noah's Ark symbolism of *Peace Concluded*,[61] at least they could decipher what those toy animals denoted. *Autumn Leaves* tended to baffle them, although the *Saturday Review* found it impressive, evidencing, in its 'depth of feeling' – rather than an intellectualising 'depth of thought' – a valuable kind of artistic inwardness.[62] The *Art Journal* complained that *Autumn Leaves* was symptomatic of 'the new transcendentalism', adding 'We are curious to learn the mystic interpretation that will be put on this composition';[63] the *Athenaeum*, too, considered it over-mystical ('we do not see' the 'deep meaning');[64] the *Daily News*, despite having been quick to put down *Peace Concluded* for the fact that one had to pick out the meaning 'piecemeal from various frivolous symbols', and being immune to the implications of apples and gathered flowers held by young girls, comments that 'The meaning would have been suggested much more forcibly, and contrast obtained, if a very old man had been introduced mournfully contemplating the children's thoughtless mirth.'[65] Ruskin, whilst very generous towards *Peace Concluded* and *Autumn Leaves* – perhaps surprisingly generous, given how things stood in personal terms between him and Millais at this juncture – had nothing to say about *The Blind Girl* in his *Academy Notes*. In fact, only *The Times*, pointing out the fact that in *The Blind Girl* 'there is so much of symbolical meaning quite consciously expressed in the

15 John Everett Millais, *Autumn Leaves*, 1855–6. Oil on canvas,
104.1×73.6 cms.

composition of this artist', but without unpacking the detail any further, goes any way towards suggesting that this is a landscape to be 'read'.[66]

However, it is possible to interpret this apparent failure to read the overt symbolism of the painting in a different way. George Landow comments, in relation to the problems the *Athenaeum*'s reviewer had in comprehending Hunt's *The Scapegoat*, that whilst the symbolism was not in itself iconographically obscure, the difficulty lay in the gulf between the intense realism with which the actual scene is set out on canvas, with its consequent appeal to an aesthetics of fact, and the abstract emblematic message which it carried.[67] Hunt here, just like Millais in *The Blind Girl*, was attempting to do what the contemporary critic P.T. Forsyth explained was his aim in *The Triumph of the Innocents* (1876–87):

> to see with two eyes at once, with the bodily eye and the soul's; to gain one vision of two worlds; to read one system in two spheres. The world is a double world . . . The veriest materialist is living two lives. He is performing a conscious part in this world, but he is shaping unconsciously a character which will be all that remains when this material frame shall vanish like a cloud.[68]

Such blinkered readings as were offered, whatever their cause, may plausibly have had a dissuasive effect on Millais's own methods: he produced no more works so densely crammed with allusive detail. More importantly than that, however, when it comes to our own understanding of the painting, contemporary critical responses serve to exemplify how, as Paul de Man put it in his essay 'The Rhetoric of Blindness', 'blindness can take on the form of a recurrently aberrant pattern of interpretation', and that writing critically about critics 'becomes a way to reflect on the paradoxical effectiveness of a blinded vision that has to be rectified by means of insights that it unwittingly provides.'[69] In this case, the insights are two-fold. Firstly, there is the unstartling fact that the modes and sophistication of interpretive methods applied to Pre-Raphaelite painting not only exhibit no homogeneity, but do not necessarily recognise as legible the signs encoded in paintings by the artists themselves. The critics had not learnt the methods which would have been most appropriate for understanding this mode of painting, or were failing to employ such competence that they might have. Secondly, and consequently, we would be unwise to assume that our own understanding of the visual components of the culture of the period, our own knowledge of 1850s systems of representation, in fact constitutes anything like an unproblematised reconstruction of Victorian modes of 'reading' art. What we put together as having been available to a Victorian viewer is no guarantee that a painting was interpreted with all, or even a substantial number, of these potential points of reference in mind. The language of the eye has quite literally changed, as is brought home by the comment of the *Art Journal*'s critic that *Autumn Leaves* contains 'a significant vulgarism' because 'the principal figure looks out of the picture at the spectator'.[70] The limitations, or at least the visual parameters, of contemporary critics, looking very selectively at the canvas surface, blinded them, in the case of *The Blind Girl*, to a crucial (and, in the case of a painting, a troubling) meaning of Millais's painting: that the most powerful form of vision may be inward, rather than directly dependent on the visible, material world.

A couple of years after Millais painted *The Blind Girl*, Elizabeth Barrett Browning explained why she had found it necessary to blind Romney Leigh, the central male character of her narrative poem *Aurora Leigh*: 'He has to be blinded . . . to be made to see.'[71] These are words which closely parallel Romney's fervent sigh of gratitude:

> Thank God, who made me blind, to make me see!
> Shine on, Aurora, dearest light of souls,
> Which rul'st for evermore both day and night![72]

Illumination shines doubly from Aurora: as woman and as poet. The whole poem is shot through with references to eyesight and to vision, and their contemporary relevance is amplified if one places them in the broader context of discourses of blindness. The explicit ways in which these allusions are made allow one to be more confident about them being recognised and understood than when one is dealing with the visual medium.

In *Aurora Leigh*, actual processes of seeing take one, through the imagination, beyond the visible. Aurora's mother's 'rare blue eyes were shut from seeing me / When scarcely I was four years old'.[73] Instead of gazing on the live woman, her daughter perused her portrait, this face becoming a repository for all kinds of mythic, mutable projections of womanhood, even though it did not change in its actual lineaments, so that her mother became by turns a Muse, a loving Psyche, a still Medusa, Our Lady of the Passions, and Lamia: 'That way went my thoughts / When wandering beyond sight.'[74] The poem clearly privileges the inner over the outer form of sight, despite celebrating 'the grace / And privilege of seeing' beauty in the natural world.[75] This natural beauty, at its most intense, is looped back to tropes of divine illumination. When Aurora and Marion arrive in Italy,

> morn and eve
> Were magnified before us in the pure
> Illimitable space and pause of sky,
> Intense as angels' garments blanched with God,
> Less blue than radiant.[76]

By contrast to the rapturous appreciation of the natural world, with its tokens of God's goodness, social practices of seeing are figured as potentially cruel. That gaze which seeks to penetrate, to discover, to trespass on the inner self is an oppressive one, as Aurora finds on arrival at her aunt's, who, 'with two gray-steel naked-bladed eyes / Searched through my face – ay, stabbed it through and through'.[77] Later, believing Aurora loves Romney even though she has just refused him, this aunt 'drew her probing and unscrupulous eyes / Right through me, body and heart'.[78] From this point the whole house, maidservants included, put her under torturing observation, turning her intimate core into an object of drawing-room ornamentation, a freakish display to be wondered at:

> I lived on and on,
> As if my heart were kept beneath a glass,
> And everybody stood, all eyes and ears,
> To see and hear it tick.[79]

These same eyes of the aunt haunt Aurora at her death, even if in the same breath she tries to express incredulity that these blank, open organs had the power to unsettle her.

The poem suggests that to scrutinize entirely, as it were, from the outside – without taking account of the subjectivity of the person perceived – is, limitingly, to force your vision on the world. This is the kind of philanthropy practised by Romney himself, for all his social idealism, and by Lady Waldemar, whose effect on Marion, the girl notes, was like that of the cruellest glare of light –

> Though Lady Waldemar was kind
> She hurt me, hurt, as if the morning-sun
> Should smite us on the eyelids when we sleep,
> And wake us up with headache.[80]

Such scrutiny leaves no room for the imagination, only attempting assessment through facts, and imposing its view of truth through their mustering. As Aurora tells Romney, to balance the work of the economists and the reformers, it is necessary for the artist to 'keep open roads / Betwixt the seen and unseen . . . your Fouriers failed, / Because not poets enough to understand / That life develops from within'.[81]

This, consistently, is the role of imaginative, poetic vision that Aurora claims for herself. 'Inward evermore / To outward',[82] she reiterates in Book v, in a section which amplifies the precise qualities of seeing which are necessary:

> poets should
> Exert a double vision; should have eyes
> To see near things as comprehensively
> As if afar they took their point of sight,
> And distant things as intimately deep
> As if they touched them.[83]

These are lines, incidentally, which surely owe something to Robert Browning's 1852 essay on Shelley, where he reflects upon the 'objective poet's' 'double faculty of seeing external objects more clearly, widely, and deeply, than is possible to the average mind, at the same time that he is so acquainted and in sympathy with its narrower comprehension as to be careful to supply it with no other materials than it can combine into an intelligible whole'.[84] Such a poet is contrasted with the 'subjective' type, who is more a seer than a fashioner, more a mystic than an interpreter, one whose infusion of personality into his writing is figured through a metaphor which contrasts the social display of the objective poet with the formation of vision in the mind's eye: 'He does not paint pictures and hang them on the walls, but rather carries them on the retina of his own eyes.'[85] Barrett Browning's poem dramatises the possibility for the co-existence of both types of vision within the poet–subject, the dialogue of inward and outward vision that characterises not just Aurora, but her own oscillation between outer and inner – albeit ultimately and consistently privileging the latter – in the focus of her gaze.

Again, in Book VII, Aurora muses at length about how the natural is impossible without the spiritual to give it form and motion, and, rather in the spirit of early Ruskin, considers how the artist – the word's used broadly –

> holds firmly by the natural, to reach
> The spiritual beyond it – fixes still
> The type with mortal vision, to pierce through,
> With eyes immortal, to the antitype
> Some call the ideal – better called the real.[86]

Explaining her intentions in writing this 'autobiography of a poetess' in a letter to John Kenyon, Barrett Browning stated even more explicitly that she was setting out to oppose 'the practical & the ideal lifes . . . showing how the practical & real (so called) is but the external evolution of the ideal & spiritual – that it is *from inner to outer*, . . . whether in life, morals, or art'.[87] In all of this, Barrett Browning was writing under the influence of Emanuel Swedenborg, the Swedish philosopher and mystic who maintained that the universe consists of two worlds, that of the spirit and that of nature, the reality of the latter assuming secondary importance to the idealism of the former.

In *Aurora Leigh*, as in contemporary sermons, physical blindness, as we have seen, can be presented as something good, something even – albeit temporarily – to be sought out, as the young Marion Earle

> liked, she said,
> To dazzle black her sight against the sky,
> For then, it seemed, some grand blind Love came down,
> And groped her out, and clasped her with a kiss;
> She learnt God that way.[88]

In this context, it is, perhaps, troubling that at the death of Aurora's aunt, and, even more so, at the early death of Aurora's mother, sightlessness is linked with death. This can probably be explained away, however, by saying that there is no brilliant inward vision ready to take the place of physical sight, as in the case of Romney, ecstatically wreathed by Aurora in the language of the Book of Revelation in the final lines of the poem, despite his sad acknowledgements of what he has lost, and despite his recognition that he has been 'mulcted', or punished, for his earlier views, and left 'A mere blind stone in the blaze of day', the language deliberately echoing *Samson Agonistes*.[89] What he has gained is a quickened sense of the gross materialism of the age, and recognition of the need to listen to God's demands. This has come about partly through experience, but largely through contact with art, in the form of Aurora's latest poem: 'this woman from her crystal soul / Had shown me something which a man calls light'.[90] He alludes, suitably enough, to the story in John 9 of Christ – 'the light of the world' – making the blind man see: thus Aurora's writing, with all its apparent celebration of the importance of inward and creative vision, is also presented as partaking of the Divine.

When one casts around in the 1850s and 1860s, confirmation of the importance of inward vision – of the importance, indeed, of the imagination, couched in ocular terms – continually recurs. That 'Infinite' for which Aurora claimed art and life are hungry has much in common with Tyndall's sense that a physicist's vision must expand into that which the mortal eye cannot see. Throughout the remainder of his career Tyndall promoted the necessity of employing the imagination in scientific inquiry, to allow one to hypothesise about the invisible: 'the vocation of the true experimentalist may be defined as the continued exercise of spiritual insight, and its incessant correction and realisation. His experiments constitute a body, of which his purified intuitions are, as it were, the soul.'[91] As we shall see in the next chapter, perhaps the most articulate of all commentators on this issue, who comfortably bridges the two cultures – and the one, moreover, whose arguments become the least entangled with the language of spirituality – was G. H. Lewes.

The necessity for clear vision lies behind Barrett Browning's 'Art's the witness of what Is / Behind this show', too.[92] Whether this 'what Is' is spiritual in a conventional Christian sense, or whether it merely figures the capacity to imagine, to see with the mind's eye – 'the act of *shutting the eyes* that one may see the more, inwardly', as Walter Pater put it in *The Renaissance*[93] – the problem for artist and writer lies in mediating between vision and representation. It is this consciousness of the transformative process, this awareness of the difficulty of making insight manifest, that is alluded to, I have been arguing, through artistic references to blindness.

In the context of eighteenth-century French interest in the relationship between blindness and language, William Paulson writes: 'blindness poses the problem of an opposition or connection between two properties of language, two ways of understanding language: the externally referential (or representational) and the internally referential (or systematic, or formal), language as a set of signs overlaying the universe and as a self-centred system of hierarchical interrelations'.[94] In its visual representation of blindness, Millais's painting is caught in a double bind. It encourages us to read the details it carefully places before us, and makes our full understanding of its potential meaning dependent on our competence in doing precisely this. Thus it reinforces the link between the mind's ideas and sensory experience that had been gaining in credence since Locke. Yet it also touches, implicitly, on the fact that fascinated Diderot in his *Lettre sur les aveugles*: that since blind people cannot attach visual concepts to the words which they encounter as signifiers, they must rely on abstract, figurative understanding, which they build out of the formal and contextual, rather than the referential, qualities of language. It is precisely this recognition of the importance of inward seeing which is articulated through the figuring of sight, both literal and metaphoric, in *Aurora Leigh*. Both *The Blind Girl* and *Aurora Leigh*, then, function as a reminder of the fact that for all the Victorians' interest in the visible world, we are ourselves demonstrating a form of blindness if we confine our own interest to that which is directly made visible within their culture.

CHAPTER 4

Lifting the veil

> So long as the events are veiled, the imagination will run riot and
> depict all sorts of horrors, but as soon as the veil is lifted, all
> mystery disappears and with it the sense of terror.
>
>   Henry James to the heart specialist, Sir James Mackenzie[1]

In 1844, a wax model went on show in London. On entering the
room where this was displayed, 'we see what seems to be the corpse
of a handsome female who has just expired. It is moulded in wax;
the face is removed like a mask, and the exterior of the limbs and
bosom being lifted, representations of what would appear in a real
subject are pointed out. Anatomical explanations are supplied with
great clearness by the gentleman who attends'[2] (figure 16). This
model was one of a number used to illustrate the structure and
functions of the human body, demystifying the regions beneath the
skin, and allowing members of the public access to sights – albeit
artificially constructed – normally accessible only to the physician.

For nowhere was the Victorian fascination with the possibility,
the necessity of making things visible more in evidence than in the
sphere of medical science. This fascination evolved out of the
work of Enlightenment scientists, who developed, as Barbara
Stafford has put it:

> proper and improper rituals for scanning, touching, cutting,
> deforming, abstracting, generating, concerning, marking, stain-
> ing, enlarging, reducing, imagining, and sensing. Constituting
> visual styles or manners of behaviour, these procedures provided
> right or wrong sensory and intellectual strategies for 'opening'
> recalcitrant materials and otherwise impenetrable substances.

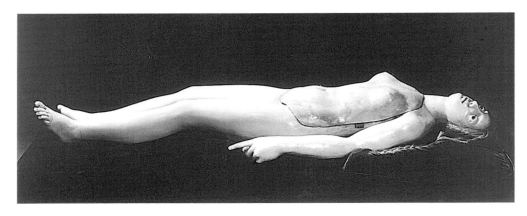

16 Wax anatomical teaching figure (French, eighteenth- century): female, with removable layers revealing internal anatomy.

Normal or abnormal processes and modes for proceeding could assure one, or not, of getting a glimpse into secretive physiognomies. Body tropes thus provided critical clues for how insight might be gained into the interior of any concealed territory.[3]

The task of the medical clinic, as Michel Foucault wrote in *The Birth of the Clinic*, was no longer 'simply to read the visible; it has to discover its secrets'.[4] The secrets of the body are complicated in their concealment, however, since they are apparently contained in two types of system. On the one hand, there are blood, muscle, bone, organs; on the other, the complex workings of the mind. Moreover, these dichotomised systems are still further bifurcated when one considers that invasive practices were increasingly being used to explore the recesses, and hence the specificities, which differentiated women's bodies from men's. The colonisation of this invasive vision is exemplified with startling clarity by the wonderment expressed by the American gynaecologist Marion Sims, when he first inserted a rudimentary speculum into the vagina and was astounded by the unfamiliar intimacy of the organ he viewed: 'I saw everything as no man had ever seen before ... I felt like an explorer in medicine who first views a new and important territory.'[5]

On 17 March 1878, Edith Simcox paid a visit to Eliot and her companion, George Lewes. She recorded their conversation in her

Autobiography of a Shirtmaker: 'I asked about the Lifted Veil. Lewes . . . asked what I thought of it. I was embarrassed and said – as he did – that it was not at all like her other writings, wherefrom she differed.' Diving into another language to carry her point, 'she said it was "schauderhaft" [horrible, ghastly] was it, and I said yes; but I was put out by things that I didn't quite know what to do with'.[6] *The Lifted Veil*, which Eliot wrote in the early months of 1859, and which was first published in *Blackwood's Magazine* in June of that year, has long been a work that critics have not known quite what to do with. It has been seen as a Tale of Mystery and Imagination, in the style of Edgar Allan Poe; a short novel dealing with moral problems; an early example of the sensation fiction which was to become so popular in England during the 1860s. It has stimulated questions concerning the part it plays in Eliot's career as a writer – particularly considering the fact that this is a work in which she conspicuously and deliberately adopts a first-person male persona.[7] The relationship between gender and knowledge – important, as we shall see, to a reading of the tale in the context of medical science – is raised by the implications of the title itself. Veils are inescapably associated with eroticism, exoticism and fetishism. To lift the veil is to peep at the forbidden, to access taboo knowledge; to occupy, by connotation, a masculine, even a godlike position.[8] The equation of veiled mystery with the divine sanctioning of natural processes, rendering them somehow, and desirably, opaque to scientific investigation or explanation, was something of a mid-Victorian commonplace, particularly when it came to the apparent evidence offered by evolutionists. Thus a writer on science, in the *Temple Bar*, commented that 'It is in all respects consistent with what we know, that some intermediate veil should intervene between mortal gaze and the display of infinite power';[9] a contributor to the *Eclectic Review* referred to the 'veil of mystery' which must surely envelop the production of species.[10] Nor should it be assumed that, on lifting the veil, one relishes what one finds: this is the message of Shelley's sonnet where he advises one *not* to shed one's illusions: 'Lift not the painted veil which those who live / Call life', and the horrors of looking, voluntarily or involuntarily, 'behind the veil' inform Eliot's novella.

Latimer, the narrator, does not welcome his unbidden powers of prevision: moreover, the fascination exerted on him by the Water-Nixie, Bertha, is in great measure due to the fact that hers is the only mind he cannot read: 'my oasis of mystery in the dreary desert of knowledge'.[11] Eliot's story is, among other things, a dramatisation of the folly of pursuing Woman on the grounds that she represents a mysterious Other.

Composed at a time when Eliot was developing her theories concerning realism, *The Lifted Veil* is a story which bends laws of probability in order to investigate questions which are implicit throughout many of her later novels: what would happen if we could lift what Latimer calls 'the curtain of the future'?[12] If we could foresee the consequences of our actions, would we act differently? If sympathy towards others is a desirable thing, is it only possible to express this sympathy when we do not know as much as it would be possible to know about the other person? To what extent does personality colour perception? All these questions tend towards a wider issue: if we could have more strongly developed powers of vision, if we could lay bare the future, and the thoughts of others, as a physiologist can lay bare the hidden workings of the mysteriously veiled human body, would we choose to accept such powers?

This question goes beyond a poser for fiction. It was inseparably linked to a developing contemporary debate about the relationship between physiology and psychology. For much of the nineteenth century, the workings of body and mind were commonly believed to be inseparable.[13] However, such assumptions did not pass unquestioned, and I want to suggest, in this chapter, that *The Lifted Veil* may usefully be read as an intervention in this scientific arena. Notably informed by contemporary science, it implicitly poses the question of whether identical hypotheses and modes of investigation are indeed suitable when it comes to understanding the workings of the mind and of the body. In writing *The Lifted Veil*, Eliot, unlike a physiologist, is unhampered by laws of corporeal possibility. The novella provides a controlled space in which she can set up her own experiment, ask 'what if?' At the same time, she carefully ties in the blood transfusion episode, the most ghoulish and incredible of all the scenes in the story – incredible since others than Latimer are witness to it, and it cannot thus be accounted for by hallucinatory peculiarities and coincidence – to contemporary medical science. The novella's interrogation of the limits of positivism are dependent for their importance and credibility on this very definite scientific grounding.

Edith Simcox, like many subsequent critics, may have felt that *The Lifted Veil* was something of a cuckoo in Eliot's fictional nest. In the autobiographical passage quoted above, she records Lewes's contribution to the discussion that she and the novelist were having: 'He Oh, but the moral is plain enough – it is only an exaggeration of what happens – the one-sided knowing of things in relation to the self – not whole knowledge because "tout comprendre est tout pardonner" '.[14] It is notable that Lewes felt that he *could* comment so confidently upon the text's import – even if his explanation may not be crystal-clear to us – since his own connection with *The Lifted Veil* and its themes is a crucial one. For Eliot's novella would have been impossible without Lewes's physiological researches, and in many respects her work should explicitly be seen as being in dialogue with them.

Many of the critical problems posed around *The Lifted Veil* centre on the quality of prevision. Yet prevision is not, in itself, a particularly strange characteristic. On the one hand, it is a term used to describe visionary experience, of the kind employed throughout Victorian writing to give an ominous *frisson* to a story. Thus the bereaved, melancholy hero of Rhoda Broughton's and Elizabeth Bisland's *A Widower Indeed* (1892), gazing at the incomplete inscription of his own name below his wife's on her tombstone, sees the date of his own death appear engraved on the stone before him: for the few remaining pages of the book, he is an inevitably doomed man.[15] Whilst this is a waking vision, dreams were a literary device commonly employed to prophesy misfortune, as we see in the figure of the murderously inclined woman who appears in another work of 1859, Wilkie Collins's 'The Dream-Woman'.[16] Eliot herself returns to the concept of prevision in *Daniel Deronda* (1876), where she describes Mordecai, waiting to speak to Daniel about Jewish history: 'His exultation was not widely different from that of the experimenter, bending over the first stirrings of change that correspond to what in the fervour of concentrated prevision his thought has foreshadowed.'[17] Yet there is also something of the visionary about him, something which Daniel briefly and mistakenly thinks might be 'hallucinations of thought' resulting from a 'diseased organism', but he then realises that 'madness' is far too easy an explanation to describe a consciousness which inhabits 'regions beyond his own experience'.[18] The implications for theories of vision when one examines the uneasy borderland between the illusion and the hallucination, between real and imagined acts of seeing, are considerable, and will be returned to in a later chapter.

As this mention of the term in *Daniel Deronda* suggests, prevision also has its function as a concept within scientific and sociological investigation. Praising Auguste Comte in the final chapter of *The Biographical History of Philosophy*, which he published in 1845–6, Lewes maintained firmly that it is 'easily proved' that 'the positive Method is the only method . . . on which truth can be found on it alone can *prevision* of phenomena depend. Prevision is the characteristic and the test of knowledge. If you can predict certain results and they occur as predicted, then you are assured that your knowledge is correct.'[19] Prevision may be a goal not just of philosophical endeavour, but of physiology. The more we know about the constitution of the body and the relations of its various parts, the more accurately will we be able to understand its functioning, and diagnose and treat its disorders. The importance of the body and its indicative manifestations runs through *The Lifted Veil*. Latimer characterises himself, once his affliction of penetrating, unbidden, into the mental processes of others becomes habitual, as suffering not so much from a mental aberration as from 'the stamp of a morbid organization, framed for passive suffering'.[20] He does not describe his strange 'diseased participation in other peoples' consciousnesses'[21] in supernatural terms, but complains that it results from experiencing 'the lot of a being finely organised for pain, but with hardly any fibres that respond to pleasure';[22] he compares it, in language prefiguring the passage in chapter 20 of *Middlemarch* which contemplates the pain of having too keen a vision of human life, to 'a preternaturally heightened sense of hearing, making audible to one a roar of sound where others find perfect stillness'.[23] Throughout *The Lifted Veil* (as, indeed, throughout all Eliot's subsequent fictions), the workings of the body are inseparably bound in with the emotions. Thus we are presented with the image of Latimer looking back to the fading of what little happiness he has known in his marriage 'as a man might look back on the last pains in a paralysed limb'.[24] Latimer's narrative gains credibility from the fact that he, schooled in science, confidently employs medical vocabulary not just in the examples cited, but as he gives the specifics of three deaths: his brother's, through 'concussion of the brain',[25] Mrs Archer's (peritonitis) and his own foreseen demise, from angina pectoris. Moreover, Eliot, via Latimer, drops a strong hint that not only are bodies important in their own right, but that our comprehension of their workings may be analogous to our interpretation of texts: 'We learn *words* by rote, but not their meaning; *that* must be paid for with our life-blood, and printed in the subtle fibres of our nerves.'[26] *The Lifted Veil*, in its very construction, is based on a paradigm of morbid anatomy: a narrative which keeps pace, to quote Lawrence Rothfield writing of Eliot in a different context, with 'the temporality of the body, its organic growth and decay, its duration of illness, its descent towards death, its complicated finitude: the narrative, in short, of a pathological organicism'.[27]

The speculative, imaginative, fiction-creating mind, with its capacity for prevision, has the ability to travel backwards and forwards in time. The human body, however, has no such ability, and nor, suggests Eliot through Latimer, can our deep-seated responses adjust themselves according to rational knowledge about the one thing which is certain, not speculative, about our futures: 'Our impulses, our spiritual activities, no more adjust themselves to the idea of their future nullity, than the beating of our heart, or the irritability of our muscles.'[28] This language takes us straight into physiology, and the implications of *The Lifted Veil*'s relations with contemporary medical science, with its interest in the connections between mental and physical activity.

The importance of conventional medical science in relation to *The Lifted Veil* has hitherto been passed over in favour of exploring the possible relevance of more tendentious forms of inquiry. Beryl

Gray has usefully illuminated some of the ways in which Eliot's novella relates to practices which lay on the very borders of acceptable science in the mid-nineteenth century, particularly mesmerism, animal magnetism, and clairvoyance.[29] 'Indications of claire-voyance witnessed by a competent observer', Eliot wrote in a letter of 1852, 'are of thrilling interest and give me a restless desire to get at more extensive and satisfactory evidence.'[30] Eliot had become familiar with such highly topical subjects in the 1840s, through her friendship with Charles and Arthur Bray. In 1851, Charles Bray had introduced her to the Edinburgh phrenologist George Combe, with whom she corresponded until her relationship with Lewes put an end to the connection. It should be noted that phrenology proves an inadequate guide to an individual's innate propensities in *The Lifted Veil*. Mr Letherall, friend of Latimer's father, takes the small head of the boy 'between his large hands, and pressed it here and there in an exploratory, suspicious manner – then placed each of his great thumbs on my temples',[31] before detecting supposed deficiencies and excesses of sensibility, and prescribing a course of scientific, classificatory education which ran counter to the young Latimer's natural inclination towards unpractical literary pursuits. Perhaps Eliot was looking back with scepticism at her own experience under a phrenologist's probing thumbs. Through Combe, Eliot became alerted to the work of William Gregory, Professor of Chemistry at Edinburgh University. In his *Letters to a Candid Inquirer on Animal Magnetism* (1853), he writes, as Gray has shown, of the experiences of one of his patients, Mr 'D', who became clairvoyant when in deep mesmeric sleep, developing the capacity to describe accurately places he had never seen, such as Cologne, and people he had never met – in a manner very like that in which Latimer intensely visualises Prague before he has travelled there. Moreover, Professor Gregory believed strongly in the possibility of 'sympathetic clairvoyance', the ability both to read the thoughts of others, and to see into the future, for: 'If past occurrences leave a trace behind them, may not "coming events cast a shadow before?"'[32] *The Lifted Veil* undoubtedly owes a good deal to Eliot's interest in the moral and metaphysical questions raised by such quasi-scientific investigations and speculations. But the relationship between *The Lifted Veil* and more mainstream science is much closer than has previously been recognised, and, as has already been suggested, the main agency of that closeness is, unsurprisingly, G. H. Lewes.

The most sensational scene in the whole work occurs near the end, when the doctor, Meunier, performs an experiment on Bertha's maid and companion, Mrs Archer. This is not a scene which critics have dwelt on with any comfort – if, indeed, they have chosen to confront it at all.[33] 'The blood transfusion incident is a piece of tawdry melodrama, a grotesque and infelicitous flaw, a *fiction*', writes Terry Eagleton; 'We can't believe it; and yet of course we must, for this is a "realist" tale, and within those conventions what Latimer as observer says goes. It *must* have happened – Bertha must therefore be guilty – and yet, somehow, it didn't.' He wriggles out of this problem by suggesting that here we have nothing less than the theoretical problem of realist fiction to ponder upon: how do we know that what Latimer writes is 'truth'? How do we account for Latimer's previsionary powers having failed him with regard to his wife, except by recourse to an explanation which reads into his specific situation a paradigm for the fact that all narrative fiction must pretend 'not to know', to some extent, in order to function *as* a narrative?[34]

Other critics are less subtle than Eagleton, but no less dismissive. Judith Wilt, seeing the novella as a mid nineteenth-century staging post between *Frankenstein* and *Dracula*, labels this 'the most splendidly Gothic scene of all'.[35] 'A lurid scene', Mary Jacobus calls it.[36] Beryl Gray passes hastily over it in her Afterword to the Virago edition, after having initially termed it a 'ghoulish, quasi-scientific resurrection from the dead': 'On the surface, the transfusion of Mr Meunier's own blood straight into the neck vein of the corpse does seem preposterously melodramatic, but it is described quite perfunctorily. The narrative drives on towards the climax, which is not the momentary success of the operation, but the shock of the posthumous release of Mrs Archer's malice.'[37] Even in the article where she concentrates on Eliot and science in relation to this novella, Gray writes of George Eliot's 'unorthodox means', and remarks that the operation emulates 'that remarkable efficiency displayed by many a Gothic doctor when coping with macabre apparatus'.[38] Jennifer Uglow and U. C. Knoepflmacher perhaps comes nearest to offering satisfactory remarks about the episode. Uglow writes that the culminating scene of the novel is one which serves to contradict the wish of Latimer's father, and of his teacher, Dr Letherall, to 'correct the boy's over-sensitivity by a dose of scientific education . . . by a nice twist of the plot, George Eliot shows that they were wrong to see science as devoid of imagination, for in the end, through the activities of Meunier, it will be used to break the barriers of normal reality in the most terrifying way'[39], and Knoepflmacher, in a thoughtful chapter on *The Lifted Veil*, notes that Meunier's response functions as a comment on the limitations of pathological investigations, and this points forward to Eliot's later fiction: '"Life for that moment ceased to be a scientific problem for him", as it will be for that other physician in Middlemarch who must adjust his scientific view of women.'[40]

Yet this blood transfusion is no melodramatic invention on Eliot's part, but is very much in keeping with the theme of medical investigation and questioning which has been raised by Latimer's own condition. Indeed, rather than being sensationalist and improbable, Meunier's experiment is directly linked to contemporary physiology. When Latimer introduces Meunier in his story, as a young man with whom he became friendly in Geneva, he lets us know that he describes him under a pseudonym: 'I shall call him Charles Meunier; his real surname – an English one, for he was of English extraction – having since become celebrated. He was an orphan, who lived on a miserable pittance while he pursued the medical studies for which he had a special genius.'[41] Eliot had, surely, a particular prototype in mind. Born in Mauritius in 1817, Charles-Edouard Brown-Séquard was the son of a French mother and of a captain in the American merchant marine, who died before his child was born.[42] Sometime before the end of 1838, the family's friends clubbed together to send this academically promising boy from Mauritius to Paris, where he quickly passed his baccalaureate and enrolled in the Ecole de Medecine. He had notably little money to live on, and seems to have been something of a social outsider at the time. By 1846, he had begun his experiments in blood transfusion, using the bodies of animals which were on the point of death.

Two of his experiments are of particular interest. In June 1851, Brown-Séquard was provided with the decapitated corpse of a healthy young murderer of twenty, freshly guillotined at eight in the morning. By nine p.m., the muscles had lost their irritability (the irritability of muscles figuring in Eliot's terminology concerning the instinctual movements of the body). The doctor had two medical friends, Dr Bonnetin and Dr Deslauriers, draw half a litre of blood from his own arm, defibrinate it (that is, rid it of the properties which cause clotting) by beating it and then straining out the clots through a piece of linen, and this blood, at a temperature of 19°C – considerably lower than normal body temperature – was then slowly injected into the radial artery of the corpse's arm over a period of ten minutes, and allowed to flow out of the veins which had been opened. In about forty-five minutes at least twelve separate muscles had become irritable, or responsive to sensation, again.[43]

Later the same year, Brown-Séquard attempted an experiment on a dog suffering from peritonitis – the very same ailment from which Mrs Archer expires. He waited until all movement had stopped, the dog had emptied itself of faecal matter and urine, its pupils had dilated and he could no longer hear the heart beat. At this point, he made a transfusion of blood from another, live dog into the right carotid artery. The first sign of temporary recovery was the recommencement of the heartbeat, and then, albeit aided at first by artificial respiration, the dog began to breathe again, and eventually 'all the main functions of animal and organic life returned to it. Although feeble, the animal raised itself on its forepaws and wagged its tail when stroked.' Four or five hours later it died: 'I almost said, died *again*.' Brown-Séquard wrote up this experiment in an article of 1858, 'Research into the possibility of temporarily bringing back to life individuals dying from illness'. This appeared in his own newly launched magazine, *Journal de la Physiologie de l'homme et des animaux*. He concluded his account with a speculation:

Would it be possible to extrapolate from these experiments some consequences relating to the combined application of transfusion, artificial respiration and the blood-letting of the jugular, to the human dying from inflammatory, or other, ailments? It is evident that, in the vast majority of cases, it would be useless, if not cruel, to keep from death, for what would have to be a very short length of time, an individual of our species whose irreparable physical injuries condemned them to die. But one could have cases in which it mattered that understanding, speech, the faculties of the senses and voluntary movement were given back to the suffering patient. For, the facts mentioned in this study, in showing that *all functions of animal life can be reestablished for several hours in animals in which their agony had already almost completely ensured that death had taken place*, make it extremely probable that the intellectual faculties, the faculties of the senses, speech, etc., may be re-established, for several hours, in those sick people who have just lost the use of their faculties.[44]

Such methods were to provoke speculation in other medical researchers, notably in France (and, as a sidenote, it is worth remarking that the transfusion scene itself in *The Lifted Veil* evidently stimulated French artistic imagination: a painting depicting it, by H. E. Blanchon, *La Transfusion du Sang*, was hung in the French Salon in 1879).[45] A. Vulpian, in his *Leçons sur la physiologie générale et comparée du système nerveux faits au muséum d'histoire naturelle*, of 1866, recounts yet another of Brown-Séquard's experiments, in which he transfused blood into the neck arteries of a decapitated dog. After several minutes, the muscles of the eye and the face showed that 'brain functions had been reestablished'. 'Perhaps', continues Vulpian,

I might be taxed with temerity in putting forward the idea that this experiment might be successful with a Man. If a physiologist tried this experiment on the head of an executed criminal, a few moments after death, he would perhaps be witness to a great and terrifying spectacle. Perhaps he could give back its brain functions to this head, and reanimate the eyes and the facial muscles, movements which, in Man, are provoked by the passions and by the thoughts of which the brain is the seat.[46]

Such an idea was taken up by Weir Mitchell, medical practitioner and writer of a substantial amount of sensationalist, sometimes comic, and habitually gruesome fiction, in his 1870 short story for the *Atlantic* magazine, 'Was He Dead?'[47] This tale contains a certain amount of discussion between medical men about the way in which blood transfusion raises questions relating to individual identity, and a recitation of experiments which have been carried out on men and dogs in the past, before they carry theory into practice, and transfuse blood into the corpse of a recently hanged man, a known criminal, who, revivified in this way, confesses to the murder of an elderly woman for which an innocent young man has already swung.

Eliot, however, had already seized on the imaginative possibilities of such a resurrection. She would certainly have been familiar with Brown-Séquard's work. Although she and Lewes were in Germany when he gave his series of six lectures on the Physiology and Pathology of the Nervous System at the Royal College of Surgeons in May 1858, Lewes cites his *Journal de la Physiologie* (which he had in his own library) at some length in his chapter on 'The Structure and Uses of our Blood' in *The Physiology of Common Life*. Moreover, at the time *The Lifted Veil* was published, Brown-Séquard not only had lectured in London, but conducted a fashionable, Harley Street practice: *Blackwood's* readership might well have recognised something of his identity in Meunier.

The Physiology of Common Life came out in 1859, the same year as *The Lifted Veil*. Lewes's interest in the relationship of the life of the mind to that of the body had, as we shall see, a good deal in common with the broad preoccupations of Eliot's novella. Eliot's publisher certainly saw the connections between the two writers, albeit in a fairly narrow way, writing to her that 'I very much dislike the revivifying experiment at the end, and would strongly advise its deletion. I cannot help thinking that some of our excellent scientific friend's experiments on some confounded animalcule must have suggested it.'[48] Although disclaiming that blood may be any more significant in its vital properties than any other part of the human organism, Lewes records the beliefs of those who have thought otherwise, including William Harvey, who first developed a theory of the blood's circulation. He quotes from Harvey's

Anatomical Exercitations concerning the Generation of Living Creatures, (1653): 'Life consists in the blood (as we read in Holy Scripture), because in it the Life and Soule do first dawn and last set ... The blood is the genital part, the fountain of Life, *primum vivens, ultimum moriens*.'[49] He himself attributes considerable vital force to this fluid, describing its circulation through the body as 'a mighty river of life ... the mysterious centre of chemical and vital actions as wonderful as they are indispensable, soliciting our attention no less by the many problems offered to speculative ingenuity, than by the important practical conclusions to which our ideas respecting the Blood necessarily lead'.[50] Strikingly, Latimer's affliction of prevision is described by Eliot in terms which are highly similar to those in which Lewes writes of blood's circulation. Latimer asks whether the reader is 'unable to imagine this double consciousness at work within me, flowing on like two parallel streams which never mingle their waters and blend into a common hue?'[51] This closely echoes the passage in *The Physiology of Common Life* which describes the circulation of the blood in highly suggestive terms:

> If for a moment we could with the bodily eye see into the frame of man, as with the microscope we see into the transparent frames of some simpler animals, what a spectacle would be *unveiled*! Through one complex system of vessels we should see a leaping torrent of blood, carried into the depths and over the surfaces of all the organs, with amazing rapidity, and carried from the depths and surfaces through another system of vessels, back again to the heart: yet in spite of the countless channels and the crowded complexity of the tissues, nowhere should we detect any confusion, nowhere any failure. Such a spectacle as this is *unveiled* to the mental eye alone, and we cannot contemplate it, even in thought, without a thrill [my italics].[52]

Yet the 'uninterrupted throbbing stream' of life,[53] to quote Lewes again, is itself not unmitigatingly positive in its associations. Blood also carries with it the connotations of a pollutant, and hence its representation carries with it a range of superstitions and taboos. These are briefly alluded to when Latimer refers to the Faust myth:

'It is an old story, that men sell themselves to the tempter, and sign a bond with their blood, because it is only to take effect at a distant day.'[54] As Lewes reminds us, 'By some the Blood is regarded as the source of all diseases.'[55] It bears associations of violence, wounds and the shedding of waste products. Furthermore, it differs from the other major category of pollutant, the excremental, precisely because of something which is latent in those lines from Harvey: its relationship to sexual difference. For blood is not just that which flows through each living being's veins, but is that which is shed by the menstruating woman. The threat which it presents in this connection has been summarised by Julia Kristeva in *Powers of Horror*: she differentiates it from 'Excrement and its equivalents (decay, infection, disease, corpse, etc.)' which 'stand for the danger to identity that comes from without: the ego threatened by the non-ego, society threatened by its outside, life by death. Menstrual blood, on the contrary, stands for the danger issuing from within the identity (social or sexual).'[56] Blood is troublesome as it belongs to the category which Kristeva designates as the abject: for her, it is 'not lack of cleanliness or health that causes abjection but what disturbs identity, system, order. What does not respect borders, positions, rules.'[57]

Blood transfusions, especially when, as in Eliot's story, they are between a man and a woman, provide a powerful image for this disturbing challenging of symbolic as well as physical boundaries. We find this in a late short story by the sensation novelist, Mary Braddon, *Good Lady Ducayne* (1896): Lady Adeline Ducayne, a very elderly aristocrat, draws young blood in order to keep up her own strength from the arm of her companion, Bella Rolleston. The syringe is inserted whilst the girl is chloroformed, and she only slowly comes to realise that the marks on her arm are not mosquito bites, but a medicalised form of vampirism. Medical writings themselves helped to sexualize the practice of blood transfusion, since it was most commonly carried out on women about to give birth or who had just given birth. It was recommended, too, that men rather than women supplied the vital fluid, since they were less liable to faint.[58] This challenging of boundaries is most famously played upon in Bram Stoker's *Dracula* (1897).

In Stoker's novel, the implications of blood transfusions are unmistakably sexualised. Dr Seward writes in his diary, after his blood has first been used to reanimate Lucy's white, wan body, that: 'it was with a feeling of personal pride that I could see a faint tinge of colour steal back into the pallid cheeks and lips. No man knows till he experiences it, what it is to feel his own life-blood drawn away into the veins of the woman he loves.'[59] There is an illicit thrill involved in this exchange of fluids: Professor Van Helsing reminds Seward not to breathe a word of this to Lucy's fiancé Arthur, since it would engender jealousy; '"A brave man's blood is the best thing on this earth when a woman is in trouble"', a donor is told – '"You're a man, and no mistake."'[60] In this context, it has become something of a commonplace to call on the remark of Freud's follower, Ernest Jones, made in his study of 1931, *On the Nightmare*, that 'in the unconscious mind blood is commonly an equivalent for semen'.[61] Moreover, as Elisabeth Bronfen has pointed out, the 'artificial reanimation' which takes place 'is also a representation of paternal birthgiving ("a feeling of personal pride"), pitched against natural decay, and implicitly against the maternal function'.[62]

The mingling of bodily fluids in Mrs Archer's body, ensuring her temporary resurrection, reveals her intense hatred for Bertha. 'The scene', as Mary Jacobus puts it, 'presents as self-evident the proposition that women are murderously commonplace, morally debased, loving neither men nor each other, but only themselves; and that this essential, unredeemably carnal feminine nature persists even beyond death – residing in the body itself.'[63] But the transfusion leads to more than this. Mrs Archer's words are not so much inward-looking as oracular, pointing – literally – an accusing finger at Bertha, pronouncing the authoritative evidence for her mistress's murderous intentions towards Latimer. The intake of *male* blood, through the combined power of Meunier's body and profession (for class as well as gender boundaries are traversed in this transfusion), gives Mrs Archer new power to speak. This is something which may be related back to the way in which this text functions as an experiment in, among other things, Eliot's awareness of the complications involved in a woman author writing with masculine authority – whether one uses 'masculine' in the

sense of personal identity, or dominant discourse. Such an awareness is voiced more explicitly much later in the century, once again
in connection with images of blood, women's modesty and uncovering. In an essay of 1896, 'The Colour of Life', the poet Alice
Meynell writes that:

> Red has been praised for its nobility as the colour of life. But the
> true colour of life is not red. Red is the colour of violence, or of
> life broken open, edited, and published. Or if red is indeed the
> colour of life, it is so only on condition that it is not seen. Once
> fully visible, red is the colour of life violated, and in the act of
> betrayal and waste. Red is the secret of life, and not the manifesta-
> tion therof. It is one of the things the value of which is secrecy,
> one of the talents that are hidden in a napkin. The true colour of
> life is the colour of the body, the colour of the covered red, the
> implicit and not explicit red of the living heart and the pulses. It is
> the modest colour of the unpublished blood . . . In the case of
> women, it is of the living and unpublished blood that the violent
> world has professed to be delicate and ashamed.[64]

This passage seems to express anxiety about women publishing
their innermost feelings, violating their selfhood, penetrating into
and spilling that which they want to keep for themselves, and it
then turns round on itself to speak of the world's awkwardness
when faced, head-on, with the revelation of such feelings. It is
uncomfortable about the whole question of whether to publish
involves crossing gender lines – a question highly relevant, of
course, to Eliot's own career, and, more particularly, to her choice
of publication under a pseudonym. It is notable that *The Lifted Veil*
– the one major work in which she employs an explicitly male first-
person narrative to convey the thoughts of her central figure – was
written at precisely the time that the identity, and hence gender, of
the person behind the name 'George Eliot' was becoming widely
known.

Yet in the long run, a pathologised reading of *The Lifted Veil*
invites interpreting the novella not just in the light of experiments
in transfusion, and by extension the way in which making the
inner voice public may involve entering a masculine world; it may
usefully be placed back in the context of *The Physiology of Common*

Life as a whole. In doing this, we can see that considering Eliot's interest in the operations of the conscious, the unconscious and the imagination in this work entails more than looking at the physical and figurative broaching of gender boundaries, even if the gendering of knowledge may still be at stake. Lewes's text, like Eliot's story, is concerned with the relationship of the normal and the abnormal, the connections between mind and brain, and between cerebral activity and physical functions. It is essential, Eliot shows not just in this novella, but in subsequent writings, to acknowledge, as Lewes does in his physiological and psychological works, the interrelations of mental and physical processes. This does not mean, however, that one should seek to be able to subject aspects of the mind's operations to detailed scientific scrutiny, to unveil them. Latimer's 'super-added consciousness' is in many ways a dramatisation of the desire voiced by Lewes: 'if for a moment we could with the bodily eye see into the mind of man'. The experiment, however, does not necessarily yield wondrous results, even if the promise of just such a revelatory experience is precisely that which any imaginative novelist holds out. Rather, Eliot suggests, through Latimer's unveiling of others' thoughts, the experience might be a tawdry rather than a miraculous one. Instead of providing a welcome, miraculous revelation:

> it urged on me the trivial experience of indifferent people, became an intense pain and grief when it seemed to be opening to me the souls of those who were in close relation to me – when the rational talk, the graceful attentions, the wittily-turned phrases, and the kindly deeds, which used to make the web of their characters, were seen as if thrust asunder by a microscopic vision, that showed all the intermediate frivolities, all the suppressed egoism, all the struggling chaos of puerilities, meanness, vague capricious memories, and indolent make-shift thoughts, from which human words and deeds emerge like leaflets covering a fermenting heap.[65]

The weaknesses of his brother's character, for example, may be read not through ordinary behavioural gestures, but 'in all their naked skinless complication'.[66]

In the chapter in *The Physiology of Common Life* entitled 'Feeling and Thinking', Lewes makes it extremely clear that he regards his own task, as a physiologist, as being essentially different from that of the psychologist. Whilst mind and body are, for him, in constant interplay: 'Our science does not pretend to cope with the mysteries of his.' In going along with this, as she does, Eliot is tacitly contesting the orthodoxy of her time that a woman's mental processes may be explained by the functions of her body. Lewes continues by noting that although the mysteries of the mind's workings will most probably for ever remain unsolved, the labours of physiologists have in the meantime 'made it possible that there should be at least a science of those vital phenomena connected with the Nervous System; and "thus", to use the fine expression of Professor Huxley, "from the region of disorderly mystery, which is the domain of ignorance, another vast province has been added to science, the realm of *orderly mystery*"'.[67] Yet it is important that this sense of mystery is acknowledged. It is as orderly mystery, *The Lifted Veil* suggests, that the workings of the minds of others are perhaps best preserved.

In the introductory chapter, we encountered Eliot's suspicion of physiognomy, her view that, as the narrative voice comments in *Middlemarch*, 'so much subtler is a human mind than the outside tissues which make a sort of blazonry or clock-face for it'.[68] The mind occupies a concealed, intriguing, mysterious space, operating as a submerged and at times an opaque, unreadable force, and Eliot's perception of its role is consonant with the line she took concerning important developments in contemporary science. Following the publication of *On the Origin of Species* later in 1859, she wrote to Barbara Bodichon that 'to me the Development theory and all other explanations of processes by which things came to be, produce a feeble impression compared with the mystery that lies under the processes'.[69] Moreover, this guarding of the intimate, the personal, had contemporary resonances with the scrutiny under which she increasingly felt she was being placed in her own life, as a writer whose identity was becoming public, and as a woman openly living with a man who was not her husband. Slightly later, early in 1861, she communicated to her friend Sara Hennell about her fear of uncovery and her desire for privacy:

> I have destroyed almost all my friends' letters to me, simply on that ground – because they were only intended for my eyes, and could only fall into the hands of persons who knew little of the writers, if I allowed them to remain till after my death. In propor-tion as I love every form of piety – which is venerating love – I hate hard curiosity; and unhappily my experience has impressed me with the sense that hard curiosity is the more common temper of mind.[70]

In *The Lifted Veil*, Eliot implicitly questions the idea that mental processes may most usefully be understood by examining a con-jectured continuous relationship between mind and body. In so doing, she conspicuously interrogates the positivistic implications and desires of contemporary physiological science. Moreover, in arguing that we perhaps would not want to see where we might be able to see – if science would allow us to – Eliot's novella challenges that often-assumed Victorian drive towards making things visible. Establishing the precise scientific context of *The Lifted Veil*, and demonstrating Eliot's knowledge of contemporary medical debate, allows one to see this work as a deliberate questioning of the desirability of specularity. Rendering 'the invisible visible by imagination',[71] she suggests, is far more valuable as a tool for understanding the human mind than lifting aside the fleshly veil, and looking within with the bodily eye.

The idea of the imagination as an invasive, although not repre-hensible voyeur had already been articulated by Eliot, when in *Adam Bede* she wrote, rather coyly, that 'imagination is a licensed trespasser: it has no fear of dogs, but may climb over walls and peep in at windows with impunity'.[72] In the way in which it is linked both with curiosity concerning the present and – as one sees in *The Lifted Veil* – with speculation about one's own futurity, the exercise of the imagination is a common human characteristic: 'We are all of us imaginative in some form or other, for images are the brood of desire.'[73] By the time of *Middlemarch*, however, in which this gener-alisation appears, Eliot's understanding of the imagination had come to be mediated through scientific imagery rather than through metaphors taken from social activity, and granted a power of visualisation which surpasses even that available to optical technology. The type of imagination most prized by Lydgate when a young, ambitious, intellectually energetic doctor was not that which manifested itself in artistic show – 'in indifferent drawing or cheap narration' – but the 'imagination that reveals subtle actions inaccessible by any sort of lens, but tracked in that outer darkness through long pathways of necessary sequence by the inward light which is the last refinement of Energy, capable of bathing even the ethereal atoms in its ideally illuminated space'. Lydgate, we learn in a significant phrase, 'was enamoured of that arduous invention which is the very eye of research'.[74]

If in *The Lifted Veil* Eliot entered into a dialogue with Lewes on the subject of vision and the imagination in which she implicitly pitted herself against his physiological emphasis, by the late 1860s, I would argue, these two writers had drawn closer together on this topic. Lewes's prolonged discussion of visuality and imagination in *The Principles of Success in Literature*, published in the *Fortnightly* in 1865, dwells on the issue of the inadequacy of our sight alone. He had already addressed this in an article in *Blackwood's* in 1860, entitled 'Seeing is Believing', where he writes of the danger of confounding vision with inference, using this general principle as a means of debunking spiritualism, spirit-rapping and table-turning. The fact that one sees a table move, or tongs leap from the fireplace, or a dinner table, complete with wine and fruit, rise in the air, does not provide evidence of supernatural agency: it would be more accurate, claims the pragmatic Lewes, to say that one *could not see* how something was done: 'It is one thing to believe *what* you have seen, and another to believe that you have seen *all* there was to be seen.'[75] Lewes's attitude, here, is that of the strict materialist.[76]

In *The Principles of Success*, however, Lewes devotes a whole section to 'The Principle of Vision', in which he is far less sceptical about the importance of inference, which he comes to acknowledge as necessarily going hand in hand with the information granted by the use of one's senses: perception supplements sense.

Thus sense may record a certain coloured surface; perception supplies one's knowledge of the roundness, the firmness, the fragrance and taste of an apple, the whole powers of the mind being involved in bringing the apple into one's consciousness. The suggestion of sense rapidly recalls one's experiences of the object: 'were it not for this mental vision supplying the deficiencies of ocular vision, the coloured surface would be an enigma'.[77] Inference, he continues, is only a higher form of the same process: 'We look from the window, see the dripping leaves and the wet ground, and infer that rain has fallen. It is on inferences of this kind that all knowledge depends. The extension of the known to the unknown, of the apparent to the unapparent, gives us Science.'[78]

This is a development of John Stuart Mill's inductive method: a method which found its most eloquent expression, in relation to the physical sciences, in the way John Tyndall was explicitly to harness the power of the imagination in relation to scientific investigation. He termed it 'the divining rod of the man of science': an instrument, in other words, caught between the status of the simplest of tools used to uncover the most elemental of substances, and the medium of the gifted seer. That imagination which counts, for Tyndall, is not 'an imagination which catches its creations from the air, but one informed and inspired by facts, capable of seizing firmly on a physical image as a principle, of discerning its consequences, and of devising means whereby these forecasts of thought may be brought to an experimental test'.[79] It is a facility which goes beyond all mechanical powers currently available to the scientist, and which, idealistically, refuses to take as final 'the phenomena of the sensible world, but looks behind that world into another which rules the sensible one. From this tendency of the human mind systems of mythology and scientific theories have equally sprung.'[80] At the end of chapter 2, we saw the simultaneous uncertainty and excitement which, for Tyndall, surrounded the limitations to microscopic vision, between the microscopic limit and the true molecular limit, which involves consideration of a bewildering 'excess of complexity' when it comes to considering the infinite permutations and combinations of atoms which are possible. The crisis this provokes is an ontological as well as a scientific one:

> We are struck dumb by an astonishment which no microscope can relieve, doubting not only the power of our instrument, but even whether we ourselves possess the intellectual elements which will ever enable us to grapple with the ultimate structural energies of nature.
>
> But the speculative faculty, of which imagination forms so large a part, will nevertheless wander into regions where the hope of certainty would seem to be entirely shut out.[81]

For Lewes, correct scientific reasoning involves first of all factual, material observation, and then extending this practice into 'seeing with the mind's eye', being capable of summoning up objects in their actual order of co-existence and succession, and seeing where the chain of logic thus created leads one. He acknowledges that often we do our thinking by means of signs – words – rather than images, for the whole image may be too distracting, but 'vigorous and effective minds habitually deal with concrete images'.[82] It is on this point that the scientist and the poet, for Lewes, draw close to one another, for, he asserts: 'No man ever made a discovery (he may have stumbled on one) without the exercise of as much imagination as, employed in another direction and in alliance with other faculties, would have gone to the creation of a poem.'[83]

The poet has greater freedom in what may be imagined: 'his vision includes things which might be, and things which never were':[84] that, for Lewes, is the main difference between the writer and the scientist. Poet, philosopher and scientist share in their task: to 'render the invisible visible by imagination'.[85] For each, 'without clear Vision no skill can avail. Imperfect Vision necessitates imperfect representation.'[86] Good literature, he maintains, 'rests primarily on insight. All bad literature rests upon imperfect insight, or upon imitation, which may be defined as seeing at second-hand.'[87] Talented writers will employ their mental vision to expand their sensory perception, and to build on their stored knowledge of the natural world, ready to transform it, for such writers have the gift of thinking in images, not abstractions. Although he draws a clear distinction between the affective registers of Science and the Arts – 'in Science the paramount appeal is to the Intellect – its purpose being instruction; in Art, the paramount appeal is to the Emotions'[88] – it is, in fact, precisely this talent of using a visualising imagination that the successful scientist, too, must call into play. This is how experimentation must be, literally, envisaged. Everyone, he writes, 'who has really interrogated Nature with a view to a distinct answer, will bear me out in saying that it requires intense and sustained effort of imagination. The relations of sequence among the phenomena must be seen; they are hidden; they can only be seen mentally.'[89]

'Even strictly-measuring science', Eliot wrote in relation to Mordecai and his 'visionary excitability', 'could hardly have got on without the forecasting ardour which feels the agitations of discovery beforehand, and has a faith in its preconception that surmounts many failures of experiment'.[90] One must use the imagination, as Tyndall put it, to 'rend the veil which separates the sensible world from an ultra-sensible one'.[91] It is in being able to exercise this facility fully, in being able to make leaps beyond repeating or varying previous experiments, that true originality, in whatever sphere, consists: 'The discoverer and the poet are inventors; and they are so because their mental vision detects the apparent, unsuspected facts, almost as vividly as ocular vision rests on the apparent and familiar.'[92] In sum, Lewes concludes: 'The often mooted question, What is Imagination? thus receives a very clear and definite answer. It is the power of forming images.'[93] As such, it is valuable to the artist and scientist alike.

CHAPTER 5

Under the ice

In 1891, George Joachim Goschen, Lord Rector of Edinburgh University, gave his inaugural lecture, in which, he said, he had tried to find 'some topic on which he might equally claim the attention of the students of the humanities, of medicine, of philosophy, of science, indeed, of all the faculties'.[1] The topic on which he seized was the imagination: 'The imagination which I have in view is the power of picturing absent things, of presenting to the mind's eye visions of the past or the future, of realising the mental attitude and thoughts of another person or of an alien race.'[2] This is the faculty, he went on to elaborate, which had been of such importance to Charles Darwin, piecing together the theories of temporality in its relation to animal life; this is the faculty which has been crucial to physical scientists, considering the constitution of matter: 'in all physical research, I am convinced that no powerful instrument, no lens, no microscope is more essential to your equipment than a true imaginative mind.'[3]

How may a non-specialist audience be made to see those forces and operations within nature which remain invisible to the naked eye of observation? This was a question preoccupying many early and mid-century scientists. 'How then are those hidden things to be revealed?' inquired John Tyndall, not looking meditatively inward, towards mental imaging as part of his own investigative technique, but drawing in his lecture audience to share in this problem: 'How, for example, are we to lay hold of the physical basis of light, since, like that of life itself, it lies entirely without the domain of the sense?'[4] Although he was himself famous for his public scientific demonstrations,[5] Tyndall presents his task in terms of debunking theatrical showmanship, wishing, if possible, to take his auditors and readers 'behind the drop-scene of the senses, and to show you the hidden mechanism of optical action', the aim being 'to uncover to some extent the unseen things of nature . . . to lighten the darkness which surrounds the world of the senses'.[6]

On the occasion of the delivery of that seminal lecture, 'On the Scientific Use of the Imagination', Tyndall's illustrative subject was, as we saw in chapter 2, the cause and mechanism of light: something not only compelling in its own right, but which provided, through its inherent vocabulary of illumination and obscurity, a powerful figurative vehicle for dramatising the way in which the imagination can reveal the invisible. There is a suggestion, too, in the choice of vocabulary through which Tyndall describes bringing illumination to obscurity, of the scientist taking over something of the authority commonly associated with the divine.

Tyndall approached the theme of light through invoking our knowledge of transmission of another quality: 'The bodily eye . . . cannot see the condensations and rarefactions of the waves of sound. We construct them in thought', and he asks us to extend our inquiries from the auditory nerve to the optic nerve.[7] Instead of sound waves passing through the air, with their origin in a given vibrating body – whether this be human vocal chords or an organ pipe – his audience is invited to envisage a similar train of waves through the dense, elastic matter which is the ether, emanating, in their turn, from a particle of vibrating matter. 'Such a particle we name an atom or a molecule. I think the seeking intellect when focussed so as to give definition without penumbral haze, is sure to realise this image at the last.'[8] Tyndall confidently makes one's cognitive apparatus a symbiotic whole with the object of its inquiry.

It is not with Tyndall's consideration of the operations of light, however, important as they are, that I shall primarily be concerned in this chapter, but with his participation in a different debate, that concerning the explanations for glacial movement. Rather, I shall be looking at the ways in which 'those charming word-pictures for which [Tyndall] is so famous' – as the *Lancet* put it[9] – the sense of obligation which he felt was incumbent upon the scientist to

17 Joseph William
Mallord Turner,
*Source of the Arveron
in the Valley of
Chamouni, 1803,
Liber Studiorum.*

project his conclusions 'into language which shall leave no mistake
as to his meaning',[10] were part of a widespread search among scientists and those concerned with investigating the phenomena of
physical science to find an adequate vocabulary, an expressive set of
visual images through which to convey their particular explanations for the operations of the unseen.

The glacier was a paradoxical phenomenon to nineteenth-century
observers. It appeared static, yet could suddenly roar into life,
destroying what lay in its path. Icy and barren, it lay side by side
with cornfields. Dorothy Wordsworth, in 1820, looking at where
the Arveiron glacier turned into a river, claimed that: 'no spectacle
that I ever beheld – not even the ocean itself – has had an equal
power over my mind in bringing together thoughts connected
with duration and decay – eternity, and perpetual wasting – the
visible and *invisible* power of God and Nature'.[11]

To all intents and purposes, the glacier, unlike other objects of
geological investigation, was mysteriously alive. John Ruskin
praised Turner's drawing for the *Liber Studiorum* of 1803, *Source
of the Arveron in the Valley of Chamouni* (figure 17) in terms which

indicate this central interpretive challenge facing mid-century *sci-entists* confronting the natural phenomenon of the glacier: Turner had 'fastened on this means of relating the glacier's history. The glacier cannot explain its own motion; and ordinary observers saw in it only rigidity; but Turner saw that the wonderful thing was its non-rigidity. Other ice is fixed, only this ice stirs.'[12] As Byron observes in *Manfred*, a poem constantly quoted by later geological commentators, and painted by later artists, like John Martin (1838), the 'glacier's cold and restless mass / Moves onward day by day'.[13] The *Pall Mall Gazette* in 1887 noted that it was 'a remarkable instance . . . of poetic insight that the geologists' "laws of glacier action" should have been anticipated' by Byron,[14] but, as we shall see, figurative language was essential to the means by which scientists came to find an enabling language in which to explain their researches.

This chapter is concerned with the implications of such metaphoricity. More particularly, it is concerned with the operations of 'physical analogy' in figuring the invisible. 'Physical analogy' is James Clerk Maxwell's term, invoked to describe 'that partial resemblance between the laws of a science and the laws of another science which makes one of the two sciences serve to illustrate the other'.[15] The expression 'science' may, in this context, be extended to include the operations of the visible natural world, as, for example, when Maxwell himself strove to explain how the movement of molecules might be envisaged:

> If we wish to form a mental representation of what is going on among the molecules in calm air, we cannot do better than observe a swarm of bees, when every individual bee is flying furiously, first in one direction, and then in another, while the swarm, as a whole, either remains at rest, or sails slowly through the air.[16]

The implications that I wish to investigate are two-fold. First, the ways in which mid nineteenth-century scientists build on contemporary cultural associations in order to clarify their technical points to a non-specialist audience are readily revealed. More importantly still, glacial studies can be seen to have had implications for the development of methods of non-biological scientific investigation which reach beyond the investigation of rivers of ice. The glacier forms a privileged site for the observation of the interplay of metaphors between 'literary' and scientific texts, something which simultaneously emphasises, of course, the difficulties during much of the Victorian period of drawing clear cut distinctions between such texts in terms of rhetorical practices. This conjunction was succinctly stated by Charles Kingsley when writing of James Forbes's pioneering work of 1843, *Travels through the Alps of Savoy*:

> We have heard Professor Forbes's book on glaciers called an Epic Poem, and not without reason. But what gives that noble book its epic character is neither the glaciers, nor the laws of them, but the discovery of those laws; the methodic, truthful, valiant, patient battle between man and Nature, his final victory, his wresting from her the secret which had been locked for ages in the ice-caves of the Alps, guarded by cold and fatigue, danger and superstitious dread.[17]

It was a conjunction which could be regarded with anxiety. In the Preface in which John Tyndall explains the organisation of *The Glaciers of the Alps* (1860), he claims that he has quite deliberately separated it into two parts, 'Narrative' and 'Science', 'believing that the mind once interested in the one, cannot with satisfaction pass abruptly to the other'.[18] His own need for telling metaphor in both sections, however, not to mention his concern to tell the history of glaciology as an organised narrative in the scientific section, belies this desire for neat generic classification.

Shelley's glaciers, in 'Mont Blanc', are menacing, deadly, encroaching presences.

> **The glaciers creep**
> Like snakes that watch their prey, from their far fountains,
> Slow rolling on; there, many a precipice,
> Frost and the Sun in scorn of mortal power
> Have piled: dome, pyramid, and pinnacle,
> A city of death, distinct with many a tower
> And wall impregnable of beaming ice.

Yet not a city, but a flood of ruin
Is there, that from the boundaries of the sky
Rolls its perpetual stream; vast pines are strewing
Its destined path, or in the mangled soil
Branchless and shattered stand; the rocks, drawn down
From yon remotest waste, have overthrown
The limits of the dead and living world,
Never to be reclaimed. The dwelling-place
Of insects, beasts, and birds becomes its spoil
Their food and their retreat for ever gone,
So much of life and joy is lost. The race
Of man flies far in dread; his work and dwelling
Vanish, like smoke before the tempest's stream,
And their place is not known.[19]

They find their analogue in Mary Shelley's *Frankenstein*, where the monster stalks his creator over the same Alpine phenomenon, the Mer de Glace, on the slopes of that mountain – 'the most desolate place in the world', she called it in her diary entry of 25 July 1816.[20] Percy Shelley, in the letters to Peacock describing his trip to the Alps (letters copied up by Mary), wrote of the verge of a glacier presenting 'the most vivid image of desolation that it is possible to conceive', an example of continuous destructive motion: 'the enormous pinnacles of ice perpetually fall, & are perpetually reproduced', in the process smashing the pines which lie at the forest's edges. This motion and forcefulness of the glacier seemed to him to signify a power, a will, with an intensity which can only be expressed through comparison with human volition:

> This vast mass of ice has one general process which ceases neither day nor night. It breaks & rises forever; its undulations sink whilst others rise. From the precipices which surround it the echo of rocks which fall from their aerial summits, or of the ice & snow scarcely ceases for one moment. One would think that Mont Blanc was a living being & that the frozen blood forever circulated slowly thro' his stony veins.[21]

Although refusing to personify the mountain in his poem, he is searching, in both letter and verse forms, for an adequate language in which to describe the force which lies behind the operations of nature.

The fact that the Shelleys could endow their glaciers with such sinister power is due in no little part to the fact that they considered them not just as magnified manifestations of malice, whatever its origins, but that they interpreted them in the light of available scientific theories. 'Within this last year', Percy Shelley wrote in the same letter:

> these glaciers have advanced three hundred feet into the valley. Saussure the naturalist says that they have their periods of increase & decay – the people of the country hold an opinion entirely different, but, as I judge, more probable. It is agreed by all that the snows on the summit of Mt Blanc & the neighboring mountains perpetually augment, & that ice in the form of glacier subsists without melting in the valley of Chamounix during its transient & variable summer. If the snow which produces the glaciers must augment & the heat of the valley is no obstacle to the perpetual subsistence of such masses of ice as have already descended into it, the consequence is obvious. – The glaciers must augment, & will subsist at least until they have overflowed this vale. – I will not pursue Buffons sublime but gloomy theory, that this earth which we inhabit will at some future period be changed into a mass of frost.[22]

In looking backwards to Buffon, whom he had been reading during the summer of 1811, Shelley was, as he half concedes here, deliberately choosing to align himself with that scientific writing which appeared to offer proof of the apocalyptic advance of a frozen world. He was, in fact, flying in the face of contemporary scientific trends. Whilst Buffon had argued that the world was slowly cooling, taking the advance of Alpine ice-caps as proof, geologists and naturalists were beginning to take note of the fact that glaciers, over time, adopted patterns of advance and retreat. They were considering the causes which inhered within the make-up of the glacier and ensured its movement, rather than attributing this movement to some external spirit.

Later in the nineteenth century, the notable Alpinist Leslie Stephen looked back to the early years of the century as the time when the high Alps were first written about with a combination of intense poetic awe and admiration, and accurate, scientific observation.[23] It was not that glaciers had previously been absent from poetry. In 1798, Helen Maria Williams, explicitly seeing the high Alps through Rousseau's eyes as a site of 'tranquil rapture', sat down on the edge of the Mer de Glace, gazed at the 'theatre where the divinity has displayed the most stupendous of his earthly works' and wrote a hymn concluding:

> where the moss forbears to creep,
> Where loftier summits rear
> Their untrod snows, and frozen sleep
> Locks all th'unclouded year;
>
> In every scene, where every hour
> Sheds some terrific grace,
> In nature's vast, overwhelming power,
> THEE, THEE, my GOD, I trace![24]

The same year, William Coxe attempted to redress the unfair emphasis which he felt Erasmus Darwin had placed in the *Botanic Garden* on the 'Nymphs of Primeval Fire' who inhabit the earth's centre, by writing the Complaint of 'The Glacier-Goddess, on her chrystal sphere'.[25] At a lighter level, 'Eliza', in 1796, wrote a comic account of an outing of women tourists to the Mer de Glace.

> Suppose the sea heaving and swelling,
> Arrested in act of that motion,
> With colours the rainbow excelling,
> And you'll faintly conceive the Ice Ocean.
>
> The torrents that scare you withal,
> The deep fissures that strike ye with wonder,
> The immense rocks of ice, as they fall,
> With reverb'rating noise loud as thunder.
>
> Yet though 'twas enchantingly fine,
> *Très superbe, magnifique*, the rude murmur,
> Still the part I thought nearest divine,
> Was when my feet touched *terra firma*.[26]

The presumed familiarity with the location exemplifies the remarks made by Gibbon in his *Autobiography* that in 1755 the fashion of 'climbing the mountains and reviewing the glaciers' had not yet been introduced by foreign visitors, but that when he returned to Lausanne in 1783, this fashion for excursions on the ice had 'opened us on all sides to the incursions of travellers'.[27]

Rather than focus on new philosophical attitudes, most particularly the questioning of God's absolute power within nature, Leslie Stephen linked the changes which took place within literary writing to changing methods of scientific inquiry:

> The judgement passed on mountain scenery in different generations would, I imagine, curiously illustrate the relation between the poetical and the scientific stage of thought characteristic of any given period . . . The mountains are now intensely real and, so to speak, alive to their fingers' end; they began by being empty metaphysical concepts, and the difference is simply due to the fact that nobody had then taken the trouble to look at them, and that a great many highly-skilled observers have been working at them very carefully ever since.[28]

Along with observation went classification. The late eighteenth century not only saw the development of classical mineralogy into a new science of geognosy (to use Abraham Werner's contemporary term) which made possible the historical investigation of the earth, but witnessed an increasing scientific emphasis on the internal structuration of plants and animals which brought the function of these organisms into prominence, and led to the introduction of a rigid distinction between living and non-living things. The study of glaciers was an area which was extremely relevant to geognosy, and which both invited and apparently justified the application of experimental models. Thus John Tyndall wrote of the Lower Glacier at Grindelwald in 1860: 'At first the ice presented an appearance of utter confusion, but we soon reached a position where the mechanical conditions of the glacier revealed themselves, and where we might learn, had we not known it before, that confusion is merely the unknown intermixture of laws, and becomes order and beauty when we rise to their comprehension.'[29]

It was not, however, the appearance and functions of glaciers themselves as they made themselves visible which formed the initial object of investigation, but the peculiarities of those deposits which were subsequently proved to be glacial in origin: geological rubbish; matter out of place.. Across Northern Europe, vast areas were mysteriously covered in chaotic assemblages of sediments ranging from muds, silts, sands and gravels to till (pebbles and boulders of rocks embedded in fine-grained matrix). It was frequently impossible to make out any simple sequence of deposit for these sediments. Still more strange were the large erratic boulders deposited on hill, plateau and plain, differing in rock type from their surroundings, and themselves containing rock and pebble deposits which originally belonged many miles away.[30] They were initially as mysterious in their origins as Wordsworth's Leech Gatherer:

> As a huge Stone is sometimes seen to lie
> Couch'd on the bald top of an eminence,
> Wonder to all who do the same espy;
> By what means it could thither come, and whence.[31]

Such a mixture of types of rock can be seen in the foreground of John Brett's *The Glacier of Rosenlaui* (figure 18), a painting of 1856 which, through its tumbled rock deposits, directly alludes to topical debate.[32] A glacial erratic is central to William Dyce's *The Man of Sorrows* (1860) (figure 19), in which Christ is juxtaposed with the material evidence that a geological, rather than theological, timescale must be held responsible for the appearance of the earth. In 'Resolution and Independence', Wordsworth went on to compare both man and stone to 'a Sea-beast crawl'd forth':[33] appropriate enough at a time when the common explanation for the strange distribution of rocks and other deposits rested in the belief that this could have resulted from 'no power of motion with which we are acquainted' (to quote Sedgwick in 1825),[34] but must have been caused by a great flood, widely identified with the Biblical deluge. Gradually, however, this diluvial theory was replaced by drift theory, with non-catastrophic causes being invoked, such as the alternating glaciation and deglaciation of the

18 John Brett, *The Glacier of Rosenlaui*, 1856. Oil on canvas, 44.5×41.9 cms.

northern and southern hemispheres. The deposits, including the boulders, were thought – according to the theory advanced by Lyell in *The Principles of Geology*[35] – to have been carried on icebergs breaking off from the edges of the frozen areas, a hypothesis fuelled by the increasing attention paid to icebergs by such travellers as Darwin on the *Beagle*. Although De Charpentier, working in Switzerland in the early 1830s, developed a theory, based on the

19 William Dyce,
The Man of Sorrows,
1860. Oil on canvas,
34.29 × 49.53 cms.

observations of a chamois hunter in the Val de Bagnes and on the beliefs of local peasants, that the deposits had been left by glaciers which had now long since retreated, and that the scratches on rocks in valleys were traces of the earlier progress of such glaciers, this hypothesis, with its concomitant hypothesis that there had once been periods when much of Northern Europe and, indeed, Northern America had been covered by glaciers, was relatively slow in being accepted. Crucial to this acceptance was the research and writing of Louis Agassiz. Here, incidentally, one can see an unusually direct example of the influence of poetry on scientific study. Agassiz's friend, Karl Schimper, wrote a poem in 1837 to commemorate Galileo's birthday, *Die Eiszeit: für Freunde gedruckt am Geburtstage Galilei.*[36] The earliest reference to an Ice Age, the term was quickly adopted by Agassiz, who handed out copies of the poem at his lectures. Agassiz's *Etudes sur les glaciers* (1840), together with his lectures, private discussions and correspondence, helped spread his ideas throughout Europe, and they were widely accepted by the mid 1850s, something signified by the changes made to the ninth revised edition of Lyell's *Principles of Geology* in 1853.

It is time to return to an examination both of the problems which glaciologists encountered when developing an adequate language in which to describe and evoke glacial phenomena, and of the transactions which took place between different modes of writing. Glaciers presented their internal evidence in terms which invited linguistic comparisons. Glacial movement showed itself most obviously in sound: the sharp report of an opening crevasse, the sudden crash of a falling avalanche. Mary Shelley's Frankenstein describes the sound of 'the cracking, reverberated along the mountains, of the accumulated ice, which, through the silent working of immutable laws, was ever and anon rent and torn.'[37] To quote Alfred Wills in *Wanderings Among the High Alps* (1858), 'the glacier speaks with almost ceaseless utterance'.[38]

But written rather than aural testimony was more commonly adduced. Wills notes that the tiny scratches on the polished rocks at the sides of a glacier, the superimposition of different layers of snow which one can see when peering into a crevasse, 'are specimens of the language in which they reveal their origin, their composition and their history'.[39] Tyndall, in *Hours of Exercise in the Alps* (1871), develops this idea of a language which needs deciphering, writing of the Grimsel region of Switzerland as 'a weird region – a monument carved with hieroglyphs more ancient and more grand than those of Nineveh or the Nile. It is a world disinterred by the sun from a sepulchre of ice. All around are evidences of the existence and the might of the glaciers which once held possession of the place'.[40] The glacier itself could also be read as the medium on which the passage of time is inscribed. James Forbes, in *Travels through the Alps of Savoy*, exclaimed: 'What a curious internal historical evidence, then, does a glacier bear to the progress of events which have modified the surface! It is an endless scroll, a stream of time, upon whose stainless ground is engraven the succession of events, whose dates far transcend the memory of living man.'[41]

How did a glacier come to manifest these traces of its own history? To recap on familiar knowledge: these researches passed through successive phases. First it was believed that the body of ice slid along its own channel by the force of its own weight, obeying the laws of gravity – but then it was realised that the glacier did not in fact obey gravitational forces. Next was advanced the theory of dilation: the little fissures and air cavities which the ice contains filling up with melted water during the day, and re-freezing at night-time, creating the movement which slowly propelled it forwards. But the whole glacier moves, not just the top few feet affected by these constant changes. It was left to Forbes to show why the glacier truly moved: it is fluid, a viscous body. 'Now,' wrote Wills, paraphrasing Forbes, 'upon reading this definition, the mind is involuntarily startled . . . ice, in the masses in which we are accustomed to see it, appears so devoid of plasticity, that the conception of its viscosity presents, undoubtedly, at first sight, a formidable difficulty.'[42]

The problem faced by geologists was one of how to describe this invisible process so that the lay public would come to comprehend it. John Ruskin, who was fascinated by glaciers and their movements, was concise in his explanation. Accept, he said, that whilst one herring is unmistakably solid, a whole heap of these fish being poured out of a net may indeed be thought of as liquid.[43] Forbes concludes his *Travels Through the Alps* with a less disconcerting surreal image: 'Poets and philosophers have delighted to compare the course of human life to that of a river; perhaps a still apter simile might be found in the history of a glacier.' It is brought forth from the 'hidden womb' of the mountains; at first soft and ductile, it takes on a character and firmness of its own. It must, however, obey some familiar laws. 'Having at length attained its greatest width and extension, commanding admiration by its beauty and power, waste predominates over supply, the vital springs begin to fail; it stoops into an altitude of decrepitude; – it drops the burdens, one by one, which it had borne so proudly aloft; – its dissolution is inevitable' – although it then turns into a 'noble, full-bodied, arrowy stream, which leaps rejoicing over the obstacles which before had stayed its progress, and hastens through fertile valleys towards a freer existence, and a final union in the ocean with the boundless and the infinite'.[44]

Forbes was building, in both his language and his conclusions, on a number of ideas inherent in the way in which people had come to write about glaciers. Not all of these concepts drew parallels between the form of the glacier and the human body, however, although I shall shortly return to the anthropomorphic implications of the language used to describe this phenomenon. A significant number of allusions developed the idea that a glacier is a type of historical monument with a history that might be elucidated. These metaphorical devices go back to the earliest accounts of the Alps. Bishop Burnet, in 1687, refused to believe that the mountains themselves, in their obstructive ugliness, could be 'the primary productions of the Author of Nature, but are the vast ruins of the first world, which at the deluge broke here into so many inequalities';[45] his son, William Burnet, writing in 1708, could not, however, resist describing the snow-fields themselves in terms of ecclesiastical architecture. Going up to the Grindelwald glacier – the most accessible, and hence the most written-about glacier in all the late seventeenth and early eighteenth centuries – 'There I saw, between two Mountains, like a River of Ice, which divides it self into two Branches, and in its way from the Top of the Mountains to the bottom swells in vast Heaps, some bigger than St *Paul's* church'.[46] Such architectural tropes continued. Agassiz wrote how the needles of ice on the sides of the Mer de Glace are 'like the fret-work on an ancient cathedral'.[47] Others looked even further back in history seeking to emphasise, in human terms, the stretches of time invoked by glacial phenomena. Again looking at the Mer de Glace, Forbes wrote of 'the pillars of ice, with their rocky capitals, studded over the plain like fantastic monuments of the Druid age',[48] and Leslie Stephen observed that

> the accurate observation of Alpine phenomena . . . supplies the mountains with a new language as imposing and sublime as that which is spoken by the ruins of human workmanship. The Pyramids or the broken arches of a Roman amphitheatre are not more impressive to the rightly prepared understanding than the vast obelisks and towers that have been raised and carved and modelled by mysterious forces throughout ages of indefinable antiquity.[49]

A further type of figurative language extended the anthropomorphic and bestial attributes of the glacier into the realm of myth. Shelley, again, had been here before the scientists, imagining, in his letter to Peacock, the glaciers to be the dwelling-place of the destructive god of Zoroastrian mythology, Ahriman, the subject of Peacock's unpublished *Ahrimanes*, with the tyrant:

> throned among these desolate snows, among these palaces of death & frost, sculptured in this their terrible magnificence by the unsparing hand of necessity, & that he casts round him as the first essays of his final usurpation avalanches, torrents, rocks & thunders – and above all, these deadly glaciers at once the proofs & the symbols of his reign.[50]

As Shelley had been fascinated with the perpetual renewal which seemed to characterise a glacier's existence, so was James Forbes. For him, the glacier of Miage did not just resemble a ruminating monster, with its 'series of unformed ridges, like the heaving of a sluggish mass struggling with intestine commotion', but manifested on its surface a puzzling glacial phenomenon, reflecting 'the strange law of the ice-world, that stones always falling seem never to be absorbed – that, like the fable of Sisyphus reversed, the lumbering mass, ever falling, never arrives at the bottom, but seems urged by an unseen force still to ride on the highest pinnacles of the rugged surface'.[51] The *British Quarterly Review* similarly recorded, perhaps with 'Kubla Khan' and Coleridge's subterranean 'caves of ice' in mind: 'Sometimes the stony ridges are found to disappear, the blocks being swallowed up in great chasms, and sometimes they return to the surface, like the classical waters of Alpheus and Arethusa.'[52] Often, the mythological imagery employed, like that of the predatory snakes in 'Mont Blanc' (a figure echoed in the 'crawling glaciers' of *Prometheus Unbound*),[53] echoed superstitions which had been held within Alpine regions until quite recent times. Kircher, a leading Jesuit, visiting the Alps around 1666, noted the common belief in the high Alps as the dwelling-place of demons. Scheuchzer, on his Alpine tours between 1702 and 1711, despite being the first person to invent a theory of glacier motion, also found evidence of dragons inhabiting the rivers of ice.[54] Returning to the mid nineteenth century, Ruskin, finding a serpent on one of the stones in Turner's *Liber Studiorum* plate of the Mer de Glace, considered the glacier itself as a serpent, issuing forth

venom where it melted.[55] Volume 9 of the *Alpine Journal* contains
an account of a village priest exorcising a glacier which was
advancing on the fertile fields of a village, which resulted in its
retreat.[56] Even in 1860, this mythological imagery, redolent of
predatoriness, stealthiness and sin, provided a powerful frame-
work for discussing scientific glacial theory. J. R. Leifchild, writing
in the *British Quarterly Review*, opens his survey article by claiming
that one can hardly help regarding a glacier but 'as some huge
monster which has just been convulsed with passion, and suddenly
paralysed with all its agonies imprinted on its frame'. Despite
going on to elucidate the rival theories concerning the movement
of ice under stress, he concludes by reinvoking this 'huge serpent'
stealing down from its mountain solitude: 'Slowly, warily, doubt-
fully it proceeds. With many a fearful wrench, and many a muffled
cry of agony, it drags its ponderous frame, all agape with wounds,
across the sharp rocks and along the jagged ravines. On it creeps
until, reaching the valley, it pauses with head upreared, as if preparing to strike its prey.'

Most frequently of all, the metaphors used to describe and
explain the glacier were human ones. The glacier could be compared with parts of the human frame – especially the hand, or foot,
each with their capacity to encroach and advance. Particularly
influential was the comparison which Henry Longfellow made in
Hyperion (1839), writing that the glacier is glove shaped, 'lying with
the palm downwards, and the fingers crooked and close together.
It is a gauntlet of ice, which, centuries ago, Winter, the king of
these mountains, threw down in defiance to the Sun; and year by
year the Sun strives in vain to lift it from the ground on the point of
his glittering spear.'[57] Forbes began an article in *Good Words* in 1862,
popularising glaciation theory, with this quotation,[58] and his
scientific rival Tyndall, in *Glaciers of the Alps* (1860), also explicitly
recalled Longfellow, and then reappropriated his terms with
greater topographical precision: 'the glacier resembles a vast
gauntlet, of which the gorge represents the wrist; while the lower
glacier, cleft by its fissures into finger-like ridges, is typified by the
hand'.[59] Elsewhere in his writing, crevasses are 'jaws'. For Gerard
Manley Hopkins, visiting the Alps in 1868, just before he began his

novitiate, and recording his impressions with a Ruskinian attention to detail, the base of the same glacier was like a 'foot, a broad limb opening out and reaching the plain, shaped like the fan-fin of a dolphin or a great bivalve shell turned on its face, the flutings in either case being suggested by the crevasses and the ribs by the risings between them, these being swerved and inscaped strictly to the motion of the mass'.[60]

More frequently, the glacier was compared to the whole being. Unknowable, untouched, remote, frigid, dangerous, the glacier was, as one wearily might anticipate, readily referred to as feminine. Particularly vulnerable to feminisation was the peak above Lauterbrunnen which the Swiss themselves call the *Jungfrau*. Wordsworth, for example, in one of the Ecclesiastical sonnets, 'Illustration. The Jung-Frau and the Fall of the Rhine near Schaffhausen', wrote of:

> The Virgin-Mountain, wearing like a queen,
> A brilliant crown of everlasting snow,
> Sheds ruin from her sides; and men below
> Wonder that aught of aspect so serene
> Can link with desolation.[61]

Longfellow's hero Flemming gazes up in awe: 'There it stood, holy and high and pure, the bride of heaven, veiled and clothed in white, and lifting the thoughts of the beholder heavenward.'[62] Tyndall, however, figures the mountain as rather more moody: 'During our journey upwards the Jungfrau never once showed her head, but, as if in ill temper, had wrapped her vapoury veil around her. She now looked more good-humoured, but still she did not quite remove her hood; though all the other summits, without a trace of cloud to mask their beautiful forms, pointed heavenward.' For him, the mountain is one among a bevy of celestially beautiful females: 'Surely, if beauty be an object of worship, those glorious mountains, with rounded shoulders of the purest white – snow-crested and star-gemmed – were well calculated to excite sentiments of adoration.'[63] Once a glacier's movement, rather than sublime remoteness, began to form the focus of attention, so, too, could typically 'feminine' motion be called upon by scientists, or those

with scientific interests. Ruskin, in the third of the lectures which
formed *Deucalion* (1875) – a lecture with a title, 'Of Ice-Cream',
which indicates his search for memorable examples of melting
solids by which he might convince his listeners of the principles of
glacier motion – is preoccupied by a glacier's moistness. One must
recognise this, he says, in acknowledging the consequent 'subsid-
ing languor of its fainting mass, as a constant source of motion'.[64]
The full implications of the feminised glacier are brought out in a
letter from Ruskin to Effie Gray, just before their marriage in 1847 –
a letter in which he also calls her 'a pitfall – a snare – an ignis –
fatuus – a beautiful destruction – a Medusa'. In this epistle, the mis-
ogynistic apprehension inherent within the feminised metaphor is
laid bare: 'You are like the bright – soft – swelling – lovely fields of a
high glacier covered with fresh morning snow – which is heavenly
to the eye – and soft and winning on the foot – but beneath, there
are winding clefts and dark places in its cold – cold ice – where men
fall, and rise not again'.[65]

Investigation of glacial movement, like the excitement generated by the conquest of Alpine peaks, was essentially a mid nineteenth-century phenomenon. As the Alps became more and more
frequented, so the tourist, rather than the mountains themselves,
came to form a new object of scrutiny. The glacier did not lose its
effectiveness as an occasional metaphor in this new form of study,
as geology ceded to anthropology. 'The British Tourist', commented *Blackwood's Magazine* in 1867, was a force of desolation,
propelled by commercialism: a 'power that, like the glacier, moves
coldly, steadily, and slowly onwards, pressing out all verdure and
beauty and geniality wherever it lays its heavy icy load'.[66] Ruskin
expressed his distaste for the undiscriminating hordes by drawing
attention to their littering habits, leaving the 'glaciers covered with
chicken-bones and egg-shells'.[67] Tourists, for him, were a symbol
of despoliation and commercialisation, just as the shrinking glaciers themselves were a result of increasing pollution. Whilst apoc-
alypticism could be signalled by Shelley through the image of
encroaching ice, its retreat fulfilled the same function for Ruskin,
writing in *Fors Clavigera* 34 (October 1873): 'More than the life of
Switzerland, – its very snows, – eternal, as one foolishly called

them, – are passing away, as if in omen of evil. One-third, at least, in
the depth of all the ice of the Alps has been lost in the last twenty
years; and the change of climate thus indicated is without any parallel in authentic history.'[68]

As glaciation theory itself receded as a controversial issue, there
were some signs that scientific and literary treatments of the Alps
were beginning, slowly, to drift apart. Moreover, self-consciously
literary writing was starting to reclaim the power of the invisible,
addressing itself again to the glacier's hidden forces and, in turn, to
the allegorical or metaphorical potential which these exemplified.
This separation was heralded by the observations of John Grey in
Trollope's *Can You Forgive Her?* (1864-5): ' "The poetry and mystery
of the mountains are lost to those who make themselves familiar
with their details . . . In this world things are beautiful only because
they are not quite seen, or not perfectly understood." '[69] E. J. Davis
set his Utopian fantasy *Pyrna: A Commune; Or, Under the Ice* (1875)
under the Rhone glacier. He praised the architectural beauty of the
city his narrator finds there, the pyramids, pillars and colonnades of
shining ice and marble echoing earlier descriptions of the glacier's
surface. He extols the success of the inhabitants' guiding maxim –
'Love your neighbour as yourself' – in this society where self-con-
sideration was merged into the well-being of others, and where,
'The principle of the existence of the community being Freedom,
the women were as free as the men.'[70] He makes great play of the
fact that this is a society where the arts and sciences complement
each other and knowledge of both is considered essential. Davis's
own uneasiness, however, about the degree to which science and
imagination can work together in the non-Utopian world is conveyed by the disclaimer he felt obliged to issue in an end-note: 'it is
scientifically asserted that the Glacier is in continual motion. The
surface would naturally be so, but I am not aware that there is any
reason to believe that the under layers of ice change their formation. Indeed, from the situation of "Pyrna", such a conjecture
would be impossible.'[71] Yet whether scientific exactitude was at
stake or not, the power of the glacier as a metaphor for human life
continued. Clara, in George Meredith's *The Egoist* (1879), rebels
against the desire of Willoughby, the egocentric landowner who

wishes to marry her, that they should form a hermetically sealed unit against the world. She would rather accept its more unpredictable aspects: 'The world has faults; glaciers have crevices, mountains have chasms; but is not the effect of the whole sublime? Not to admire the mountain and the glacier because they can be cruel, seems to me . . . And the world is beautiful.'[72] Rather than offering a threat, the glacier, for the constrained Clara, seems to offer promise, even if Clara cannot put into words quite what that promise may be.

What, finally, is so useful about the glacier to a consideration of the relationship between science, writing and the imagination? As we have seen, a glacier possesses a set of characteristics which are readily anthropomorphised. Hypotheses based upon human or animal energies, and on patterns of human history and human methods of recording the past could be, and often were, imposed on the workings of these rivers of ice. Glaciation studies in themselves provide an unusual case, in that unlike many Victorian scientific methodologies, proceeding through inductive methods – that is, accumulating much observational and measured data, and then seeing what one made of this – glaciologists worked through deductive means. They looked for evidence to fit their hypotheses, and, it would seem, it was the established mythological tradition, which figured the mysteriously moving glacier as being alive, rather than as being an inert mass somehow propelled by a force outside itself, that was one of the major factors that led them towards their conclusions. Then, in turn, they were led to express their discoveries through the employment of vivified metaphor.

Moreover, although geology and biology had seemed to be developing as different disciplines towards the end of the eighteenth century, the field of glaciation studies was one in which the sciences could be seen to draw together again, as well as one which demonstrated the mingling of aesthetic and scientific registers. The *North British Review*, in 1859, noted that in both solid ice and in more recent snow, botanists had discovered organisations of vegetable life, and zoologists had found myriads of minute creatures.[73] More than this: the growth of particle physics in the second half of the nineteenth century led to a completely new understanding of the potential for life within apparently inert matter: a question which tied in, of course, with the issues raised by evolutionary theory – 'Does life belong to what we call matter, or is it an independent principle inserted into matter at some suitable epoch – say when the physical conditions became such as to permit of the development of life?'[74] So asked John Tyndall. His answer, based on the examination of molecular energy, was, indeed, that life was inherent in all matter. To have reached this conclusion in itself involved several imaginative leaps. I've already noted the importance in general terms of his 1870 essay, 'On the Scientific Use of the Imagination'. More particularly, this acts as a justification of the ways in which he and other glaciologists used the language of poetry and myth in shaping their theories just as much as it supports his investigations of the operations of molecules within the air. Again, the term which links the disciplines, the faculty which permitted the mental imaging crucial both to Tyndall's hypotheses and to his explanation of the theories to which they led, is 'Imagination': 'Nourished by knowledge patiently won; bounded and conditioned by cooperant Reason, Imagination becomes the mightiest instrument of the physical discoverer.'[75] The study of glaciers over the preceding couple of decades provides an example *par excellence* of imaginative figuration and scientific inquiry operating in inseparable co-operation with one another.

CHAPTER 6

The buried city

The desire to excavate the subterranean, to bring to the surface that which lies hidden and dormant, is encountered in many Victorian cultural forms. The language in which archaeological investigation was excitedly described demonstrates that, in some contexts, to make the hidden visible was not just to access knowledge about past geological formations and earlier civilisations, but provided topographic metaphors for the very writing of history and the examination of both the social and the personal past.

In their turn, these metaphors famously feed into Freud's *Civilization and its Discontents* (1930). Here, Freud imagines Rome's past ages visually superimposed upon one another: 'an entity, that is to say, in which nothing that has once come into existence will have passed away and all the earlier phases of development continue to exist alongside the latest one', so that, for example:

> where the Coliseum now stands we could at the same time admire Nero's vanished Golden House. On the Piazza of the Pantheon we should find not only the Pantheon of to-day, as it was bequeathed to us by Hadrian, but, on the same site, the original edifice erected by Agrippa; indeed, the same piece of ground would be supporting the church of Santa Maria sopra Minerva and the ancient temple over which it was built. And the observer would perhaps only have to change the direction of his glance or his position in order to call up the one view or the other.[1]

Freud invokes this multi-layered image of Rome in order to figure a version of the human memory as palimpsest, a view of mental life in which nothing which has once been formed can ever perish, and may, indeed, be 'brought to light' in suitable circumstances. Rather, he invites a mental gymnastics of three-dimensional imaging in order to demonstrate the impossibility of adequately representing historical sequence – whether of a civilisation or of an individual – in these spatial terms. It develops out of the piece he wrote in 1925 on the Mystic Writing Pad, that child's toy which allows for the production of inscriptions which may be largely effaced by the lifting of the top transparent sheet on which words are written, leaving a clean surface, ready for re-inscription. This offers a tempting model for the psyche, with its contradictory features of 'an unlimited receptive capacity and a retention of permanent traces'.[2] Freud argues, however, in *Civilization and its Discontents*, that in order to represent historical sequence, we must use juxtaposition in space, since 'the same space cannot have two different contents'. The game of imaging which he has provoked has, however, he maintains, one particular advantage: 'It shows us how far we are from mastering the characteristics of mental life by representing them in pictorial terms.'[3]

Yet, when Freud's nineteenth-century predecessors set out to map mental life, and, in particular, when they searched for an adequate language in which to describe the life of the mind, and to investigate the presence and workings of the unconscious and of the memory, they were continually drawn to a register of terms which were not only spatial, but highly visual. Above all, these terms drew on a vocabulary of surface and depth, of the hidden and the revealed, of dark and of light. In this chapter, I shall be exploring the relationship of these spatial terms, which concern the inner life of the individual, to a different topography: that of the modern city. What lay under its rapidly mutating surface was frequently perceived as threatening. As Rosalind Williams has remarked in her suggestive and stimulating *Notes on the Underground*, the personal and the social are connected by the shared imagery of the subterranean: 'Both Marx and Freud depend so much upon subterranean imagery that it is now virtually impossible to read a text about the underworld without filtering it through a Marxist or Freudian interpretation – without reading the buried world as the subconscious, or the working class, or both.'[4] I shall argue, however, that uncovering what lies beneath the city's streets does more than diminish this apparent threat through rendering it available to scrutiny. It also provides continuity: links with the buried past, and hence with memory both individual and communal.

Freud's imagery harks back to Thomas De Quincey's influential description of the human brain as a 'natural and mighty palimpsest', a scroll on which experience is forever rewritten, and yet on which traces of the past cannot be entirely obliterated, but remain as ghostly presences: 'Everlasting layers of ideas, images, feelings, have fallen upon your brain softly as light. Each succession has seemed to bury all that went before. And yet in reality not one has been extinguished.'[5] By way of confirmation, he cites the case of a girl who, on the point of drowning, finds her whole past life radiantly arranged and illuminated in her consciousness; and tells how those who are 'martyrs' to opium are, likewise, subjected to experiencing visions of their past. Such revelations are compared to the effects of organised display: it is as though a deep pall or shroud has been thrown over the past, and then, suddenly, 'the pall draws up, and the whole depths of the theatre are exposed'.[6] Yet parallels are made by De Quincey with natural as well as with cultural contexts. Whilst the contents of the memory are analogous to some great library, containing mysterious, multi-layered 'handwritings of grief or joy which have inscribed themselves successively upon the palimpsest of your brain'[7] – 'memorial archives', to use the term of Forbes Winslow, mid nineteenth-century specialist in the insane[8] – they are also 'like the annual leaves of aboriginal forests, or the undissolving snows on the Himalaya'.[9] Or, one might say, they are like the successive layers of ice which go to make up the glacier, recollecting James Forbes's description of that phenomenon as 'an endless scroll . . . upon whose stainless ground' history is recorded.[10]

Where was the memory thought to be located? In physiological terms, the part of the brain in which, somehow, we store the past, could be located with apparent accuracy.[11] Thus, summarising physiological research relatively late in the century, F. W. Edridge-Green stated, with confidence, that memory '*is* a definite faculty, and has its seat in the basal ganglion of the brain, separate from, but associated with, all the other faculties of the mind'.[12] Earlier, George Lewes, in the third series of *Problems of Life and Mind*, was among those who had explained how every impression leaves a trace. The excitation caused by this impression produces a change in the neural plasmode, 'which may leave a temporary or perманent trace or modification of the molecular structure'.[13] By way of support, he quotes Sir James Paget's statement that 'the effect once produced by an impression upon the brain, whether in perception or in intellectual act, is fixed and therefore retained'.[14]

How, though, may one recover these impressions? Lewes draws a distinction between Memory, when 'images and ideas arise spontaneously; they are "unbidden", and intrude themselves into the current of thought', and Recollection, in which process there is 'an effort, a search, and a finding':[15] in trying to retrieve a date, fact or name, we will try various potential pathways of suggestivity. Moreover, according to Lewes, Memory differs from Imagination. In the case of Imagination, the 'rise of images that were once sensations, and the spontaneous combination of these images, take place incessantly in waking thought, in reverie, and in dreams. It differs from memory in that its personal escort has reference to the present or future, not to the past.'[16]

Once one moves beyond efforts to explain physiological workings in non-embellished language, the figurative placement and mapping of that 'room whereinto no one enters / Save I myself alone' – in Christina Rossetti's terms[17] – becomes revelatory both of desires about accessing the past, and also of the need to contain it in manageable fashion. This is symptomatic, too, of the proliferation of information available in print and image by the mid-century, related to, but going beyond, what Thomas Richards has seen as the project of the archive: a fantasy of state-controlled gathering and mustering of knowledge – 'not a building, nor even a collection of texts, but the collectively imagined junction of all that was known or knowable, a fantastic representation of an epistemological master pattern, a virtual focal point for the heterogeneous local knowledge of metropolis and empire'.[18] Frances Power Cobbe suggests that the workings of the memory may be analogous to such a vast, and collaborative, project when, as part of her attempt to explain the entire separability of the conscious self from its thinking organ, the physical brain, she considers the phenomenon of forgetting a word, or a line of poetry. Cobbe notes how it can be effective to turn deliberately away from the lost item, and let it return to one unbidden – or rather not unbidden, since we haven't abandoned the act of searching, but rather it is as if 'we were possessed of an obedient secretary or librarian, which we could order to hunt up a missing document, or turn out a word in a dictionary, while we amused ourselves with something else'.[19]

Other commentators substituted images taken from a yet more contemporary register than the library or archive, or Quintillian's model of a house and its separate rooms, or St Augustine's 'large and boundless chamber',[20] when it came to pictorialising this faculty's location. The critic E. S. Dallas, in *The Gay Science*, made it sound as though the recovery of acquired knowledge is similar to the uncovering of a concealed item of evidence in a sensation novel: 'How and where we hide our knowledge so that it seems dead and buried; and how in a moment we can bring it to life again, finding it in the dark where it lies unheeded amid our innumerable hoards, is a mystery over which every one capable of thinking has puzzled.'[21] A little later, he describes the kleptomaniac, magpie-like mind, assimilating everything, indiscriminately: 'Absolute as a photograph, the mind refuses nought. An impression once made upon the sense, even unwittingly, abides for evermore.'[22] Cobbe, again, employed this same image in discussing how those scenes in which we have experienced strong mental tension are particularly likely to remain with us: 'While our conscious selves have been absorbed in speculative thought or strong emotion, our unconscious cerebration has photographed the scene on our optic nerves *pour passer le temps!*'[23] William Carpenter – who coined the phrase 'unconscious cerebration' – explained, in his *Principles of Mental Physiology*, that there are strong physiological reasons to believe that the storing-up of ideas in the memory is the psychological expression of physical changes in the cerebrum, and that these impressions 'may be revived again in full vividness under certain special conditions'. Once again, the materiality of the body is rendered peculiarly modern when he searches for the image which will best convey this. Scenes from the past may be recalled, he says, 'just as the invisible impression left upon the sensitive paper of the Photographer, is developed into a picture by the application of particular chemical re-agents'.[24] The same trope was also readily deployed in more populist works on improving the memory. William Stokes, a self-styled 'teacher of memory', maintained that 'skilfully used Pictorial Mnemonics is a species of MENTAL PHOTOGRAPHY.'[25] Photographs can themselves accumulate into archives. John Samson, writing in 1896, claimed that he had

> sometimes fancied that there is a resemblance between the collection of impressions which we call memory, and the photographer's storeroom for negatives. Past scenes and events seem to be impressed and recorded upon the cells of the brain in some mysterious and permanent manner . . . But there seems to be some power in the brain – I picture it as the store-keeper of the negatives – who knows where to find every plate.[26]

In *Middlemarch*, George Eliot, as Cobbe was to do, writes of the way in which memories return not only when they are deliberately hunted down, but return unbidden, just as if they have been stored away as visual resources: 'Our moods are apt to bring with them images which succeed each other like the magic-lantern pictures of a doze.' Thus 'in certain states of dull forlornness Dorothea all her life continued to see the vastness of St Peter's', the figures in the mosaics on the dome, and – in an image which simultaneously suggests Dorothea's growing realisation that her marriage was not what she had hoped, and her desire to blot out this knowledge – she would also recollect 'the red drapery which was being hung for Christmas spreading itself everywhere like a disease of the retina'.[27] The ways in which the 'gigantic broken revelations of that Imperial and Papal city' thrust themselves abruptly into Dorothea's defenceless mind; the forms 'both pale and glowing' which, like architectural spectres, 'took possession of her young sense, and fixed themselves in her memory even when she was not thinking of them, preparing strange associations which remained through her after-years', return one to the image of Rome, the multi-layered, much-excavated city. In *Pictures from Italy* (1846),

Dickens records the simultaneity of present and past, and indeed of differing cultures, when he writes of the way in which narrow streets and heaps of dunghill rubbish suddenly give way to broad squares containing a haughty church or an Egyptian column. He describes how a Roman ceremonial pillar will be topped by a statue of a Christian saint; how obelisks and columns are recycled into granaries and stables. The sense of Rome as a site of cultural bricolage is summed up by the way in which a squat pyramid, the burial place of Caius Cestius, stands alongside the graves of Keats and Shelley.

Importantly, however, this inter-layering of past and present does not limit itself to material culture. It can be observed at a spiritual level: a level which functions in terms of corporate, social memory as well as individual recall. Architecturally, the ruins of old mythology, obsolete legends and observances have been incorporated into the physical structures used for Christian worship, just as their traces remain at the level of cultural practices. In a still less tangible dimension, this archaeological blurring of past and present raises questions, in Dickens's mind, about the persistence of ethnic traits. Dickens is clearly uneasy about the evidence for cruelty in former times which he has encountered whilst travelling. Is the capacity for cruelty latent within the national character, he ponders? Are the atrocities of the past proleptic of some coming apotheosis in Italian society? Can the people help themselves? His anxieties become focussed on what the Coliseum – 'now, a ruin. GOD be thanked: a ruin!' – represents.[28] Just as it outtowers the other ruins in Rome, however:

> so do its ancient influences outlive all other remnants of the old mythology and old butchery of Rome, in the nature of the fierce and cruel Roman people. The Italian face changes as the visitor approaches the city; its beauty becomes devilish; and there is scarcely one countenance in a hundred, among the common people in the streets, that would not be at home and happy in a renovated Coliseum to-morrow.[29]

In *Pictures from Italy*, Dickens is especially fascinated with the act of seeing, and with the consideration of how his memory operates in relation to what he has observed. He presents his mind as an open screen which receives impressions. By entitling the chapter in which he journeys from Rome to Naples 'A Rapid Diorama', he suggests that he then re-presents these impressions in a manner informed by that highly popular form of visual entertainment and education. In *Charles Baudelaire*, Walter Benjamin comments that it is no accident that 'a special literary genre . . . panorama litera-ture' came into vogue – he is writing about France, but the same holds true for England – at the same time as dioramas were in fashion: 'These books consist of individual sketches which, as it were, reproduce the plastic foreground of those panoramas with their individual form and the extensive background of the panora-mas with their store of information.'[30] Dickens's book belongs to this type, and his speculations about the interactions that take place between one's physiological registering of the external world, and one's mental apprehension of the facts received, occur in relation to both natural and aesthetic phenomena. In Mantua, he looks with fascinated revulsion at Giulio Romano's frescoes in the Palazzo Te: ugly and grotesque giants, humanoid monsters with 'swollen faces and cracked cheeks . . . immensely large, and exaggerated to the utmost pitch of uncouthness'.[31] The way in which he describes the nature of his response is curious, attempt-ing to convey an unpleasant physical immediacy whilst at the same time trying to abnegate his own active role as perceiver and inter-preter: 'the colour is harsh and disagreeable; and the whole effect more like (I should imagine) a violent rush of blood to the head of the spectator, than any real picture set before him by the hand of an artist'.[32] If he can only compare the role of 'the spectator' – a term which distances his own presence – to something he imagines, from what position, one might ask, has he been describing these aesthetic aberrations? A yet more self-conscious, self-interroga-tory discussion of the way one may receive, retain, process and remember scenes when travelling and constantly exposing oneself to new (and simultaneously quasi-repetitive) visual experiences occurs when Dickens describes his approach to Venice. The lan-guage emphasises the perceiver as passive receptor:

> The rapid and unbroken succession of novelties that had passed before me, came back like half-formed dreams; and a crowd of objects wandered in the greatest confusion through my mind, as I travelled on, by a solitary road. At intervals, some one among them would stop, as it were, in its restless flitting to and fro, and enable me to look at it, quite steadily, and behold it in full distinctness. After a few minutes, it would dissolve, like a view in a magic-lantern; and while I saw some part of it quite plainly, and some faintly, and some not at all, would show me another of the many places I had lately seen, lingering behind it, and coming through it. This was no sooner visible than, in its turn, it melted into something else.[33]

Here, Dickens is still using the relatively familiar vocabulary of the public entertainment, the language of the phantasmagoria: magic lantern shows turned to the production of supernatural effects, which had become even more effective and flexible after the invention and perfection (1807–18) of 'dissolving views'. These were to become, as Richard Altick puts it in *The Shows of London*, 'one of the most widely attended of all forms of Victorian entertainment'.[34] The idea of the city street as a magic lantern is one to which Dickens was to return (in a letter quoted by Benjamin). He wrote from Lausanne, whilst composing *Dombey and Son*, that he cannot function for long in quiet seclusion, but needs the constant procession of scenes in front of him: 'the toil and labour of writing, day after day, without that magic lantern, is IMMENSE'.[35] In one further, striking passage, however, Dickens, whilst he appeals to his readers' recognition of the phenomenon of which he writes, does not filter his rendition of the scene and his responses to it through the language of artifice, unless one counts the underpresence of a Gothic terminology. Rather, he describes how in certain, unpredictable moments of visionary intensity, we experience a confusion of perception and imagination, of true and false memory:

> At sunset, when I was walking on alone, while the horses rested, I arrived upon a little scene, which, by one of those singular mental

operations of which we are all conscious, seemed perfectly familiar to me, and which I see distinctly now. There was not much in
it. In the blood red light, there was a mournful sheet of water, just
stirred by the evening wind; upon its margin a few trees. In the
foreground was a group of silent peasant girls leaning over the
parapet of a little bridge, and looking, now up at the sky, now
down into the water; in the distance, a deep bell; the shade of
approaching night on everything. If I had been murdered there,
in some former life, I could not have seemed to remember the
place more thoroughly, or with a more emphatic chilling of the
blood; and the mere remembrance of it acquired in that minute,
is so strengthened by the imaginary recollection, that I hardly
think I could forget it.[36]

Dickens's fascination with violence against the body, with
torture, imprisonment and cruelty, can be read as more than a personal quirk, a recurrent and unbidden habit of the mind. In this
book, he uses its recurrent underpresence in his imagination as a
means of providing a continual commentary on the prevalence of
violent political oppression within the modern country: a mental
filter through which, consciously or otherwise, he experiences his
social environment. Along with the exuberance of the Carnival is
the continual presence of state control, as dragoons and troopers
control the progress of carriages. In the poor villages of mid-Italy,
'the soldiers are as dirty and rapacious as the dogs',[37] bringing
them down to an unsavoury and predatory level. He records the
inscriptions scratched by prisoners on the wall of the Doges'
palace; the instruments of torture hanging in the Venetian
armoury. The visionary moments are frequently infused with
guilty, blood-red hues, as with the sunset that stains the dungeon
walls where Parisina and her lover were beheaded in Ferrara; the
Turnerean 'crimson flush' that irradiates the Venetian lagoon.[38]
Most chilling of all is the old prison cell which might have been St
Peter's in Rome, where:

> hanging on the walls, among the clustered votive offerings,
> are objects, at once strangely in keeping, and strangely at vari-
> ance, with the place – rusty daggers, knives, pistols, clubs, divers

instruments of violence and murder, brought here, fresh from use, and hung up to propitiate offended Heaven: as if the blood in them would drain off in consecrated air, and have no voice to cry with.[39]

In other words, Italy's present is continually written onto a map of the past. The potential for violence is never far from the surface, and, for Dickens, this is not merely a fact of the country's history, but is written into its natural topography. When he is in Naples, he cannot take his eyes off the compelling, smouldering presence of Vesuvius. Whilst ostensibly fascinated by the potential for destructive energy in the volcano itself, there is an implicit suggestion that the repetition of violence is inherent within Italy. Dickens sees in the volcano 'the doom and destiny of all this beautiful country, biding its terrible time'.[40]

Dickens, here, hovers between reading promise and threat into the figure of volcanic eruption. Habitually, however, the instability of the earth's crust functioned as a signal of doom, a metaphor for unwanted instability and unpredictability. Hence, whilst the archaeological investigations which had been taking place south of Naples since 1748 must have informed the hopeful language of Dickens's conclusion to *Pictures from Italy*, where he hopes that this 'noble people may be, one day, raised up from these ashes',[41] Edward Bulwer-Lytton's popular historical novel, *The Last Days of Pompeii* (1834), is full of references which are far from optimistic ones. Just before the catastrophic eruption, the hero, Arbaces, wakes from a series of admonitory nightmares to find a seer before him: 'he beheld the ghastly features, the lifeless eye, the livid lip – of the hag of Vesuvius!'[42] The physical appearance of this woman functions metonymically: she herself has stared over the lip of the volcano's crater that dawn, and seen the stream of lava below 'broader, fiercer, redder than the night before . . . The walls of Pompeii are built above the fields of the Dead, and the rivers of the sleepless Hell. Be warned and fly!'[43]

Two recurrent modes of figuring subterranean danger stand out here. First, the interior of the earth, particularly its fiery aspects, is associated with the infernal, the underworld: home of

20 John Martin, 'The Fiery Gulf', 1825–7, steel engraving to John Milton, *Paradise Lost*.

evil and death. This is the damp, cavernous gloom which John Martin depicts in his illustration, executed between 1825 and 1827, to Milton's *Paradise Lost*: 'The Fiery Gulf' (figure 20). Although some attempted to discuss the riches to be found underground – here, claimed W. H. Davenport Adams, 'are laid the foundations of the glorious palace which man is permitted to inhabit'[44] – even Adams found himself pulled into the darker rhetoric of tradition, and tourist exploitation of a love of dread, as soon as he started to explore actual subterranean locations. In Kentucky's Mammoth Caves, for example, he visits not only the 'Chamber of the Dead' (complete with liquor-dispensing restaurant and the daily papers, presumably to lift one from the gloom) and the 'Devil's Chair', but the 'Bottomless Pit', site of lovers' suicides, and into which two pursued fugitive slaves from Alabama threw themselves: 'For a moment they were visible, by the glare of the torches flung in their direction, standing erect, hand clasped in hand, in the recess which opens on the awful gulf; then they flung themselves into its silence, and earth knew them no more!' Davenport Adams readily turns this story into a parallel for the 'horrors' of slavery: the dark history underlying America's nineteenth-century narrative of progress.[45]

Second, we have the conflation of the earth with the body, almost inevitably the female body. A gynophobic response as to what the Earth Mother might actually bring forth is a long-standing one: Spenser, for example, presented Earth as the 'uncouth mother' of the hideous Giant with whom the Red Cross Knight joins in combat in the first book of the *Faerie Queene*: she

> trebling the dew time,
> In which the wombes of women do expire,
> Brought forth this monstrous masse of earthly slime,
> Puft up with emptie wind, and fild with sinfull crime.[46]

As well as fears based upon the specifics of a woman's body, the continued troping of earth and body again, as in the case of vampires, allows one to read anxieties about what happens when it exceeds its apparent margins through ideas originally developed around the leaky human container. Mary Douglas expands the connection between bodies and wider structures of ideas when, in *Purity and Danger* (1966), she argues that apprehension about the maintenance of rigid bodily boundaries is most intense in societies which in one way or another perceive their own actual or metaphorical boundaries to be under attack:

> Any structure of ideas is vulnerable at its margins. We should expect the orifices of the body to symbolise its specially vulnerable points. Matter issuing from them is marginal stuff of the most obvious kind. Spittle, blood, milk, urine, faeces or tears by simply issuing forth have traversed the boundary of the body. So also have bodily parings, skin, nail, hair clippings and sweat. The mistake is to treat bodily margins in isolation from all other margins.[47]

Social vulnerability is frequently manifested through figurative language which suggests the matter of the earth destructively breaking through to the surface. This movement from body to state is found, say, in the manner in which Dickens treats Krook's spontaneous combustion in *Bleak House*, making it into an allegory of the fate of 'all authorities in all places under all names soever, where false pretences are made, and where injustice is done. Call the death by any name Your Highness will, attribute it to whom you will, or say it might have been prevented how you will, it is the same death eternally – inborn, inbred, engendered in the corrupted humours of the vicious body itself.'[48] In this passage, he implicitly draws on the prevalent mid-century metaphor which equates political, particularly urban, unrest with the fiery, rumbling matter which seethes under the earth's crust. Charlotte Brontë, writing in 1848 of political disruption in France to her publisher, W. S. Williams, is apprehensive that it will spread, unseen and unchecked, in strata which lie beneath obvious geographical boundaries: '[England] is divided by the sea from the lands where it is making thrones rock, but earthquakes roll lower than the ocean, and we know neither the day nor the hour when the tremor and heat, passing beneath our island, may unsettle and dissolve its foundations'.[49] The image is one which clearly fascinated Charlotte Brontë: she employs it to suggest the violence with which individuals might experience the insecurities of their own lives, either because of their concealed pasts (Rochester confesses that 'To live, for me, Jane, is to stand on a crater-crust which may crack and spue fire any day')[50] or because they believe the world to be intrinsically a threatening place, demanding courage and endurance. Hearing the wild noises of the storm whilst at Miss Marchmont's, Lucy Snowe:

> fancied, too, I had noticed – but was not philosopher enough to know whether there was any connection between the circumstances – that we often at the same time hear of disturbed volcanic action in distant parts of the world; of rivers suddenly rushing above their banks; and of strange high tides flowing furiously in on low sea-coasts. 'Our globe', I had said to myself, 'seems at such periods torn and disordered; the feeble amongst us wither in her distempered breath, rushing hot from steaming volcanoes.'[51]

Brontë's language both internalises the characteristics of the sublime, making the very business of living one of almost pleasurable terror, and disperses it where it might break out unpredictably.

The metaphor of the precariously thin surface of the civilised world endured the Victorian period – William Hale White, in *Mark Rutherford's Deliverance* (1885), comments that 'our civilization seemed nothing but a thin film or crust lying over a volcanic pit'[52] – as did the promise of penetrative discovery: the laying bare of the conditions which might give rise to social and political unrest. 'Throughout the century', as Peter Stallybrass and Allon White put it, 'the "invisibility" of the poor was a source of fear.' They quote the Select Committee of 1838 noting 'that there were whole areas of London through which "no great thoroughfare passed" and, as a consequence, "a dense population of the lowest classes of persons" were "entirely secluded from the observation and influence of better educated neighbours"'.[53] This phenomenon was not limited to London, as Friedrich Engels graphically demonstrated in relation to Manchester, where urban architectural arrangements – the shops that line the streets which lead in from the quarters where the better-off live, hiding the dirty and tumbledown dwellings in the side streets – form a buffer between the workers and the middle classes. The latter are spared the sight of 'the misery and squalor that form the completing counterpart, the indivisible component, of their riches and luxury'.[54] 'I have never seen', Engels writes, 'so tender a concealment of everything which may affront the eye and the nerves of the bourgeoisie, as in Manchester.'[55] The language of social explorers in the latter decades of the century specifically offered glimpses into 'the abyss' of urban society. Together with announcing the performance of necessary revelatory acts, their titles simultaneously sustained the fear of social eruption emanating in fact, as well as figuratively, from underground: James Greenwood, *Low-Life Deeps* (1876); C. F. G. Masterman, *From the Abyss* (1902); Jack London, *The People of the Abyss* (1903); Mary Higgs, *Glimpses into the Abyss* (1906).

Some virtually lived underground. Commenting on those who inhabited the Adelphi arches in the mid-century, Thomas Miller wrote:

> Thousands who pass along the Strand never dream of the
> shadowy region which lies between them and the river – the
> black-browed arches that span right and left, before and behind,
> covering many a rood of ground on which the rain never beats
> nor the sunbeam rests, and at the entrance of which the wind
> only seems to howl and whine, as if afraid of venturing further
> into the darkness.[56]

However, for thousands of others, these arches figured strongly in
the imagination. 'The dark arches of our own dear riverside
Adelphi', wrote John Hollingshead, author of an obsessively infor-
mative study on *Underground London* (1862),

> are still looked upon as the favourite haunt of the wild tribes of
> London, or City Arabs, whatever these may be.
>   A popular notion exists that those few sloping tunnels are a
> vast free lodging-house for hundreds of night-wanderers; and
> that to those who have the watchword they form a passage
> leading to some riotous hidden haunt of vice. This belief prevails
> very largely amongst very quiet, respectable people; the class
> who live in the suburbs, feed upon 'serious' literature, shudder
> when the metropolis, the modern Nineveh, is only mentioned in
> conversation.[57]

Gustave Dore, in his engraving 'Under the Arches', showed the
miserable, uncomfortable, crowded reality of those who took
shelter under the bridges at night (figure 21) The reference to
Nineveh, however, reminds one once again of the apocalyptic
threat offered by London's under-classes. The great river wall of
the ancient city of Nineveh was not only its protection from the
Tigris, but was the site of its sustained defence against Arbaces,
Beleses and Rabsaris: once broached, the invaders flooded into this
site of – as John Martin figured it in *The Fall of Nineveh* (1829) – rich-
ness. (figure 22).
     The present-day barbarians were frequently compared, in their
social positioning, to what lay under the earth's surface: a form of
categorisation that naturalised them. 'To borrow a figure from
geology,' as John Parker put it, 'the working classes are composed

21 Gustave Dore, 'Under the Arches', steel engraving to William Blanchard Jerrold, *London, A Pilgrimage*, 1872.

of strata', and this includes 'a great substratum, a chaotic mass, in which brutality, sensuality, filthiness, and ignorance are conspicuously present'.[58] This is the sector of society which, according to Alexander Thomson, the 'searching eye' will discover to be – like the floor of an equatorial forest – composed of 'an unstable agglomeration of mixed materials, often decaying and rotting away, whose corrupting influences are perpetually spreading upwards'.[59] The threat of the barely human rising from the subterranean is refigured countless times in imaginative writing. It is manifested through the most feckless, lawless members of the working classes in George Gissing's unsubtly entitled *The Nether World*, or the morlocks, living underground but ready to break to the surface with their carnivorous desires in H. G. Wells's *The Time Machine*.[60]

The anxieties about the condition of England which were expressed through the dread of what lay under the earth, were bound in with apprehension about other, more distant illegible environments. Patrick Brantlinger has written, in relation to late Victorian imperial Gothic fiction, of 'the nightmare of being

22 John Martin, *The Fall of Nineveh*, 1829. Mezzotint, 53.66 × 81.28 cms.

swallowed by the world's dark places', invoking in this context Rider Haggard's fantasy landscapes 'as his characters are swallowed up or temporarily entombed in chasms, tunnels, crypts, and caves: the Place of Death in *King Solomon's Mines*, the underground river down which the explorers plummet to the land of the Zu-Vendis in *Allan Quatermain*, the Caves of Kôr in *She*'.[61] This imagery looped symbiotically back to the metropolitan centre, as parallels between the 'savage' state in which the urban working classes were found and the condition of those who inhabited more far-flung corners of the Empire became a commonplace. William Booth, in *In Darkest England and The Way Out*, in which he compares 'The Equatorial Forest traversed by Stanley' to the vast stretch of 'Darkest England', both sharing monotonous darkness, inhabited by 'dwarfish de-humanized inhabitants' subjected in their different ways to slavery, describes, enumerates and classifies the appalling features of English urban life: 'the stony streets of London, if they could but speak, would tell of tragedies as awful, of ruin as complete, of ravishments as horrible, as if we were in Central Africa; only the ghastly devastation is covered, corpse-like,

with the artificialities and hypocrisies of modern civilisation.[62]
Booth's desire, here, to prise open London's roadways and pavements is a figurative stripping of the urban skin to reveal the diseased body beneath.

What lay beneath the city's floor, however, presented far more
direct dangers in its unhealthiness, whilst it simultaneously stimulated the imagination. As Hollingshead succinctly stated: 'there is a
fatal fascination about sewers'.[63] Indeed, 'Imagination generally
loves to run wild about underground London, or the sub-ways of
any great city.'[64] He writes of the ways in which in popular culture,
sewers – rather like the Adelphi arches – were seen as hiding places
for criminals fleeing from justice; as containing 'secret caverns full
of metropolitan banditti'.[65] More immediate, and less fanciful,
concerns predominated, however. Under London ran a number of
underground rivers, which for a long time doubled as sewers: the
Fleet Ditch and Tyburn, Stamford Brook and Westbourne,
Walbrook and Shoreditch, and a dozen others. The biggest sewer
of all, of course, was the highly visible River Thames, but even in
this case there was a discrepancy between its smoothly flowing
surface and what lay beneath it. As Hollingshead remarked, when
Wordsworth stood on old Westminster Bridge and wrote his
famous sonnet about the sleeping city, pernicious dead and living
organisms even then formed part of the river, but, since his nostrils
were unoffended (unlike those of Londoners during the 'Great
Stink' of 1858), he was unaware of the fact: 'It was left for a later and
more sanitary age to destroy part of the poet's dream by introducing the microscope in no friendly spirit.'[66] The rivers, and the
sewers themselves, carried a great deal of extraneous material: the
'main arteries' of the city's body, Hollingshead termed them, and
when they became clogged and silted, the healthy circulation of
the city was halted.[67] Henry Mayhew, visiting the old Westminster
sewers, recorded that the deposits found in them comprised the
ingredients from breweries, gas works and chemical and mineral
manufactories; dead dogs, cats, kittens and rats; offal from slaugh-
terhouses, including animal entrails; 'street-pavement dirt of
every variety; vegetable refuse; stable-dung; the refuse of pig-
styes; night-soil; ashes; tin kettles and pans (pansherds); broken

stoneware, as jars, pitchers, flower-pots, &c.; pieces of wood; rotten mortar and rubbish of different kinds'.[68] Other commentators added to this catalogue: a dead seal and sets of false teeth; silver spoons, marbles and bad half-crowns; human arms and heads, the residue of body-snatchers and medical students; a live hedgehog and dead children.[69] In terms of the everyday cargo of the sewers, particularly repulsive were those which ran under the meat-markets, and those which received the by-products of manufacturing chemists and soap- and candle-makers. Poisonous gases built up in them; houses that were built over conduits for sewage had 'the very stench of death' rising through their boards.[70] Charles Kingsley, in *Alton Locke*, employed an infernal register to describe the 'phosphorescent scraps of rotten fish gleaming and twinkling out of the dark hollows, like devilish grave-lights – over bubbles of poisonous gas, and bloated carcases of dogs, and lumps of offal, floating on the stagnant olive-green hell-broth'.[71] Those who lived in such conditions could all too readily be equated with the waste products which undermined their own physical health. 'Moral sewerage', Sidney Godolphin Osborne termed 'the dregs of life which exist at the depths of civilization . . . the living nastiness and offensive living matter which we have been content to allow to accumulate in streets', and he went on to inform his readers that 'there are moral *miasmas* just as there are physical'.[72] Sewage resembled the lowest categories within society: it 'is very much like our convicts, everybody wants to get rid of it, and no one consents to have it'.[73] Yet, as Stallybrass and White pointed out, the sewer also disrupts the topographically arranged hierarchy on which these versions of class depend. However much sanitary reformers, like early anthropologists, attempted to draw rigorous distinctions between the clean and the unclean, the pure and the impure, the civilised and the savage, the sewer, to quote Victor Hugo, is the place where the 'last veil is stripped away'. The sewer, he wrote in *Les Misérables*, is not only the 'conscience of the town', it is a place of levelling, of intimacy, of what we all come to: 'No false appearance, no white-washing, is possible; filth strips off its shirt in utter starkness, all illusions and mirages scattered, nothing left except what is, showing the ugly face of what ends.'[74] This point is brought graphically home in an anonymous popular serial of 1863, *The Wild Boys of London; Or, The Children of the Night*, where the narrator, invoking the 'mighty secrets' which are contained within 'those vaulted receptacles', the sewers of London, prioritises upper-class infanticides among these: 'Secrets that would ruin many of the proudest families in the land are carried away by that black tide, as it rushes through the murky arches bearing the murdered forms of many a newly-born infant, children of sin, who had come into the world but to utter one wailing cry.'[75]

The very fact of being exposed to the smelliness of sewers, of having the evidence of one's nose forced upon one and hence becoming aware of one's sense of smell, was not only relevant to the general belief – until Pasteur's development of germ theory – that stench was a major source of disease, but dragged the nose's possessor back down the evolutionary chain. 'The suppression of the sense of smell was one of the defining characteristics of "civilized man"' in the later part of the nineteenth century, claim the authors of *Aroma. The Cultural History of Smell*, reminding one that 'Darwin had postulated that humans lost their acuity of smell in the process of evolving from animals.'[76] The tendency to privilege visual symbolism inevitably means diminishing the impact of the symbolic, as well as actual, impact of the other senses, but this was simply not possible when being assaulted by the reek of sewers or the Thames in summer.[77] Moreover, the pervasive, invasive characteristics of smell give it a power akin to sound. It has the ability to disrupt an individual's spatial ordering of him or herself. '*Sound*', Walter J. Ong has explained, '*situates man in the middle of actuality and in simultaneity, whereas vision situates man in front of things and in sequentiality.*'[78] Both sound and smell situate the individual experiencing them in the middle of the world, bombard them with simultaneity. One cannot see in front and behind of one, above and below, in the same instant, but one can smell and listen. 'Hearing', Ong continues, 'makes me intimately aware of a great many goings-on which it lets me know are simultaneous but which I cannot possibly view simultaneously and thus have difficulty in dissecting or analyzing, and consequently of managing. Auditory syntheses overwhelm me with phenomena beyond all control.'[79]

The very necessary control over waste products which was obtained through the building of London's great sewage system began in 1858 and was completed by 1865, by which time there were over eighty miles of sewers.[80] These works were preceded by numerous schemes and plans which never came to fruition, including a number by John Martin. His apocalyptic canvases contain versions of the grandiose architecture he would have liked to have seen on the banks of the Thames in London, and demonstrate the destruction he felt was imminent if an embankment as solid as the one at Nineveh was not built, 'the breaching of which', as William Feaver reminds us in his discussion of Martin's urban plans,

> marked the end of civilization as Sardanapalus, at any rate, knew it.

> . . . It has been said
> For ages, 'That the city ne'er should yield
> To man, until the river grew its foe'.[81]

Even despite its unarguable necessity, the very vastness of the new sewage system provoked apocalyptic apprehension in some, regarding the new honeycomb of tunnels carrying waste as potential 'volcanoes of filth; gorged veins of putridity; ready to explode at any moment in a whirlwind of foul gas, and poison all those whom they fail to smother'.[82] Images of the earth's fragile corrupt are here conflated with the idea of the corrupt individual body, and the precarious state of the body politic. Sewers, however, were not the only channels of communication and circulation under London. They formed only part of the city's corporeal figuration, as Hollingshead explains:

> The bed of a London thoroughfare may be compared to the human body – for it is full of veins and arteries which it is death to cut. There are the water-mains, with their connecting drains; the gas-mains, with their connecting pipes . . . and very often the tubes containing long lines of telegraph wire. If the gravel and clay be opened at any time a few yards under our feet, we catch a glimpse of these tubular channels, lying nearly as close together

as the pipes of a church organ. The engineers of the Metropolitan Railway . . . have had to remove all these old channels to
the sides of the roadway, steering their tunnel in between, with
the delicacy of a surgical operation.[83]

A few pages earlier, Hollingshead produces a symptomatically confused set of metaphors and similes to describe the jumble of
human-made routes which lie beneath the surface. Underground
London is at once a 'vast grave of iron', as pipes and mains rot away
into plumbago. These pipes are 'crowded together like tramps in a
threepenny bed', without even the room for a rat to run between
them: the city's human detritus conflated with its subterranean
structures. Then, again, these structures are also described in
terms which blend engineering with the human skeleton, since
they suffer from 'defective joints': simultaneously the places where
gas dangerously escapes, and symbolic of the whole creaking foundations of the city.[84] The co-presence of underground routes of
communication is well displayed in an engraving in the *Illustrated
London News* in 1867, showing the Thames Embankment under
construction at Charing Cross. On the left is the Metropolitan
District Railway running through its tunnel, and in the centre,
sewers and a proposed – though never constructed – 'pneumatic'
railway which was intended to run from Charing Cross under the
river to Waterloo. Subways were constructed through which gas,
electricity and water pipes could be accessed: the oldest of these,
under Garrick Street, was built in 1861. Telegraphic forms were
carried underground by pneumatic tubes through which com-
pressed air propelled cylinders.[85] In 1862, the Pneumatic Despatch
company installed a parcels tube, which operated along the same
principles. Some forms of technological transmission, to be sure,
ran overhead. By 1842, the telegraph had come up from below
ground, and when London's first telephone exchange opened in
Lombard Street in 1879, its ten lines also went overhead. In both
cases, it was as though the silent, invisible transmission of words
was somehow rendered as visible sound, as Dickens described the
telegraph lines in *Hard Times*: 'the electric wires which ruled a
colossal strip of music-paper out of the evening sky'.[86]

In 1860, work began on the Metropolitan Railway, the first of London's underground rail routes, following the findings of the Parliamentary select committee which had been set up in 1855 to consider how to combat congestion in London's streets.[87] John Fowler, the engineer, originally envisaged trains being blown through tunnels like giant pneumatic tubes, but it was impossible to develop a tight enough seal on the tunnels; he then proposed a tyreless locomotive, recharged with high-pressure steam at each terminus, but again the technical problems were too great. The use of conventional coke-burning steam locomotives when the railway opened on 10 January 1863 inevitably led to unpleasantly smoky tunnels, despite the boring of blow-holes along the route, and the trains being fitted with condensing gear. In turn, new forms of underground mobility brought new dangers, and new stimuli to the imagination. These took both imaginative, and actual, form. Dion Boucicault composed a climactic scene of his melodrama *After Dark* in which the villains tied the hero to the lines of an underground railway in an attempt to murder him: his rescue takes place whilst, according to the stage directions, a bell rings, a whistle sounds, and first an approaching train is heard, then comes into view.[88] The Underground also became vulnerable to politically motivated terrorist attacks. The Fenians exploded a charge of nitro-glycerine in the tunnel of the District Railway between Charing Cross and Westminster, to be followed by further explosions in February 1884, January 1885 and April 1897.

The excavations for all these underground passages resulted in previous layers of London's past being brought to the surface: an archaeological pathologising. Prestwich, investigating the London basin between Dulwich and Peckham, found masses of old leaf deposits in the clay, the remains of forests that had once grown upon the banks of a mighty, but now unknown, river, he hypothesised.[89] During the works for the subterranean tunnel which began at Paddington and ran under the Edgware Road, Maida Vale and St John's Wood, the vertebral remains of a crocodile were found. At Old Ford, once the site of a Roman ferry, and now the point of cross-over for the new sewage system, workmen picked up decayed skulls, pieces of huge items of pottery, and early coins.

When excavations for a new sewer were being conducted at Smithfield in 1849, a mass of unhewn, fire-blackened stones, covered with ashes and human bones, were uncovered: the spot probably used for burning martyrs.

If the Fleet Brook's nineteenth-century role was as a notorious subterranean sewer, this did not prevent historians refiguring it in their idealising imaginations:

> They have pictured the period when Roman villas studded its banks; when Snow Hill was famous for its snowdrops; when Saffron Hill was a wooded slope like the Thames's banks at Richmond; and when the stream wandered down from its source in the Hampstead Hills, carrying swarms of silver trout into the Thames. They have dreamed over the time when large vessels may have floated up as high as King's Cross, where this black river is now carried over the underground Metropolitan Railway in an iron pipe or tunnel.[90]

These are the infinitely aged knotted roots, the skeletons and treasure that lie beneath Mrs Dalloway's London; or, more ominously, the rhododendron forests, harbouring the iguanodon, the mammoth and the mastodon, that Mrs Swithin, in *Between the Acts*, imagines were once growing in Piccadilly. A sense of different time scales underlying the present has, as Woolf was to recognise, the capacity to disrupt one's sense of modernity. Rosalind Williams has written about the ambivalent responses of the Victorians to the process of excavation. On the one hand, such projects represented a supreme example of what the period understood as progress, achieving a physical domination of nature, as scientific investigations had achieved a dominance in other areas. Yet, they also stood for social disruption: for the destruction of neighbourhoods, of ways of life. 'The conflict between the two responses to excavation projects', Williams argues, '– between seeing them as cruelly disruptive and seeing them as wonderfully heroic – represents the fundamental ambivalence of the middle classes toward the advent of a technological environment.'[91]

What I want further to suggest is that the concern with what lies underneath the city, and the desire to make it visible, is intimately connected to the ways in which memory is figured within the developing discourses of Victorian psychology. In both cases, what is at stake is a desire not just to render the invisible present to the eye, and hence to diminish the sense of threat that is anxiously present in that which cannot be seen, but a desire to restore a sense of order, of sequentiality.

William Carpenter, believing as at least probable what Freud was later to challenge – that all memories are potentially recoverable – linked the means by which such recovery might be effected to two tropes which we have already seen were closely connected in the figuration of the city: the existence of transportation systems, and the workings of the body. It is by the association of ideas, Carpenter thought, that we have the best chance of recovering that which seems to have faded from the conscious memory. This is because all our ideas are, he maintains, linked in 'trains' or 'series', 'which further inosculate with each other like the branch lines of a railway or the ramifications of an artery'.[92]

To make the past of the city visible is to restore to it a sense of depth. Both archaeological investigation, and a laying bare of the circulatory system of the modern metropolis, demonstrate a set of characteristics which relate its spatial being to time. When Michel de Certeau wrote of seeing Manhattan from the 110th floor of the World Trade Center, he describes how elevation transfigures one into a voyeur. 'It transforms the bewitching world by which one was "possessed" into a text that lies before one's eyes. It allows one to read it, to be a solar Eye, looking down like a god'; it represents the exaltation of a scopic and a gnostic drive.[93] The experience allows one an imaginary totalisation unavailable to those who experience the city through walking, making use of spaces that they do not and cannot perceive themselves. It is a late twentieth-century equivalent of the panoptic desires expressed by balloon flights over the city, by aerial topographers, by the observation platform on the dome of St Paul's Cathedral, designed to track the dangerous miasmas which, it was believed, rose like infectious exhalations of the mephitic Thames. Whether in the case of New York or London, however, such illusions that one can surmount and articulate 'the contradictions arising from urban agglomeration',[94] as De Certeau calls them, can refer only to the present, and not to the hidden histories of place, of individuals, of ideologies which form and underpin it.

Depth is, by its nature, resistant to visibility. It is never spread out before our eyes, but appears to them only in foreshortened form – that is, if what we wish to see is not quickly obscured by impenetrable density of matter. When we conceive of depth, figure it in our mind's eye, it becomes tacitly equated with breadth seen from the side: depth made visible by, as it were, turning it on its axis. We thus perform a sort of mental acrobatics when we envisage depth, which severs imaginary perception from any actual possible positioning as a spectator. 'What makes depth invisible for me', Merleau-Ponty explains, 'is precisely what makes it visible for the spectator as breadth: the juxtaposition of simultaneous points in one direction which is that of my gaze . . . In order to treat depth as breadth viewed in profile . . . the subject must leave his place, abandon his point of view on the world, and think himself into a sort of ubiquity.'[95] By rendering depth as breadth viewed in profile, one is also, necessarily, spreading it out according to the same dimensions as linearity, temporality.

Making history visible in a period of rapid urban change has a stabilising function. It gives the city a temporally based solidity: its description is not just thick in the anthropologist's sense of crowded with circumstantial detail, but in the sense of being comfortably wadded with layers of the known past. The city becomes a palimpsest in its own right, composed of strata of previous (and, it was often implicitly suggested, more savage, more uncouth) inhabitants and their relicts. Carlyle, in 1830, figured history itself as a palimpsest, a 'complex manuscript, covered over with formless inextricably entangled characters': one must, he argued, search and explore the past since it is the true foundation of knowledge, and only by uncovering it – so far as one can – will we come to understand the present and future.[96] What is being uncovered is not so much the memory of an individual, the location of which so fascinated Victorian writers on psychology, but communal memory – or, as Herbert Spencer christened it in *The Principles of Psychology* (1855), 'organic memory'.[97] This memory, in its turn, forms a part of each human's composition, and its traces, according to G. H. Lewes, are to be found both in the contents of our minds, and in the palimpsestic make-up of our own bodies: 'All sensations, perceptions, emotions, volitions, are partly connate, partly acquired: partly the evolved products of the accumulated experiences of ancestors, and partly of the accumulated experiences of the individual, when each of them have left residua in the modification of the structures'.[98]

Yet, this recovery of the past, whether of individual, society or metropolis, has its limitations, if one allows oneself to end with this image of the palimpsest, the continually written-over surface of the present that always allows the traces of the past to be seen. For, as Derrida pointed out in his essay 'Freud and the Scene of Writing', in which he places the 'Note on the Mystic Writing Pad' under intense scrutiny, what is, and what has been, recorded on the surface of this device is not, in itself, productive of meaning. Not only must one engage with 'the deletions, blanks, and disguises of writing' – or, indeed, of any mode of representation; 'The subject of writing', Derrida continues, 'is a *system* of relations between strata: the Mystic Pad, the psyche, society, the world.'[99] All the items recovered by archaeologists under London, all the conduits for waste and information, exist in huddled juxtaposition to one another, but are only brought into communication by human activity, by the secret operations of the brain, in which memory necessarily plays an inseparable part. Other forces come into play, however, when it comes to the interpretation of material objects. Focussing on the activity of looking, and stressing the relationship between perceiver and object, has the tendency to privilege that object, even if the object exists only in the mind's eye, to be called into presence through writing and through the operations of figurative language. It will be my task, in the following two chapters, to move away from fascination with the workings of the eye, the problems of perception, and the Victorians' conscious articulation of the dialogue between visibility and invisibility. Rather, I shall place the act of looking in a broader social context, and show how it intersects with a further type of the invisible: the hidden forces of ideology.

CHAPTER 7

The rôle of the art critic

In 1859, Thomas Roberts exhibited *The Opinion of the Press* at the Society of British Artists (figure 23). It shows a despairing artist in front of his easel, right hand on his brow, left hand clutching a crumpled letter, being consoled by his young wife. Their son, sitting on the floor, paints on, a sentimentalised suggestion not just of the family unity that may suffer with coming financial hardship, but of a continuity that may also be shattered if the artist loses confidence in himself, or worse. For financial circumstances are not good. Not only is the attic room sparsely furnished, the rug threadbare on the floorboards, but the figure of a portly, top-hatted man can be seen descending the stairs, oblivious, or uncaring, of the scene he has left behind him. The circumstances of the narrative told by the painting are filled in by the text which accompanied its exhibition: 'Mr. – has just left us. He bought one of the public journals containing a criticism on my dear husband's picture, and a letter from – declining to complete the purchase . . . Come as soon as you can, for we are in much trouble.' So far as one can tell from the canvas in question, and the sketches pinned to the wall, Roberts's artist has devoted himself to religious art in the grand manner (even if he was presumably unable to afford a grand-scale canvas): the antithesis of the modern subject painting which Roberts's own work represents, and to which the accompanying text – with its similarity to Augustus Egg's gloss on *Past and Present* – alludes.

Ruskin used *The Opinion of the Press* as the occasion for a little homily, warning young painters against assigning 'too much

23 Thomas Roberts,
*The Opinion of the
Press*, 1859. Oil on
canvas,
63×76 cms.

importance to press criticism as an influence on their fortunes. If sharp and telling, it is a disagreeable thing to look at when damp from the type', he acknowledges, and appears in 'an unpleasantly convenient form for one's friends to carry about in their pockets. But, ultimately, it is quite powerless, except in so far as it concurs with general public opinion.' If one does one's work well, he assures the artist, 'no enemy can harm you. So soon as your picture deserves to be bought, it will be bought.'[1] Ruskin's appeal to abstract and nebulous values concerning what is or is not deserving stands out as a form of idealistic impotence against both the stark message of Roberts's canvas, and the realities of the commercial art world which he disregards in a cavalier fashion with the phrase 'except in so far as'. For the art critic was increasingly influential in the Victorian period, as the market for pictures among those with little or no training in formal aesthetic matters widened, and as the expansion of the press offered a growing number of outlets – both specialist and generalist – for writers on art. The rôle of the critic was not to problematise acts of spectatorship; not to make his or her readers think about the relationship between the visible world and the world of the imagination; not, even, very frequently, to educate them in looking carefully at the techniques and means of representation used in publicly displayed works. Rather, a commentary tended to be offered on the painting's contents: a commentary which often assumed an unquestioned continuity between the world represented and the world inhabited by the reader of criticism. Ironically, it was this refusal to take art *as* art, which united, at least at one level, those who otherwise were implacably at odds in their attitudes towards painting.

'Let there be no critics', cried James McNeill Whistler in 1878.[2] He was pleading for works of art to be received in silence, as, he asserted, was the practice 'in the days to which the penmen still point as an era when art was at its apogee'.[3] 'Whistler v. Ruskin: Art and Art Critics', the pamphlet in which Whistler's demand appeared, was printed less than a month after the conclusion of the notorious libel case of *Whistler* v. *Ruskin*.[4] It is a vindication and an expansion of the position he took during the trial, when he aligned himself with those 'some people' contemptuously designated by the Attorney General 'who would do away with critics altogether'.[5] The pamphlet is also, paradoxically, an effort to gain recognition through print for the seriousness of his own critical ideas, particularly his belief that there is such a thing as an autonomous language of painting. By attempting to open up a theoretical debate, Whistler hoped to show the views he articulated during his trial to have been more than a self-publicising gesture.

Unmistakably, there was a considerable amount of personalised animosity on display in 'Art and Art Critics'. Although Whistler had emerged the legal victor from the trial, Ruskin had won a moral victory, the damages against him reckoned, famously, at a farthing. His critical values, emphasising the connections between Art and Ethics, had been left undented so far as the broad mass of the public was concerned. During the trial, Whistler had left

Ruskin's status as art critic unassailed: 'to have said that Mr Ruskin's pose among intelligent men, as other than a *littérateur*, is false and ridiculous, would have been an invitation to the stake; and to be burnt alive, or stoned before the verdict, was not what I came into court for'.[6] He invited post-trial assassination, however, in this pamphlet, through querying Ruskin's very credentials for writing about art. Indeed, as Merrill notes, 'this time the verdict of the press was unequivocal: there is scarcely a word of sympathy for Whistler in the numerous reviews of *Art & Art Critics* that appeared in the papers'.[7]

A life spent, like Ruskin's, among pictures, does not in itself qualify one to express opinions about them, Whistler maintained – otherwise the policeman who guards the works in the National Gallery would have equal justification for asserting himself. The only type of criticism which Whistler had acknowledged as valid during the trial was technical criticism, voiced by 'a man whose life is passed in the practice of the art he criticises',[8] but in the pamphlet, feigning ignorance of Ruskin's experience as a practical artist (or choosing to ignore it), he condemns him in outraged terms for having the impudence to preach to young men what he cannot perform himself. This assertion, that painting could only be understood by a practising artist, belonged to a long tradition: Dürer, for example, wrote around 1513 that 'The art of painting cannot be truly judged save by such as are themselves good painters; from others verily it is hidden even as a strange tongue.'[9] Within English criticism, this position harks back to Reynolds's placing of artistic competence above literary skill when it came to the ability to assess a picture: 'the knowledge which an artist has of his subject will more than compensate for any want of perspicuity in the matter of treating it'.[10] Early in the Victorian period, distrust of 'pleasant' practitioners of fine writing, exercising their talents in respect to canvases, drew scorn upon them and upon their propensity to pour forth, as a contributor to the *New Monthly Magazine* put it, 'whole pages of Twaddle written, not on the picture, but on supposed beauties and intentions never intended by the artist'.[11]

Whistler's campaign was not, in the long run, as the contemporary writer on art Frederick Wedmore noted, 'so much against Mr

Ruskin personally as against the rights or claims of criticism'.[12] The introductory paragraphs of 'Whistler v. Ruskin: Art and Art Critics' complain that the essence of the trial seems to have been either missed or willingly winked at by reporters in their comments. What they should have noticed, according to Whistler, was that 'the war, of which the opening skirmish was fought the other day in Westminster, is really one between the brush and the pen; and involves literally, as the Attorney-General himself hinted, the absolute "raison d'être" of the critic'.[13] He notes that critics are creatures of relatively recent growth, and laments that the press gives them ample opportunity to spread their foolishness and prejudice, so that through the newspapers, 'thousands are warned against the work they have yet to look upon'.[14] His fundamental case is that judgement upon a work of art should not be a question of personal preference. Since art should be regarded as based upon laws as rigid and defined as those of the known sciences, the layperson, however much they might pride themselves on their 'taste', should remain as discreet and taciturn on the subject of painting as they would on engineering or astronomy.

Whistler carried this theme further in his 'Ten O'Clock Lecture', originally planned as an article for the *English Illustrated Magazine*, and finally delivered in London on 20 February 1885.[15] Although not printed until 1888, it received wide press coverage at the time of its delivery. Opposition to Ruskin is still very much present, not just in the thinly disguised portrait of the haranguing, exhorting, denouncing 'Sage of the Universities – learned in many matters, and of much experience in all, save his subject',[16] but in Whistler's attack on the belief that art is linked, either as product or as determinant, to the society in which it is executed. Ruskin is far from being Whistler's only target, however. He also protests against the work of the 'unattached writer' – an epithet apparently applied to the freelancing newspaper or periodical critic who falls into the common trap (discussed at length in the next chapter) of seeing a work of art solely in terms of the story it tells or fails to tell, and who thus brings about 'the most complete misunderstanding as to the aims of the picture'.[17] He mocks, too, the stance of William Morris and other backward looking inhabitants of the 'little hamlets [which] grow near Hammersmith',[18] asserting that the notion of the one-time existence of an artistic period or an art-loving nation is mere idealistic fallacy. As with his censures on Ruskin, this attack is linked to Whistler's denial of the existence of any valid relation subsisting between art and history. He has no greater sympathy for the 'Dilettante' or the 'voice of the aesthete',[19] and he quickly disposes of what he sees as the clerical, pigeon-holing labours of the new breed of art historians, such as Crowe and Cavalcaselle, 'sombre of mien, and wise with the wisdom of books, who frequent museums and burrow in crypts; collecting – comparing – compiling – classifying – contradicting', since they reduce art to statistics and hence kill it.[20] To the artist, Whistler claims, these various forms of response which he gathers together are inseparable from both vulgarisation and popular pre-tension. They foster the illusion that the mysteries of art are easily accessible, and that the majority of the population have the ability to enter the privileged 'gentle circle' of this goddess.[21] In this, he was in direct opposition not just to Ruskin, but to such critics as Francis Palgrave, the principal critic of the *Saturday Review* in the 1860s, with his firmly democratic belief that 'art, like poetry, is addressed to the world at large'; that its purpose is to produce pleasure, and that to 'point out the degree in which a work fulfils this condition, and thereby to assist the artist in fulfilling it, and the spectator in feeling it, is the province of criticism'.[22] At the same time, however, he was not alone in his fastidiousness. The very popularity of painting caused other writers as well to rail against the effects of public exhibition on many of the paintings which were being produced, with their compulsive reaching after a low common denominator in the taste of the public. Their language readily betrays the social elitism behind the aesthetic position-taking. J. B. Atkinson, for example, took up the spirit of Whistler's polemic when he wrote a few years later about how the arts 'obtain applause by realising through low expedients the greatest happi-ness of the greatest number',[23] and Frederic Harrison, likewise, lamented the fact that the competitive nature of the exhibition system means that 'the conspicuous alone catches the public eye. *Il faut sauter aux yeux*, and that in the eyes of the silly, the careless, the vulgar, in order to be popular.'[24]

What lies at the heart of Whistler's objection to art critics was the commercial role which they had come to fulfil, acting, as he put it, as a 'middleman' between public and artist.[25] This, in turn, is a part of his desire to emphasise what he sees as the decontextualisation necessary to a 'pure' aesthetic response. His repudiation of the need for artistic mediators, however, was the aspect of his polemic to which both his supporters and detractors most frequently objected. Even such a committed admirer as Sheridan Ford, the compiler of the unauthorised collection of Whistler's letters to the press, was to take up the remark made by Oscar Wilde in his assessment of the 'Ten O'Clock Lecture' that 'an artist is not an isolated fact',[26] adding: 'While Art has no need of the Pen, the Public, of which the Newspaper is the Voice, has need of Art, and the Pen must be reckoned with.'[27] However, what Henry James termed Whistler's 'little diatribe against writers on art' was no isolated outburst drawing attention to the problematic role of the art critic, but needs to be placed in the broad context of the debate which had been taking place during the preceding decades. That Whistler was not alone in his unease is stressed by James: 'The painter's irritated feeling is interesting, for it suggests the state of mind of many of his brothers of the brush in the presence of the bungling and incompetent disquisitions of certain members of the fraternity who sit in judgement upon their works.'[28]

Yet James, writing in 1875, also understood that the critic had a particular and developing function to fulfil: 'Art, at the present day, is being steadily and rapidly vulgarised (we do not here mean in the invidious sense); it appeals to greater numbers of the people than formerly, and the gate of communication has had to be widened.'[29] The critic became, in other words, the eyes of the growing middle-class public. But what was expected of these critics, a group with an increasingly professionalised role?[30] Did they see their function as being to teach the public to see, training their unpractised vision? Was their task, as Whistler suspected, less concerned with aesthetics, and more concerned with commerce?

The answer, of course, lies in a combination of these possibilities. Ironically, the writing of Ruskin, however much it might be interspersed with forcefully expressed moralising, or narrative extrapolations, or idiosyncratic asides, did more than that of anyone else to encourage a readership to actually *look* at pictures. He continually emphasised the importance of the eye – 'that for ever indescribable instrument'[31] – and the importance of seeing. His well-known statement that 'the greatest thing a human soul ever does in this world is to *see* something, and tell what it *saw* in a plain way'[32] calls attention to the integrity he believed must be invested in both observation and communication. He believed fervently that this need for integrity was related to judging art for the combination of objective and personal honesty it contained, leading him to condemn as well as praise, to write criticism that was much more evaluative than that of most of his predecessors.[33] For him, too, the right use of the eye was inseparable from an individual's personal and moral qualities.

This was where Ruskin parted company from contemporary scientific thinkers, as well as from Whistlerian aestheticians. He vehemently opposed Thomas Huxley's remark that: 'sight was "altogether mechanical". The words simply meant, if they meant anything, that all his physiology had never taught him the difference between eyes and telescopes. Sight is an absolutely spiritual phenomenon; accurately, and only, to be so defined'.[34] Although he acknowledged that 'the science of optics is an essential one to us',[35] what mattered to him was a person's capacity to go beyond 'ordinary sight' and see 'within the temple of the heart'.[36] As he famously asserted in *Modern Painters* I (1843), 'the first great mistake that people make . . . is the supposition that you must *see* a thing if it be before their eyes'. Impressions made on the 'outward parts' are nothing if they do not reach the mind, 'if they are not taken notice of within; there is no perception'. It is the habit of the bodily organ to see, but if the objects of perception do not register on the brain, they 'pass actually unseen'.[37] Moreover, and this is where Ruskin established the more controversial ground on which both acclaim and opposition were to rest, we do not all see equally. Although we may train our sight – 'No human capacity ever yet saw the whole of a thing; but we may see more and more of it the longer we look . . . Every advance in our acuteness of perception will show us something new '[38] – some people, he believed were better equipped as producers and spectators of art than others. Their 'bodily sensibility to colour and form', he asserted, is intimately connected to

> that higher sensibility which we revere as one of the chief attributes of all noble minds, and as the chief spring of real poetry. I believe this kind of sensibility may be entirely resolved into the acuteness of bodily sense of which I have been speaking; associated with love, love I mean in its infinite and holy functions, as it embraces divine and human and brutal intelligences, and hallows the physical perception of external objects by association, gratitude, veneration, and other pure feelings of our moral nature.[39]

The impassioned importance with which Ruskin invested an individual's power of seeing, and the moral existence which he believed lay behind it, can be seen in his vehement opposition to the 'mechanical' art of photography. He draws an analogy between using the cornea and retina for the reception of an image, and employing a lens and a piece of silvered paper for the same purpose: what has the power to turn the former process into art is 'that inner part of the man, or rather that entire and only being of the man, of which cornea and retina, fingers and hands, pencils and colours, are all the mere servants and instruments'. A man may see, says Ruskin, 'though the eyeball be sightless'.[40] Whilst he was prepared to acknowledge photography's usefulness as a means of recording some kinds of facts – like details of architecture or buildings under threat, or drawings by old masters – this 'truth of mere transcript . . . has nothing to do with Art properly so called'.[41]

The impact of art criticism, in any period, is complicated by the very nature of its object. For whereas the mechanical reproduction of writing allows for the possibility of a relatively widespread diffusion of a literary text, 'even the most perfect reproduction of a work of art', as Walter Benjamin reminds us, cannot replicate an original's 'unique existence at the place where it happens to be'.[42]

Undoubtedly, influential Victorian critics could build up or demol-
ish an artist's reputation, but those people with the purchasing
power to acquire a work by a popular painter remained a privileged minority, despite the growing market for engravings and
photogravures. Moreover, many of the paintings by the best-
known artists had been commissioned before they were ever hung
on an exhibition wall.[43] Hence, critical opinions had the power to
influence future commissions, but not to effect the sale of the particular work under scrutiny. Buying an entrance ticket for an exhibition represented a modified form of primary consumption,
founded upon collective participation in a ritual occasion, and
serving, then as now, much the same function, at one level, as
theatre or concert attendance, fostering social and ideological
cohesion (and aspirations) within a group, the whole process of
consumption (including the consolidating effects of criticism)
ensuring, to use Pierre Bourdieu's formulation, 'adherence, at the
deepest level of the habitus, to the tastes and distastes, sympathies
and aversions, fantasies and phobias which, more than declared
opinions, forge the unconscious unity of a class'.[44] Representations of exhibitions could be used to suggest, on occasion, an
intensity of public interest in the works on show – the gazes in
George O'Neill's *Public Opinion* (c. 1863) are turned away from
artist and spectator, directed towards the popular, rail-protected
work on display or towards the information contained in catalogues: the active and focussed nature of looking is emphasised by
the woman with opera glasses who is positioned near the centre of
the canvas (figure 24). But by concentrating on the mobile faces of
a crowd, however aesthetically motivated one might take them to
be; by offering up their dress, their fashionability, their interaction,
as tokens to be read and interpreted; by stressing, in other words,
social gathering rather than the paintings themselves, depictions
of art shows, whether in paintings or in periodical publications,
ultimately serve to reinforce the point that spectators are partici-
pating in social rituals, however much any individual act of spectatorship may involve individualised, subjective apprehension and
judgement (figure 25).

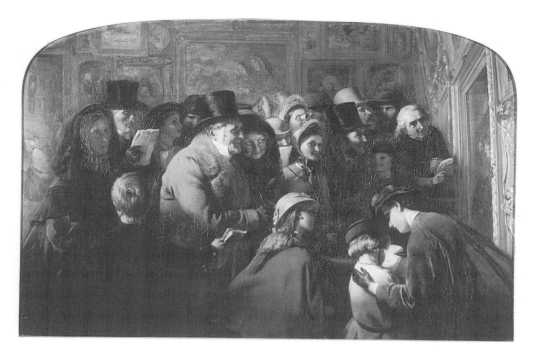

24 George O'Neill, *Public Opinion*, c. 1863. Oil on canvas, 53.2×78.8 cms.

Reading and assimilating art criticism meant, as with literary criticism, the acquisition of knowledge. Whereas, in the case of fiction or poetry or a travel book, this gained knowledge, whether of fact or opinion, might lead to the purchase of these volumes (either directly, or through placing demands on a circulating library's stock), the consumption of art inevitably tended to remain at a secondary rather than a primary level, with the possession of knowledge or opinion taking the place of the acquisition of the work itself. This possession acted, to use Bourdieu's useful term, as 'cultural capital', and, necessarily, 'the apprehension and possession of cultural goods as symbolic goods' – even at one remove – 'are possible only for those who hold the code making it possible to decipher them'.[45] Victorian critics were also frequently aware not only of their responsibility in moulding the success or failure of individual artists, but also of what they believed to be their responsibility towards the education of the growing numbers of the middle-class public – the principal consumers of the newsprint and journals which contained art criticism – who

25 William Small,
'At the Royal
Academy', *Graphic*,
26 June 1880.

became more and more vocal in their demands for direction. The demonstration of one's ability to articulate information and opinion on artistic matters was increasingly an indication of one's achieved status, or an aid to upward social mobility. The prominent critic Philip Hamerton – prominent enough for Henry James to remark of him, hyperbolically, in 1868, that 'the profession of art critic, so largely and successfully exercised in France, has found in England, but a single eminent representative'[46] – succinctly summed up the situation as he saw it in the early 1860s: 'Every day thousands of new human beings come into the world whose future social position will require them to pretend to appreciate pictures. Is this pretension to be a hollow make-belief, degrading to manliness, destructive to honesty, and thus vitally injurious to character? or is it to be the simple assertion of a well-founded right to a real opinion?'[47]

Hamerton's article in the *Cornhill Magazine* on 'Art Criticism' attempts to outline the grounds on which a critic should attempt to educate this new audience for art, and the demands which he makes upon the critic are formidable. Their exhaustive inclusiveness makes this piece a useful one on which to pause, however, for his numbered list of a critic's eleven duties or functions was regularly recycled, for the rest of the century, in the advice offered to young critics, and may fairly be seen as representative of the expectations which were held regarding the critic's ideal role. The public must be made aware of the claims of the past, through the exalting of 'the fame of dead artists whose example may be beneficial',[48] and the weakening of 'the fame of dead artists whose names have an injurious degree of authority'.[49] Otherwise, the first and most important function of the art critic is to utter unpopular truths, 'truths which others do not yet perceive'.[50] Popular truths, he claims, are well enough stated already: a critic should do more than reproduce perfectly valid received opinion. He further proposes that the critic must 'instruct the public in the theoretical knowledge of art';[51] must 'defend true living artists' – especially young ones – 'against the malice of the ignorant',[52] and must prevent 'false' living artists 'from acquiring an influence injurious to the general interests of art',[53] thus opposing the opinion, often uttered by insipid critics, that one should withhold adverse criticism because of financial compassion for a painter's livelihood. Writers must 'speak always with absolute sincerity',[54] and must not fear being inconsistent in their judgements, since those who are both honest and intelligent will be perpetually reviewing their own conclusions. The flexibility of critics is stressed in two further demands: they must be continually enlarging their own powers of sympathy, which, since Hamerton sees painting as being an expression of human feeling, is essential; and they must do their best to resist the formation of prejudices.

The most demanding of Hamerton's precepts is the obligation he places on the critic to 'make himself as thoroughly informed as his time and opportunities will allow about everything concerning the fine Arts, whether directly or indirectly'.[55] The entry of Ruskin onto the reviewing scene with his *Academy Notes* (published as independent pamphlets between 1855 and 1859) had laid down a standard in this respect, since Ruskin declared in his first Preface that 'Twenty years of severe labour, devoted exclusively to the study of the principles of Art, have given me the right to speak on the subject with a measure of confidence.'[56] Hamerton's qualification 'time and opportunities' is certainly a necessary one: to follow Hamerton's programme would demand a substantial private income and relatively unlimited leisure. He was not alone, however, in acknowledging the need for lengthy training, even if Frances Verney's remarks in the *Contemporary Review* that 'good criticism demands at least as long and severe an apprenticeship as that in ironmongery'[57] deliberately suggests that what is required is a practical course in familiarising oneself with the tools of the trade rather than a prolonged exposure to high culture. Such acknowledgements of the need for carefully learning the skills of art criticism, however phrased, are surely, though, in part a response to those who consider the task a soft option, a most 'pleasant mode of earning a livelihood, . . . constantly feeding one's eyes upon pictures by clever painters'.[58] For, as Hamerton puts it, 'painting seems so simple, the object which it proposes to itself is apparently so obvious, that everyone secretly believes himself competent to judge of it'.[59]

The critic's comprehensive self-education, according to Hamerton, should be first a practical one. He or she should start by making up to 1,000 careful studies from nature, and then turn to the copying of parts of paintings and drawings by different masters. Critics must travel, in order to prepare themselves to comment on the representation of types of scenery with which they are not familiar; and they must travel, also, to see as many original examples as they can of artists' work, for 'to grasp the whole mind of a great artist we must see *all* his works, for every great artistic nature is so large that each picture is a new revelation of power before unknown to us'.[60] Then more academic study must be entered into:

> It is unnecessary to indicate the immense range of literary culture essential to the art critic. The success of historical paint-ing is not to be estimated by persons ignorant of history, nor can illustrations of poets be intelligible to spectators who never read

verse. And there is this peculiarity about the position of every art critic, that his knowledge must embrace the knowledge, not of one artist only, but of thousands.[61]

Contextual cultural information was widely noted as being what many of the public wanted: by the same token, the *naïveté* of this public in the arena of high culture could provide the opportunity for the rhetorical display of superiority on such matters on a critic's part, in turn an act of implied flattery which served to consolidate their relations with their readership – for the implication is that the truly cultured critic, like the truly cultured reader, will not have had to resort to second-hand sources of information about classical sources in the first place. Thus in 1883, the *Saturday Review's* critic elaborated – in mildly condescending terms – on their duty of explaining 'to a not particularly well-educated world the matter in hand'. Young ladies who have never heard of Penelope may learn from the critic that she was the wife of Ulysses and occupied herself with embroidery. Moreover:

> The public cannot imagine why Mr Calder Marshall's Thetis is holding a baby up by the heel. Their natural inclination is to think of Solomon, and to blame the unnatural mother. Then the critic, by virtue of his researches into Lemprière and other heathen writers, is able to inform his readers that Thetis is merely giving her boy a dip in the water which makes men invulnerable. Thus the character of the silver-footed goddess is cleared, and every one is happier and wiser.[62]

Reviewing the Academy exhibition in 1888, the *Athenaeum's* critic felt it necessary to quote seventeen lines from the *Iliad* as a gloss to Leighton's *Captive Andromache*, and accompanied his remarks on Alma-Tadema's *Roses of Heliogabalus* with a potted biography of this Roman Emperor who suffocated whilst enjoying a bath of rose petals.[63] This provision of information was, necessarily, not always as disinterested as this. When the *Art Journal's* critic expanded on the subject matter of W. L. Windus's *Burd Helen* (1856) (figure 26), it was in a Janus-like fashion, educating (this time in antiquarianised popular culture) in order to be able to condemn:

26 William Lindsay Windus, *Burd Helen*, 1856. Oil on canvas,
84.46 × 66.67 cms.

> The subject is from an old Scottish ballad —
>> Lord John he rode, Burd Helen ran,
>>> A live-long simmer's day,
>> Until they cam' to Clyde Water,
>>> Was filled frae brank to brae.

> We instance this as an example of the worst taste in the selection of subject. The lady appears as a page running by the side of her mounted lover, who was a dastard; not to say anything of the discredit attending such a course on the part of the lady. The greater the success in the treatment of such a subject, the more painful it becomes.[64]

In all of Hamerton's *Cornhill* brief for constituting the art critic, there is little stress placed on the importance of training the picture-viewing public to use their eyes. Hamerton's piece – however laudable the demands he makes for critics to enter into their task with the utmost preparation, seriousness and sense of responsibility may be – ultimately conveys the impression that looking at art has everything to do with knowledge, education and the acquisition of socially acceptable taste, and involves very little practice in visual engagement.

However, this was far from being Hamerton's last word on the subject of seeing, and in an article in the *Art Journal* three years later, he wrote in much more careful detail about 'how artistic sight differs from ordinary sight', adding that it is 'the business of artists to see artistically; it is the bounden duty of all who write on Art to learn to see in that manner'.[65] Hamerton's writing is clearly informed by a knowledge of contemporary debates about the nature of vision and perception. He acknowledges that seeing is an activity that differs from individual to individual, whether the object of the gaze is natural or culturally produced: 'It is an optical fact, easily proved, that no two men ever saw the same rainbow. It is an aesthetic fact, scarcely more difficult of proof, that no two men ever saw the same appearance in any object whatever. What men will see is determined beforehand by very complex conditions of faculties, experience, and education.'[66] The scientific justification for a statement such as this could be found in Lewes's comments in his chapter of *The Physiology of Common Life* entitled 'Feeling and Thinking', when he argues in terms which go beyond the exercise of one's eyes, but which start with the very act of looking:

> Of two men looking from the same window, on the same landscape, one will be moved to unutterable sadness, yearning for the peace of death; the other will feel his soul suffused with serenity and content: the one has a gloomy background of Consciousness, into which the sensations excited by the landscape are merged; the other has a happy background of Consciousness, on which the sensations play like ripples on a sunny lake. The tone of each man's feeling is determined by the state of his general consciousness. Except in matters of pure demonstration, we are all determined towards certain conclusions as much by this general consciousness as by logic. Our philosophy, when not borrowed, is little more than the expression of our personality.[67]

One's ways of seeing may also, of course, be drawn more broadly from one's cultural and national context, as Robert Louis Stevenson showed himself to be well aware when crossing the plains of Nebraska with a carriage-load of Chinese immigrants. 'Heaven knows', he muses, 'if we had one common thought or fancy all that way, or whether our eyes, which yet were formed upon the same design, beheld the same world out of the railway windows.'[68]

What Hamerton makes clear, in his *Art Journal* piece, is that the ordinary spectator of a picture will observe it with criteria drawn from, and relevant to, the whole material world in which she or he lives, and hence their spectatorship will be informed by the social expectations and prejudices that they bring with them. This accompanying baggage of cultural knowledge also, necessarily, brings limitations too – as Lewes acknowledged: 'If Perception is enlarged by Preperception, and Conception by Preconception, they are also thus restricted as by *blinkers*.'[69] Thus the bourgeois mind admires wealth, order and cleanliness, whilst 'to the artistic eye, the costliness or cheapness of an object is always a matter of

the most supreme indifference'.[70] Yet rather than looking beyond
the object itself – in other words, turning seeing into cultural
judgement and classification – artistic sight consists of 'trying to
grasp all the facts, so far as they are visible, yet no farther':[71] this
involves learning to see 'true' colours, 'true' proportion and the
'true' relations of things. Those who presume to comment on
artistic work, he continues, should also endeavour to have artistically trained eyes themselves.

Yet certain general considerations continually interfered with
the idealistic agendas set down by Hamerton, whether he was
writing in a generalist periodical or for a publication in which a
more informed and involved engagement with aesthetic issues
and the act of seeing could be anticipated. It was not just, as we
shall see in the following chapter, that the vast majority of the
picture-viewing public looked at art, and were encouraged to look
at art, with a quite different set of priorities from the development
of their powers of vision. The particular conditions under which
writers on contemporary art exhibitions operated were hardly
conducive to the optimum exercise of their visual and judgemen-
tal practices. First, as Whistler recognised and condemned, commercial pressures could weigh upon a reviewer. As the
curmudgeonly critic Harry Quilter pointed out when looking
back at his career – a career which began as art correspondent for
the *Spectator* in 1876 – painters need to live, and to live they must sell
pictures. The critic, 'if he is to have any reason for existing at all, is
placed between the picture-buyer and the picture-producer for the
express purpose of gauging the artistic value of the latter's
achievement, and interpreting its meaning to the world at large'.[72]

Much more explicitly, Quilter demystified the job of critics by
casting them in the role of a tradesman's agent: describing the
artist as a particular type of tradesman who was peculiarly dependent on popular opinion and fashion, since his commodity is not
purchased out of true necessity. This popular opinion, he asserts,
can only find expression in the press, and he employs a comparison which deliberately underscores his understanding of works of
art as a market commodity. Suppose one were, in a newspaper, to
attack the quality of silk on sale at Marshall and Snelgrove and the

ignorance of the proprietors in such matters, whilst insinuating that, nonetheless, they inveigled the public into purchasing in their store through an enticing window display, the certain result would be a libel suit with the vendor receiving heavy damages. The artist who is misrepresented or misunderstood, however, traditionally takes no such redress.[73] However, whilst he believes the critic should be free to show partisanship where the intrinsic value of a work merited it, he deeply resented editorial interference, pointing out the fact that the direction of favouritism might not be left up to the critic, since newspaper proprietors could not afford to offend those whose advertisements were a continual source of revenue. The principal medium for the distribution of advertisements designated for the art world, and for art criticism, was, after all, identical. Quilter claimed that he wrote from experience; that he had himself been ordered by his editor to review certain engravings and photogravures more leniently than he wished. He knew that such a policy resulted in a lower standard being 'admitted for those phases of art which are commercially profitable to the paper, and that critics are forced, or at all events tempted, to bestow upon the exhibition, for instance, of large picture dealers or the publications of the great art publishing firms, an amount of praise and attention which are very frequently entirely undeserved'.[74]

Yet over and beyond Quilter's typically outspoken, if indicative, pronouncements on the issue, resentment of the linkage between art and commerce was something of a commonplace throughout the period. This disapproval, this distaste was expressed both in relation to general attitudes towards art, and with reference to specific practices. As early as 1830, *Fraser's Magazine* had grumbled that 'art has too grovelling and mercantile a spirit; it keeps its ledgers, its debtor and creditor accounts, and smacks of the counting house'.[75] The protests became persistent around the late 1850s and early 1860s, a period when the Royal Academy exhibitions were dominated by anecdote and landscape, when the Pre-Raphaelites had lost their initial bite and there were few controversial continental products to be seen. 'Pictures are now but a portion of domestic furniture',[76] complained the *Saturday Review*'s critic after visiting the Academy's Summer Exhibition in 1857. In 1861, the smaller galleries, too, were accused of promoting paintings as if they were 'a mere manufacture and a dull routine of trade',[77] and in 1862, the critique of 'the growing demand for what may be called "furniture pictures"' was repeated in the *Saturday*.[78] Whilst the tone of this criticism betrays a class-based unease at the fact that the artist is infused with nothing more remarkable than those skills which elsewhere find their outlet in mass commodity production – something which in turn reflects in derogatory fashion on the tastelessness of the picture-buying public – the converse was the complaint that critics and artists operated in too intimate and uncritical a proximity to one another. 'Much of even the best writing on art has usually the stamp of special cliques and art friends about it, the flavour of mutual admiration societies', complained Emilie Barrington in 1879,[79] and numerous anecdotes and representations of art critical activity support her accusation. She herself noted that the influence of practising artists is particularly apparent when the newspaper writer passes from treating the 'literary aspect of art' to the technical matters about which she or he knows little. Personal intervention could take forms which had even less to do with the execution of the canvas. Archibald Henderson recalls how Bernard Shaw, at the last press show that he attended, was in the capacity of art critic to a Sunday paper

> which had just then passed into the hands of a Jewish lady. 'My Academy notice', as he once told me, 'appeared padded out to an extraordinary length by interpolations praising the works of the Jewish lady's acquaintances – "No.2744 is a sweet head of Mrs – by that talented young artist Miss –" and so on. Naturally I resigned in a highly explosive manner.'[80]

Ella Hepworth Dixon, who herself worked as an art critic (and had trained as an artist) has a sharply satirical scene in *The Story of a Modern Woman* (1894) in which her heroine, Mary, temporarily takes over the position of exhibition reviewer for the newspaper for which she writes. 'It was press day at the galleries of the Society of United Artists', she writes: 'Scotch mountain streams, eastern bazaars, young ladies reading love-letters, fishermen mending nets, ran promiscuously up the walls to the very cornice, or modestly hung on a level with the boots of the spectator. Everywhere was the obvious, the threadbare, the *banal*; everywhere there was a frank appeal to the Philistinism of the picture-buying public.'[81] As Mary walks slowly round the show – taking in the buffet spread with a York ham, bath buns and sherry decanters, not to mention the cigar-smoking, Inverness-caped male critics gossiping to each other, rather than looking at the paintings – she conscientiously stops in front of every picture she could possibly mention in her article:

> and stopping, too, before pictures which an editorial hint had advised her she would have to mention whether she liked them or no. Yonder was a yellow and blue 'Rome from the Pincian Hill', by a man with whom, she remembered, her editor constantly dined; while close beside it was a portrait of Mr Bosanquet-Barry himself, by a lady more celebrated for her charms than her talent. She must find, of course, some phrase which might encourage the fair artist to go on painting editors' portraits.[82]

As Helene Roberts points out, the fact that 'artists and dealers tried to court or bribe critics was a testimonial to the widespread belief in their influence'.[83]

The second inhibiting factor which weighed upon some art critics lay in the frequent assumption that the exercise of criticism was to be considered as a branch of manners. A code of gentlemanliness prevailed. Norman MacColl, editor of the *Athenaeum* in the 1870s, wrote to his art correspondent Frederick Stephens about the pragmatic etiquette of reviewing, considering that a critic, whilst never praising a bad picture, should find no more fault with it than necessary: too great a severity defeats its own ends. Rather than attacking two of his particular targets, Frith and Orchardson, Stephens is advised to consult the passage in Matthew Arnold's *Essays in Criticism* where Arnold contrasts Francis Palgrave's vehement prose with the more temperate offerings of Gustave Planchet, to the latter's advantage:

It seems to me a canon in literature that the appearance of reserved force is the great thing to be aimed at in hostile judgements. You produce a much greater effect if you make the reader think that, badly as you have spoken of a picture, you could be far more severe on it if you chose – in fact if instead of throwing all the mud you possess, you make him see how much more you could throw.[84]

Rhetorical pragmatics mingled with the force of commercial considerations in the advice offered by Mr Bowen, the solicitor acting for Ruskin in the 1878 trial, when he suggested that the average person (in the person of a jury member) would, on balance, tend to have more sympathy with favourable rather than with aggressive criticism. He advocated, therefore, getting recognised artists, such as Burne-Jones, to speak in favour of Ruskin's point of view, rather than assuming that the critic's prose would of itself have the power to convince, for the jury 'would look to the language used rather than to the provocation + their sympathies would rather lean to the side of the man who wanted to sell his picture than to the side of the outspoken critic whose criticism interfered with the sale of a marketable commodity'.[85] Persuading the reader, whatever the context, was not the only point of writing well-mannered criticism: it was asserted that the very quality of painting itself would benefit if the language used to write about it was kept within decorous bounds. The artist, a 'thin-skinned, impressionable being, with sensitive nerves and perceptions', was often described as someone who would benefit from criticism in general terms, but who would respond particularly readily to praise, to anything which lightened the depressing 'chill of fashionable indifference'.[86]

The complete novice who followed the advice laid down in *The Reporter's Handbook* (1884) was left in no doubt as to where to begin: 'Get a catalogue.'[87] The list of questions with which he or she was then furnished indicate the habitual emphasis of reviews in the provincial press: the primary importance of the exhibition was as a social event in the calendar of a local community. The reporter should, therefore, inquire about the specific significance of the exhibition. How much money are the organisers trying to raise, and for what purpose? Should the aim of the show be, for example, to finance some new building, the writer should obtain the particulars of this prospective edifice from the architect. Who originally conceived the idea of holding the exhibition? The names of the committee must, as one might expect, be prominently mentioned. The number of oil paintings, water-colours, etchings, engravings and sculptures must be carefully counted. When the question of providing a commentary on the works themselves finally arises, the reporter is issued with a glossary of the most common words and phrases used, followed, in this journalist's *dictionnaire des idées reçues*, by a list of noted painters, arranged according to their choice of subject matter, from which informed remarks and comparisons can be drawn. Thus, if conveniently faced with a representation of a bowl of fruit, the critic can praise or damn this by means of the reference to be found under '*Grapes*' to 'Zeuxis, who is said to have painted grapes so well that the birds came and picked at them'.[88]

Nonetheless, most reviewers of art exhibitions, however provincially situated, were exhorted by the writers of self-help manuals to obtain a far wider knowledge of art than could be gleaned from the pages of a handbook. This knowledge, it was continually stated, required a dual, and familiar foundation: 'to write on art requires two distinct educations; one in literature and philosophy, the other in practical art-work'.[89] Art history, through the successive periods of its evolution from classical times, should be thoroughly mastered; the lives of the principle painters and sculptors read, and the results of this mass of reading verified by the study of actual paintings and statuary – feasible in any large English city by the 1870s. The understanding of contemporary art, it is suggested, will be greatly aided by visits to artists' studios: permission to visit these was usually readily granted (often, no doubt, by those anxious to obtain some free publicity in the many columns in the art press devoted to work in progress) and, whilst: 'many excellent painters and sculptors have neither the time, inclination, nor the requisite literary training to enable them to write on their art, . . . some of these will discourse in their studio in such a way that teaches more than most of the professionally written pages published in the best art journals of the day'.[90]

Third, Hamerton's desiderata seem to assume not just abundant leisure in which to acquire a thoughtful competency in the field of art, but all the time critics might wish for in which to write up their impressions of exhibitions. Yet even those who were trained in looking did not necessarily have the time to do so very carefully, particularly if they were writing for the daily or weekly press. Complaints about the size of exhibitions combined with tight deadlines were a commonplace. Harry Quilter estimated that between 1872 and 1890, he saw and wrote of 'nearly half a million pictures and sculptures, and criticised several hundred books, chiefly relating to art'. He goes on, however, to say that this work 'has been done for the most part at a few hours notice, and generally with no time for revision or reflection. This is one of the conditions of newspaper writing.'[91] The *Saturday Review*'s critic asked in 1883:

> Does anyone imagine that the art critic likes having eight hours, at the utmost, in which to inspect and form his opinion about eighteen hundred works of art? Suppose a man goes to the Academy at ten, on the morning of the Press view, and stays till six, lunching on a cake of chocolate as he walks round, and denied even the refreshment of a cigarette, he will probably be removed in the condition of a colour-blind idiot before dinnertime. Yet even this conscientious critic would only have, we think, twenty seconds and a trifle over to give to each exhibited masterpiece.[92]

Henry Morley had made a similar calculation a decade earlier, estimating that if a critic gave one minute's viewing time to each work in the 1872 Royal Academy exhibition, it would take twenty-five hours to see them all.[93] It was this mid-Victorian habit of crowding walls – a habit deliberately broken by the policy of the Grosvenor Gallery when it opened in 1877 – which led Francis Palgrave, an earlier critic on the *Saturday Review*, to warn his readers against jading their responses. Whilst the 'eye may not be satisfied with seeing', the 'Imagination is quickly wearied by attending; the vast mass of different works which must fill all collections fatigues and blunts the judgment'.[94] Yet even though the cramming together of pictures could lead to visual fatigue, and even though it damaged appreciation of the particular aesthetics of individual paintings – Henry Blackburn complaining, for example, that in the newly hung National Gallery many works 'are injured in effect by close juxtaposition – the style and colour of Turner's work seeming especially to demand space and isolation'[95] – such enforced juxtaposition might be thought to have encouraged a comparative mode of picture viewing; to have led the spectator, whether consciously or not, into the habit not just of considering like with like in terms of subject matter and style, but of bringing different works into dialogue with one another.

There is scant evidence that this was the case. The effect of the more traditional mode of display was not to encourage the formation of any dialogue between the apparent chance juxtapositions set up by a hanging policy driven by the demands of fitting together a geometric puzzle of rectilinear forms, even though the resulting bricolage created the potential for just such a dialectic manoeuvring between contesting emphases of representation. Rather – with the exception of those reviews which doggedly progressed by chronological catalogue number – the majority of critics imposed their own taxonomies on the confusion of canvases. The most common technique was to group discussion according to genre – paintings of historical subjects, of contemporary life, landscapes, portraits and so on – with notable, or perhaps separate, attention given to works by prominent Academicians, or by those such as the Pre-Raphaelites, or Frith, whose paintings had occasioned special controversy or debate, or been great popular favourites the previous year. In this stultifying way, each Royal Academy exhibition, in particular, tended to set up the terms in which the next one was written about.

In respect of the crowded nature of exhibition walls, the *Saturday Review*'s correspondent pointed out, the rôle of the art critic was quite unlike that of the novel-reviewer, even if the number of novels published each year is on a par with the number of pictures exhibited at the Academy. For, even if the 'general run' of the latter is much superior to the former, the fiction reviewer has leisure to read the books that come in to him or her during the year, and, moreover, can do so in the comfort of their own home. Additionally, the paucity of facilities at the Academy press views – let alone the fact that only one day was allocated to them – formed a further perennial ground for grouching. Harry Furniss, artist and occasional writer, turned these deprivations into a comic attack in a letter he wrote to the *Daily News* in 1877, dwelling on the lack of refreshment, the provision of only one catalogue per critic, only one invitation per publication, and describing critics retiring into quarters where they nervously eat sandwiches and, 'when the doorkeeper's eyes are turned, sip sherry and water from a travelling flask'.[96] Furniss further reinforced his point about the uncomfortable conditions under which an art critic had to pursue their task with his 1890 *Punch* cartoon, 'Strictly Private View, Royal Academy' (figure 27) in which barriers of top hats and bustles get in the way of scrutinising the paintings.

As Hepworth Dixon's fictional depiction of the woman correspondent suggests, the social atmosphere of the private view was overwhelmingly male. Whilst there were women who wrote for the press, as Pamela Gerrish Nunn has noted, 'In the welter of articles, essays, reviews, comments and letters which appeared in print from the late 1850s on the general theme of women and art (fine and otherwise), the topic of women as art critics practically never occurred.'[97] The Victorian period produced some distinguished women art historians and critics – Elizabeth Eastlake, Anna Jameson, Emelia Dilke[98] – and their numbers increased from the 1880s, including Vernon Lee (Violet Paget) and Mrs (Emilie) Russell Barrington. Whilst the earlier writers, particularly Jameson, conspicuously paid attention to women painters of the past, and gave more prominence to the decorative arts than most of their male counterparts, it is hard to detect anything like a feminist agenda, let alone to identify any particular ways of seeing as specific to women, in the later practitioners. Quite the reverse, in fact: as Nunn puts it, their own authority tended to rest on their ability to voice the dominant social values, and they contrasted 'with their early Victorian predecessors not only in the relatively uncontroversial status they enjoyed but in their lack of or disdain for a feminist or woman-identified stance'. Only a couple of more

27 Harry Furniss, 'Strictly Private View, Royal Academy', *Punch*, 3 May 1890.

occasional writers on art, such as Florence Fenwick-Miller and Alice Meynell, wrote 'emphatically as women'.[99] What is, however, apparent in the writing of most women art critics is the depth and extent of their knowledge, despite the fact that they lacked the formal educational background which was assumed to underpin the authority of their male counterparts.

There was no guarantee, in many publications – particularly the provincial press – that those writing about art would have any specialist knowledge of their subject whatsoever. Nothing brings this home more pointedly than the guidance offered by Ruskin, elsewhere so emphatic about the importance of the careful, direct, honest use of the eye, when he was asked what advice he would give a country reporter, with no specialised knowledge of art. He replied that he considered it a newspaper writer's duty to point out to the paper's readers things in a picture which they would have missed without his help. The reporter should stick to commenting on content: 'the best thing he can do is to describe carefully the

subject of the pictures he thinks likely to please simple people, if
they are shown what is in them, and, so far as his editor will allow
him, to take no notice of pictures attracting merely by their tricks
of painting'.[100] By describing the already perceivable content of a
work, such critics, however, fulfilled the function of confirming a
spectator's own powers of vision. The long lists of paintings which
appeared in the daily press, summarising the contents of each
canvas, represented safe, well-defined ground for both reviewer
and reader. Their compilers relied upon total recognition and
acceptance of both subject matter and treatment – treatment
which required no comment other than a few chosen adjectives of
unspecific commendation. The more progressive art critics complained constantly that 'the English public only like pictures of
familiar subjects, and only understand painters who see such subjects with the same vulgar unthinking eyes as they themselves are
accustomed to contemplate common objects'.[101] Such depictions
of common objects provided in themselves the temptation for
scathing critics to list the offending items and expect their own discerning readers to react against the itemisation with little need for
further explanatory comment. Thus *The Monster* by a recognised
master of 'kids and kittens', Burton Barber, stands condemned:
'the canvas contains a pug dog, a kitten, a tiger's skin, a baby, a box
of bricks, a spelling-book, and a cane arm chair. I expect to see this
reproduced in a Christmas number, and copies purchased by thousands of simple-minded boobies who delight in the mock sentiment of mismanaged nurseries.'[102] D. S. MacColl, together with R.
A. M. Stevenson, one of the most thoughtful and innovative 'new
critics' of the last decades of the nineteenth century, ridiculed the
taste of suburban mothers and Manchester cotton-mongers for
using art as they might use cheap tea or tobacco – 'even so',
lamented MacColl, 'does the cheap Baby or Bishop or Poodle act as
a symbol, pull strings of association in the heads of those for
whom the visible world does not exist except as a gaudily ticketed
catalogue of sentiments'.[103]

The type of predictable associations that were stirred forms
the topic of the next chapter. What emerges clearly from an
examination of the role of the art critic is that very frequently, the

information which, it was presumed by many, should underpin reviews, make them authoritative, was not intended to startle the reader into any new understanding or way of seeing, but was used to confirm their membership of the social grouping to which they belonged, or to which they aspired to belong. Possession of shared knowledge, and shared opinion, was considered far more important than the activation of the individual eye.

CHAPTER 8

Criticism, language and narrative

For many mid-Victorian spectators, their favourite paintings were those which told stories. Art had the function of confirming the narratives which they used to make sense of their lives. This preference was repeatedly lamented in criticism. William Michael Rossetti wrote in 1867 that 'The public want, above all, something that tells its story in a salient way, and in which the pictorial conception of the subject – the means of representation which constitute pictorial, as other means constitute poetic, art – shall not be made very prominent.'[1] By contrast, he identified himself, and the kind of art criticism for which he stood, as believing that 'a work professedly of fine art shall above all things fulfil this profession, be primarily a work of *art*, and that *fine* art'.[2] A decade later, Whistler was still complaining that 'the vast majority of English folk cannot and will not consider a picture as a picture, apart from any story which it may be supposed to tell'.[3]

Whistler's protest was part of his objection against what he called the amateur writer on art, who lacked specialist art training:

> For him a picture is more or less a hieroglyph or symbol of story. Apart from a few technical terms, for the display of which he finds an occasion, the work is considered absolutely from a literary point of view; indeed, from what other can he consider it? And in his essays he deals with it as with a novel – a history – or an anecdote. He fails entirely and most naturalistically to see its excellences, or demerits – artistic – and so degrades Art, by supposing it a method of bringing about a literary climax.[4]

The comments of both Rossetti and Whistler may be seen as representative of the growing gulf between writers for the general press, and those who saw their role as that of the distinctively professional critic. The shibboleth of narrative remained a target for those critics who wished to assert the autonomous demands of art – and who at the same time wished to sever themselves from any identification with mass taste – well into the twentieth century.

Many generalist critics fell readily into using a vocabulary equally or better suited to fictional prose when it came to discussing the moral implications or sentimental appeal of painting.[5] Professional critics, by contrast, came to develop a more distinctive range of technical vocabulary with which to describe effects of colour and modelling, line and tone. Both foreign writing on art, and the rapidly expanding literature of art history, played a part in the growth of a distinctive register for discussing visual productions. This served as a line of demarcation between those writing for a broad public, and those who served, or flattered, or went some way towards producing, an audience who considered themselves more discriminating.[6]

Yet the popularity of narrative works during the Victorian period, with their mass of particularities inviting identification and exemplification, was unarguable.[7] A picture which told, or could be made to tell, a story served the requirement both of those who required art to instruct, and of those who expected it to entertain. If fiction could generically be used by some to condemn this pictorial approach, so others invoked excellence in novel writing as a standard by which to judge painting. Mrs Russell Barrington, asking 'Is a Great School of Art Possible?', expresses the hope that it would be possible for a modern artist to treat, successfully, the same 'subtler thought and moral fervour' which 'finds expression pre-eminently in the writings of "George Eliot"'.[8] From the knowledge that it was possible to 'read' certain types of pictures in narrative fashion, thus enabling a sequence of events to be deduced from them (and hence introducing those notions of cause and effect which were so crucial to moralising readings), developed the popular, if usually unarticulated, critical premise that stories so told should be subject to the same criteria as verbal fiction. It was assumed, in fact, that paintings could be written about using the same vocabulary, and employing the same modes of discussion, which were conventionally regarded as appropriate to prose fiction, particularly that fiction which dealt with recognisable, often domestic, settings and incidents.

More than anything else, this was the assumption which prevented so much writing about art from engaging the spectator's eye – whether physiological or imaginative – and from addressing the spectator's visual faculties. Still less did it engage with the visualisation and artistic skills which had gone into the composition and execution of a picture. The belief which underpinned this, not so much theorised about as taken, undiscussed, as a common working supposition, was that 'language' was a concept which applied across media, and hence commentators could slip readily between genres. This assumption is encapsulated by the inaugural introduction to the *Magazine of Art*, in 1878. The writer set out to emphasise the seriousness of the magazine's subject matter by claiming that the importance of art lies not just in its potential to create pleasure, but in the fact that it is 'the embodiment of a conception of the mind'. To bring the point home, the functioning of high culture was homogenised: 'the great works of great masters, though simple, are not easy to understand. Their language must be studied as carefully as the language of Homer, Dante, and Shakespeare.'[9] Using a still broader sense of 'language', the *Saturday Review*'s critic of 1883, when faced with Whistler's worth, could enthusiastically praise the painter's ability to render the effects of Venetian water, but constantly attacked the lack of finish and form in his figures. The people represented in *Wool Carders*, for example, had no discernible merit: 'they are ridiculous shadow-like suggestions which are as much worth understanding as gibberish language'.[10] In a more deliberated and expansive consideration of the relationship between various forms of communication, and following the premise that 'writing . . . is but a simpler form of drawing',[11] Walter Crane had no hesitation in speaking of line as language: poor drawing, he wrote, could be considered as analogous to undeveloped, ungrammatical language. The endless variations which result from the fact that each designer and draughtsman uses lines in a different way, he termed 'dialects'.[12]

The assumption that art behaves like already-known and evaluated verbal practices enabled statements to be made about the implicit aesthetic value and status of a given work of art in accordance with parallels drawn with established hierarchies of literary genres. There was an enduring belief that a novel was a lesser form of composition than poetry, and this added to the degree to which, if only by implication, a relatively low aesthetic value was placed on narrative art in 'high' cultural circles. In the eyes of *its* detractors, particularly in the earlier decades of the Victorian period, the novel was no more than an entertainment, more likely to engage the imagination than the moral or speculative faculties. Ruskin himself differentiated between Holman Hunt and those who painted merely 'the outward verities of passing events': the latter, if they 'worked worthily of their mission would become, properly so called, historical or narrative painters', whilst Hunt and his Pre-Raphaelite peers were designated, because of their faculties of originality, invention and feeling, '*poetical* painters'.[13] For others, the emphasis on detail which they saw Ruskin as encouraging, the 'keenness of [the] eye and the cunning of [the] hand' which this involved, showed technical merit, but it did not invite the eye to rest, and hence it admitted no reflective space for the spectator.[14] It approached too closely the denotive characteristics of prose fiction loaded with circumstantial detail. Poetry, on the other hand, it was argued, allowed for imaginative freedom, and, in the same way that Tyndall and Lewes argued for the role of the imagination in science, so poetry might act as a kind of optical tool, allowing a writer: 'to describe, with truth and force, those objects which are too vast, and those which are too minute for ordinary ken; the former escaping common observation, from the inability of an ordinary eye to take the range of the whole at one view; and the latter, from the delicacy of observation required for their survey'.[15]

The more apparently banal the subject matter, the more pejorative the literary associations invoked to condemn this misspent attention to meticulous detail. Having acknowledged that a 'picture is sometimes religion, sometimes philosophy, sometimes history, sometimes poetry', J. B. Atkinson, writing in *Blackwood's*, condemned the 'trivial' choice of scene painted by George Hicks in *The General Post-Office, One Minute to Six* (1860) as being no more than meretricious hack journalism, 'at best mere clever penny-a-lining'.[16]

In canonical terms, poetry, with its connotations of inspiration and imagination, counted for far more than prose. 'It is to the poetical literature of an age that we must, in general, look for the most perfect, the most adequate interpretation of that age, – for the performance of a work which demands the most energetic and harmonious activity of all the powers of the human mind', Matthew Arnold maintained in his 1857 inaugural lecture as Professor of Poetry at Oxford.[17] This hierarchisation was confirmed by the art and literature critic Francis Palgrave when he wrote that 'the world would always rank poetical art as the highest thing, in the same way as poetry ranks at the summit of literature'.[18] If, at one end of the spectrum, something like documentary travel art could be devalued as the work of 'conscientious draughtsmen' who refuse to allow emotion any space in their works, and 'only use the language of art as a plain and useful prose wherewith to register facts', by contrast, the *Artist*, in 1893, maintained that what the public chiefly admired in painting, and what distinguished it from photography, was that something extra which it gave to nature, a quality which the writer found it easiest to term 'poetry'. 'Art of the highest order is necessarily associated with poetry', Sarah Stickney Ellis confidently proclaimed in *The Beautiful in Nature and Art* (1866).[19] This preference, she declared, in turn influenced the type of writer whom the journal itself chose to interpret works of art: 'it is to the "literary" critic that the public will turn, simply because this "mood", this power of addition, in the painter is the poetic – the literary – quality in him, only to be fairly interpreted through the same quality in the critic'.[20] The term 'literary', as is illustrated by a juxtaposition of both Stevenson's and the *Artist's* terminology with that of Whistler, was itself a usefully, if confusingly, mutable one, suggesting either an inviolable distance from the proper end of visual art, or else a particular quality which allowed such art to be distinguished from its more prosaic counter-parts.

The idea of art's literary, or, more especially, its poetical ana-logues could be used, moreover, to differentiate it from science. We have already seen that parallels were made between the work-ings of the imagination in art and in the sciences, and noted the insights which scientific investigations brought to understanding the complex processes involved in the act of seeing. Yet resistance to the scope of authority which could be attributed to science could be expressed through juxtaposing it to the formulations of high culture: 'the finer Art, with written poetry, being reserved for those who, believing that the Almighty has endowed his human creatures with imagination, ideality, and *even with the power of con-ceiving beautiful things peculiar to the human brain, desire to see those faculties*' exercised in painting.[21] The crucial aesthetic site on which was centred the debate about whether art and science worked in tandem with one another, or were at cross-purposes, was, of course, photography.[22] Those paintings which also seemed to their spectator to substitute scientific 'truthfulness' for imagination came under similar censure. Palgrave, whilst admiring the 'anatomy' of the rock painting in Dyce's *Pegwell Bay*, (figure 28) lamented that there is in this work 'no feeling for the poetry of the dying day';[23] for Bayley, apparently immune to those scientific thinkers of the 1860s who were attempting to harness the power of the imagination to science, that art which attempted to 'compile external facts together, by dint of mere hard-staring eyes', to mani-fest 'an *idolatry* of the mere physical material of facts',[24] is betray-ing a damaging allegiance to science: 'For it is not all that is before the outer glass of the eye, but only that which is drawn by con-sciousness inwards to the sentient mirror of the brain, that we actually see; and this knowledge is very much directed by knowl-edge and feeling.' Explaining that the 'great artist', unlike a scien-tist, is both highly selective, and then 'humanises the objects of his contemplation, by impressing on them a tenderness and grandeur peculiarly his own', he concludes by asking: 'would the severe and minute analytical toil needful to perfect Science be compatible with those habits of imaginative feeling, and its dry demonstra-

28 William Dyce, *Pegwell Bay: A Recollection of October 5ᵗʰ, 1858*, *c.* 1858–60. Oil on canvas, 63.5×88.9 cms.

tions with the free play of invention, and tender sentiment primarily indispensable to Art, as *muta poesis*? We fear not.'[25]

The most extreme reaction to the traditional view that art could be spoken of as a potentially accessible language was to declare it untranslatable, the mediating word of the commentator redundant. Whistler himself posed the rhetorical question: 'Art, that for ages has hewn its own history in marble, and written its own comments on canvas, shall it suddenly stand still, and stammer, and wait for wisdom from the passer-by?'[26] This idea, that art speaks with its own language, demanding no further interpretation, was already, of course, something of a cliché in popular criticism. Here imagined self-sufficiency was invoked as a rhetorical device which concealed the fact either that the critic lacked the technical expertise necessary to discuss the work more fully, or that his or her readers would be bored or bewildered by such an exercise. Furthermore, the notion that a work of art needs nobody to speak on its behalf could be given support on moral grounds. For example, the editorial writer in the *Fine Art Annual* for Christmas

1872 commented that 'All good pictures speak for themselves much more eloquently than humanity can speak for them, and as their eloquence is that of silence, the most sensitive cannot call it egotism or vanity.'[27]

What we witness here, whether in Whistler's writing or in more popular prose, is the expression of a particular form of desire: a desire for the plenitude of the visible. As W. J. T. Mitchell has effectively put it:

> Perhaps the best answer to the purist who wants images that are only images and texts that are only texts is to turn the tables and examine the rhetoric of purity itself. In painting, for instance, the notion of purity is invariably explicated as a purgation of the visual image from contamination by language and cognate or conventionally associated media: words, sounds, time, narrativity, and arbitrary 'allegorical' signification are the 'linguistic' or 'textual' elements that must be repressed or eliminated in order for the pure, silent, illegible visuality of the visual arts to be achieved. This sort of purity, often associated with modernism and abstract painting, is both impossible and utopian, which isn't to dismiss it, but to identify it as an ideology, a complex of desire and fear, power and interest.[28]

The idea that paintings were in some way untranslatable received what was ultimately to be the most influential articulation not within art reviewing *per se*, but in Walter Pater's writing. In his essay 'The School of Giorgione', Pater criticised the mistake, as he saw it, of much popular criticism in regarding poetry, music and painting as 'but translations into different languages of one and the same fixed quantity of imaginative thought', supplemented only by certain technical qualities – colour in painting, sound in music, and rhythmical words in poetry. He believed that the starting point of all aesthetic criticism lay in the recognition of the opposite principle: that each art brings with it an individual quality which is directly traceable to its physical medium – 'Each art, therefore, having its own peculiar and untranslatable sensuous charm, has its own special mode of reaching the imagination, its own special responsibilities to its material.'[29] This truth, in Pater's opinion, most needs reinforcing with regards to art criticism, because of the popular idea, already encountered in this chapter, that painting can be emphatically praised through comparing it with poetry. For Pater, 'the possession of the pictorial gift, that inventive or creative handling of pure line and colour', is 'quite independent of anything definitely poetical in the subject it accompanies'.[30] The weaving of light that is colouring, the arabesques traced in the air that are drawing, are the essential pictorial qualities that first of all delight the senses. This remains the case despite the admitted tendency of all arts not to fill the place of each other but, reciprocally, to lend each other new force. Despite the familiarity of Pater's essay, one further point is also worth emphasising, since it articulates most clearly one end of the later nineteenth-century aesthetic spectrum: his belief that design and colouring can be in themselves all-satisfying. Here are to be found the foundations of certain principles which were to be repeated in much abstract art theory. He considers that in its primary aspect, a 'great picture has no more definite message for us than an accidental play of sunlight and shadow for a few moments on the wall or floor'[31] – indeed, in truth, it is itself a space of just such fallen light. The subject of a poem or picture is nothing without its form, and this form, or mode of handling, 'should become an end in itself, should permeate every part of the matter'.[32] Although Pater does not explicitly suggest that the form could become the matter, the work hence becoming self-referential, this potential is implicit in his argument, particularly when he maintains that art is continually striving to get rid of its responsibilities to its subject or material, providing food for the eye rather than for the intellect.[33]

Crucial to this discussion is the anxiety as to what actually constitutes 'art', or, more particularly, what modes of translating visual impressions into language serve to confirm an individual's membership of which specific, self-defining, exclusive groups. Certainly, there were writers on art in the later part of the century, particularly D. S. MacColl and R. A. M. Stevenson, and to a lesser extent Edward Rashdall and Philip Hamerton, who largely directed their responses towards what was taking place on the canvas surface, to the intrinsic properties of paint and ground, to methods of composition and paint application, line and colour and space. A good deal of their more innovative criticism, which focussed on technical issues, was prompted by their desire to explain new developments in painting, especially Impressionist art. They needed to make comprehensible, among other things, the optical and technical theories which lay behind these developments.[34] Necessarily, they participated in a blindingly obvious contradiction: using verbal language in order to assert the autonomy of the visual. Ironically, it was the much mistrusted Ruskin who, of all Victorian art critics, made the most striking refusal of verbal description in order to convey the power of a work of art when, in *The Stones of Venice*, he guides his reader carefully round the Tintorettos in the Scuola di San Rocco, directing their sight to technical details and to overall impression, to perspective and to colour, to the arrangement of figures and to the treatment of light, to carefully finished painting and that which has deliberately been left sketchy and impressionistic: this is an extensive effort to direct a reader in a slow and informed understanding and appreciation of the art before them. His rhetoric is deployed so that one can understand what choices on the painter's part lead to the spectator's eyes being led in a particular way to assimilate and respond to a particular composition. He thus explains, in relation to *Christ Bearing His Cross*, the penultimate canvas in Tintoretto's series:

> instead of the usual simple expedient of the bright horizon to relieve the dark masses, there is here introduced, on the left, the head of a white horse, which blends itself with the sky in one broad mass of light. The power of the picture is chiefly in effect, the figure of Christ being too far off to be very interesting, and only the malefactors being seen on the nearer path; but for this very reason it seems to me more impressive, as if one had been truly present at the scene, though not exactly in the right place for seeing it.

However, when Ruskin comes to the sixty-second and final painting, *The Crucifixion*, he ends with a dramatic flourish of silence: 'I must leave this picture to work its will on the spectator; for it is beyond all analysis, and above all praise.'[35]

'Reading' the narrative implications of a picture involved interpreting it according to commonly held expectations and associations concerning gender, race, class, occupation: expectations which were both overtly and tacitly invoked in critical responses as, to a greater or lesser extent, they had already been exploited by the artists themselves. The dissociation of any consideration of the relationship of the physiological act of seeing – including the eye's journey around the canvas – from the practices of comprehending and assimilating the apparent implications of the practices of visual representation was almost invariable.

What were the different types of painting which the Victorians found most amenable to a narrative approach? First, and most obviously, there are those works which directly serve as illustrations to print, or which draw their inspiration directly from a readily identifiable text. An examination of catalogues for the Royal Academy Summer Exhibition reveals the frequency with which painters depended on pre-existent verbal formulations either to provide the subject matter for their canvases or, in the shape of a quotation, to explain, or give added authority, to the message contained within their picture.[36] Although the originating work itself may have had a definite narrative structure, these paintings freeze this structure at one particular moment, turning it into a tableau. They have the capacity to be read as a form of literary interpretation in their own right, directing a spectator's attention and sympathy, pulling out the emotive resonances of a scene.[37]

More clearly illustrative of paintings begging to be understood as painted fictions, in precisely the way that caused Whistler, MacColl and others to recoil, were those works which contained within themselves elements which allowed them to be read as if they were equivalent to episodes in novels. There are a small number of works which follow the eighteenth-century tradition of Hogarth's *Rake's Progress* or *Marriage à la Mode* in that they were painted and hung so as to form a sequence within themselves, frequently with some didactic purpose. It was something of a commonplace among Victorian commentators to describe Hogarth's method through pairing him with the prose writers who were more or less his contemporaries. Francis Palgrave drew the obvious parallel – 'He first . . . put into painting what Fielding put into novel-writing', adding, a little later, 'In Hogarth's pictures a direct moral is generally dominant; they are De Foe on canvass.'[38] Hippolyte Taine turned the comparison into a question of making the invisible visible: 'Hogarth, the national painter, the friend of Fielding, the contemporary of Johnson, will show us the externals, as these authors have shown us the internals.'[39] One conspicuous inheritance of the sequential aspect of the Hogarthian tradition was the practice of circulating engravings with an accompanying text (drawing on the pattern established by John Trusler's *Hogarth Moralised* (1768)), thus ensuring that their moral reached a far larger audience than that of the public who would visit an art exhibition. This is the model followed, say, by George Cruikshank's temperance fable, *The Bottle* (1847) and its sequel, *The Drunkard's Children* (1848) (figures 29–36). In this latter sequence, Cruikshank parallels and counterpoints the downwardly spiralling effects of gin and bad company on a young man and a young woman. The former becomes a robber, is sentenced to transportation for life, and dies on the convict ship; the latter falls into prostitution and ends by committing suicide, joining the considerable litany of Victorian fallen women who end up in the Thames. Robert L. Patten, in his expanded, illuminating discussion of this series of prints, draws attention to Cruikshank's power in manipulating line and space, when he shows how form is used to produce meaning both within an individual print, and by subtle reference back to earlier elements in the sequence. 'All the poetry of motion', he writes,

> that subversively undercut the animadversions against dancing [in figure 31] reappears, now eerily transformed so that the beauty is the beauty of a body releasing itself from earthly pleasures and restraints in an uninhibited flight downward to death. The girl's black-and-white shape partially echoes the clouded moon, cold, indifferent, heedless of human affairs. But while the remote lunar disk has risen above and beyond the masts, her shape seems about to impale itself on a forest of spars.[40]

29

30   29–36 George Cruikshank, *The Drunkard's Children*, 1848. Glyphograph.

31

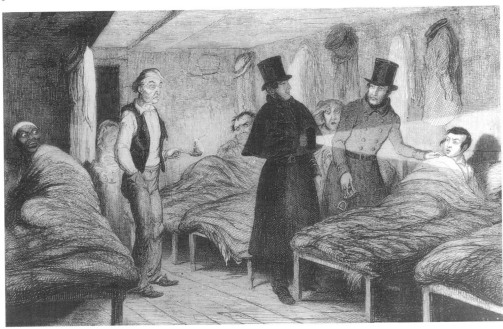

32

33

34

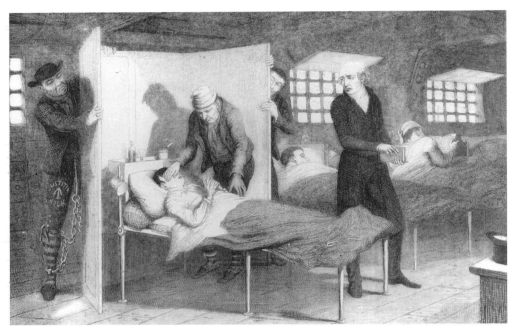

35

36

However, this tension between beauty and moral purpose was not what drew the attention of Victorian commentators, focussed on the logic of narrative rather than on any oppositional resonances created through its mode of expression. The same could be said to be true – unless one takes into account the complaints which were made against sloppiness of execution – of the two sequences of paintings by William Powell Frith which I discuss later in this chapter: *The Road to Ruin* (1878) and *The Race for Wealth* (1880).

The second type of narrative reading involves the deciphering of symbolic elements which the artist has deliberately included in a single picture. Again, the manner in which Hogarth crammed his works with images demanding that their signification be unpacked provided the model. The critical cue came from Charles Lamb: 'other pictures we look at – his prints we read'.[41] Theophile Gautier, commenting on the British art on show at the 1862 International Exhibition (which included *The Rake's Progress* and *Marriage à la Mode*), reminds his readers that 'every thing in his pictures shows significance, observation, volition. The slightest detail has meaning. The clock, the chair, the table, are as those which should and must be *there* and not anywhere else, and which would be wholly out of place to furnish another room withal.'[42] In the Victorian period, when the habit of both painting and decoding in this way had temporarily passed out of vogue, Ruskin provides the well-known paradigm for the resuscitation of such a mode of reading. In *Modern Painters* III (1856), he wrote of painting beginning 'to take its proper position beside literature'.[43] By this, he meant that narrative painters were no longer employing themselves merely in showing 'the outward verities of passing events – battles, councils, etc.',[44] but were abandoning the rôle of chronicler in favour of inventing the stories they paint. As an example of this commendable tendency, he cites Holman Hunt's *The Awakening Conscience*, shown at the Royal Academy that summer (figure 37). This was the intervention, R. A. M. Stevenson was later to maintain, which helped to launch 'the confusion between literary aims or conceptions and those proper to the plastic arts, a confusion now common, and in a great measure due to Ruskinian influence'.[45]

37 William Holman Hunt, *The Awakening Conscience*, 1853–4. Oil on canvas, 76.2×55.9 cms.

Ruskin claims to be baffled by the fact that Hunt's work is not more readily understood. No one, surely, he believes, could remain unmoved by the countenance of the 'lost girl, rent from its beauty into sudden horror'. He maintains that the full meaning of the picture is wasted through a spectator's reluctance to look at the details which make up the whole: in other words, to abandon, temporarily, a visually perceivable aesthetic unity for a thematic unity which can be grasped only through conscious, and sustained, mental activity. In employing our own imaginative involvement, one will come, Ruskin thought, closer to a form of perception which, interestingly, he suggests that we share not so much with the artist, but with the main figure represented: 'Nothing is more noticeable than the way even the most trivial objects force themselves upon the attention of a mind which has been fevered by violent and distressful excitement.' Our consciousness of the objects in the room is channelled through our response to the woman's situation, through the sympathy which has initially been stimulated in us by her despairing expression. This apparent fusion of the emotional state of the principal protagonist with that of the spectator is used to underscore the mimetic fallacy inherent in Ruskin's narrative explication: that what is depicted has actual existence. His certainty that we should interpret the pictures in a literary fashion is inherent in his verb: 'There is not a single object in all that room . . . but it becomes tragical, if rightly read.' He continues by pointing to the single meaning he believes is designated by each of the visual signifiers:

> That furniture so carefully painted, even to the last vein of the rosewood – is there nothing to be learnt from that terrible lustre of it, from its fatal newness; nothing there that has the old thoughts of home upon it, or that is ever to become part of a home? Those embossed books, vain and useless – they also new – marked with no happy wearing of beloved leaves; the torn and dying bird upon the floor; the gilded tapestry, with the fowls of the air feeding on the ripened corn; the picture above the fireplace, with its single drooping figure – the woman taken in adultery; nay, the very hem of the poor girl's dress, at which the

painter has laboured so closely, thread by thread, has story in it, if we think how soon its pure whiteness may be soiled with dust and rain, her outcast feet failing in the street; and the fair garden flowers seen in that reflected sunshine of the mirror, – these also have their language –

Hope not to find delight in us, they say,
For we are spotless, Jessy – we are pure.[46]

The danger in such a complete commentary is that it may come to function as a substitute for the picture itself, inviting the reader to believe that the deciphering is now closed. Yet not only may the accuracy of Ruskin's reading be questioned on several points – that figure above the fireplace, for example, is not the woman taken in adultery, but is an engraving of a painting by Frank Stone called *Cross Purposes*[47] – but Ruskin's determination to read the inevitability of the familiar downward spiralling narrative of the Fallen Woman into this led him to ignore such redemptive hints as the large gilt star on the frame of the picture, and the fact that it was intended as a companion work to Hunt's *The Light of The World* – shown at the same Academy exhibition – with its message that Christ may knock at the heart of the most hardened sinner.[48]

Even if Ruskin, with some justification, believed that he was writing for a readership which found such decipherment of a canvas unfamiliar, from the mid-1850s onwards, this mode of composition and explication took hold. It was dependent on a belief in an *a priori* meaning, or set of meanings, resting within the picture waiting to be unlocked and described. 'The faces should be individual; they should each tell a story, contain lines of history, and marks of joy and sorrow', commanded the *Art Journal*'s critic, writing about domestic painting in the mid-1860s, continuing: 'The details, too – the furniture, for example, in a room, – must have a meaning and even point a moral.'[49] This type of detailed reading was aided by Victorian fashions for crowded, heavily ornamented decoration, which allowed symbolic objects to be placed within naturalistically rendered settings, creating a dense superflux of signification. Such a mode of reading is closely dependent upon the growth of consumer society during the nineteenth century: a society in which status could be consciously projected through the purchase and arrangement of objects which demonstrated one's taste – a world in which, as Marx put it, '*all* the physical and spiritual senses' are replaced by 'the sense of *having*'.[50] Identity, rather than being regarded as something innate, pre-inscribed on the body, was increasingly recognised as something which could be deliberately constructed for others to read. The thoughtful, sensitive Fanny Assingham in Henry James's *The Golden Bowl* (1905) recognises that her voluptuous Oriental appearance is absolutely no physical guarantor of her personality, but is something which she might as well playfully exploit:

> She wore yellow and purple because she thought it better, as she said, while one was about it, to look like the Queen of Sheba than like a *revendeuse*; she put pearls in her hair and crimson and gold in her tea-gown for the same reason: it was her theory that nature itself had overdressed her and that her only course was to drown, as it was hopeless to try to chasten, the overdressing. So she was covered and surrounded with 'things', which were frankly toys and shams, a part of the amusement with which she rejoiced to supply her friends. These friends were in the game – that of playing with the disparity between her aspect and her character.[51]

The increasingly commodified world of the middle-class Victorian stimulated an awareness of the significations of the object which has endured into our own times:

> We read clothes, possessions, interiors, and exteriors as representing more or less successful accommodations to a world of goods, and in so doing we rehearse in our minds the appropriation of that social world via the commodity . . . Each display invokes, satisfies, and reinvokes a cognitive drive, what Jean Baudrillard calls 'the passion for the code'. . . What modern consumer culture produces, then, is not so much a way of being (profligate, miserly, reserved, exhibitionist) as a way of seeing – a way best characterised as visually acquisitive.[52]

As Ronald Paulson has noted in *Emblem and Expression*, 'the higher the level of denotation, the more particular the objects

38 Robert
Martineau, *The Last
Day in the Old Home*,
1861. Oil on canvas,
107.95 × 144.78 cms.

represented . . . the greater its potential for verbalization'.[53] The
ease with which this verbal narrativisation may be performed –
with no reference to the impact made by brush technique or
colour, with spatial arrangements signifying only in relation to the
connections between personages, with no acknowledgement of
spectatorial subjectivity or emotional investment – can be illustrated if we look at Robert Martineau's *The Last Day in the Old
Home* (1861), a painting dramatising the dreadful effects of gambling (figure 38). 'A novel in colour', Palgrave called it, in case
anyone was likely to miss the narrative possibilities contained in its
plenitude of signification.[54] An old home, and an old, wealthy
family: the portraits, the suit and pieces of armour, the date of 1648
on the old oak chest on the left tell us this. But it is now up for sale.
Little auctioneer's lot numbers appear on the furniture. There is a
sale catalogue on the floor, plainly legible: 'Catalogue of the valuable contents of Hardham Court, the Seat of Sir Chas. Pulleyne,
Bart. Christie and Manson. October 22, 1860.' From being objects
whose meaning has been derived from the particular social and

cultural sediment in which they had been embedded for genera-
tions, and from the personal and familial histories which they contained, the possessions are becoming mere commodities, entering
onto the market. 'Every material inheritance is, strictly speaking,
also a cultural inheritance', Bourdieu has commented: 'Family
heirlooms not only bear material witness to the age and continuity
of the lineage and so consecrate its social identity, which is inseparable from permanence over time; they also contribute in a practical way to its spiritual reproduction, that is, to transmitting the
values, virtues and competencies which are the basis of legitimate
membership in bourgeois dynasties.'[55] It is this membership which
is being forfeited.

The old woman at the window table is paying off the family
retainer, who is handing over the keys. The newspaper on the table
is open at a page headed 'Apartments'. Unmistakably, the family
have fallen. The familiar motive of Adam and Eve, carved on the
left-hand panel of the fireplace, informs the spectator of this – even
if there is no hint of sexual transgression in this particular instance,
human greed and uncontrolled desire have been to blame. The
financial plight has caused family division: the wife stretches her
hand across to her husband, but he ignores it; the positioning of
the fireplace suggests that any fire of passion is now burning low
between them.[56] Her desolate-looking daughter, holding a doll
which might be read as a model for the affection which is not being
shown towards her, has the potential to suggest that prayer could
offer some kind of consolation, since she looks towards a small
triptych with a crucifix at its centre, but religion does not seem to
have provided much by way of support or example to the family as
a whole, and this item of furniture, too, bears a sale ticket. The
father prefers to lift an optimistic glass to the future with his son
and heir, but – quite apart from the fact that one might question
the wisdom of introducing him to strong drink, from either the
decanter or the bottle on the table behind him – this man's optimism, rather than prudence, has proved to be his downfall, and the
downfall of his family. The crucial clues are given by the racehorse
picture propped up on the far left – the one item of furnishing
which does not seem to bear a sale ticket – by the betting book, and
by the dice box on the floor; and by the miniature gold dice-box on

39 Clarkson Stanfield, *The Abandoned*, 1856. Oil on canvas, 88.9 × 152.4 cms.

the man's watch-chain (ironically juxtaposed with a gold fish, symbol of baptism or redemption).[57] The damage has been caused by gambling.

In planting these visual references, Martineau would appear to assume a certain cultural awareness among his spectators. The mode of explication invited by *The Last Day* fosters the sense of a common cultural and social identity. Stefan Morawski, in *Inquiries into the Fundamentals of Aesthetics*, coined the term 'paraquotation' to signify the use of a certain type of interpolation 'with a stimulatory-amplificatory function', as he put it – like the presence of Clarkson Stanfield's depiction of a shipwreck, *The Abandoned* (1856) on the wall behind the wrecked family in Egg's *Past and Present* (figures 39 and 40). Not only, argues Morawski, is paraquotation a means adopted particularly by artists with theses to prove (as in the case of Hunt or Egg or Martineau), but quotations habitually 'accumulate in art when the boundaries between it and other forms of social consciousness become vague'.[58] The overlap between 'readable' pictures, and the combination of elaborate-yet-resolved plots and solid specificity of detail embraced by the mid-Victorian novel, is no accident.

One further variant of narrative reading assumes not so much that there is one definite story, and perhaps moral, to be disinterred from a painting's visual evidence, but rather, granting the basic

40 Augustus Leopold Egg, '*August the 4th. Have just heard that B——has been dead more than a fortnight, so his poor children have now lost both parents. I hear she was seen on Friday last near the Strand, evidently without a place to lay her head. What a fall hers has been!*' (known as *Past and Present*), no. 1, 1858. Oil on canvas, 63.5×76.2 cms.

explanation of the activities portrayed to be self-evident enough, they are used as a starting point for speculating about possible aspects of the behaviour of the depicted characters. Like Ruskin, reading *The Awakening Conscience*, Tom Taylor, in his pamphlet on William Powell Frith's *The Railway Station* (1862) offers a paradigm for this mode of interpretation, providing not so much a key to this crowded work as a set of viable alternative readings (figure 41). On the right, a man is being arrested on the steps of the railway carriage which would have conducted him to sanctuary: he is 'a fraudulent banker, or actuary, bank cashier or railway clerk – who has long been carrying on his embezzlements'.[59] Taylor interprets

41 William Powell Frith, *The Railway Station*, 1862. Oil on canvas, 116.84 × 256.54 cms.

expressions on the faces of individuals: the detective preparing this criminal's handcuffs is smiling as he anticipates the satisfaction of his employer, the honour in store for himself and his companion, the newspaper glory when the trial comes up, and the financial reward. Taylor does not fail to seize an opportunity for sermonising. He focusses on the wedding group 'which forms the centre of the picture, both pictorially and morally'.[60] Its brightness and beauty are juxtaposed with 'the sickening fear and agony of the felon incident' in both moral and visual chiaroscuro: 'So it is that the darkest shadows and brightest lights of life come together; that joy is intensified by sorrow, and sorrow deepened by joy, as the painter uses his lights and darks to relieve each other.'[61] The alternation of brightness and shade serves as an elementary symbol for the wheel of fortune: perhaps the broken-hearted wife of the criminal, who shrinks under her husband's shame, had just as gay a group of bridesmaids: 'who knows if her hopes were not as high, the prospect before her as sunny to the eye, as this young bride's?'[62]

Taylor, however, does not see himself as possessing any specially privileged insights into this composition. Rather, the essence of this mode of criticism – of this mode of painting, too – lies for him in its democracy, its accessibility – by which he means that he feels confident that he shares the same values as his audience, and that they will respond to that which is represented according to dominant Victorian ethical and interpretive codes. Frith's *Railway Station*, he claims, is typical of any platform:

> There is nothing here that does not come within the round of common experience. We are all of us competent to understand these troubles or pleasures, anxieties or annoyances: there is no passage of these many emotions but we can more or less conceive of ourselves as passing through. The painter in choosing such a subject, makes every spectator his critic.[63]

To some extent Taylor is abnegating his own responsibilities, arguing himself out of a job. His stance emphasises the subjectivity inherent in every act of spectatorship: subjectivity which has nothing to do with the physiological variability of each set of eyes, but which is dependent both on the individual experiences which everyone brings to their interpretation of the events depicted in a work of art, and on the capacity and inventiveness of their imaginations. Moreover, in the context of narrative criticism, Taylor is underlining the mimetic principles on which it is based. Taylor assumes unquestioningly that the same methods of interpretation can be used for art and for non-mediated experience. Hence, it becomes that much easier to draw connections between the two in the sphere of morality. Moreover, the spatial practices of interpretation that are necessary to a careful reading of *The Railway Station* more closely mimic those of everyday experience than of aesthetic spectatorship. If the latter is characterised by the adoption of perspective, which centres everything, as John Berger, Norman Bryson and others have argued,[64] on the eye of the beholder, the privileged centre of vision, here the gaze must be non-centred, mobile, existing within variables of space and time, and hence compelled towards a narrativisation of what is observed. This is the gaze of the *flâneur*, the urban crowd-scanner,[65] an observer formed through the habit of walking through city streets and endlessly using the eyes to record and categorise the visual information on offer; standing back from actual contact with individuals, intrigued and intoxicated by the phenomenon of the crowd.[66]

How variable, how free, in fact, is the interpretation practised by Taylor, and envisaged by him as being practised by others? It would seem that both the internal logic of the paintings which demand narrative readings, and the criticism which performed such readings, in fact relied upon certain highly predictable trajectories, "strong narratives" in prevalent circulation within Victorian culture. In relation to such works, the operations of the eye were indissolubly linked to the affirmation and recirculation of these dominant narratives. 'Reading' these paintings involved the careful accumulation and combination of the deliberately placed detail, and then the decoding of such details according to certain pre-inscribed narrative assumptions. Rather than the spectator being granted a liberating independence of interpretation and free association – as might legitimately be argued on behalf of someone facing the indistinct blue-grey suggestivity of a Whistler *Nocturne*, for example – the role of this spectator was in fact extremely circumscribed.

This can be very well demonstrated if we return to a consideration of the theme of gambling as it is depicted in painting. Gambling fascinated the Victorians. It offered a challenge to the apparently iron laws of economic life and financial accountability: the amount of chance which it incorporated disrupted recognisable patterns of cause and effect. It promised gain without duty, without responsibility, without long-drawn-out periods of effort. Yet, a potentially addictive obsession, it could destroy the individual and all who depended on him, or her. In her essay 'The Reader's Wager: Lots, Sorts, and Futures', Gillian Beer explores the resonances of gambling for the Victorian – and contemporary – reader, arguing that part of the fascination with gambling finds its parallel in the activity indulged in by the reader, predicting the future from a set of givens and then matching these against the unfolding of a novel's plot, investing their own desire in willing a certain end, 'persistently inventing possibilities and alternatives as they play, conjuring an experience of freedom before the game concludes'.[67] She notes the particular interest excited by the juxtaposition of women and gambling within literature, whether Lily Barth in Wharton's *The House of Mirth*, Polina in Dostoevsky's *The Gambler* or Gwendolen in *Daniel Deronda*, reminding us of the social disapproval that was brought to bear on the idea of a woman taking chances, risking all and flouting the slow pace of that other form of gambling, the betting on a safe future through making a socially reputable match to a secure husband. This fascination with the woman gambler, and with the erotics inherent in her position, are to be found in a couple of paintings. In Alfred Elmore's *On the Brink* (1865), speculative and sexual transgression are brought together – the woman is liminally positioned between garden and gaming room, between respectability and seduction (figure 42).[68] Discarded pieces of paper – perhaps a torn-up marking card – lie in the foreground; on the right of the painting a passion flower is blooming with iconographic pointedness, flourishing above a drooping example of that symbol of purity, the lily. The shadowy male who hangs over her right shoulder would seem to be offering an easy way out of what one presumes is her financial dilemma. Behind her, in the luridly lit salon, women flirt openly with men, and reach out greedily, desperately, over the gaming table. The large window frame between the two spaces of the picture, however, and the fact that the woman's gaze is still directed outwards, if downwards, make the outcome of the episode as yet uncertain, even if the signs are ominous. So, in a less emotionally charged scene, Millais's *Hearts are Trumps* (1872), are the futures of these three young women uncertain (figure 43). Despite the sentimental triumphalism of the title, and despite the apparent levity of the women's play, it is hard, in the light of Gillian Beer's comments, not to read a far more serious gambling with their futures into the painting's setting. Three society beauties are here set up as potential objects of exchange with the speculative risks of marriage before them.

Just as much Victorian fiction, however, obeyed formulaic demands, so that the readers – unlike a gambler – could place their emotional bets with confidence, enjoying the *fort-da* game of pretend uncertainty, so the vast majority of paintings of gambling either worked to reinforce a predictable narrative of loss and ruin, or relied on such an internalised narrative being in the observer's, and interpreter's, possession. William Orchardson's *Hard Hit* (1879) (figure 44) shows the young gambler exiting the scene of his ruin. The cards from 200 packs which lie scattered on the floor, together with the champagne bottles on the side table and the over-turned chair, tell of the length and extent of the night's dissipation. The apparently inevitable results of gambling were rehearsed by many

42 Alfred Elmore, *On the Brink*, 1865. Oil on canvas, 114.3 × 83.18 cms.

43 John Everett Millais, *Hearts are Trumps*, 1872. Oil on canvas, 165.7 × 219.7 cms.

moralisers, its participants offering a tempting challenge. If he were a 'zealous missionary', proclaimed the fallen hero of Percy Fitzgerald's *Fatal Zero. A Diary Kept at Homburg* (1869):

> I would come here; I would stand at the door of this place; I would preach in the street, in front of this red sandstone palace – charnel house of infamy – and warn, dissuade, and exhort, passionately, with my whole heart and soul . . . One soul saved from that den, stopped at the threshold, would be worth all the blacks who ever simulated Christianity for a musket or two strings of glass beads.[69]

Again and again, participation in the practice was seen as addictive. The Reverend E. Newton Jones, for example, in *The Love of Money the Root of all Evil, or The Sin of Gambling* (1856), warned his listeners and readers against betting even once, and flattering oneself that one can stop, 'lest in approaching even its margin only, you be drawn in, imperceptibly to yourselves, into the midst of the

44 William
Orchardson, *Hard
Hit*, 1879. Oil on
canvas,
83.82 × 123.19 cms.
Present
whereabouts
unknown. Etching
by P. A. Massé.

sweeping torrent and thus come to destruction of both body and soul'.[70] Whilst Newton Jones particularly railed against 'the deadening and pernicious influence of the race-course',[71] C. H. Spurgeon, the author of a number of admonitory works on gambling, highlights the snares of Monte Carlo – 'a man-trap' – and warns parents against taking their offspring anywhere near the place, which had become something of a tourist attraction, for:

> The way of destruction was smoothed even to the jaws of hell: first, there was a walk in the lovely gardens with mother and sisters; then the music in the hall was enjoyed in mixed society; next came a sly visit to the rooms and a trifling speculation, followed by frequent sittings at the table, diversified with wine and questionable company, and in the end brought to a climax by actual vice and ruin.[72]

This is the story told in William Powell Frith's *The Road to Ruin* (1878), intended, the artist wrote in his autobiography, to 'show some of the evils of gambling, my idea being a kind of gambler's progress . . . I desired to trace the career of a youth from his college

45 William Powell Frith, *The Road to Ruin, No. 3: Arrest*, 1878. Oil on canvas, 69.85×90.17 cms.

days to his ruin and death – a victim to one of the most fatal vices'.[73] The five frames include origins of the trouble, which lay in card-playing in *College*; the escalation into racecourse gambling in *Ascot*; and the shameful disruption of very comfortable family life in *Arrest*. The newspaper which has been tossed down on the carpet, *Bell's Life in London and Sporting Chronicle*, tells of the irresponsible young husband's obsession (figure 45). In *Struggles*, the family have exchanged an opulent home for sparse rented lodgings, where an exasperated landlady is presenting the bill. The gambler seems as unprompted to take consolation or inspiration from the religious paraphernalia that surrounds him – a crucifix is on the wall; there are images of Christ preaching and of John the Baptist on the mantelpiece – as was Martineau's family. The final picture of the series shows his desperate demeanour just before he takes what, one is led to presume from the gun on the table, is the final step: *The End* (figure 46). Painted two years later, Frith's *The Race for Wealth* effectively illustrates the same theme (figure 47).

"*THE ROAD TO RUIN.*" By W. P. Frith, R.A.

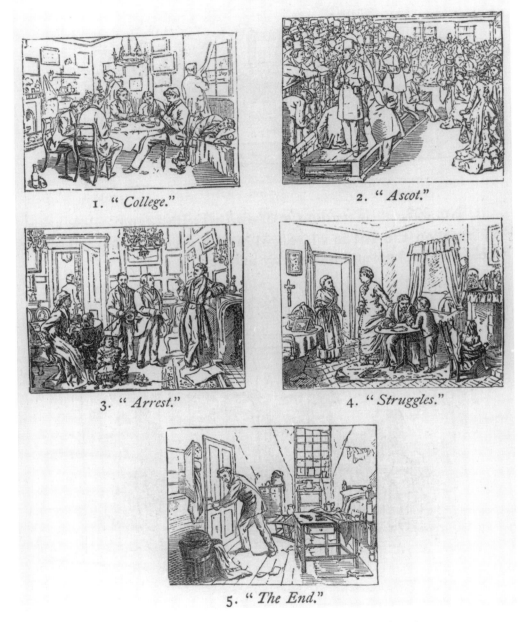

46 William Powell Frith, *The Road to Ruin*, 1878. Sketches of paintings.

"THE RACE FOR WEALTH." By W. P. FRITH, R.A.

1. *"The Spider and the Flies."*   2. *" The Spider at Home."*

"Altogether we are glad to be able heartily to congratulate the painter on a work which shows not only unimpaired but enhanced power, and which, now that election agitation has settled down, ought to attract as dense and interested crowds to the exhibition rooms in King Street as the "Road to Ruin" two years ago drew round it on the walls of the Royal Academy."—*The Times.*

3. *"Victims."*   4. *" Judgment."*

"And so the curtain falls solemnly and impressively upon Mr. Frith's telling drama; but after a moment's reflection, mental applause follows the successful work. There can be little doubt about the interest and instruction with which the public will study this painted play." — *The Daily Telegraph.*

"The didactic purpose of pictorial art is enforced with brilliant ability and powerful effect in a series of new paintings by Mr. W. P. Frith, R.A., collectively entitled 'The Race for Wealth.'" — *Morning Post.*

5. *" Retribution."*

47   William Powell Frith, *The Race for Wealth*, 1880. Sketches of paintings.

His declared moral was 'that both those who, in their eagerness to become rich, rush into speculation, and the man who cheats them, should all be punished'.[74] Whilst the subject this time is financial speculation, rather than gambling, for many Victorians the two were synonymous. Andrew Steinmetz, in the Preface to his magisterial history *The Gaming Table* (1870), drew no difference between them in asserting that 'a spirit of speculation and gambling has taken hold of the minds of large classes of the population'. Men who were formerly content with modest gain now seem 'ready to embark their fortunes, however hardly gained, in the vain hope of realizing immense returns by premiums upon shares'.[75] Spurgeon, again, after outlining why gambling is wrong – it breaks the commandment forbidding us to covet; it verges closely on that which forbids us to steal; it hardens the heart; it brings one in contact with other forms of vice – and whilst acknowledging that there is a necessary speculation involved in all commercial activity, maintained that: 'Whether a man gambles with Government stock, or cotton, or wool, or what, or merely risks his cash upon the cast of dice, or the turn of a ball, is of small consequence to the moral quality of the action.'[76] He asserts the vulnerability of private individuals who are induced to become 'the prey of designing men, who know their way about among stocks, shares, mines, and bubble companies'.[77]

This would seem to be the line taken by Frith, as he laid out the progression towards ruin through his five pictures: *The Spider and the Flies* (the ante-room of the Financier's office, full of speculators and potential investors in a mining company); *The Spider at Home* (the Financier's outer drawing-room, where he is greeting his fashionable dinner guests in surroundings of tasteful opulence); *Victims* (the news of the collapse of the speculation hits the breakfast table in a country rectory); *Judgment* (the fraudulent Financier stands in the Old Bailey dock, surrounded by readily identifiable legal personalities); and *Retribution* (the Financier walks in an exercise circle in the dreary confines of Millbank prison). 'The Race for Wealth has been run', commented Tom Taylor, in the pamphlet he produced to accompany the exhibition of these pictures. 'We see the end of one of "the favourites".'[78]

In this pamphlet, Taylor draws the obligatory parallels between Frith and Hogarth, and explains that just as Hogarth wrote 'I have endeavoured to treat my subjects as a dramatic writer; my picture is my stage',[79] so 'These five pictures are to be looked at as the five acts of a domestic drama dealing with the real life of the day.'[80] This suggests that narrative painting has links not just with the process of flux represented by fiction, but with the stage convention of holding a moment of action frozen into a tableau.[81] The interiors, however, are to be read with a carefulness not normally invited by stage sets. Once again, paraquotation plays an important role in the construction of the narrative, as Taylor explicates. In the second painting, we are invited to identify 'good modern pictures' on the walls – works by Turner, Egg, Leslie, Stone and Linnell. Within the setting of the inveigling Financier's habitation, these are used as part of the means by which it is shown that money 'can command splendour, "society", fine art, and voice authoritative upon it'.[82] Either Midas can be seen to have taste, or, as Taylor sardonically comments, 'his furnishers and art-advisers have, which comes to the same thing'.[83] Revealing in a different way are the works hanging above the country rector's breakfast party in 'Victims'. They – according to Taylor – 'suggest dreams of cathedral preferment, of deaneries and canonries, who knows? even a bishopric, perhaps; and, alas, side by side with these high hopes, hangs an ominous foreshadowing of a shipwreck'.[84] The ruined vicar ends up giving evidence against the swindling Financier. Unlike Dickens's Merdle, in *Little Dorrit*, or Melmotte in Trollope's *The Way We Live Now*, the Financier does not end up following the path of these fictional models – perhaps because Frith had already made his gambler end up suicidally – but in prison. Here Frith shows his subject almost uncomfortably exposed to scrutiny. His punishment is that not of oblivion, but of visibility.

The nature of this punishment, however, still less its fact, seemed to surprise few critics of the exhibition:[85] so conventional was the narrative told by Frith and amplified at elaborate, even wearisome length by Taylor that its didacticism was either passed over without comment, or recounted in all its predictability. The focus of the criticism falls most frequently on Frith's unremarkable technical display, and on the disparity between the grandiose claims made by Taylor and the actual execution of the works: 'Mr Frith's productions are dramatic in the same sense in which the performances of a bad actor are dramatic.'[86]

Hippolyte Taine claimed for Hogarth's pictorial sequences what Taylor was doing his best to argue for Frith's, even if, in so doing, he was opening up the field for the paintings to be judged in the same terms as hammed-up performances. When we gaze on them, Taine wrote:

> we forget the painting and become spectators of a tragedy or a domestic comedy. Figures, costumes, attitudes, all the accessories, are summaries of characters, biographical abridgements. They form a conceited series, they compose a progressive history, they are the illustrations of a text half revealed; under the surface, chapter by chapter, we read the text itself.[87]

It is, many nineteenth-century critics would have argued, the task of the reviewer to verbalise this painted text, to translate it into terms which would be recognised and shared by those who read art criticism, thus confirming their vision. As we have seen, opposition to this mode of explication came from those – both artists and writers on art – who wished to fracture the bonds between verbal and visual languages, asserting the relative autonomy of the latter. Paradoxically, of course, the commercial success of experimental art was to come to depend upon the mediating presence of the written word: as Tom Wolfe put it in *The Painted Word*, in relation to abstract expressionism, this resulted in 'an art more truly Literary than anything ever roared against in the wildest angers of the Fauvists and Cubists'.[88]

The narratives in this case, however, were to be ones internal to art history. What is so striking about mainstream Victorian art criticism during the latter half of the century is its closeness to the social and moral narratives circulating outside the sphere of aesthetics. This reinforces the necessity which the paintings themselves seem to demand from us for as full an inter-textual interpretation of them as possible, seeing the act of 'reading' a picture as more than sorting out its internal syntax and grammar.

More than that, however, the dominance of narrative as a form both of painting and of interpretation points to a need within Victorian middle-class culture which the act of spectatorship helped to serve. Charles Taylor, in *Sources of the Self*, has argued that it is 'a basic condition of making sense of ourselves, that we grasp our lives in a *narrative*'. This – he says, drawing on Heidegger's description, in *Being and Time*, of the inescapable temporal structure of being in the world – is not an 'optional extra': our lives exist in 'this space of questions, which only a coherent narrative can answer. In order to have a sense of who we are, we have to have a notion of how we have become, and of where we are going'.[89] It may well be that many of the stories the Victorians told themselves, or had reinforced, through reading paintings, were woefully predictable and familiar ones. Their consumership served not so much to confirm their membership of an aesthetic elite, or their pretensions to such an elite, as to assure them of the unexceptionalness of their position within society, and hence their safety within a world of changing and competing values.

CHAPTER 9

Surface and depth

The importance of the surface is built into the very subject matter of Edward Burne-Jones's *The Mirror of Venus* (1877) (figure 48). The beauty of the young women who stare into a pool is reflected back to them: the single gaze which is directed away from the water looks up at the standing figure, attempting to stall any departure and re-enclose her in this intensely self-regarding female world. Only in this suggestion of onwards movement from the taller woman – identified as Venus herself, by some contemporary critics – and in the fact that the women's reflected heads are framed by forget-me-nots is there any slight hint of temporality. The multiplication of similarly styled, similarly featured women may further be read as signifying an excess of generic femininity, and a concomitant erasing of individuality.

In post-Lacanian theory, the mirror has often been invoked as a metaphor for the act of self-fashioning, reflecting back a desirably united, if ultimately illusory, view of the 'whole' person, an isolate being utterly separate from all others. The relevance of this mirror-metaphor has, however, been challenged in relation to woman's self-presentation. Susan Stanford Friedman has argued that when a woman looks in a mirror, she sees not isolate selfhood but an image of 'woman', a member of a social and cultural category,[1] and Lynda Nead has elaborated further on the theme of social placement when observing one's reflection in *The Female Nude*: 'Woman looks at herself in the mirror; her identity is framed by the abundance of images that define femininity. She is framed –

48 Edward Burne-Jones, *The Mirror of Venus*, 1877. Oil on canvas, 120×200 cms.

experiences herself as image or representation – by the edges of the mirror and then judges the boundaries of her own form and carries out any necessary self-regulation . . . The formless matter of the female body has to be contained within boundaries, conventions and poses.'[2] The surface of the mirror, or of the crystalline pond, in other words, may be a barrier between a woman's image and her interiority.

This gap between interior and exterior, between imaged reflection and the contemplative mode of reflection that takes place in the mind of the perceiver, is important for our understanding of the representation of women in late nineteenth-century painting. It has, however, far wider ramifications. It can be made to stand for the ways in which aesthetic understanding was becoming problematised; the ways in which a dialogue was developing between the practice of observation and the role of subjectivity, and – this is crucial to my particular argument – the manner in which physiology functioned as a mediating force between these two modes of approach.

For one contemporary observer at least, the female circle of self-referentiality symbolised the aesthetic attitude of the school of art to which Burne-Jones belonged. Henry James, acknowledging that he was not in sympathy with this school, described its products as:

> the art of culture, of reflection, of intellectual luxury, of aesthetic refinement, of people who look at the world and at life not directly, as it were, and in all its accidental reality, but in the reflection and ornamental portrait of it furnished by art itself in other manifestations; furnished by literature, by poetry, by history, by erudition. One of Mr Burne-Jones's contributions to the Grosvenor is a very charming picture entitled 'Venus's Mirror', in which a dozen young girls, in an early Italian landscape, are bending over a lucid pool, set in a flowery lawn, to see what I supposed to be the miraculous embellished image of their faces. Into some such mirror as this the painters and poets of Mr. Burne-Jones's turn of mind seem to me to be looking; they are crowding round a crystal pool with a flowery margin in a literary landscape, quite like the angular nymphs of the picture I speak of.[3]

Yet it was precisely the fact that this picture calls attention to the importance of its surface, to its decorative qualities, to its detachment from the world 'in all its accidental reality' that permitted it to be a site on which the inviolability of the surface was in fact called into question. It exemplifies Charles Harrison's claim about painting in general, that 'what gives us pleasurable pause is the strange and distinctive form of scepticism about appearances that is set in play when the allure of imaginative depth meets resistance from the vividness of decorated surface'.[4] Moreover, the elimination of suggestions of individual personality in the decorative nature of the women represented might be a spur, rather than a hindrance, to the acknowledgement of individuality in the spectator's response to such a work. Likewise, the featureless landscape, whilst refusing to provide details which might distract the viewer from the female subjects, offers a contemplative space in which to site one's own specific response. Seeing the painting in relation to a developing matrix of ideas about the connections between art and science, especially the developing science of psychology, provides,

I shall show, a means of breaking open not only its apparent self-enclosure, but the solipsistic aestheticism against which James complained.

The Mirror of Venus was first displayed at the opening show of the Grosvenor Gallery, in May 1877. Critical attention on this occasion was very much drawn to surfaces: not to the works exhibited, in the first instance, but to their striking surroundings. The young Oscar Wilde wrote approvingly in the *Dublin University Magazine*:

> The walls are hung with scarlet damask above a dado of dull green and gold; there are luxurious velvet couches, beautiful flowers and plants, tables of gilded wood and inlaid marbles, covered with Japanese China and the latest 'Minton', globes of 'rainbow-glass', like large soap-bubbles, and, in fine, everything in decoration that is lovely to look on, and in harmony with the surrounding works of art.[5]

Not everyone shared in his enthusiasm: the *Daily Telegraph* complained that the incessant brightness of the decor strained 'the fatigued optic nerve of the spectator';[6] the *Morning Post*, after protesting against the 'blaze of heterogeneous colour', singled out for complaint the fact that the paintings were covered in glass, something all very well for water-colours, 'but glass over the deeper shadows produced by the stronger medium of oil gives back an obtrusive reflection, mocking the spectator with the semblance of his own face and figure as through a mirror'.[7] It was something of a commonplace that fashionable people went to art exhibitions as much to look at each other as at the paintings: here the implications of narcissism inherent in this mode of spectatorship are hinted at.

Sir Coutts Lindsay's exhibition marked Burne-Jones's return to public exhibition after some seven years. The innovative practice of hanging all the works of one artist together facilitated the critical concentration on his works demonstrated by most of the reviewers. As well as *The Mirror of Venus*, he showed *The Days of Creation* – the painting of his on which the most critical attention in fact focussed – *The Beguiling of Merlin*, and five single figures of

Temperantia, *Fides*, *Spes*, *St George* and a *Sibyl*. 'From that day', wrote his wife Georgiana in her *Memorials of Edward Burne-Jones*, 'he belonged to the world in a sense that he had never done before, for his existence became widely known and his name famous.'[8] The *Globe* was moved to superlatives: 'There is nothing in modern art more beautiful or more artistically complete';[9] J. Comyns Carr, in the *Pall Mall Gazette*, listed the qualities of his friend:

> In expressive and subtle draughtsmanship, in a system of colour carefully regulated according to the laws of tone and yet preserving an almost gem-like quality in each separate tint, and in the ability to imitate the most delicate appearances of nature wherever such imitation can be made serviceable to the particular scheme of his art, we scarcely know of any living painter who can be reckoned his rival whether in the English School or in the schools of the Continent.[10]

Although there were some dissident voices – the *Morning Post* termed his paintings 'eccentricities', although this was perhaps mild compared to the insults it hurled at Whistler ('monstrosities') and Spencer Stanhope ('crimes in colour')[11] – the general message was clear: Burne-Jones's status was assured, at least among critics; the *Illustrated London News* reminded one, nevertheless, of the fact that there were too many 'Philistines' who were put off by his pronounced mannerisms '– possibly because they fail to understand them –' and that they 'considerably outnumber the chosen people of critics and connoisseurs who are able to comprehend and to enjoy'.[12] The fact that Burne-Jones's work was successful among critics who considered themselves discerning, and who appreciated its aesthetic, as opposed to populist literary qualities, was underscored by the *Spectator*'s remarks concerning *The Days of Creation*, claiming first that it is one of those paintings 'of which the charm can only be felt, and of which words can give but a faint idea', and continuing:

> Nothing would be easier than to pull it to pieces, and the majority of the remarks which we have heard while standing before it (and we have been five times) have been of this kind: – 'What's all this

about it? Oh, angels, ah! I don't care about them; wonderful frame, isn't it? Who is it by? Burne Jones! Who's he?' – and so on, *ad infinitum*.[13]

The reception of *The Mirror of Venus* itself largely rested, as we shall see in a moment, on an assessment of how successfully the artist has mastered the technical challenges which he had set himself. Inevitably, however, Burne-Jones's very project – summed up by the *Globe* as 'the manifestation of physical beauty in its purest forms'[14] – was out of sympathy with those Philistines who approached their art through narrative criteria, like Heathcote Statham in *Macmillan's*, claiming to be baffled by 'these inexplicable females who, in front of a landscape mapped out with conventional regularity, gaze with such unaccountable agony of solemnity on the reflection of their own faces in the pond'.[15] This critic was equally frustrated by the inscrutability of a single woman figure in Albert Moore's *The End of the Story* (figure 49):

> a title which rather unfortunately forces upon our attention the limits of his art. Such a title naturally excites our interest; we expect to see in the expression of the figure something that may suggest to our imagination the nature of the story and of its effect on the reader. But Mr Moore gives us nothing of this. His figure is a graceful woman, charmingly draped, and she holds a book; but that is all he tells us.[16]

It is a relief to Statham to move from the *Mirror* to those single figures of Burne-Jones's which have 'a more masculine and healthy feeling':[17] the dread of feminised morbidity also turning up by way of a token of disparagement in the *Morning Post*, noting that the girls' faces 'are delicate even to the look of consumptiveness', despite the fact that their 'limbs are as round, solid, and compact as those of so many dairymaids' – a ridiculing of the presumed elitism of the aesthetic project.[18] This detection of degenerative disease was, incidentally, to become a feature of critical comment about Burne-Jones's women at the next year's Grosvenor exhibition, in terms proving the point about the tendency to assess womanhood through the 'abundance of images that define femininity'.[19]

49 Albert Moore,
The End of the Story,
1877. Oil on canvas,
87.6×33 cms.

Such a concentration on the socially mimetic aspects of painting was, according to Sidney Colvin in the *Fortnightly*, missing the point. The beauty that mattered was not the replication of human form, but the beauty of line. He laments that those who complain about the downcast, yearning eyes and expressions in Burne-Jones's paintings do 'not turn their minds, instead, to the happiness which the maker of these melancholy things has prepared for them if they were capable of receiving it, – the happiness and glory and delight of living line and visible rhythm, the fire and rapture of colour poured forth in profuse and perfect harmonies unseen till now'.[20] Others, if less rhapsodic, make much the same points, often turning to Renaissance art to validate Burne-Jones's skill: 'The purest charm of the true Renaissance is here in perfection', maintained the *Athenaeum*.[21] 'The forms and draperies are made out in a way that Perugino himself might have admired', commended the *Standard*'s critic (almost certainly Frederick Wedmore);[22] 'In many ways it recalls the primitive art of the earlier 15th century Venetian painters, but especially in its colour',[23] claimed the *Globe*. This critic, probably A. L. Baldry, also had reservations about the way in which the phenomenon of reflection was treated: not so much the mirroring of the girls in the water, but something more technical to do with the representation of colour, 'the influence which, in nature, every tint has on those surrounding it'.[24] Despite being in sympathy with the painter's 'highly wrought poetic feeling', the *Daily News*'s correspondent – although not going so far as the perennially carping *Morning Post* in claiming that 'the shadows are to the full as strong as the substances, so that it would matter very little, if at all, though the painting were turned upside down'[25] – explained his objection:

> It is sufficient to point out the falsity of painting only as much of a reflection as a painter chooses, and that so strong in colour and exact in its imitation as to be more forcible than the real object. The reflection upon the polished surface of the leaves is omitted, that from the edge of the bank is also on which the figures stand, so that all pictorial illusion is destroyed, if the painter intends to represent objects as they really are seen in nature.[26]

What unites all these responses, critical as well as favourable, is not just their preoccupation with what is going on on the canvas surface, but their assumption that they can call on objective standards, standards that will be recognised and held in common by their audiences, as a means by which to describe and to assess the painting. These are the assumptions which have been explored in the last couple of chapters. The particular response on which I wish to concentrate, however, did not come from a regular art critic, but from the pioneering psychologist James Sully, and it is a response that suggests that there may be other ways of approaching art than reading a canvas with the assumption that one's reaction depends on the painting's ability to mimic life.

During the 1870s, James Sully was following a freelance career as a writer on philosophical, physiological and literary subjects. Born in 1842, and later, in 1892, to become Grote professor of the philosophy of mind at University College, London, his interest in art dated from around 1867–8, when he was studying in Göttingen and visited Dresden. Like George Eliot, he felt particularly drawn to Raphael's *Madonna*, in Dresden's art gallery. He began his literary career in London in 1871, writing for the *Fortnightly* and the *Saturday Review* on a variety of subjects, often with a psychological or aesthetic bias. In 1874, he published *Sensation and Intuition: Studies in Psychology and Aesthetics*, which concludes with his essay 'On the Possibility of a Science of Aesthetics', something which, he claims, would proceed 'by means of historical research supplemented by psychological explanation'.[27] He follows Archibald Alison, Alexander Bain and Herbert Spencer in their attempts to classify and explain aesthetic pleasure, and attempts to group such pleasures according to certain criteria. These include the pleasures of stimulation that one might receive from certain colours or treatments of form; gratification due to novelty; and pleasure deriving from memories, or from experiencing intuition which leads to other forms of intellectual activity – for example the recognition of relations of objects. He writes of the pleasures of the imagination, working on 'the tendency of the mind to idealize, and the satisfaction of the universal longings for something higher and more complete than the actual'.[28] The chapter is shot through with evolutionary assumptions – the person with the most advanced mental development will be rewarded by the highest number of pleasures, as opposed, say, to the momentary pleasure which a 'savage' might receive from bright colours. 'It follows from this', Sully continues:

> that the higher aesthetic appreciation is always a process of some delicacy. Pleasurable qualities which obtrude themselves on the observer's attention cannot afford a cultivated mind any appreciable delight. An essential ingredient in the more refined enjoyments of the beautiful, the ludicrous, etc., is the exercise of a certain intellectual activity. This mode of delight is the result of an extended activity of mind in discovering what is hidden, and in distinguishing elements which are closely interwoven.[29]

Yet 'an extended activity of mind' is not all that is involved in perception: first comes the operation of the eye. This is something which Sully addressed in general terms in an earlier chapter of *Sensation and Intuition*, 'Recent German Experiments with Sensation', in which he carries on the work begun by John Tyndall and others in bringing the theories of Hermann von Helmholtz before the British intelligentsia. Drawn by Helmholtz's reputation, Sully had spent the winter of 1871–2 in Berlin, having realised that he 'needed some first-hand knowledge of the physiological processes that help to condition the currents of our mental life'. He conducted anatomical studies in Dubois-Reymond's physiological laboratory, and attended Helmholtz's lectures on physiological optics: 'he was particularly kind, and soon gave us the entrée to his house'.[30] Helmholtz's work informed his April 1872 article in the *Fortnightly* on 'The Basic of Musical Sensation', which was praised highly by both George Lewes and Herbert Spencer. Its influence can also be found in Sully's article on 'Aesthetics' for the ninth edition of the *Encyclopaedia Britannica*, commissioned in October 1873. The reception of *Sensation and Intuition*, particularly Alexander Bain's enthusiastic review in the *Fortnightly*, led to him being asked to contribute to the first number of the pioneering journal of psychology, *Mind*: Darwin – whom Sully met at Lewes's for the first time – especially praised his piece on 'Physiological

Psychology in Germany'. Sully also knew Tyndall well: when Sully gave his 1880 lectures on 'Art and Vision' at the Royal Institution, Tyndall lent him apparatus for his optical experiments.[31]

In November 1878, Sully's article 'The Undefinable in Art' appeared in the *Cornhill Magazine*: it builds on some of the precepts put forward in *Science and Intuition*, and adds to these a far more precise consideration of what may actually happen when we look at a picture. In his earlier accumulation of ideas about what might constitute aesthetic pleasure, the possibilities for subjective, personal pleasures mingle with more objectively formulable qualities. By the late 1870s there was nothing startlingly fresh in asserting the importance of the individualised and subjective when it comes to viewing, or indeed producing, art: Burne-Jones, to put its synoptically, knew his Pater. What Sully does that is new is to blend physiology with more philosophically grounded theories of perception, and he thus lays down a claim for the importance of the developing science of psychology when it comes to aesthetic spectatorship.

In this article, Sully starts from the premise that there are two distinct kinds of mind in his contemporary world: on the one hand the mind with a 'curious enquiring and scientific' turn, 'and on the other side, the dreamily contemplative and the emotional attitude'. Both cultivate a taste for the beautiful, but in clearly demarcated ways: 'The former are mainly concerned with clarifying their aesthetic impressions, with apprehending the sources of pleasure in nature and art; the latter live rather to enjoy beauty without understanding it, and to have the delights of art with the least admixture of definite thought.'[32] Need it be like this, though? Might it not be possible for an aesthetically trained mind to suspend the intellectual functions, in order, as he puts it, 'to taste of the mysterious delights of the unthinking dreamer'?[33] Just as Tyndall acknowledged the access to the sublime which scientific inquiry gave him, that opening up of infinite spaces which could be afforded by the contemplation of dust or the stretch of the horizon, so, Sully explains, emotional satisfaction does have its part to play in intellectual culture, which in its 'highest degrees . . . takes the form of a sense of the undefined and the mysterious'.[34] What specifically intrigues Sully above all in this article is the fact that the intellect and the emotions may indeed be simultaneously engaged when looking at a painting, and that this is so is due in part to the way in which the perceiving eye operates. We cannot assimilate all of a picture in one go, and our consciousness is bound to vacillate: 'One impression or feeling is reflected on, and so appears clear and distinct; but outside there are circles of consciousness, feelings, and thoughts, which are vague and undefined. Thus at any given moment the impression we receive from a work of art consists of clear and obscure feelings, which latter can only be made luminous in their turn at the expense of the former.' In emphasising the pleasure of the obscure, he is not just drawing on the traditional repertoire of the sublime, but on much more recent work by Robert Schumann which demonstrated the intellectual appeal of the undefined in art.[35] He may also have been influenced by the work of Emile Javal (Helmholtz's translator into French), who, in his *Annales d'un oculiste*, also published in 1878, explained the process of 'saccader': the fact that the eye is never still, but always in motion, moving from one centre of attention, from one focus, to another.

By way of bringing home to the reader his point about the possibility of sustaining dual modes of viewing, Sully provides an actual example:

> let us take a picture which has attracted a good deal of notice of late – the Venus' Mirror of Mr Burne Jones. When, for example, we are passing the eye over the several details – the gracefully set figures, the water with its soft reflections, the quiet landscape behind – we are at each successive moment elevating one impression or group of impressions after another into clear consciousness, while the rest fall back into the dim regions of the sub-conscious. Each ingredient – the illuminated and the unilluminated – is alike essential. When, for instance, we are deriving an intellectual satisfaction from some particular virgin-shape or gentle face, the many other pleasing elements of the picture contribute each a little rillet of undiscriminated emotion; and these obscure or 'sub-conscious' currents of feeling serve to swell the impression of any single instant, making it full and deep.[36]

Here, our perception of a work of art is itself described in terms which make the mind a simulacrum for the experience of encountering the painted canvas. We first approach it with the intellect, that part of our being which is, as it were, clear and visible, since we can be in conscious control of its operations. Then, however, follows the plenitude and depth of understanding and knowledge of the work of art by the workings of our own depths, or 'subconscious'.

At no time, according to Sully, will the whole of the work of art be available to us: we concentrate on either part or generality, but the specific will always inform the general, and vice versa. If we concentrate on colour, or on the sense of the ensemble given by the scene, we will not be able to prevent an underpresence of our consciousness of the separate details of the picture affecting our sense of the ensemble of the whole. All the time, some of the impressions that the picture effects on us may remain beyond analysis, since, Sully writes, 'our power of taking apart the contents of our consciousness is always limited'.[37] That which lies hidden will inform that of which we are aware. We cannot always be definite about the sources of our pleasure, they lie deeply embedded in our memories: 'the impressions which objects produce in our minds are a growth of many past experiences', but these themselves may be 'lost to view'.[38] He even acknowledges the fact that some of our emotions may be peculiarly unrecoverable in their origins, since they belong not to our own experiences, but to those of our ancestors, and are part of racial, not personal, memory.

Sully maintains that 'Certain modes of aesthetic pleasure directly depend on vague mental representation as their essential condition, and disappear as soon as reflection seeks to give exactness and definiteness to the ideas.'[39] In particular, poetry, with its demands on the imagination, and music are privileged art forms in this respect: significantly, he calls on his own physiological assumptions about the workings of the eye, to the extent of figuring its impersonal mechanism as a desiring subject replicating his own taste, in order to justify his own prejudices about what he encountered at the Grosvenor: 'it may safely be said that vague suggestion cannot be introduced into pictorial art to the same extent as into music. The eye desires clear and well-defined objects: it is the organ of perception *par excellence*, and it could never be long satisfied with misty "nocturnes" or with a dreamy symbolic type of art.'[40] Indeed, the terms of his argument – although he does not become specific about particular works other than mentioning the Burne-Jones painting and making that dismissive reference to Whistler – suggest that he might not have felt too uncomfortable with, say, Frith's *Railway Station*. Despite his promotion of the role of the unconscious within the visualising process, Sully was completely unresponsive to the interpretive potential offered by indefinite horizons, shifting perspectives, and the refusal of stable depth of field that characterise Whistler's experimental painting of the 1870s. For Sully's Darwinian principles inform his aesthetic judgement when he argues that 'higher works of art are distinguished from lower and elementary ones by being more complex, by having more numerous elements, also a larger number of uniting relations; in other words, a more intricate unity, dominating a wider diversity'. It follows that 'the more complex a work of art, the larger must be the region of the obscure and undiscriminated at any single moment.'[41] Yet, he is completely unspecific about the nature of the 'uniting relations' – whether these be narrative or aesthetic – and the potential for them partaking solely of the latter category can be understood when he remarks that ideas – albeit 'vague ideas' – may be produced by abstract forms, by the straight line or circle, or the presence of white in a work.

Among other things, James Sully's work may be seen as a contribution to that debate which runs through the second half of the nineteenth century and which has played such a central work in my own study: the relationship between art, science and aesthetics. Writing in the new journal *Mind* in 1876, Sully claimed that 'there is probably no region of phenomena which has received less illumination from the activities of the modern scientific spirit than the processes of the Fine Arts'.[42] His remedy for this is psychology, a discipline which he defines quite widely: 'an appeal not only to the study of mental operations by individual self-reflection but also to the newer inquiries into the laws of mental development in the race, and of the reciprocal actions of many minds in the social organism'.[43] This interest in the social as well as the individual is a sign of the influence of Herbert Spencer upon him, yet Spencer's remarks in *The Principles of Sociology* about the importance of the concept of duality across cultures usefully function to return us to the topic of reflection, and the co-presence of the seen and the unseen – 'apparent and unapparent states of being',[44] as Spencer also calls them – which the fact of reflection suggests. These categories, whilst not identical with Sully's intellectual and emotional, the realm of fact and the realm of suggestion, clearly have a good deal in common with them. What Spencer is playing with is an early version of the mirror-phase, the troublesome but intriguing gap between one's physical and mental existence.

The Fijians, according to Spencer, claim that each person possesses an Other – his likeness reflected in water or a looking-glass:

> This belief in two spirits, is, indeed, the most consistent one. For are not a man's shadow and his reflection separate? and are they not co-existent with one another and with himself? Can he not, standing at the water-side, observe that the reflection in the water and the shadow on the shore, simultaneously move as he moves? Clearly, while both belong to him, the two are independent of him and one another; for both may be absent together, and either may be present in the absence of the other.
>
> Early theories about the nature of this duplicate are now beside the question. We are concerned only with the fact that it is thought of as real. Here is revealed another class of facts confirming the notion that existences have their visible and invisible states, and strengthening the implication of a duality in existence.[45]

This co-presence of visible and invisible states is at the core of Sully's own understanding of the process of aesthetic perception. One may describe, and respond to, the formal qualities on the canvas, as contemporary reviewers habitually did, but this is not an adequate summation of the activity that takes place in looking at a painting. The science of psychology, blending, as it did, an understanding of the physiology of looking, with an acknowledgement of an individual's interiority – memory, associationism and so on –

insists that we pay attention to both the body and mind of the spectator: in other words, to the simultaneous presence of the visible and the invisible in their own constitutions. In sum, what Sully does is to deflect critical attention from the surface of *The Mirror of Venus*, and to focus it on the interior. This is not, however, some presumed interiority of depicted character, nor is it the deduced state of mind of the artist, lying behind the female reflections in what Oscar Wilde termed the 'mirror of polished steel',[46] the preternatural clarity of the painted pool. Rather, what Sully privileges is the inescapable duality – intellectual and emotional, physiological and mental – involved in the practice of spectatorship itself.

James Sully's interest in the practice of visualisation extended into the ways in which others experienced its powers. He records how George Eliot told him that 'she could carry about so distinct a picture of the faces of her friends, that not only photographs, but nearly all portraits, disappointed her by their incompleteness'.[47] Eliot's own interest in visuality, as made manifest in the pages of another work of the mid-1870s, *Daniel Deronda* (1876), encompasses, however, not just the tensions between inward and outward vision, between the material and the imaginative objects of sight – as was discussed in chapter 4 – but comes to centre on exactly the same issues which were preoccupying Sully at this time: issues of perspective and subjectivity, of the variations between perception and judgement that characterise the viewing habits of each individual.

The difficulties of arriving at a clear cut view of any issue, or formulating a straightforward judgement concerning any individual, that make *Daniel Deronda* taken as a whole such an interpretively provocative text are exemplified by the uncertainties of the narrative's first sentences – 'Was she beautiful or not beautiful? and what was the secret of form or expression which gave the dynamic quality to her glance? Was the good or the evil genius dominant in those beams?'[48] – another woman gambler not just coming under the scrutiny of a male observer (a disquieting, 'measuring gaze'[49] as Gwendolen herself characterises it a few pages later) but having the characteristics of her own gaze interrogated. 'The wish to look again' which she exerts on Deronda is felt 'as coercion and not as a longing in which the whole being consents'.[50] This is a novel in which point of view is embedded within the third-person narrative, shifting from character to character with far less self-conscious authorial positioning than in Eliot's earlier fictions; these assessments are voiced from within Daniel's culturally formed consciousness, his repertoire of ways to read women, the social construction of masculinity which Eliot investigates through him. At the same time, they are symptomatic, as Jacqueline Rose has pointed out, of the broader 'problem of fixing the identity of a woman, of judging the origins of her power', that the narrative as a whole explores.[51] The sexualised energy and exchange involved in the act of men and women looking at each other, assessing each other, acknowledging the workings of fascination and compulsion and curiosity when eyes meet or the directions of their looking fail to coincide, is a theme to which Eliot continually returns in this novel. The intensity with which the moment of looking is charged can be as apparently slight as the 'smile of irony' in Daniel's 'eyes as their glances met'[52] at the gaming table, or the emotion articulated may be as strangely compelling as the 'wild amazed consciousness in [Gwendolen's] eyes'[53] as Grandcourt's drowned body is brought to shore, but, throughout, Eliot invokes both the dynamics of the gaze and the innate and mutable expressiveness of the eye to direct the reader's attention towards interpretive cruxes.

For these repeated moments of vision are important not just in their own right, as elements in the dramatic unfolding of the story, and as indications of uncertain and uneasy exchanges of understanding between characters, but as they symbolise the very uncertainties inherent in the figurative act of seeing, or interpreting. Eliot oscillates in the novel between writing about seeing as a process in which the physiological and the associative are blended, and invoking this process in more metaphorical ways.

These ways can, on occasion, be conventional. Gwendolen's attitude towards her cousin Rex when they go hunting together – 'Gwendolen was apt to think rather of those who saw her than of those whom she could not see; and Rex was soon so far behind that if she had looked she would not have seen him'[54] – acts as a concise summary of her social attitudes as a young woman. Similarly, Eliot employs – as she did to such effect when juxtaposing Hetty and Dinah in *Adam Bede* – the familiar device of the looking glass to suggest self-regard or its obverse. Gwendolen's engagement with mirrors can signify her dissatisfaction with herself – 'she took no conscious note of her reflected beauty'[55] – as she sits before the glass after receiving the letter telling her of her family's financial ruin. For once her identity cannot be 'framed by the abundance of images that define femininity', as it was when she admired herself and the symbiotic prettiness of her surroundings in the bedroom mirror when first arriving at Offendene, although Eliot's pointed use of the word 'conscious' suggests her awareness of the part played by repetition and unacknowledged reiteration of past associations involved in the act of looking. For Gwendolen was well used to posing herself in attitudes of aesthetic attractiveness, aware of the effect such contrived positioning would have on spectators. At the archery meeting, for example, Eliot emphasises the artificiality inherent in her appeal – 'She was the central object of that pretty picture, and every one present must gaze at her.'[56] So aware was Gwendolen of this that there was no need for her eyes to follow the direction of her thoughts, an episode of simultaneous display and concealment.

Artifice, however, is little help when it comes to dealing with actuality, as Gwendolen discovers when she meets with Lydia Glasher. Although the initial visual reference is to pictures formed in the mind rather than with the eye – 'Gwendolen's uncontrolled reading, though consisting chiefly in what are called pictures of life, had somehow not prepared her for this encounter with reality'[57] – Eliot turns this into a more general, ironised critique of those who aestheticise the unpleasant, which therefore makes its impact the sharper when it is encountered: 'Perspective, as its inventor remarked, is a beautiful thing. What horrors of damp huts, where human beings languish, may not become picturesque through aerial distance!'.[58] Through analogy, Gwendolen's personal experience, and the revelation to her of her social blindness, is thus made to serve for the generalised English blinkeredness towards other races, other peoples, which forms a powerful under-current throughout the novel.[59]

Here, however, as with the gambling scene with which the novel opens, the emphasis falls on the act of observation, and the gap that may exist between appearance and reality. Eliot is certainly aware of the individualised processes of cogitation which take place in the mind of the gazer, as they attempt to make sense of what they see, and of the ways in which speculation is ready to fill out knowledge: 'By dint of looking at a dubious object with a constructive imagination, one can give it twenty different shapes.'[60] She saves her most complex assessment of the subjective element involved in the act of perception, however, for the mental processes of her hero, Daniel, and for his mentor, the prophetic figure of Mordecai. When she describes Daniel rowing on the Thames, in chapter 17, Eliot first reminds one, in passing, of the earlier ways in which she has treated vision: recalls the 'peculiarity of [his] gaze which Gwendolen chose to call "dreadful"';[61] describes how looking in a mirror, for Daniel, had for many years been associated with clues to his parentage and hence to his identity. His reflective processes are halted when he catches sight of a girl on the river bank, not caught up in the pleasures of her own reflection, but looking, as it were, beyond it: 'her eyes were fixed on the river with a look of immovable, statue-like despair'.[62] Their eyes meet, in a moment which is both a mirror image and a sharply differentiated occasion from Daniel's encounter with Gwendolen: 'It was but a couple of moments, but that seems a long while for two people to look straight at each other',[63] and, though she turns away and he rows on, the image stays with him – not least because he acknowledges its aesthetic attractiveness. As the shadows lengthen and the light mellows, and just before he sees Mirah again and moves to stop her from drowning herself, he pulls his boat up on the bank, and passes into reverie:

> He lay with his hands beside his head propped on a level with the boat's edge, so that he could see all around him, but could not be seen by any one at a few yards' distance; and for a long while he never turned his eyes from the view right in front of him. He was

forgetting everything else in a half-speculative, half-involuntary
identification of himself with the objects he was looking at,
thinking how far it might be possible habitually to shift his centre
till his own personality would be no less outside him than the
landscape.[64]

Daniel is practising a kind of evacuation of himself through
looking, although in reflecting upon the process even as he carries
it into practice, Eliot shows how inseparable the motion of the
mind is from the act of looking. Similarly, she describes Mordecai's
responsiveness to the visual effects of London, in a passage which
foreshadows the potential parallels between the two men, especially since the scene is again the river. Mordecai, we are told, 'was
keenly alive to some poetic aspects of London':

> his thought went on in wide spaces; and whenever he could, he
> tried to have in reality the influences of a large sky. Leaning on the
> parapet of Blackfriars Bridge, and gazing meditatively, the
> breadth and calm of the river, with its long vista half hazy, half
> luminous, the grand dim masses or tall forms of buildings which
> were the signs of world-commerce, the oncoming of boats and
> barges from the still distance into sight and colour, entered into
> his mood and blent themselves indistinguishably with his think-
> ing, as a fine symphony to which we can hardly be said to listen
> makes a medium that bears up our spiritual wings.[65]

It is as if Eliot were providing illustrations of the ideas about the
connection of mental with physiological process that George
Lewes had put forward in the first series of *Problems of Life and Mind*
(1874). Lewes reminded his readers first of the whole complex
system of associationism that is built into the act of perception –
'The organic seat of Vision is too often assumed to be the retina;
whereas that is only the seat of the visual excitation, which in the
Perceptive Centre is blended with the residua of other excita-
tions.'[66] Memory, which includes our stored knowledge of sensations of taste, fragrance, resistance and so on, thus enters into the
operations of sight. As M. H. Pirenne, writing a century after
Lewes, puts it in his authoritative study, *Optics, Painting &*

Photography: 'As to the problem of the precise relationship between the physiological events occurring within the brain and the psychological processes of vision, it is part of the philosophical riddle of the relationship between body and mind, and largely remains a mystery.'[67] Lewes was certainly well aware that the relationship existed, however, and that it was a crucial one.

In addition to his familiarity with English physiologists and scientists who studied the workings of the mind, Lewes was exceptionally well informed about Continental scientific theory. In chapter 4, we traced some specific instances when he borrowed from French medicine: more influential to his work on perception were those Germans who considered the relationship between mind and body, such as Johannes Müller, Ernst Wilhelm von Brücke, Jacob Moleschott and Carl Vogt. As he moved from a more objectivist to a more subjectivist position in the early 1860s, the work of Hermann von Helmholtz became increasingly important to him, as it had been to both Tyndall and James Sully.[68] He had read the complete version of Helmholtz's *Handbuch der physiologischen Optik* by the mid-1860s, and visited him when in Heidelberg in 1868. His influence can be felt strongly throughout *Problems of Life and Mind*, and nowhere more than in his incorporation of Helmholtz's principle that: 'Perceptions of external objects being . . . of the nature of ideas, and ideas themselves being invariably activities of our psychic energy, perceptions also can only be the result of psychic energy. Accordingly, strictly speaking, the theory of perceptions belongs properly in the domain of psychology.'[69]

Lewes, as the case of Sully demonstrates, was far from alone in picking up on and disseminating the interactions between physiology and psychology that Helmholtz was so instrumental in formulating. What is striking, however, is not so much the link that he draws between the dual processes involved in vision, but the further factor involved: language. Perception, he sets out to show in *Problems*, is the result of a slow process of evolution, like all organic forms (he betrays an internalisation of precisely the kind of prejudices of his time that Eliot looks to undermine in *Daniel Deronda* when he situates the polar extremes of human intelligence, so inseparable from the complex process of perception, in, 'say a Tasmanian and a Shakespeare'):[70]

> not only will it be shown that many thousands of years passed before even man was able to *perceive* the colour blue, for instance (though of course he felt a difference between a blue object and a brown one) it will be shown that no animal can possibly perceive blue as we perceive it; and the reason in both cases is not to be sought in physiological processes of Vision, but in psychological processes of Thought. The possibility of this perception is due to Language; and Language exists only as a social function.[71]

For Lewes, it matters little whether the images that are perceived exist in the material world, or have been conjured up in the mind's eye, in the imagination, like Mordecai's 'yearnings, conceptions' which, like Latimer's presentiments, 'continually take the form of images which have a fore-shadowing power'.[72] What is of concern are the means by which these acts of vision are translated and communicated. This dual stress on physiology and psychology, the material and the intangible, the objective and the subjective, had little immediate effect on writing about art – Burne-Jones's painting was, for Sully, an example rather than the focus of his piece in its own right. Its foregrounding in more general writing about perception in the 1870s allows us to appropriate these concerns. Even if an overt acknowledgement of the double operations involved in perception did not penetrate very far into the narrative and moralistically hidebound language of much art criticism itself, they may still be found elsewhere: not just in writing, like Lewes's, which bridged body and mind, but in the way vision was treated in certain works of art and literature in the closing decades of the century.

CHAPTER 10

Hallucination and vision

By the later decades of the nineteenth century, many art critics, as we have seen, became impatient with easy-to-read narratives, in which interpreting the actions depicted and drawing moral conclusions relied on conventional responses held by the spectator. Whilst indubitably popular among the public, their production, and a liking for them, was held to be a mark of vulgar taste. A further type of narrative painting encountered less scorn, however: the problem picture, the picture which left its viewers asking questions about what, exactly, might be happening on the canvas. Such pictures are the visual equivalents to, say, the fiction of Henry James's mid or late career, in which the reader is left speculating what leads Isobel, in *The Portrait of a Lady*, to return to Gilbert Osmond, or interrogating their own judgement concerning the moral justifications, or otherwise, behind Merton's and Kate's actions in *The Wings of the Dove*. Problem pictures inevitably stimulated readings based on narrative formulations, sets of possible outcomes, already established in a spectator's cultural consciousness, but they were not predicated on there being any one reading of the depiction, any predefined didactic conclusion to be drawn from it.

Many of these problem pictures – by Frank Dicksee, John Collier and William Orchardson, in particular – set up sexually charged scenes. What, precisely, is being confessed in Dicksee's *The Confession* (1896), in which an anaemic-looking young woman – wearing a wedding ring – and a haggard and unhappy man sit together? *The Times*, in noting that Collier's *The Prodigal Daughter*

50 John Collier, *The Prodigal Daughter*, 1903. Oil on canvas, 160.02 × 215.9 cms.

(1903) (figure 50) was 'the popular attraction, and to a certain extent the popular puzzle' of that year's Academy exhibition, went on to discuss what one might make of 'English Magda – the runaway daughter of a quite old couple', returning in her finery to their simple home: 'The details of the dramatic moment are a little difficult to understand; has she just entered the room, or is she leaving it, repelled? Is she telling a story, or has she told it, unforgiven, and is she about to pass out again into the night? These things want explaining, for a narrative picture ought to have no ambiguity.'[1]

Orchardson, in calling one of his pictures *An Enigma*, said that he was himself uncertain of the precise narrative explanation of this depiction of a young man – in fancy dress? – and young woman sitting on a sofa together.[2]

Here, I want to consider two pictures with very similar themes, Frank Dicksee's *A Reverie* (1894) (figure 51), and John Everett Millais's *Speak! Speak!* (1895) (figure 52). Whilst both involve very

51 Frank Dicksee, *A Reverie*, 1894. Oil on canvas, 104.14 × 137.16 cms.

uneasy dynamics between a man and a woman, neither pivot on orthodox, familiar questions of sexual morality. In the former, an ethereal figure of a woman appears to a man as he sits listening to another woman play the piano. Reviewers were once again divided about what could possibly be going on in this work, and, in particular, projected with confidence their own particular versions of family dynamics. Claude Phillips, in the *Academy*, described the 'young white-robed lady' singing at the piano 'while her father, leaning his head on his hand, dreams bitter-sweet dreams of the past, visible to him only: a diaphanous vision of one who long ago sang the song now heard floats through the air, evoked by the magic of the music and the passionate melancholy of the listener'.[3] Marion Spielmann, in the *Magazine of Art*, reads the relationship differently but conspicuously unconfidently: 'a modern poetic scene of a girl at the piano, while her brooding husband (?) sees the memory rise behind her, ghostlike, of a former love'.[4] In Millais's painting, which has a loosely defined medieval setting, a

52 John Everett Millais, *Speak! Speak!* 1895. Oil on canvas, 67.6×210.8 cms.

man sits up in his bed, where he has been reading old love letters, to see the form of his bride before him. Is this a material being, or a ghostly apparition, or a hallucination caused by some internal disturbance in the man's mind? Millais himself claimed to be unsure, to have painted a work in which the possibilities for interpretation as to what exactly was the nature of the apparently visible were left uncertain. Spielmann, again, records: 'When I remarked that I could not tell whether the luminous apparition was a spirit or a woman he was pleased: "That's just what I want", he said; "I don't know either, nor", he added, pointing to the picture, "does he"'.[5] Certainly, one can look at these two paintings, like any problem pictures, as examples of the democratisation of art criticism of which Tom Taylor wrote, in which each spectator is granted their own interpretive license, and the subjectivity of their point of view is hence acknowledged.[6] There is, however, a different way of considering the modes in which Dicksee and Millais have, in Odilon

Redon's phrase, put 'the logic of the visible at the service of the invisible',[7] and that is to use these paintings to open up issues about the relationship between hallucination and the practice of vision. When may someone be believed to have seen something which is not actually there? This question, which forms the pivot for countless Victorian ghost stories, which lies at the heart of debates about spiritualism and the degrees of fraud and deception inhering within its practices, is intimately entwined with developments in the physiology and psychology of vision during the period.

At the simplest level, fallacious perception may occur because of sensory delusions that all of us experience: delusions which have an objective foundation. Edmund Parish, in *Hallucinations and Illusions*, runs through some of these: the illusion that a straight stick bends as it enters a pool; the doubling of an object seen in a prism; or the nerve disturbance in the eye which results in 'diplopia monucularis', causing the double image normally formed by the lens to be developed on the retina as two distinct images. 'Other fallacies of perception are caused by confused or ambiguous stimuli', like darkness or fog, or occur because 'the image seen does not fall on the point of clearest vision'.[8] Sensory deception, too, occurs when an individual's attention is directed away from the point of action, or when they believe that they have seen that which they would expect to have seen in a given situation: this is the type of swindle that, as we have seen, Lewes thought that spiritualists practised on their gullible public, and that formed the basis for magicians' acts.

Both hallucination and illusion are forms of perception which demand more complex consideration. Theories of hallucination have a long history, going back to the place of visions in the writings of St Augustine of Hippo (354–430), who drew distinctions between corporeal vision, imaginative vision and intellectual vision (the last of these being primarily concerned with the figuring of abstract concepts), but acknowledged that mystical experiences could occur at any of these levels. These theories move through the texts of the scholastics, who drew a far sharper dividing line between apparently normal and abnormal vision, and then again, between the sources of the latter, it being of crucial importance to determine whether they emanated from God or the Devil. The fear that visions and voices were of satanic origin had cruel consequences in the fifteenth and sixteenth centuries. By the beginning of the nineteenth century, however, members of the medical profession had gained ascendancy over theological interpreters when it came to understanding those whom one might deem to be insane in terms of what they claimed to see.[9]

Opinion differed, however, as to whether or not there was a sharp dividing line between hallucination and other forms of perception, or whether they all belonged in some kind of continuum. T. Arnold put forward the dominant view at the beginning of the century when he asserted the distinction between 'ideal insanity' – in other words, pathological hallucination – and normal perceptual experience. S. Hibbert-Ware, however, in his *Sketches of the Philosophy of Apparitions* (1825), believed that hallucinations were far more commonplace and less sensationalist events, aligned to the workings of the imagination. The most influential pronouncement on the nature of hallucination, and its distinction from illusion – a distinction which continues to be widely used today – came from the French physician Esquirol, who wrote in 1832 that:

> In *hallucinations* everything happens in the brain (mind). The visionaries, the ecstatics, are people who suffer from hallucinations, dreamers while they are awake. The activity of the brain is so energetic that the visionary, the person hallucinating, ascribes a body and an actuality to images that the memory recalls without the intervention of senses.
>
> In *illusions* on the other hand, the sensibility of the nervous extremities is excited; the senses are active, the present impressions call into action the reactions of the brain. This reaction being under the influence of ideas and passions which dominate the insane, these sick people are mistaken about the nature and cause of their present sensations.[10]

In other words, illusions bear a perceptual relation to that which lies outside the perceiver – the kind of Radcliffean Gothic examples that later nineteenth-century commentators used were a man mistaking a rock for a tower, or the play of moonlight through forest leaves for running water, or a sheet hanging up for a ghost. Hallucinations, on the other hand, usually are independent of external stimulus, caused by some 'subjective irritation of the optic or auditory nerve'.[11]

This apparent separation between illusion and hallucination could function as a necessary demarcation in the later nineteenth century, at a time when anxieties about increasing amounts of psychological disturbance and nervous disorders were growing in circulation. It was hard to police, however. This, in turn, is connected to the growing interest in the unconscious, and in the relation, to use Allon White's formulation, of 'mystery, deception, repression and deceit par excellence' which forms 'that boundary between the conscious and the unconscious'.[12] White calls upon Eliza Lynn Linton's article 'Our Illusions' (1891) to illustrate the ways in which *fin-de-siècle* anxieties about the uncertain borderlands between truth and falsity, the rational and the irrational, demonstrate a realisation of the disturbance of relativity. Linton comes to the conclusion that there is essentially no difference between a fervent Christian believer, trembling at the presence of Satan, and a man suffering from persecution mania, thinking he is pursued by the Furies:

> The state of mind is the same – but the objective truth of the appearance? Was not that maya, illusion, in each case alike? If this be not so, then we have no line of boundary between madness and sanity. If we affirm the truth of spiritual impressions, however we may name them, we open the doors of Bedlam and make its haunted inmates free citizens like the rest.[13]

Invoking the spiritual, in this context, shows how difficult it could be to make or maintain a separation between illusion and hallucination. J. H. Blount, writing in 1856 'On the Terms Delusion, Illusion, and Hallucination', commented despairingly that:

> scattered through the various writers on insanity every here and there, these terms seem to occur with a distinctive character; and then again, a few pages further, and each term is found with quite

a different signification, so that it is impossible, in any English work, or from the mass of them, to deduce any precise or distinctive definitions for these terms.[14]

Slade and Bentall claim that distinguishing hallucination by its pathological quality was fostered by medical discourse on the mentally unstable or insane and their treatment: 'the view', as they put it, 'that hallucinations are medical phenomena has led to a relative lack of interest in them by psychologists' in this century.[15] As they suggest, however, without examining at any length, pioneering psychologists of the late nineteenth century tended to be far more flexible in their definitions than their twentieth-century successors. Thus James Sully opens his important work *Illusions* by avowing that:

> Hardly anybody is always consistently sober and rational in his perceptions and beliefs. A momentary fatigue of the nerves, a little mental excitement, a relaxation of the effort of attention by which we continually take our bearings with respect to the real world about us, will produce just the same kind of confusion of reality and phantasm which we observe in the insane . . . Our luminous circle of rational perception is surrounded by the misty penumbra of illusion.[16]

One of the things that a student of optics soon finds, Sully goes on to explain, in terms consistent with his discussion of perception in relation to painting, is how many things hover around on the edge of our consciousness without us ever paying full attention to them: the 'startling discovery' for such a student is that 'his field of vision has all through his life been haunted with weird shapes' – the language is pointedly borrowed from a supernatural register – 'which have never troubled the serenity of his mind just because they have never been distinctly attended to'.[17] In part, these weird shapes belong to the memory, to one's personal storehouse of recollections of previous sensations – not just of size and distance, crucial components of recognition, but of tactile and muscular experiences: this is a Helmholtzian understanding of the mechanisms of perception, to which Sully adds that another thing 'worth noting with respect to this process of filling up a sense-impression is that it draws on past sensations of the eye itself'.[18]

Not everyone, however, uses the eye in the same way, and with the same attention. This is not just a commonplace relating to divergent subjectivities, nor to Ruskin's belief, passed on by many popularisers, that one can and should train oneself to observe more carefully, particularly in respect to the natural world. It is a fact that may be related to the practice of mental imaging, of seeing with the mind's eye. Francis Galton conducted a series of questionnaires and personal inquiries designed to test the relative powers of visualisation among individuals. He asked each of his subjects, before responding to his questions, to

> think of some definite object – suppose it is your breakfast table, as you sat down to it this morning – and consider carefully the picture that rises before your mind's eye.
> 1. *Illumination.* – Is the image dim or fairly clear? Is its brightness comparable to that of the actual scene?
> 2. *Definition.* – Are all the objects pretty well defined at the same time, or is the place of sharpest definition at any one time more contracted than it is in a real scene?
> 3. *Colouring.* – Are the colours of the china, of the toast, bread crust, mustard, meat, parsley, or whatever may have been on the table, quite distinct and natural?[19]

Further questions ask about the apparent location of the images – in the head, in the eye ball, in front of the eyes, at a 'normal' distance; about the ability to recall people's features, or to remember scenery: 'Can you easily form mental pictures from the descriptions of scenery that are so frequently met with in novels and books of travel?'[20]

The answers that Galton received surprised him in some ways, particularly since he found that 'the great majority of the men of science to whom I first applied protested that mental imagery was unknown to them',[21] whilst many members of general society claimed to be able to see, and to report what they saw, in minute detail. Galton concludes that 'an over-ready perception of sharp mental pictures is antagonistic to the acquirement of habits of highly-generalised and abstract thought, especially when the steps of reasoning are carried on by words as symbols'.[22] However, not only does he learn that one can train oneself in mental imaging – several of his respondents claim that the very act of replying to the questionnaire led them to practise this – but he determines that there are certain categories of people who do make considerable use of the faculty, from blacksmiths, carpenters and architects to 'strategists, artists of all denominations, physicists who contrive new experiments'.[23] This latter category fall very much within those whom G. H. Lewes had in mind when considering the rôle of the imagination within scientific inquiry. Galton also notes – although he does not offer any explanation for the fact – that 'the power of visualising is higher in the female sex than in the male',[24] and that there are racial differences when it comes to the faculty of making mental images: he singles out the French, the South African Bushmen and the Eskimo for their powers, in a way which cuts across any relationship between visualisation and theories of racial development or degeneration.

More than this, Galton is adamant that one does not have to be insane to experience hallucinations. On the contrary, 'a notable proportion of sane persons have had not only visions, but actual hallucinations of sight, sound, or other sense, at one or more periods of their lives'.[25] He concluded that there is a continuity between all forms of visualisation, 'beginning with an almost total absence of it, and ending with a complete hallucination'.[26] Whilst Galton's questionnaire was sent to people who were asked specifically to concentrate on calling up a picture in their mind's eye, exercising the images stored in the memory, others record the vivid appearance of scenes in their mind's eye, even though the perceiver harboured no illusion as to the externality of their existence. The astronomer Sir John Herschel, in a lecture 'On Sensorial Vision', records the shadowy, unpleasing faces that pass through his consciousness when his eyes are closed: 'Landscapes present themselves much more rarely but more distinctly, and on the few occasions I remember, have been highly picturesque and pleasing, with a certain but very limited power of varying them by an effort of the will'.[27] Some years previously, recovering from a fever, '[his] chief amusement for two or three days consisted in the exercise of a power of calling up representations both of scenes and persons, which appeared with almost the distinctness of reality'.[28] What distinguishes these internal apparitions, like more disconcerting hallucinations, from the workings of the imagination, are their felt objectivity, the sense that they have an existence independent of the conscious, voluntary and active workings of the imagination.

The question of ghosts, and of the supernatural more generally, with the apparent autonomy which accompanies their appearance, shows quite how grey an area is occupied by the problems of hallucination and perception. Without doubt, spiritualist practitioners preyed upon their patrons' desire for reassurance that there existed some kind of life after death, a continuum between the visible and the invisible worlds no longer provided, for many, by conventional religion. They practised the deceptions which we have already seen G. H. Lewes scorn, producing 'materializations' of the dead who appeared from behind curtains or from a closed cabinet, and spinning 'ectoplasm' out of a medium's body, aided by suggestive lighting and rooms crowded with furnishings. As Alan Gauld asserts: 'Certainly there does not seem to be the slightest reason for supposing that the vast majority of the spectacular physical phenomena reported in the eighteen-seventies and eighteen-eighties were anything other than fraudulent.'[29]

Yet those who saw these 'materializations', and were willing to testify to the reality of what they had seen, tended to be more than credulous: they were sympathetic to the mediums' enterprise, anxious to believe, receptive to suggestivity. Such receptiveness, too, seemingly characterised those who claimed to see ghosts or other hallucinations in less controlled circumstances. The Society for Psychical Research, founded in 1882, carried out a 'census of hallucinations' between 1889 and 1892, to which it received 17,000 answers. To the question 'Have you ever, when believing yourself to be completely awake, had a visual impression of seeing, or being touched by a living being or inanimate object, or of hearing a voice; which impression, so far as you could discover, was not due to any external physical cause?'[30] Of the respondents, 673 claimed that they *had* experienced first-hand perceptions of human figures. As with any questionnaire, one needs to be sceptical about the implications of such statistics, considering both the motivations behind bothering to reply to such questioning, and desires to come up with interesting or desired answers. What further emerges from the replies, and is more relevant to the subjectivity involved in vision, is the degree to which ghost sightings were frequently prompted by suggestions that particular houses or rooms were haunted, or by a wish to share in an experience already undergone by a family member.[31]

The question of whether or not the apparently paranormal could be explained rationally was the recurrent issue posed by the Victorian ghost story, whether tacitly, as in James's *The Turn of the Screw* (1898), or openly. 'What of the appearance Maria Lease saw? . . . Was it reality or delusion?', asks the narrator of a short story by Ellen Wood, which takes this very question as its title: 'That is (as the Squire put it), did her eyes see a real, spectral Daniel Ferrar; or were they deceived by some imagination of the brain?'[32] The open-endedness was highly similar to the uncertainties raised by the ghostly problem paintings of Dicksee and Millais: it was in this vein that Sheridan Le Fanu wrote to his publisher, George Bentley, saying of 'The Haunted Baronet' that he was striving for 'the equilibrium between the natural and the *super*-natural, the supernatural phenomena being explained on natural theories – and people left to choose which solution they please'.[33] More specifically, however, the query was frequently raised in fiction concerning the role which scientific, and, in particular, physiological factors might play in explaining the presence of ghosts.

Margaret Oliphant's 'The Open Door' (1881) exemplifies well this play on the overlap between body and mind in the dramatisation of the uncanny. The narrator's son is terrified by the wailing cry he hears in the grounds of their new home near Edinburgh. This is an auditory hallucination, it would seem, perhaps stimulated by atmospheric conditions: '"Noises? – ou ay, there'll be noises – the wind in the trees, and the water soughing down the glen"', Jarvis, the coachman, offers by way of explanation, albeit with evident evasiveness, for he comes to admit that the cries, the moaning, the pathetic words ' "Oh, mother, let me in!" ' had been heard by others.[34] 'Hallucinations of hearing', as plenty of Victorian comment attested, 'are more common than those of sight'.[35] The narrator himself is horrified not just at his son's evident distress, but at what it may signify, a form of effeminate unhealthiness: 'My blood got a sort of chill in my veins at the idea that Roland should be a ghost-seer; for that generally means a hysterical temperament and weak health and all that men most hate and fear for their children.'[36] Bent on investigating what has so distressed his boy, and charged by Roland with righting the ghost's wrongs, he heads off to the ruined site where the sounds materialise, and himself experiences a 'long, soft, weary sigh'. The terror, for the time being, lies not so much in what he sees, but in what he does not: 'This is the thing that human nature trembles at – a creature invisible, yet with sensations, feelings, a power somehow of expressing itself.'[37] He returns with Bagley, his matter-of-fact butler, whose customary decorum is shattered by the wailing, the apparent knocking, before the vacant doorway in the old house, that potent symbol of the liminal.

Next morning, Simson, the doctor, is unequivocal. There is an 'epidemic' in the narrator's house: collective hysteria with 'delusion' at the bottom of it.[38] Nonetheless, he volunteers to go to the apparently haunted site that night, bringing with him 'his materialism, his scepticism':[39] those qualities which habitually stop spiritualist manifestations dead in their tracks. At first he is vindicated; then he starts to hear the voice – a child out late, he tries to maintain – sees before the door, as Bagley and the narrator did before him, something – a juniper bush. But the bush had formerly been on the other side. The next morning, in daylight, the mobile shrub is not there at all. Science being little help, the narrator turns to religion, in the form of Dr Moncrieff, the minister. The three once again return to the ruins of the old house, hear the voice: the minister talks to the low sobbing sound, addressing it as 'Willie', praying to the Lord to take him, like his mother, home – he then explains the story of the prodigal son of the ruin's former housekeeper, who had returned, distraught, to find his mother just dead. What gives the story its power, apart from the unravelling of a

mystery, the structure of which is itself dependent on the rhetorical underpinning given by a folkloric structuring of repetition, is
its coda, which transforms it from being just a tale of the exorcism
of an unhappy soul in which old-fashioned religion is given the
determinate power. Simson and the narrator subsequently visit
the ruin together, and find a little hole in the corner of the ruin,
containing a quantity of straw, and some crusts. Simson feels vindicated: he always believed what they experienced had been caused
by human agency; but he 'forgets, I suppose, how he and I stood
with our lights seeing nothing, while the space between us was
audibly traversed by something that could speak, and sob, and
suffer'.[40] More than that, there was the matter of the juniper bush,
which the narrator produces as a kind of trump card, both to
subdue the rationality of medical science, and to conclude the
story:

> To me that was a matter of little importance. I could believe it
> was mistaken. I did not care about it one way or other; but on his
> mind the effect was different. The miserable voice, the spirit in
> pain, he could think of as the result of ventriloquism, or reverber-
> ation, or – anything you please: an elaborate prolonged hoax exe-
> cuted somehow by the tramp that had found a lodging in the old
> tower. But the juniper-bush staggered him. Things have effects so
> different on the minds of different men.[41]

Visual evidence here takes on a powerful and paradoxical status.
Somehow more real, more plausible, than sound, it stands first as
evidence that the apparently supernatural can be explained away,
and then, when its own recollected movements defy such explanation, it takes up its role as a guarantor of the supernatural. Even in
the mind of the scientific sceptic, the bush's mobile materiality
seems to offer proof of the inexplicable.

One further factor about the narrator of this story should be
noted, together with the fact that Oliphant constructs a voice for
him which reveals that he is more rattled by his experience than he
wishes to own – he stays out the rental period for the property, but
does not renew it. That is the fact that he, and his 'shaken and
ghastly Bagley', who left his service as soon as he got well again,

had served in India. Whilst this fact is delivered up in the first sentence, almost nothing is made of it, other than the country being used to form a climatic contrast with the renovating Scottish environment: 'The warmth of Indian suns was still in our veins. It seemed to us that we could never have enough of the greenness, the dewiness, the freshness of the northern landscape. Even its mists were pleasant to us, taking all the fever out of us, and pouring in vigour and refreshment.'[42] The narrator nonetheless feels a certain pull to India still – or at least to 'the interests with which all his previous life has been associated'; calls himself 'an old Indian'. Perhaps his own bodily purging is not as complete, his veins not as replenished with the circulation of new blood and a new way of life, as at first he seems to wish to claim. It is certainly in his veins that, he said, he registered his son's disturbance. Might his earlier career, his service abroad, in fact have a bearing on how this story can be read, and how pressures on the mind, of an unconscious kind, may be understood as working?

I want to approach this question through examining another story from the same decade, in which medical scepticism again interacts with powerful hallucinatory experience. In Kipling's 'The Phantom 'Rickshaw' (1885), two explanations are offered near the beginning of the story for Pansay's death. The doctor, Heatherleigh, 'maintained that overwork' was responsible;[43] and laughs at the unnamed narrator's 'theory that there was a crack in Pansay's head and a little bit of the Dark World came through and pressed him to death'.[44] In the written version that Pansay leaves behind, he records how he was haunted by the spectre of a yellow panelled 'rickshaw pulled by four piebald horses, belonging to a Mrs Keith-Wessington, with whom he had unwisely become entangled on a voyage out to India, spent a season at Simla, and whom he had then tired of – to her dismay. He becomes engaged to a young woman; Mrs Wessington dies, yet keeps reappearing to Pansay around Simla, interfering with his new relationship, and yet somehow becoming more real than the 'impalpable fantastic shadows' of the other people around him,[45] to the extent that he becomes more comfortable in her presence: 'vaguely unhappy when I had been separated too long from my ghostly companion'.[46] Eventually Pansay sickens and himself dies, seeing his haunting and fatal illness as 'punishment'.[47] Certainly, this is one plausible interpretation for his hallucinations, if that is what they are: that he has suffered fatally as a result of the effect of his past actions on his guilty conscience, his imagination defying the rational organisation of space and time in a way which is simultaneously liberating and lethal.[48]

Alternatively, 'The Phantom 'Rickshaw' may be seen less as the drama of a split individual mind than as an enactment of what Zohreh Sullivan, in connection with Kipling's fiction, has called 'the symptomatic anxieties of colonialism'.[49] Not just Pansay's state of mental equilibrium is as stake, but the narrator may be seen as projecting his own fears, denials and repressions onto him, creating that disjuncture between the two parts of the story which occurs so frequently in Kipling's narratives about India – an 'unresolvable disturbance at the heart of the story'[50] which is marked by the slippage between two types of discourse: that which deals with the knowable, the masterable, and that which deals with the Other. The Other is simultaneously, therefore, the unconscious, the spirit world and the Unknowability of India. 'One of the few advantages that India has over England is a great Knowability',[51] the story opens, a comment which is so markedly ethnocentric, especially when set in its immediate context of the English community within the Empire, that its irony resonates throughout all that follows. One tool for accessing, or defining, knowledge which this story renders particularly inadequate is the professional language of physiology. Pansay points to an invisible It: Heatherleigh reacts: ' "*That* may be either DT or Eyes for aught I know. Now, you don't liquor. I saw as much at dinner, so it can't be DT. There's nothing whatever where you're pointing, though you're sweating and trembling with fright like a scared pony. Therefore, I conclude that it's Eyes" '[52] – a ' "spectral illusion" theory, implicating eyes, brain, and stomach',[53] which the doctor attempts to treat through liver-pills, cold-water baths and exercise. Neither mind, body nor the malaise of colonialism responds, however, to such a practical prescription. The ghost of Empire, the perturbation caused by the collision of different modes of understanding experience that the encounter with the Indian Other demands, cannot be exorcised here, any more than Oliphant's unnamed narrator may, in the long run, be said to be free of the legacy of his exposure to a non-British world. As unprovable as the presence or absence of the supernatural, this is the further ghost that hovers as an underpresence in 'The Open Door'.[54] It is another ghost that hangs around James's *The Turn of the Screw*, too: Miles and Flora were orphaned in India.

The question of cultural difference and alternative modes of seeing is one which surfaces in a late nineteenth-century craze which overlapped with the practice of spiritualism: crystal-gazing. Frank Dicksee, in *The Magic Crystal* (1894), captured the popular somewhat bohemian image of this practice when he depicted a woman in a flowing dress holding up a crystal ball (figure 53). The activity of crystal-gazing – or of gazing into other shiny surfaces – has a long and culture-crossing tradition, and Dicksee's dark-featured woman may be seen as potentially Oriental, exotic, and in herself bearer of nineteenth-century cultural clichés that constructed the Orient as 'a world elsewhere, apart from the ordinary attachments, sentiments and values of *our* world in the West'.[55] Andrew Lang

> found, by studying works of travel and anthropology, that many savage and barbarous races gaze into water, polished basalt crystals, and so on, for the purpose of seeing distant events, foreseeing the future, detecting criminals, and so forth. Polynesians, Hurons, Iroquois, Apaches, the Huille-che, the people of Madagascar, the Zulus, the Siberians, the people of Fez, the Arabs, the Australian black fellows, the Maoris, the Incas, not to forget the Hindoos, all unite in the same practice.[56]

The Egyptians practised the scrutiny of drops of ink, as Edward Lane investigated at some length in *Customs of the Modern Egyptians* (1833–5):[57] this is the power that the narrator seeks to co-opt in the service of historical fiction at the opening of *Adam Bede* ('With a single drop of ink for a mirror, the Egyptian sorcerer undertakes to reveal to any chance comer far-reaching visions of the past. This is what I undertake to do for you, reader').[58] A similar practice of interpreting images seen in lamp-black placed on the hand of a child seems to have been introduced into India by Muslims.[59] The

53 Frank Dicksee, *The Magic Crystal*, 1894. Oil on canvas, 165.1 × 99.06 cms.

Maori used to gaze into a drop of blood.[60] In Sarawak, the manang, or shaman, used *Batu ilan*, or *Batu enggan meda samengat* (quartz crystals), to view the condition of his patients' soul;[61] T. L. Mitchell, travelling in Australia in the 1830s, recorded how crystals for scrying were carried around by *coradjes*, who took care that no-one should see them unnecessarily (and women not at all);[62] there was, claimed D. G. Brinton, hardly a village in Mexico's Yucatan peninsula which did not have a sanctified bit of crystal or other translucent stone;[63] and Apache medicine men used crystals to recover lost property, especially ponies: 'Na-a-cha . . . could give no explanation except that by looking into it he could see everything he wanted to see.'[64] In Siberia, native peoples looked into water poured into a vessel to discover, among other things, what sacrifices the gods required;[65] Zulus revered a kind of Chief's vessel in which, when it was filled with water, they practised divination;[66] and in Ashango-Land, witch-doctors used a black earthenware vessel for the same purpose.[67] Thus seeing or summoning up images within glistening spheres may be related to the same fascination with the possibility that other cultures may see differently, or rather, that they may differ from Western modes of understanding and interpreting perception, that Kipling raises in some of his short fiction.

The potential of crystal-gazing's ability to produce powerful images is exploited by H. G. Wells's story, 'The Crystal Egg' (1897). The magic crystal of the story has its powers validated by the observations of a Mr Jacoby Wace, Assistant Demonstrator at a London hospital, even if its original location is among the bric-à-brac of a junk shop, the shabby proprietor of which, a Mr Cave, realises that he is in possession of an object with exceptional properties. This crystal egg, after a thin shaft of daylight has been shone upon it, glows luminously: more than that, Mr Cave notices that 'the crystal, being peered into at an angle of about 137 degrees from the direction of the illuminating ray' – Wells's matter-of-fact observational tone granting authority to the extraordinary – 'gave a clear and consistent picture of a wide and peculiar country-side. It was not dream-like at all; it produced a definite impression of reality'.[68] Mr Wace assured the narrator that Mr Cave's statements about what he saw 'were extremely circumstantial, and entirely free from any of that emotional quality that taints hallucinatory impressions',[69] which, in the absence of any dissenting opinion from the narrator himself, sets up the reader to believe that Cave actually did see in the crystal the scenes which are subsequently described: a plain bounded by reddish cliffs; terraced buildings with thickly vegetated terraces, and winged creatures flitting around, something like bats, something like cherubs, something like butterflies. It dawns on him, after seeing the stellar arrangement which was visible in the night sky from this other world, that he is looking at Mars. Moreover, Mars, or at least the Martians, are looking at him. For on the tops of masts are fixed large crystals, and into one of these a creature peers – seemingly, and disconcertingly, on one occasion looking straight back into Mr Cave's face:

> Unless we dismiss it all as the ingenious fabrication of Mr Wace, we have to believe one of two things: either that Mr Cave's crystal was in two worlds at once, and that, while it was carried about in one, it remained stationary in the other, which seems altogether absurd; or else that it had some peculiar relation of sympathy with another and exactly similar crystal in this other world, so that what was seen in the interior of the one in this world was, under suitable conditions, visible to an observer in the corresponding crystal in the other world; and *vice versa*. At present, indeed, we do not know of any way in which two crystals could so come *en rapport*, but nowadays we know enough to understand that the thing is not altogether impossible. This view of the crystal as *en rapport* was the supposition that occurred to Mr Wace, and to me at least it seems extremely plausible.[70]

These conclusions are reiterated at the end of the story, with the final and decisive comment: 'No theory of hallucination suffices for the facts.'[71]

This is not, of course, true. Andrew Lang, in *Cock Lane and Common-Sense* (1894), wrote of the revival of 'scrying', 'peeping' or 'crystal-gazing' in recent years. Some crystal-gazers, Lang notes, tended to fall back on spiritualist explanations. He particularly had Sophia de Morgan in mind: she, in *From Matter to Spirit* (1863), had written how as an explanation of crystal-seeing, 'a spiritual drawing was once made representing a spirit directing on the crystal a stream of influence, the rays of which seemed to be refracted, and then to converge again on the side of the glass sphere before they met the eye of the seer'.[72] This is a development of the answer she gave to the broader question 'How is vision produced?' – vision, that is, in the sense of manifestations of the world that is commonly unseen. Drawings in her text show a 'good spirit above' throwing their influence on the 'higher portions of the brain, namely, the organs of veneration, benevolence, ideality, and the intellectual portion', while the 'evil spirit, nearer to earth, is trying to mesmerise the base of the brain'.[73] Telepathic visions may be explained by the capacity of a spirit to send its influence into two individuals simultaneously. (figures 54 and 55). Lang, however, did not hold with such mysterious explanations. Rather, he takes crystal-gazing as an example of how

> a substratum of fact may be so overcrowded with mystic mummeries, incantations, fumigations, pentacles: and so overwhelmed in superstitious interpretations, introducing fairies and spirits, that the facts run the risk of being swept away in the litter and dust of nonsense. Science has hardly thought crystal-gazing worthy even of contempt, yet it appears to deserve the notice of psychologists.[74]

His description of those who make good crystal-gazers harks back, without making explicit reference, to Galton's vocabulary:

> A crystal-seer seems to be a person who can see, in a glass, while awake and with open eyes, visions akin to those which perhaps the majority of people see with shut eyes, between sleeping and waking. It seems probable that people who, when they think, see a mental picture on the subject of their thoughts, people who are good 'visualisers', are likely to succeed best with the crystal.[75]

He substantiates his conclusions by remarks made in the *Proceedings of the Society for Psychical Research* by a Miss X, who claims to have been able to see pictures in crystals and other polished surfaces since her childhood, and who believes that these are 'after-images, or recrudescent memories (often memories of things not consciously noted)', 'objectivations of ideas or images, consciously or unconsciously present to the mind', and – as a third and, to Lang's mind, decidedly least convincing option – visions, perhaps telepathic or clairvoyant, 'implying acquirement of knowledge by supernormal means'.[76] For him, the answer is a simple one: 'the unconscious self suggests the pictures in the ball'. Such a conclusion was supported by Edmund Parish, in his comprehensive study *Hallucinations and Illusions* (1897), where he attributes the capacities of the crystal-gazer to their ability to access what is 'latent in the percipient's *subliminal* consciousness'.[77]

As well as exploiting a contemporary craze for scrutinising images produced in the mind's eye, Wells's story may be seen as engaging with visuality in another of its aspects: the production of concrete images, visual metaphors, in which to convey the understanding of abstract concepts – in other words, scientific modelling. For 'The Crystal Egg' is one of his fictions in which he explores the possibility of the Fourth Dimension. This concept is most vividly outlined at the opening of *The Time Machine*, where it provides the pre-conditions for time travel on which the apparent plausibility of the tale depends. The Time Traveller expounds on the three dimensions of space – length, breadth, thickness – and the further dimension of time, or duration. He attempts to concretise this: 'You know how on a flat surface, which has only two dimensions, we can represent a figure of a three-dimensional solid, and similarly [some philosophical people] think that by models of three dimensions they could represent one of four – if they could master the perspective of the thing. See?'[78] Effectively, the whole narrative of *The Time Machine* is an allegory of the principle of the Fourth Dimension, designed to make the reader 'see' (whilst simultaneously raising questions of history, degeneration, human will to power, and the principles which drive social organisations and determine their collapse or survival over time).

Whilst the idea of a geometry of more than three dimensions can be traced back to D'Alembert's article on 'Dimension' in Diderot's *Encyclopédie*, and serious interest in it had been growing

54 and 55
'Mediumship –
Modes of
Influence'.
Illustrations to
Sophia de Morgan,
From Matter to Spirit,
1863.

throughout the nineteenth century, Wells's fascination with the concept seems to depend on the work of the American, Simon Newcomb (who is referred to at the opening of 'The Time Machine'), and Charles Hinton.[79] Hinton, in his essay 'What is the Fourth Dimension?', which appeared in his two-volume *Scientific Romances* (1884–5), asks the reader to visualise first three dimensions, and then four, by a complicated set of mental manoeuvres involving imagining sheets of paper, first flat, then overlain, then folded.[80] Some would doubtless have had better luck in carrying out these mental gymnastics than others: Galton reported how 'a few persons can, by what they often describe as a kind of touch-sight, visualise at the same moment all round the image of a solid body'.[81]

Wells explored this idea in another work of 1895, 'The Remarkable Case of Davidson's Eyes'. Davidson, a scientist

55

colleague of the narrator's at Harlow Technical College – as with
the assemblage of professional men at the opening of *The Time
Machine*, as with Mr Wace's position, the scientific materialist
setting is part of Wells's rhetoric of credibility – is suddenly found
blundering around the lab, running violently and undeliberately
into a big electromagnet, claiming to see a beach, some shells, a
ship rounding the headland, stranded, or so he believes, on an

island, deserted apart from the penguins who walk straight through him. He travels down into the weedy, luminous purple-red depths of the sea. Gradually, these visions and his blindness to the actual world start to fade. For a while, they blend surrealistically into one another – 'these two pictures overlapping each other like the changing views of a lantern',[82] writes Wells, invoking the language of Victorian optical toys – until the shadowy other world fades away. A couple of years later, it emerges that what he saw, what he experienced, was the landing of a ship named the *Fulmar* on an island in the South Seas, which had been co-terminous with his strange hallucinatory experience. 'It's perhaps the best authenticated case in existence of real vision at a distance', says the narrator of this fictional tale.[83] He invokes the explanation of a Professor Wade, although he is sceptical about theoretical space:

> To talk of there being 'a kink in space' seems mere nonsense to me; it may be because I am no mathematician. When I said that nothing would alter the fact that the place is ten thousand miles away, he answered that two points might be a yard away on a sheet of paper, and yet be brought together by bending the paper round. The reader may grasp his argument, but I certainly do not. His idea seems to be that Davidson, stooping between the poles of the big electromagnet, had some extraordinary twist given to his retinal elements through the sudden change in the field of force due to the lightning.
>
> He thinks, as a consequence of this, that it may be possible to live visually in one part of the world, while one lives bodily in another.

But, says the narrator: 'the whole of his theory seems fantastic to me. The facts concerning Davidson stand on an altogether different footing, and I can testify personally to the accuracy of every detail I have given.'[84]

Since the narrator manifestly is *not* Davidson himself, this is in itself a slightly troubling statement: he can attest, indeed, to Davidson's bemused and clumsy actions under the influence of his visual experience, and can report what Davidson claims that he saw. What, though, constitutes 'accuracy' under these circumstances, for which, indeed, the narrator offers no alternative explanation to counteract the notion that Davidson somehow found himself inhabiting the Fourth Dimension?[85] Although this story is not strictly speaking a ghost story, the irresolvable tension which it throws up between scientific explanation and some kind of alternative reasoning is not dissimilar.

There is, however, a twist. For in 'The Remarkable Case of Davidson's Eyes', the matter-of-fact solution would seem to lie in the idea that Davidson was somehow or another hallucinating, that he was experiencing mental instability, and that some extraordinary coincidence – not dissimilar to the experience of ghost-seeing, or materialisation, that was allegedly shared by countless sympathetic participants in apparently supernatural episodes – was responsible for the overlap in his account and that given by the Royal Navy lieutenant who confirms that Davidson's account tallies with his own South Seas sojourn among the penguins. In this story, it is science that seems far-fetched, rather than the circumstantial overlapping, the coincidences, found in two people's anecdotes, with the resulting unsettling metaphysical overtones.

Yet, like 'The Time Machine', however improbable the whole story, it serves as an embodiment of abstract theory, an opportunity for the reader to envision, in their own mind's eye, how the concept of the Fourth Dimension might be understood to exist. Once again, the binary between the visible and the invisible, between the material and the imaginary, has been called into question. Moreover, this unstable borderland, evoked within fiction, dependent upon recent scientific development, not only collapses disciplinary divisions: it indicates that the cost of such a collapse may be the destabilisation of the reader's own position, their own confident belief in what is real and what is not. This is the process of destabilisation on which successful ghost stories depend, but what these scientific tales also demonstrate is that the suspension of disbelief inherent in that genre is also, potentially, a necessary component of intellectual inquiry.

Theoretical speculation, whether in mathematics or physics, has always something of risk-taking about it, not least since it involves the projection of individual desire. 'The driest argument has its hallucinations, too hastily concluding that its net will now be large enough to hold the universe', comments George Eliot in *Daniel Deronda*: 'Men may dream in demonstrations, and cut out an illusory world in the shape of axioms, definitions, and propositions, with a final exclusion of fact signed QED.' However, she continues:

> No formulas for thinking will save us mortals from mistake in our imperfect apprehension of the matter to be thought about. And since the unemotional intellect may carry us into a mathematical dreamland where nothing is but what is not, perhaps an emotional intellect may have absorbed into its passionate vision of possibilities some truth of what will be – the more comprehensive massive life feeding theory with new material, as the sensibility of the artist seizes combinations which science explains and justifies.[86]

The whole question of hallucination and vision raises issues which slide between the different disciplines. The uncertainties that are thrown up in scientific contexts concerning what may be said to be 'true' and what not – for what kind of validity is possessed by that which an individual sees inwardly? – find their correlations in stories of the supernatural which refuse easy explanation, paintings which are deliberately ambiguous about the status and identity of the apparently visible.[87] By the closing decades of the nineteenth century, the borders between the visible and the invisible worlds were increasingly hazy. The mediating concept which linked the two, which could allow one to hypothesise about the uncertainties and variables of many types of perception, was that of the unconscious. Psychoanalysis, with its capacity to take the imagined, the fantasised, the dreamed, the intangible world as seriously as the empirical one, came to offer new forms of narrating and understanding the interactions of the unseen and the seen.[88]

Conclusion. The Victorian horizon

In John Everett Millais's painting of 1870, *The Boyhood of Raleigh* (figure 56), a swarthy, tanned sailor points energetically towards the horizon. The eyes of one of the small boys are fixed intently on him; those of the other, Raleigh himself, are directed more downwards, suggesting an inward, imaginative visualisation of the sailor's words. In his mind's eye, he sees, to quote a contemporary commentator, F. G. Stephens, 'El Dorado, and the palaces of Aztecs and Incas, temples of the sun, where the sun's face burns in gold; hidden treasures, fair Indian captives, and the fountains of eternal youth'.[1] On the left of the picture, a toy sailing ship, placed on the same diagonal as the sailor's outstretched arm, suggests how childhood enthusiasms, mediated through the narratives and inspiration of the sailor, will be transformed into adult exploration, action, adventure. The red ensign on this ship signals its Englishness; the strange feathered cap, and the exotic plumage of a dead bird behind the sailor, represent the cultural and natural trophies awaiting the voyager across the ocean.

The horizon, in this painting, marks a boundary, between sea and sky, between the visible, material world and the ether. 'Horizon' from the Greek ορίξων: a bounding circle, a demarcation, a limitation, an ending, the present participle of ορίξειν: to bound. That sailor's pointing finger, however, is carefully positioned just above the dark blue of the sea so that it indicates the apparently limitless possibilities that lie just beyond the reach of sight. The horizon, in other words, marks not just the edge of the visible, but suggests futurity, the space into which the imagination

56 John Everett Millais, *The Boyhood of Raleigh*, 1870. Oil on canvas, 120.65 × 142.24 cms.

and inner vision may travel: it connotes expansiveness. The horizon suggests empty space: that which, as Henri Lefebvre puts it in *The Production of Space*, 'unleashes desire. It presents desire with a "transparency" which encourages it to surge forth in an attempt to lay claim to an apparently clear field.'[2] The existence of a horizon brings together space and temporality: the reach of the gaze and the desire to see beyond its physical limitations. This is the concept dramatised in Stanhope Forbes's *The Seine Boat* (1904) (figure 57), where what the men in the boat look eagerly towards is only a blank, outside the material horizon of the picture frame, for the spectator to conjure with.

What is more, this potential for expansiveness goes on and on. For, as Cornelius Van Peursen has written, 'the really striking fact about the horizon is that it recedes':[3] it is always there, temptingly, far ahead of us. This phenomenon is invoked in a double way in the

57 Stanhope
Alexander Forbes,
The Seine Boat, 1904.
Oil on canvas,
114 × 157.5 cms.

best-known of all Victorian poetic horizons, when Tennyson's
Ulysses, the ocean's rim before him, links his specific voyaging
project to the wish to make one's life a continuing process of exploration, even against the odds of age and physical weariness: 'all
experience is an arch wherethrough / Gleams that untravelled
world, whose margin fades / For ever and for ever when I move'.[4]
The horizon is only to be perceived as a limitation if we do not
move ourselves, for its existence is dependent upon on our own
capacities for perception. It has no independent, objective existence apart from the rôle it plays within the human gaze. It is this
fact – that the concept of the horizon simultaneously signifies out
there, away from us, somewhere towards which we might reach,
and yet also is something that is indivisible from our individual
physical and conceptual faculties, that makes it such an ideal trope
through which to examine Victorian attitudes towards the visual,
towards the practice of seeing. For, like the very idea of 'sight', the
idea of the horizon is at once material, and figurative. Whilst the

horizon has a visible presence, marking the rim of the world, the limit of one's sight, it may also be invoked metaphorically, to signify the excitement of unfolding interpretive possibilities: exploration in a theoretical, as well as a topographical, sense.

In Millais's painting, the focus is primarily on the geographical implications of travelling towards the horizon, even if one critic saw a further and more personal point in the artist having chosen two of his own sons as models, and painting them 'with all the charm and pride of a devoted father who projects great things for his offspring'.[5] The subject was suggested to Millais by his reading of the historian J. A. Froude's *English Worthies*. Froude, in his copious writings, constantly emphasised the connection between England's 'watery dominion' and her imperial and expansionist power. 'Take away her merchant fleets,' he wrote, 'take away the navy that guards them: her empire will come to an end; her colonies will fall off, like leaves from a withered tree; and Britain will become once more an insignificant island in the North Sea, for the future students in Australian and New Zealand universities to discuss the fate of in their debating societies.'[6] The colonies, of course, were particularly identified with horizonal, forward-looking movement: 'There', wrote J. R. Seeley in *The Expansion of England* in (1881–2), 'you have the most progressive race put in the circumstances most favourable to progress. They have no past and an unbounded future', unlike India with its troubling weight of history, the 'vistas' it 'opens . . . into a fabulous antiquity'.[7] Millais's celebration of Britain's maritime importance, its hunger for over-seas conquest, possession and expansion, as represented by this popular painting, was among the factors serving to establish him as a quintessentially patriotic painter by the end of the Victorian period: his 'Art was wholly fervently British', claimed James Harlaw in *The Charm of Millais* (1913): '– direct, simple and sponta-neous . . . His nationality was a halo around the man: his patriotism the spirit of his life. "Made in Britain", is written in golden letters over all his work.'[8] It is no surprise that he chose the detail of the pointing sailor for the cover of his book on the artist (figure 58).[9]

The Boyhood of Raleigh, with its patriotic message and its assumption that the experience of one generation can form the

58 Cover of James Harlaw, *The Charm of Millais*, 1913.

59 James Clarke
Hook, *Hearts of
Oak*, 1875. Oil on
canvas,
95.25 × 143.51 cms.,
Castle Museum,
Nottingham.

ambitions of the next, had a successor in James Clarke Hook's *Hearts of Oak* (1875) (figure 59). Here, the sailor whittles away at a toy boat, watched avidly by his son and by his supportive wife. Behind, the sea stretches away into a bright horizon, the spectator's eyes drawn towards it both by its lustre, and by the way it balances the activity in the opposite corner of the canvas. The directing of our own gaze towards this horizon thus encompasses the mobility and futurity embodied in the expanse of empty sea. Here, however, the horizon also functions as a deliberate limiting line, a safe enclosure around the family and the country, to which their domestic unity stands in a metonymic relation. For the patriotic underpinning of this picture comes not just from its title, drawing on the nationalistic maritime cliché formulated by David Garrick in his song 'Heart of Oak' –

'Heart of Oak are our ships,
Heart of Oak are our Men,
We always are ready,
Steady! Boys! Steady!
We'll fight and we'll conquer again and again'[10]

60 William Gale,
The Convalescent,
1868. Oil on panel,
29 × 43 cms.

but from the Shakespearean lines appended to it when it was exhibited at the Royal Academy: 'that England, hedged in with the main, / That water-walled bulwark, still secure / And confident from foreign purposes'.[11]

A horizon can function as a line of limitation. In terms of pictorial perspective, a high horizon, without diagonals stretching out towards it, serves as a kind of wall, enclosing the subject and concentrating the viewer's attention onto the specifics of a scene. For all the redemptive possibility inherent in the subject-matter of Holman Hunt's *The Scapegoat* (figure 12), the firm high line of enclosing arid mountains has the effect of pulling the spectator's eye back to the earthly suffering of the miserable animal. More ambiguous are the rocks and cliffs of William Gale's *The Convalescent* (figure 60). Again, the dark masses draw one towards the family group, as the husband's anxious gaze, near the painting's centre, makes one focus on his pallid wife. Her own eyes, however, look outwards, past her daughter, to an imaginary horizon, the correlative of which is the stretch of sea leading out towards the right of the canvas: something which might be seen in terms of futurity, a life-line, or which could equally well be seen as a blank expanse. Differently again, in Leighton's *Flaming June* (figure 61), the high

61 Frederick
Leighton, *Flaming
June*, c. 1895. Oil on
canvas, 119 × 119 cms.

horizon pitches the viewer forwards into a consideration of a figure's interiority. Here, although the sun burns dazzlingly into the sea, drawing our attention momentarily towards this luminosity, it has no narrative or temporal suggestivity other than to provide a contrast with the reverie or dream that may be taking place within this narcoleptic body, watched over by a sign of the underworld, the aloe. Her voyaging is to be inward, downward: something which in a broader sense serves to confine the woman as a thoroughly passive object of the gaze, an aesthetic celebration of her beauty in stasis. This may be read as an anxious risposte to the way that upper- and middle-class women's horizons were figuratively expanding during the latter decades of the century. For a woman to launch herself on such seas of self discovery and social adventuring was a risky act of exposure. Edith Nesbit, in her 1889 poem 'Under Convoy', seems to figure such perilous exploration as foolhardy, setting up a woman who tries to do 'the work that I cannot – ':

> As a swimmer alone in mid-ocean
>   Breasts wave after green wave, until
> He sees the horizon unbroken
>   By any coast-line – so I still
> Swam blindly through life, not perceiving
>   The infinite stretch of life's ill.
>
> But wave after wave crowds upon me –
>   I am tired, I can face them no more –
> Let me sink – or not sink – you receive me,
>   And I rest in your arms as before.

The speaker pleads to the man to hold her, kiss her, provide a leaning post for her: he offers, he thinks, 'a haven . . . for the storm-blown and tossed'. The poem pivots, however: to rest safe is to make the ignoble choice: if 'you save me my ease as a woman . . . the life of a soul is the cost!'[12] To turn away from the horizon is an act of cowardice, denying the promise of the unknown offered by the 'infinite stretch', and retreating, fearfully, into the known.

Certainly, the horizon can suggest frightening as well as liberating space. Arnold's 'Sea of Faith' no longer stretches out into a comfortable curved plenitude, though once it 'at the full, around earth's shore / Lay like the folds of a bright girdle furl'd'. Rather, the axis has shifted, and Arnold has substituted medieval mapping, in all its suggestive flatness, for the continuity suggested by a spherical shape. This horizon cannot go on and on, but must give way to desolation, emptiness and the limits beyond which there is an utter void: the sea's 'long, withdrawing roar' retreats 'down the vast edges drear / And naked shingles of the world'.[13] Arnold moves from the visual to the auditory in terms of figuring his own bleak interiority, which in part evades the problems of representing a curveless earth. It also stresses the way his crisis of belief and purpose is turned in upon himself, the reverse of Tennyson's thumpingly optimistic rhetoric in 'Locksley Hall', where the speaker 'dipt into the future as far as the human eye could see, / Saw the vision of the world, and all the wonder that could be'.[14] For all its retrogressive cartography, however, this is still a post-Romantic poem with Arnold employing the rhetoric of the sublime, his language diminishing the human figure in relation to natural forces, whilst ensuring that the landscape is not divisible from its responses.

The capacity to shrink the individual in his or her importance is a central characteristic of the horizon's power. This power can be a thoroughly beneficial one. Thus, in *Middlemarch*, Dorothy famously faces a new day with optimism, after spending an introspective night considering her feelings towards Ladislaw and Rosamond. Looking out of the window, 'far off in the bending sky was the pearly light; and she felt the largeness of the world and the manifold wakings of men to labour and endurance'.[15] The horizon has been co-opted into Eliot's perennial solution for personal troubles: placing them in a larger context of forward-looking human duty. Arnold's fearful reaction to the imagined edges of the world, and the retreat into selfhood – or at best, by the end of the poem into a slightly shaky coupledom – which it induces, is in contrast to Charles Darwin, who, at the end of *The Voyage of the Beagle*, asks why it should be that the plains of Patagonia have taken such a firm hold on his visual memory, unlike, say, the green and more fertile Pampas? What is the appeal of these arid wastes? He answers himself by saying that:

> it must be partly owing to the free scope given to the imagination. The plains of Patagonia are boundless, for they are scarcely passable, and hence unknown: they bear the stamp of having lasted, as they are now, for ages, and there appears no limit to their duration through future time. If, as the ancients supposed, the flat earth was surrounded by an impassable breadth of water, or by deserts heated to an intolerable excess, who would not look at these last boundaries to man's knowledge with deep but ill-defined sensations.[16]

I shall be returning to the relationship between the horizon and the search for knowledge and understanding. I want to pause here, however, on two, linked types of stimulus which it offers the imagination.

In the first place, the horizon's stretch offers the type of pleasure set out by the narrator of Shelley's 'Julian and Maddalo', who rides out 'one evening with Count Maddalo / Upon the bank of land which breaks the flow / Of Adria towards Venice' (lines 1–3). Positioned, if we visualise this, on what would mark the horizon for an observer of the scene, he himself looks towards the thin line which divides land and air, and comments on the scene's effects:

> I love all waste
> And solitary places; where we taste
> The pleasure of believing what we see
> Is boundless, as we wish our souls to be. (lines 14–17)

This type of pleasure has a dimension which we may characterise as spiritual. For, in general terms, the horizon powerfully participates in the paradoxical metaphysics of the infinite. This is recognised by Ruskin when, in the second volume of *Modern Painters*, he discusses the 'pure' emotion he first felt when a child 'running down behind the banks of a high beach to get their land line cutting against the sky': an emotion stimulated by the sight of 'a light distance appearing over a comparatively dark horizon'. However much pleasure we may receive from the effects of light on foreground objects – like dew on grass, or the glitter of a birch trunk – 'there is yet a light which the eye invariably seeks with a deeper feeling of the beautiful, – the light of the declining or breaking day, and the flakes of scarlet cloud burning like watch-fires in the green sky of the horizon; a deeper feeling, I say, not perhaps more acute, but having more of spiritual hope and longing'. The aesthetic effects, according to Ruskin, which create this are not attributable to fine form, for the light above the horizon blurs the outlines of things on the ground; nor is the wan and dying light at the day's end conducive to 'sensual colour-pleasure'. There is one thing, however, which this light

62 John Martin, *The Plains of Heaven*, 1853. Oil on canvas, 78 × 120 ins.

has, or suggests, which no other object of sight suggests in equal degree, and that is – Infinity. It is of all visible things the least material, the least finite, the farthest withdrawn from the earth prison-house, the most typical of the nature of God, the most suggestive of the glory of His dwelling-place. For the sky of night, though we may know it boundless, is dark; it is a studded vault, a roof that seems to shut us in and down; but the bright distance has no limit, we feel its infinity, as we rejoice in its purity of light.[17]

This purity of light folding away into infinity is the effect chosen by John Martin in *The Plains of Heaven* (1853) (figure 62), as ever, in Martin's paintings of futurity, underpinned by the claim made in *Paradise Lost* that beyond this transient world 'is all abyss / Eternity, whose end no eye can reach'.[18] It is used to a consolatory, even inspirational effect, a visualisation of what a belief in an afterlife could give one. For the sensations which the contemplation of the horizon evokes are intimately bound up with the question of mortality, of individual endings. The horizon, through its very infinity, has the capacity to remind us of our own finitude, of the fact that, to quote the philosopher A. W. Moore, 'we are part of a world which is radically independent of us and which we can only ever glimpse from one particular point of view' – however much, we might add, this point of view is itself capable of shifting. This, he says, is an apprehension far more 'primordial than the fact that we have edges, even the temporal edges of birth and death . . . We feel pressure to acknowledge the infinite, and we feel pressure not to. In trying to come to terms with the infinite, we are in effect trying to come to terms with a basic conflict in ourselves.'[19] This, at base, is the conflict between the fact that it would not be good never to die – to be stuck, like Tithonus, with 'cruel', endless immortality[20] – and the fact that nonetheless it is never good to die.

Thus, whilst the horizon can suggest the wonder of eternity, too much of it, unrelieved, can mean monotony and tedium. Hence the relief of Louisa Clifton, writing in her *Journal* as the *Barque Parkfield* approached Australia, that her 'sickening longing' had been relieved: 'there in the far horizon, in the grey colouring of coming twilight, loomed the faint outline of our adopted land';[21] hence the exhausted visual senses of travellers on the American prairies, in desert landscapes and on the Australian plains. Robert Louis Stevenson wrote of the plains of Nebraska as presenting a 'world almost without a feature', apart from the railway which 'stretched from horizon to horizon, like a cue across a billiard-board'. Settlers there, having made 'this discovery of the whole arch of heaven, this straight, unbroken, prison-line of the horizon' were unsettled by the fact that there is no rest or shelter for the eye, were tortured by distance. They needed to rush into their cabins and find repose in things close at hand: 'Hence, I am told, a sickness of the vision peculiar to these empty plains.'[22] 'The eye becomes fatigued with so extensive a view, bounded only by the level horizon', complained William Henry Breton, travelling near the Liverpool Ranges, in the 1830s,[23] and Paul Carter, in *The Road to Botany Bay*, writes about the importance of the vertical, and of the tree in particular, to those suffering 'vertical deprivation' in inland Australia: of its connection to a sense of community and of human mastery over space.[24] Self-assertion over the loneliness of the infinite horizon is a means of differentiating oneself against one's surroundings and their metaphysical implications. The horizon cannot perpetuate its spiritually uplifting properties without being brought into dialogue with the varied visual attributes of the material world: without the eye retreating from the search for the absolute to look around the more immediate location of its possessor.

The second type of stimulus offered to the imagination by the horizon is less paradoxical: it is an aesthetic gratification, without the theological underpinning given by Ruskin. Whilst, like the first, it diminishes the individual in terms of their worldly importance, this is not necessarily a troubling experience. Again, the legacy of the Romantic sublime suffuses early and mid-Victorian representations of the visually and emotionally pleasurable horizon, wherever it may be encountered. Joanna Baillie may at one level be recording the appalling pollution caused by coal dust in the air of 'England's vast capital', which forms its own horizon blotting out the line of the Surrey hills, 'a curtain'd gloom / Connecting heaven and earth', but simultaneously and explicitly she employs the word 'sublime' to describe these effects, which add to the impression of awe created by 'this grand imperial town'.[25] The sublime provides the verbal filter through which 'Australie' describes:

> An inland sea of mountains, stretching far
> In undulating billows, deeply blue,
> With here and there a gleaming crest of rock,
> Surging in stillness, fading into space,
> Seeming more liquid in the distance vague,
> Transparent melting, till the last faint ridge
> Blends with clear ether in the azure sky
> In tender mauve unrealness; the dim line
> Of mountain profile seeming but a streak
> Of waving cloud on the horizon's verge.[26]

If this writing looks back to Wordsworth, to the ways in which he used images of mist and light in his poetry to break down the eye's search for boundaries, it also looks forward to a modernist preoccupation with the sea. This preoccupation is not with that High Victorian space of national exploration so much as with the space of contemplation opened up by the sea's vastness. Rosalind Krauss has argued, in *The Optical Unconscious*, that the sea 'is a special kind of medium for modernism, because of its perfect isolation, its detachment from the social, its sense of self-enclosure, and, above all, its opening into a visual plenitude that is somehow heightened and pure, both a limited expanse and a sameness, flattening it into nothing, into the no-space of sensory deprivation'.[27] This is the space, or no-space, offered by Conrad's horizons, which have both a literal and a figurative significance in his fictions. In *Lord Jim*, for example, Jim recounts what he saw after the *Patna* jolted and tilted: 'I could see the line of the horizon before me, as clear as a bell, above her stem-head; I could see the water far off there black and sparkling.'[28] Perhaps that verbal jolt between visual phenomenon and auditory simile – 'as clear as a bell' – ought to alert one to Jim's capacity for failing to match perception and comprehension. This has already been hinted at when we learn that 'the circular stillness of water and sky' gave him the kind of 'certitude of unbounded safety and peace' that was 'like the certitude of fostering love upon the placid tenderness of a mother's face':[29] a misplaced confidence for a sailor to adopt, and one which, if one considers the range of infant vision and concentration, implies a metaphoric shortsightedness on Jim's part. This balances his inability to choose an appropriate focus when actually gazing out to sea, when his 'eyes roaming about the line of the horizon, seemed to gaze hungrily into the unattainable, and did not see the shadow of the coming event'.[30] After the ship lurches, before he jumps, Jim has no problem in making out what is bearing down on the *Patna*:

> a silent black squall which had eaten up already one-third of the sky. You know how these squalls come up there about that time of the year. First you see a darkening of the horizon – no more; then a cloud rises opaque like a wall. A straight edge of vapour lined with sickly whitish gleams flies up from the southwest, swallowing the stars in whole constellations; its shadow flies over the waters, and confounds sea and sky into one abyss of obscurity.[31]

What counts is not the fact of his perception, but his response to it: a cowardly response – by one set of standards; an understandable act of self-preservation, by another: a choice which when Marlow comes to attempt to comprehend it ensures that he, as he put it, 'strained my mental eyesight'.[32] For what Jim's action does is to reveal the horizons of his own capacities, his fallibility, his limitations. The sense that each individual, whatever their idealism, may have such limitations is a major topos explored by the novel. When the elderly merchant Stein talks to Marlow about Jim, and about life more generally, about the importance of following one's dream as a successful code by which to live – in a sentence which tails off, tellingly, into the distance of inconclusive contemplation created by ellipses – Marlow describes how 'the whisper of his conviction seemed to open before me a vast and uncertain expanse, as of a crepuscular horizon on a plain at dawn – or was it, perchance, at the coming of night? . . . a charming and deceptive light, throwing the impalpable poesy of its dimness over pitfalls'.[33] Space, within *Lord Jim*, is interchangeably inner and outer, topographical and psychological.

This, of course, could be said to be true of the cultural representation of space throughout the Victorian period. I want to argue, however, that focussing on the idea of the horizon provides us with a means in which we can trace a shift in the relationship of the individual to such representations of space, which in turn is analogous to the changing ways in which visual perception came to be understood and problematised. The role of subjectivity, of inwardness, came increasingly to be stressed. Along with this came an increasing articulation of the fact that one must consider the physiological as well as the psychological dimensions of seeing. This development can usefully be illustrated by juxtaposing Turner and Whistler, two painters who manipulated the lure of the crepuscular, uncertain horizon in their works. The confounding of sea and sky of which Conrad writes describes well the effects to be found in earlier cultural productions, the later paintings of Turner. These offer a visual mediation between the Romantic and the modernist treatments of the sea, and the role played by the horizon within these: a horizon which is not so much a clear line between land and sea, but a vanishing point, or a succession of points, towards which the eye is led. In their fascination with the power of light, their

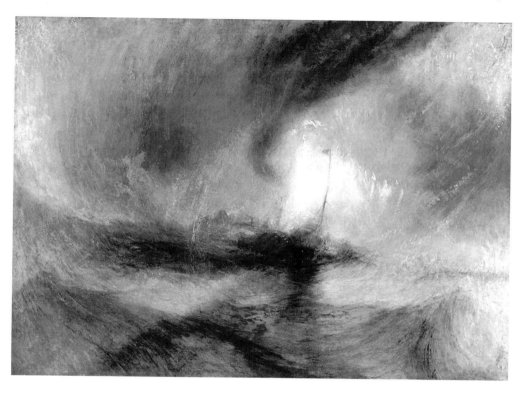

63 Joseph William Mallord Turner, *Snowstorm: Steam-boat off a Harbour's Mouth*, 1840. Oil on canvas, 91.5 × 122 cms.

denial of the bounding line, their refusal of limitations, achieved not just through the fluidity of the paint work but through the fact that they are structured around colour, rather than clear linear perspectives, these paintings present a sublime version of nature powered by energies both dangerous and awe-inspiring, as seen in the whirling vortices of *Snowstorm: Steam-boat off a Harbour's Mouth* (figure 63). In other paintings, such as *Ulysses Deriding Polyphemus* (figure 64), the menace of a fear-enducing horizon that fades off into ominous, potentially stormy and destructive darkness is paired with the suggestion of a more glorious, less turbulent future: a duality which, to quote Karl Kroeber, 'recalls the Romantic insistence on the provisionality characterizing the inexhaustible phenomena of the natural world to which humankind must accommodate itself'.[34] Furthermore, the importance of Turner's treatment of the indefinite horizon lies in the way in which it positions – or, it might be more apt to say, unsettles – the spectator, and causes one to reflect upon the very process of

64 Joseph William Mallord Turner, *Ulysses Deriding Polyphemus*, 1829. Oil on canvas, 132.5 × 203 cms.

perception. If Turner's later painting represents, as it surely does, an unfinished dialogue between artist and subject matter[35] – something exemplified by his frequent return to Norham Castle, his many reworkings of the *Fall of the Clyde*, his fascination with Venice and his endless experimentation with the sea – it also may be seen as suggesting an ongoing dialogue between spectator and canvas.

Turner's early work, in the late eighteenth-century topographic tradition, firmly places the viewer, statically, somewhere in front of the picture space, in a position which can be determined by following forwards the receding lines of the linear perspective. Such a construction of a vantage point, however, fails in front of a work like *Yacht Approaching the Coast* (c. 1835–40) (figure 65), not just because of the absence of architectural structure, or even the diagonal of a sloping beach, but because the hazy treatment of light allows no easy purchase on the depth of field. As we concentrate on the differing details – the sails, the buildings on the shoreline – what we become aware of is not so much our imagined presence within a scene, but our experience as viewers of a painting, the motion of our own eyes. The *activity* of looking takes precedence over interpretive questions concerning representation.

65 Joseph William Mallord Turner, *Yacht Approaching the Coast, c.* 1835–40. Oil on canvas, 102 × 142 cms.

Yet the intensity with which Turner invests natural forces makes it impossible to ignore his simultaneous appeal to a spectator's more traditional emotional response of human diminution in the face of the sublime. By the time Whistler was painting his *Nocturnes*, in the 1870s, the insistent tug into the depth of the painted space provided by a radiant sun burning into the horizon, or the vortex of a storm, is replaced by a self-conscious awareness, on the painter's part, that he is inviting the spectator to witness the manipulation of paint upon a flat canvas surface (figures 66 and 67). His crepuscular horizons in part result from a form of mimesis, conveying the sensations created by particular light effects in a particular location at a particular time of day. They are also deliberately suggestive through their employment of banks and washes of colour, their orchestration of tonalities, making demands on the viewer's subjectivity, associationism, and awareness of parallelism with other aesthetic forms. Moreover, as Julia Kristeva remarks in *Desire in Language*, colours 'have a non-centered or decentering effect, lessening both object identification and

66 James Abbott
McNeill Whistler,
*Nocturne: Grey and
Silver*, 1873–5.
Oil on canvas,
31.1×51.7 cms.

phenomenal fixation'.[36] Rather than recreating in the spectator the experience of self-diminishing awe which can be incorporated into the aesthetics of the sublime, these canvases invite a more individualised, interiorised personal response.[37] They use that which is outside oneself to focus the attention back on the self: the self both as a source of subjectivity, in its psychological dimension, and as the possessor of a pair of mobile eyes, in its physiological one.

The activity of the eye which Whistler's *Nocturnes* demand is not the scanning motion with which one assesses the narrative and moral connections to be drawn between the signifying objects in a mid-Victorian crowded domestic scene, such as Martineau's *The Last Day in the Old Home* (figure 38), or with which one reads the physiognomies and sartorial codes which produce the social and character juxtapositions of Frith's *The Railway Station* (figure 41). In relation to these paintings, the eye moves from right to left and along diagonals, in a manner analogous to perusing the printed page. Looking at one of Whistler's canvases, however, necessitates the expansion and contraction of the focal gaze. The act of spectatorship involved in approaching the paintings of Whistler's mid-career dramatises the double way – psychological and physiological – in which the issue of visuality was being problematised by the later decades of the nineteenth century. This is the period that

67 James Abbott
McNeill Whistler,
*Nocturne: Blue and
Silver – Cremorne
Lights*, 1872. Oil on
canvas,
50.2 × 74.3 cms.

marked the shift from the humanistic, and morally tinged,
Ruskinian emphasis – 'You do not see *with* the lens of the eye. You
see *through* that, and by means of that, but you see with the soul of
the eye'[38] – to an acknowledgement of the role which that lens has
to play in the whole system of perception. It was a period when, to
quote Krauss again, thanks to the work of 'great physiologists like
Fechner, Young, Helmholtz, Hering . . . The two planes – that of the
retinal field and that of the picture – were understood now to be iso-
morphic with one another, the laws of the first generating both
the logic and the harmonic of the order of the second; and both
of these fields – the retinal and the pictorial – unquestionably
organized as flat.'[39]

   Like spectatorship, the horizon itself is, as we have noted, a
double phenomenon – separate from the self, away from us, and
hence the focus of our desires, sometimes our fears; representing a
future towards which we move. Horizon, vision, subjectivity:
these come together in Hardy's observation in *Far from the Madding
Crowd* that 'in making even horizontal and clear inspections we
colour and mould according to the wants within us whatever our

eyes bring in'.[40] Yet the horizon is nevertheless something which is indivisible from the perceiving body. As Van Peursen puts it: 'Man's optical structure, his bodily height, his erect posture – his whole bodily organism is found to be involved in the sighting of the horizon.'[41] Whilst the view and scope afforded by a horizon is necessarily dependent on a body's physical positioning, it is also vulnerable to mistakes made by an individual in interpreting that which he or she sees. Nothing brings this point home more clearly than an anecdote told by R. H. Horne in 1871:

> Seated one evening, during the brief twilight of the antipodes, in the first floor of an inn on the stormy western coast of Australia, I contemplated the fading blue sky through an open window. The sea was, at this time, perfectly calm and colourless, and presented a faint yet clear, dark line of the horizon at an apparent distance of eighteen or twenty miles. There was no sound, either of air or sea. I thought of the ships and boats that had passed over the expanse before me – the space of sea between the window-frame and as far as the horizontal line – and thought of the living freights that those vessels had borne, long since passed away to the dead; – thought of the enormous numbers of fish that had eaten each other, and were all gone into the water, and what not, while similar races were now roaming abroad with the same destinies. I thought of the anxious eyes that had often been fixed upon yonder horizontal line, now becoming much fainter, yet still presenting its definite boundary . . . Suddenly a most enormous bird – the *roc* of the 'Arabian Nights' could have been nothing to it – alighted directly upon the distant horizontal line, which *dipped* with its weight! I started, breathless, and, for an instant, quite confounded. I sprang up, and ran across the room to the window. There was no sea at all. What I had been contemplating so intently in the twilight was the level sky, with the telegraphic line extending across the window at a distance of some twenty yards! The monster bird was an imported London sparrow, who had suddenly alighted on the line, and caused it to make a little dip down![42]

Horne tells this story, in the course of a piece on the variety of human vision, to emphasise that it made no difference to him whether the horizon around which his speculations clustered was or was not a horizon: 'There was no essential difference, to me, between what I imagined and believed I saw, and what would have been the reality.'[43] So, whilst the external world does exist, out there, for practical purposes it may also be said to exist within the mind.

Seeing within the mind: this brings us to the last important way in which I want to draw together some general notions about the horizon, and Victorian preoccupations with the visual. For the horizon is not just that thin line between the world and the air, the material and space, but may be considered in a more phenomeno-logical sense, especially according to its conceptualisation as devel-oped by Husserl. Whilst in Husserl's early writing, in *Ideas* (1913), the horizon can be thought of as a contextual field, that to which the attention is given inattentively, since it is no more than back-ground surrounding an object, an act or an experience, he came to give it a spin which related the concept far more directly to tempo-rality, to futurity. The idea of the horizon is infused with the sense of possibility: possibilities which are inherent within an experience or a perception, but which are at present latent. 'Perception', he writes in *Cartesian Meditations* (1931), 'has horizons made up of other possibilities of perception, as perceptions that we *could* have, if we *actively directed* the course of perception otherwise: if, for example, we turned our eyes that way instead of this, or if we were to step forward or to one side, and so forth'.[44] It is this 'leaving open', Husserl says, which is 'precisely what makes up the "horizon" '.[45]

Hubert Damisch, in *The Origin of Perspective*, ties in Husserl's ideas about the horizon, as well as his reflections concerning the origins of geometry, to ideas about science and history. Science, as Damisch explains, is never *the* truth, being tied to a specific time and opening onto a future in which it will necessarily challenge its own attainments: the Husserlian horizon, he writes, is 'a fact on which the future of science hinges, at every moment – on the extent to which truth exceeds knowledge, on the intention behind any founding act issuing in concepts that bring it to realization'.[46] There are copious Victorian testimonies by scientists to the power of sight, especially when assisted by new technologies of viewing:

'the eye', wrote Sir David Brewster, for example, 'carries us to the remotest horizons around, glances upward beyond the voiceless air, through the planetary regions where worlds are but stars'.[47] More significant, in this context, is the scientific desire to press beyond what is visible in the material world, seeing into the future, and actively directing the course of perception otherwise, through employing the imagination, seeing with the mind's eye.

'The grandest discoveries, and the grandest applications to prac-tice, have not only outstripped the slow march of Observation, but have revealed by the telescope of Imagination what the micro-scope of Observation could never have seen', wrote G. H. Lewes in 1874,[48] in a passage where the optical instruments parallel those which, in *Middlemarch*, Lydgate used to insist were, metaphorically speaking, essential to all scientific investigation, arguing that ' "there must be a systole and diastole in all inquiry" ' and that ' "a man's mind must be continually expanding and shrinking between the whole human horizon and the horizon of an object-glass" '.[49] Neither imagination nor observation, however, are self-sufficient. Lewes opened *Problems of Life and Mind*, from which comes that celebration of the imagination, by stating how it is a fact endemic to all research that after 'all efforts there still loom in the distance vast stretches of untrodden ground, and beyond these a region inaccessible to man'.

> He deplores, however, those who recourse to metaphysics, who, impatient to pass beyond the limits of Experience . . . will reject a solution which confines them within the human horizon. That which fascinates them is the hope of passing beyond this horizon. It will, therefore, be incumbent on me to show that such a hope is futile, and *per contra* that every question which can be stated in terms of Experience is capable of an answer on the Experiential method.[50]

As Lewes sees, the essence of the horizon is that whilst it suggests futurity, advance – the exercise of speculation, the involvement of the imagination – its existence is inseparable from materiality, both of the earth itself, and of the perceiving subject.

I wish finally to turn to another painting of Millais's from the

68 John Everett Millais, *The North-West Passage*, 1874. 176.53×222.25 cms.

1870s, *The North-West Passage* (1874) (figure 68). At first glance, this would seem to be the antithesis of *The Boyhood of Raleigh*: this is an interior scene, rather than one where a hand is expansively outstretched across the sea. Indeed, although the actual maritime horizon is visible as a sharp blue line through the window on the left, this is of no concern to the painting's protagonists, and functions only as a reminder to the viewer of the site of action and exploration. The central mariner is an elderly man, not a future English coloniser – he was, in fact, modelled by Captain Trelawny, a friend and memorialist of Shelley and the Lake Poets in his youth, and hence provides an accidental, if apposite, link back to Romantic aesthetics. The room is filled with references to the sailor's patriotic context. There is a portrait of Nelson behind his head, a chart of the northern regions lying open on his left hand, flags draped in the corner. Originally, the sense of British global domination would have been still stronger, since Millais initially placed two small children examining a globe in the right-hand corner. The painting was probably the most popular of all of Millais's works during the later part of his career: popular, according to his son, 'not only for its intrinsic merit, but as an expression more eloquent than words of the manly enterprise of the nation and the common desire that to England should fall the honour of laying bare the hidden mystery of the North'.[51] The Franklin expedition of 1847 had consolidated the association of heroic exploration and the cruelty of Arctic wastelands, whether in Landseer's picture *Man Proposes, God Disposes*, or the early poem of Swinburne's on 'The Death of Sir John Franklin', which plays on familiar tropes of patriotism, expansionism and boundaries within an icy context:

> What praise shall England give these men her friends?
> ... while the bays and the large channels flow
> In the broad sea between the iron ends
> Of the poised world where no safe sail may be,
> And for white miles the hard ice never blends
> With the chill washing edges of dull sea –
> And while to praise her green and girdled land
> Shall be the same as to praise Liberty –[52]

Millais's painting certainly managed to reach around the world as a widely disseminated cheap print: his son recounts seeing it pinned up on the wall of a Bushman shepherd's hut in the Great Karoo, in the form of 'a gaudy German oleograph'. He asked its owner what he thought of it: 'In reply to my inquiry, he pointed to the Union Jack as displayed in the picture, and said in broken English, "I like that cotton goods. It would make good clothes."'[53] John Millais tells this as a jokey tale, but the anecdote brings home strongly the Eurocentric nature of the expected response to Millais's images of the horizon, something which reinforces the cultural specificity of the ideas about the horizon which I have been discussing.[54] The phenomenon of the horizon is quite different to peoples with other notions of travel, trade and invasion.[55]

In the case of Millais's painting, however, not all the potential travel relates to actual seas. The sailor's daughter 'sits at his feet, reading', as Millais junior says,

what we may take to be the record of previous efforts to reach the
Pole. He is at home now – this ancient mariner, stranded on the
sands of life, like the hulk of an old ship that has done its duty –
but as he listens to these deeds of daring, the old fire burns within
him, and in every lineament of face and figure we see how deeply
he is moved.

He gazes straight ahead of him, but this gaze is resolutely sited
away from the yacht outside the window, as his voyaging takes
place towards and beyond an imagined icy horizon. The words of
travellers are transmitted through his daughter: if her dutiful
posture reminds one of Gwendolen's dissatisfaction in *Daniel
Deronda* when she complains 'We women can't go in search of
adventures – to find out the North-West Passage or the source of
the Nile',[56] who can tell where she may be travelling in her own
mind's eye?

Visualising in the mind's eye, observing the natural world, interpreting paintings – in all these and many other acts of spectatorship, the process of seeing incessantly moves between the
subjective and the objective, blurring the distinction between
the two. Throughout the period, Victorians were fascinated with
the technology of vision – whether the apparatus concerned was
located outside the body (as in the case of the telescope, the microscope, the camera lens or optical toys) or whether it was an integral
part of it – the eye. For them, however, problematising vision
meant a great deal more than a consideration of the conceptual
and mechanical implications of these means of seeing. It involved
acknowledging the individualism involved in perception, both the
individualism of consciously evoked social knowledge and experience, and of factors of memory and association which belonged to
the increasingly investigated world of the unconscious.

Examining visuality in an interdisciplinary context – exploring
its problematisation within science and within literary texts as well
as within art criticism – shows it to have been a continual point of
return. Visuality was crucial to Victorian debates about the place
of the individual in the world. Like the horizon, it formed a connecting line – sometimes clearly so, sometimes hazy and indistinct

– between the material and the invisible worlds, between the apparently knowable and the realm of hypothesis, between the figured and the imaginative, between the body and the mind. The essential vehicle, the mediating instrument, was the eye: something which itself partook of this dual function, both subjective and objective. One may look at eyes, and speculate upon them; in turn, one is using one's own eyes through which to see. The eye is a means of obtaining information, a data-retrieval instrument; a way of reaching beyond the body's boundary, yet inseparable from that body. A physical reality, eyes are at the same time a symbol for the spirit, the world within. 'Eyes', asked Mary Coleridge, in a poem of 1896:

> Eyes, what are they? Coloured glass,
> Where reflections come and pass.
>
> Open windows – by them sit
> Beauty, Learning, Love, and Wit.
>
> Searching cross-examiners;
> Comfort's holy ministers.
>
> Starry silences of soul,
> Music past the lips' control.
>
> Fountains of unearthly light;
> Prisons of the infinite.[57]

Notes

1 The visible and the unseen

1 Henry Mayhew, *London Labour and the London Poor*, 4 vols. (London: Griffin, Bohn and Co., 1861–2), III, p. 232.

2 Jean-Louis Comolli, 'Machines of the Visible', in Teresa de Lauretis and Stephen Heath, eds., *The Cinematic Apparatus*, (London and Basingstoke: Macmillan, 1980) pp. 122–3. See also James R. Ryan, *Picturing Empire. Photography and the Visualization of the British Empire* (London: Reaktion Books, 1977).

3 David Spurr, *The Rhetoric of Empire. Colonial Discourse in Journalism, Travel Writing, and Imperial Administration* (Durham N.C. and London: Duke University Press, 1993), p. 27. See also John Urry's comments at the opening of *The Tourist Gaze. Leisure and Travel in Contemporary Societies* (London: Sage Publications, 1990), p. 4, where he argues that by the nineteenth century, the prevalent mode of writing about travel, demanding 'eyewitness observation', led to the development of the visualisation of experience and the concomitant 'gaze', 'aided and assisted by the growth of guidebooks which promoted new ways of seeing'.

4 The literature dealing with the history of photography in the Victorian period is copious. Of particular interest and use, see: Helmut Gernsheim and Alison Gernsheim, *The History of Photography: From the Earliest Use of the Camera Obscura up to 1914* (London: Oxford University Press, 1955); Helmut Gernsheim, *The Origins of Photography* (New York: Thames and Hudson, 1982); John Tagg, *The Burden of Representation: Essays on Photographies and Histories* (London: Macmillan, 1988); Elizabeth Edwards, ed., *Anthropology and Photography 1860–1920* (New Haven and London: Yale University Press, 1992).

5   Mayhew, *London Labour*, III, p. 209.

6   See Patricia Anderson, *The Printed Image and the Transformation of Popular Culture 1790–1860* (Oxford University Press, 1991); William Ivins, *Prints and Visual Communication* (London: Routledge and Kegan Paul, 1953).

7   See Celina Fox, 'The Development of Social Reportage in English Periodical Illustration during the 1840s and early 1850s', *Past and Present* 74 (1977), pp. 90–111; W. L. Thomas, 'The Making of "The Graphic"', *Universal Review* 2 (1888), pp. 80–93; C. N. Williamson, 'Illustrated Journalism in England: Its Development', *Magazine of Art* 13 (1890), pp. 297–301, 334–40, 391–6.

8   See M. H. Spielmann, *The History of Punch* (London: Cassell and Co., 1895).

9   See J. R. Harvey, *Victorian Novelists and Their Illustrators* (New York University Press, 1971); Joan Stevens, 'Thackeray's Pictorial Capitals', *Costerus: Essays in English and American Language and Literature*, 2 (1974), pp. 113–40, and 'Thackeray's *Vanity Fair*', *Review of English Literature* 6 (1965), pp. 19–38; Patricia Sweeney, 'Thackeray's Best Illustrator', *Costerus: Essays in English and American Language and Literature*, 2 (1974), pp. 83–112; Judith L. Fisher, 'Image versus Text in the Illustrated Novels of William Makepeace Thackeray', in Carol T. Christ and John D. Jordan, eds., *Victorian Literature and the Victorian Visual Imagination*, (Berkeley, Los Angeles and London: University of California Press, 1995), pp. 60–87.

10 See Paul Greenhalgh, *Ephemeral Vistas. The 'Expositions Universelles', Great Exhibitions and World's Fairs, 1851–1939* (Manchester University Press, 1988); Charles Low, *Four National Exhibitions in London and their Organisers* (London: T. Fisher Unwin, 1892).

11 See Richard D. Altick, *The Shows of London* (Cambridge, Mass. and London: The Belknap Press of Harvard University Press, 1978); 'The Panorama and the Diorama: Aids to Distraction', ch. 2 of William H. Galperin, *The Return of the Visible in British Romanticism* (Baltimore and London: Johns Hopkins University Press, 1993); Ralph Hyde, *Panoramania* (London: Trefoil Publications and the Barbican Art Gallery, 1988); Stephan Oettermann, *The Panorama. History of a Mass Medium* (1980; trans. Deborah Lucas Schneider, New York: Zone Books, 1997).

12 R. A. M. Stevenson, 'General Impressions of the Royal Academy of 1893', *Art Journal* 21 (1893), p. 241.

13 See Susan P. Casteras and Colleen Denney, eds., *The Grosvenor Gallery. A Palace of Art in Victorian England* (New Haven and London: Yale University Press, 1996); Christopher Newall, *The Grosvenor Gallery Exhibitions: Change and Continuity in the Victorian Art World* (Cambridge University Press, 1995); and Giles Waterfield, ed., *Palaces of Art: Art Galleries in Britain, 1790–1990* (London: Dulwich Picture Gallery and the National Gallery of Scotland, 1991). The primary audiences for exhibitions, throughout the period, were the middle and upper classes, but days of reduced or waived admission fees, and exhibitions targeted especially at those who did not normally have access to art ensured that a variety of visual material was, on occasion, available to working-class spectators as well. For attempts to bring art to the urban working classes, see Frances Borzello, *Civilising Caliban. The Misuse of Art 1875–1980* (London and New York: Routledge and Kegan Paul, 1987).

14 See Kate Flint, 'The English Critical Reaction to Contemporary Painting 1878–1910', D.Phil. Oxford University, 1985 (Bodleian Ms.D.Phil.c.5579); Elizabeth Prettejohn, 'Aesthetic Value and the Professionalization of Victorian Art Criticism 1837–78', *Journal of Victorian Culture* 2 (1997), pp. 71–94; Helene E. Roberts, 'Exhibition and Review: The Periodical Press and the Victorian Art Exhibition System', in Joanne Shattock and Michael Wolff, eds., *The Victorian Periodical Press: Samplings and Soundings* (Leicester University Press, 1982), pp. 79–107.

15 Isobel Armstrong, 'Transparency: Towards a Poetics of Glass in the Nineteenth Century', in Francis Spufford and Jenny Uglow, eds., *Cultural Babbage. Technology, Time and Invention* (London and Boston: Faber and Faber, 1996), p. 143. See also Susan R. Horton, 'Were They Having Fun Yet? Victorian Optical Gadgetry, Modernist Selves', in Christ and Jordan, *Victorian Literature and the Victorian Visual Imagination*, pp. 1–26.

16 Thomas Richards, *The Commodity Culture of Victorian England. Advertising and Spectacle, 1851–1914* (1990; London and New York: Verso, 1991), p. 16. See also Rachel Bowlby, *Just Looking. Consumer Culture in Dreiser, Gissing and Zola* (New York and London: Methuen, 1985), and Lori Anne Loeb, *Consuming Angels. Advertising and Victorian Women* (New York and Oxford: Oxford University Press, 1994).

17 For expanded readings of Egg's triptych, see T. J. Edelstein, 'Augustus Egg's Triptych: A Narrative of Victorian Adultery',

Burlington Magazine 125 (1983), pp. 202–10; Lynda Nead, *Myths of Sexuality. Representations of Women in Victorian Britain* (Oxford and New York: Basil Blackwell, 1988), pp. 71–86.

18   Charles Baudelaire, *Mon Coeur mis à nu* (c. 1861), *Oeuvres Complètes*, ed. Claude Pichois, 2 vols. (Paris: Gallimard, 1975) I, p. 701. See Beatrice Farwell, *The Cult of Images: Baudelaire and the C19th Media Explosion* (University College of Santa Barbara Art Museum, 1977).

19   Michel Foucault, *Discipline and Punish. The Birth of the Prison* (*Surveiller et Punir: Naissance de la Prison* (1975; trans. Alan Sheridan, London: Allen Lee, 1977)), p. 200.

20   For a critique of Foucault's notions concerning the visible, see Martin Jay, *Downcast Eyes. The Denigration of Vision in Twentieth-Century French Thought* (Berkeley, Los Angeles and London: University of California Press, 1993), pp. 381–416.

21   Dolf Sternberger, *Panorama, oder Ansichten vom 19. Jahrhundert* (1955), quoted by W. Schivelbusch, *The Railway Journey: The Industrialization of Space and Time* (Leamington Spa: Basil Blackwell, 1986), p. 63. Schivelbusch's *Disenchanted Night. The Industrialisation of Light in the Nineteenth Century* (1983; trans. Angela Davies, Oxford, New York and Hamburg: Berg, 1988) has some interesting material on how the spread of electric lighting, rendering urban streets glaring and shadowless, did more than guarantee the security of the individual: 'it permits total surveillance by the state': 'In the course of the nineteenth century, the value placed on light as a guarantor of public morals, safety and order decreased as lights actually became brighter' (pp. 133–4).

22   'The Influence of Railway Travelling on Public Health. Report of the Commission. II', *Lancet* (11 January 1862), p. 52.

23   Dante Gabriel Rossetti, 'A Trip to Paris and Belgium', in ed. William Michael Rossetti, *The Collected Works of Dante Gabriel Rossetti*, 2 vols. (London: Ellis and Elvey, 1888), I, lines 134, 40, 21–3, 143–4. I am grateful to Matthew Beaumont for drawing my attention to this poem.

24   For a useful anthology of writings on ballooning from the 1780s to 1860, see Hatton Turnor, *Astra Castra* (London: Chapman and Hall, 1860).

25   Henry Mayhew and John Binny, *The Criminal Prisons of London and Scenes of Prison Life* (London: Griffin, Bohn, and Company, 1862), pp. 7–9.

26   Henry Mayhew, '"In the Clouds"; or, Some Account of a Balloon Trip with Mr Green', *Illustrated London News* (18 September 1852),

p. 224. For a history of balloon ascents, see L. T. C. Roly, *The Aeronauts. A History of Ballooning 1783–1903* (Gloucester: Alan Sutton, 1985).

27 Charlotte Brontë, *Villette* (1853; Oxford, Clarendon Press, 1984), p. 526. Several analyses of this novel draw Foucauldian attention to the theme of surveillance, especially Joseph A. Boone, 'Depolicing *Villette*: Surveillance, Invisibility, and the Female Erotics of "Heretic Narrative"', *Novel* 26 (1992), pp. 20–42, and Sally Shuttleworth, *Charlotte Brontë and Victorian Psychology* (Cambridge University Press, 1966).

28 Charles Dickens, *Bleak House* (1853; New York and London: W. W Norton, 1977), p. 673.

29 Charles Dickens, *Dombey and Son* (1848; Oxford: Clarendon Press, 1974), p. 620. See Jonathan Arac, *Commissioned Spirits: The Shaping of Social Motion in Dickens, Carlyle, Melville, and Hawthorne* (New Brunswick: Rutgers University Press, 1979), pp. 111–13. For a full discussion of this passage from *Dombey and Son* in the light of social criticism, see Raymond Williams, *The English Novel from Dickens to Lawrence* (London: Chatto & Windus, 1970), pp. 32ff.

30 Dickens, *Dombey and Son*, pp. 276–7.

31 Sir Arthur Conan Doyle, 'A Case of Identity' (1891), *The Penguin Complete Sherlock Holmes* (London: Penguin Books, 1981), p. 191.

32 'London from Aloft', *Strand* (July 1891), pp. 492–8. I am indebted to Upamanyu Mukherjee for finding this reference.

33 D. A. Miller, *The Novel and the Police* (Berkeley, Los Angeles and London: University of California Press, 1988), pp. viii–ix. See also Mark Seltzer, *Henry James and the Art of Power* (Ithaca: Cornell University Press, 1984), especially pp. 25–58.

34 Anthea Trodd, *Domestic Crime in the Victorian Novel* (London: Macmillan, 1989), p. 11.

35 X. Bichat, *Anatomie générale* (Paris, 1801, vol. 1, Avant-propos, p. xcix), quoted by Michel Foucault, *The Birth of the Clinic. An Archaeology of Medical Perception* (*Naissance de la Clinique*, 1963; trans. A. M. Sheridan Smith, London: Tavistock Publication, 1973), p. 146.

36 Jeremy Tambling, '*Middlemarch*, Realism and the Birth of the Clinic', *English Literary History* 57 (1990), pp. 939–60. For optical imagery and *Middlemarch*, see, in particular, J. Hillis Miller's influential essay, 'Optic and Semiotic in *Middlemarch*', in Jerome H. Buckley, ed., *The Worlds of Victorian Fiction* (Cambridge, Mass.: Harvard University Press, 1975), pp. 125–45, and Mark Wormald,

'Microscopy and Semiotic in *Middlemarch*', *Nineteenth-Century Literature* 50 (1996), pp. 501–24.

37 George Eliot, *Middlemarch* (1871–2; Oxford: Clarendon Press, 1986), p. 162.

38 Mark Seltzer, *Bodies and Machines* (New York and London: Routledge, 1992), p. 95.

39 Thomas Richards, *The Imperial Archive. Knowledge and the Fantasy of Empire* (London: Verso, 1993), p. 11.

40 Peter Brooks, *Body Work. Objects of Desire in Modern Narrative* (Cambridge, Mass., and London: Harvard University Press, 1993), p. 88.

41 See Stephen J. Gould, *The Mismeasure of Man* (1982; Harmondsworth: Penguin, 1984).

42 [Charles Dickens], 'The Demeanour of Murderers', *Household Words* 13 (14 June 1856), p. 505.

43 [Eliza Lynn], 'Passing Faces', *Household Words* 2 (14 April 1855), p. 263.

44 Mary Cowling, *The Artist as Anthropologist. The Representation of Type and Character in Victorian Art* (Cambridge University Press, 1989), p. 5. For the use of physiognomic theory in literature, see Jeanne Fahnestock, 'The Heroine of Irregular Features', *Victorian Studies* 24 (1981), pp. 325–50; Graeme Tytler, *Physiognomy in the European Novel: Faces and Fortunes* (Princeton University Press, 1982).

45 Johann Casper Lavater, *Essays on Physiognomy, Designed to Promote the Knowledge and the Love of Mankind* (1774–8; trans. Thomas Holcroft 1789–98; 9th edn London: W. Tegg, 1855), p. 16.

46 H. A. Taine, *History of English Literature* (1863; trans H. Van Laun, Edinburgh: Edmonston & Douglas, 1871, 2 vols.), II, p. 4.

47 Charles Dickens, *Hard Times* (1854; London: Penguin Books, 1995), p. 68.

48 Catherine Gallagher, *The Industrial Reformation of English Fiction. Social Discourse and Narrative Form 1832–1867* (Chicago and London: University of Chicago Press, 1985), p. 222.

49 George Eliot, *Adam Bede* (1859; London: Penguin Books, 1980), pp. 197–8.

50 George Eliot, *Daniel Deronda* (1876; Oxford: Clarendon Press, 1984), p. 170.

51 Anna Mary Howitt, *An Art-Student in Munich*, 2 vols. (London: Longman, Brown, Green and Longmans, 1853) II, pp. 40–1. Widely held beliefs about the relationship between physical and criminal type were, of course, to become consolidated with the spreading

authority of the research of Cesare Lombroso and others: see Daniel Pick, *Faces of Degeneration. A European Disorder, c. 1848 – c. 1918* (Cambridge University Press, 1989).

52 Robert Louis Stevenson, 'A Note on Realism', *The Essays of Robert Louis Stevenson*, ed. Malcolm Elwin (London: MacDonald, 1950), p. 381.

53 Sir Arthur Conan Doyle, 'A Study in Scarlet' (1888), *Complete Sherlock Holmes*, p. 23.

54 Henry James, *The Portrait of a Lady* (1881; revised edn New York: Charles Scribner's Sons, 1908, 2 vols.), I, pp. 287–8.

55 For discussion of racial disguise and 'passing' in Kipling, see Gail Ching-Liang Low, *White Skins / Black Masks. Representation and Colonialism* (London and New York: Routledge, 1996), especially pp. 200–21; Anne McClintock, *Imperial Leather. Race, Gender and Sexuality in the Colonial Contest* (London and New York: Routledge, 1995), pp. 65–71.

56 For a stimulating discussion of the ways in which work and the working environment may be seen to be written onto the body, see Elaine Scarry, 'Participial Acts: Working. Work and the Body in Hardy and Other Nineteenth-Century Novelists', in *Resisting Representation* (New York and Oxford: Oxford University Press, 1994), pp. 49–90. The work of Giovanni Morelli – 'the anthropometry (so to say) of art criticism': Charles Whibley, 'Italian Art at the New Gallery', *Nineteenth Century* 35 (1894), p. 335 – took up the identifying characteristics of physical signs (the shape of an ear-lobe, the measurements of a hand) and employed them as a touchstone of authentification when judging the provenance of paintings. For an enthusiastic account of Morelli's 'scientific' art criticism, see Mary Whitall Costelloe, 'The New and the Old Art Criticism', *Nineteenth Century* 35 (1894), pp. 828–37.

57 Carol T. Christ, *The Finer Optic. The Aesthetic of Particularity in Victorian Poetry* (New Haven and London: Yale University Press, 1975), p. 32.

58 For discussion of the slippery notion of realism, shifting, as it does, from generation to generation, see Lilian R. Furst, ed., *Realism* (London and New York: Longman, 1992); Katherine Kearns, *Nineteenth-Century Literary Realism. Through the Looking-Glass* (Cambridge University Press, 1996); and George Levine, *The Realistic Imagination. English Fiction from Frankenstein to Lady Chatterley* (Chicago and London: University of Chicago Press, 1981),

pp. 3–22. Chapter 12 of Levine's work, 'George Eliot, Conrad, and the Invisible World' (pp. 252–90), contains much that is germane to my own study.

59   Laurie Langbauer, *Women and Romance. The Consolations of Gender in the English Novel* (Ithaca and London: Cornell University Press, 1990), p. 199.

60   Ibid., p. 200, citing Mark Seltzer, *Henry James and the Art of Power* (Ithaca: Cornell University Press, 1984), p. 50.

61   Herbert L. Sussman, *Fact into Figure* (Columbus: Ohio State University Press, 1979); George P. Landow, *Victorian Types, Victorian Shadows* (London: Routledge and Kegan Paul, 1980).

62   Thomas Carlyle, *Sartor Resartus* (1831; London: Chapman and Hall, 1896), p. 57. For Carlyle and German philosophy, see Rosemary Ashton, *The German Idea. Four English Writers and the Reception of German Thought, 1800–1860* (1980; London: Libris, 1994), pp. 67–104.

63   Carlyle, *Sartor Resartus*, pp. 195–6.

64   Charlotte Brontë, 'Author's Preface', *Jane Eyre* (1847; New York and London: W. W. Norton and Company, 1987), pp. 1–2.

65   Jonathan Crary, *Techniques of the Observer. On Vision and Modernity in the Nineteenth Century* (Cambridge, Mass., and London: MIT Press, 1990), p. 16. Crary's superb *Suspensions of Perception. Attention, Spectacle, and Modern Culture* (Cambridge, Mass., and London: MIT Press, 1999) appeared when this volume was already in proof.

66   W. J. T. Mitchell, *Picture Theory. Essays on Verbal and Visual Representation* (Chicago and London: University of Chicago Press, 1994), p. 21.

67   For two short, but very valuable discussions of this aspect of Victorian visuality, see Gillian Beer, ' "Authentic Tidings of Invisible Things": Vision and the Invisible in the Later Nineteenth Century', in Teresa Brennan and Martin Jay, eds., *Vision in Context. Historical and Contemporary Perspectives on Sight* (New York and London: Routledge, 1996), pp. 85–98, and Daniel Pick, 'Stories of the Eye', in Roy Porter, ed., *Rewriting the Self. Histories from the Renaissance to the Present* (London and New York: Routledge, 1997), pp. 186–99. James Krasner, *The Entangled Eye. Visual Perception and the Representation of Nature in Post-Darwinian Narrative* (New York and Oxford: Oxford University Press, 1992), contains some excellent discussion of post-Darwinian ideas concerning visual perception and their presence within nature writing, showing how nature came to be understood as a site of optical illusion and visual failure.

68   A notable exception here, of course, is where the issues of technology and aesthetics collide in debates about the status and evaluation of photography. See Jennifer Green-Lewis, *Framing the Victorians. Photography and the Culture of Realism* (Ithaca and London: Cornell University Press, 1996); Lindsay Smith, *Victorian Photography, Painting and Poetry: The Enigma of Visibility in Ruskin, Morris and the Pre-Raphaelites* (Cambridge University Press, 1995).

69   This has long been recognised by historians of the literature of science. See Tess Cosslett, *The 'Scientific Movement' and Victorian Literature* (Brighton: The Harvester Press, 1982), especially the first chapter; Peter Allan Dale, *In Pursuit of a Scientific Culture. Science, Art, and Society in the Victorian Age* (Madison: University of Wisconsin Press, 1989). Gillian Beer, *Darwin's Plots* (London: Routledge and Kegan Paul, 1983), and George Levine, *Darwin and the Novelists. Patterns of Science in Victorian Fiction* (Cambridge, Mass., and London: Harvard University Press, 1988), have been particularly influential in demonstrating the interweaving of literary and scientific discourse, especially when it comes to linguistic cross-fertilisation.

70   Thomas Huxley, 'Science and Morals' (1886), *Collected Essays,* 9 vols. (London: Macmillan, 1893–4), IX, p. 122.

71   John Tyndall, 'Early Thoughts' [from 'Physics and Metaphysics', *Saturday Review*, 4 August 1860], *Essays on the Use and Limit of the Imagination in Science* (London: Longmans, Green and Co., 1870), p. 72. In terms of his commitment to the mystery that lies beyond the visible, the influence of Carlyle was surely very important to Tyndall. See A. S. Eve and C. H. Creasey, *Life and Work of John Tyndall* (London: Macmillan, 1945), p. 74 and *passim*, and, more generally, Frank M. Turner, 'Victorian Scientific Naturalism and Thomas Carlyle', *Victorian Studies* 28 (1975), pp. 325–43.

72   John Forster, *Life of Dickens* [1872–4], ed. J. W. Ley (London: Cecil Palmer, 1928), p. 350.

73   Mark Akenside, '*The Pleasures of Imagination*', *The Poetical Works of Mark Akenside* (1845; reprinted New York: Arms Press 1969), pp. 175–6. For a concise, stimulating discussion of the relationship between memory, images and knowledge, see chapter 5 of Mary Warnock, *Memory* (London and Boston: Faber and Faber, 1987), pp. 75–102.

74   George Eliot to Elma Stuart, 24 December 1879, *The George Eliot Letters*, ed. Gordon S. Haight, 9 vols. (New Haven and London: Yale University Press, 1954–78), VII, p. 233.

75   Eliot, *Middlemarch*, p. 186.

76   Ibid., pp. 161–2.

77   See, in particular, W. David Shaw, 'The Optical Metaphor: Victorian Poetics and the Theory of Knowledge', *Victorian Studies* 23 (1980), pp. 293–324.

78   Jerome J. McGann, *Towards a Literature of Knowledge* (Oxford: Clarendon Press, 1989), p. 2.

79   Peggy Phelan, *Unmarked. The Politics of Performance* (London and New York: Routledge, 1993), p. 1.

80   Ibid., p. 6.

81   [Sir D. Brewster], 'The Sight and How to See', *North British Review* 26 (1856), p. 146.

82   Joseph Turnley, *The Language of the Eye: The Importance and Dignity of the Eye as Indicative of General Character, Female Beauty, and Manly Genius* (London: Partridge and Co., 1856), p. 8.

83   Ibid., p. 16.

84   Ibid., p. 38.

85   Ibid., p. 99.

86   Ibid., p. 103.

87   Ibid., p. 44.

88   Ibid., p. 52.

89   Ibid., p. 67.

90   Thomas Bull, *The Senses Denied and Lost* (London: Longman, Green, Longman and Roberts, 1859), p. 10.

91   Joseph Wood, 'Sight and Insight', *Modern Review* 1 (1880), p. 225.

92   John Tyndall, *Six Lectures on Light. Delivered in America in 1872–1873* (London: Longmans, Green and Co., 1873), pp. 8–9. Hermann von Helmholtz's strictures against the eye can be found in 'The Eye as an Optical Instrument', the first section of 'The Recent Progress of the Theory of Vision', *Popular Lectures on Scientific Subjects* (trans. E. Atkinson, London: Longmans, Green and Co., 1873), pp. 197–228. He does make the point, however, that the eye is remarkably adept at compensating for its inherent defects, hence providing a fascinating model for the character of organic adaptation generally. For Helmholtz's importance, see David Cahan, ed., *Hermann von Helmholtz and the Foundations of C19th Science* (Berkeley: University of California Press, 1993).

93   George Eliot, *The Impressions of Theophrastus Such* (1879; London: J. M. Dent, 1995), p. 129.

94 See Lisa Cartwright, *Screening the Body: Tracing Medicine's Visual Culture* (Minneapolis: University of Minnesota Press, 1995); Stanley Joel Reiser, *Medicine and the Reign of Technology* (Cambridge University Press, 1978). For a Victorian survey and celebration of such exploratory techniques, see Robert Brudenell Carter, 'Medicine and Surgery', in Thomas Humphry Ward, ed., *The Reign of Queen Victoria*, 2 vols. (London: Smith, Elder, and Co., 1887), II, pp. 388–444.

95 Alfred Meadows, 'Description of Two New Vaginal Specula', *Lancet* (14 May 1870), p. 692.

96 See Lindsay Smith, *The Politics of Focus* (Manchester University Press, 1998).

97 Walter Benjamin, 'A Short History of Photography', *Screen* 13 (1972), p. 9.

98 Thomas Huxley, 'The Progress of Science 1837–1887' (1887; first published in *The Reign of Queen Victoria*), *The Works of Thomas Henry Huxley*, 6 vols. (New York: D. Appleton and Co., 1897), vol. I, *Methods and Results. Collected Essays*, p. 111.

99 Richard A. Proctor, 'The Photographic Eyes of Science', *Longman's Magazine* 1 (1883), p. 442.

100 Ibid., p. 462.

101 See Carolyn Marvin, *When Old Technologies Were New. Thinking About Electric Communication in the Late Nineteenth Century* (New York and Oxford: Oxford University Press, 1988).

102 Georg Simmel, 'The Metropolis and Mental Life' (1903), in David Frisby and Mike Featherstone, eds., *Simmel on Culture* (London: Sage Publications, 1997), p. 175.

103 Norman Bryson, *Vision and Painting. The Logic of the Gaze* (Basingstoke and London: Macmillan, 1983), p. 85.

104 Here I draw on Pierre Bourdieu's employment of the term in 'Cultural Reproduction and Social Reproduction', in Richard Brown, ed., *Knowledge, Education and Cultural Change: Papers in the Sociology of Education* (London: Tavistock, 1973), p. 73.

105 I have discussed this at much greater length in 'Moral Judgement and the Language of English Art Criticism', *Oxford Art Journal* 6 (1983), pp. 59–66.

106 [James Sully], 'The Undefinable in Art', *Cornhill Magazine* 38 (1878), pp. 559–72.

107 Ibid., p. 561.

108 The phrase is Patrick Brantlinger's, in *Rule of Darkness. British Literature and Imperialism, 1830–1914* (Ithaca and London: Cornell University Press, 1988), p. 240, who goes on to link the fascination with the occult in the later years of the nineteenth century with the craze for literary romance, quoting Andrew Lang: 'As the visible world is measured, mapped, tested, weighed, we seem to hope more and more that a world of invisible romance may not be far from us' (Andrew Lang, 'The Supernatural in Fiction', *Adventures in Books* (London: Longmans, Green and Co., 1905), p. 279).

109 James Sully, 'Art and Psychology', *Mind* I (1876), p. 467.

110 Ibid., p. 471.

111 She blames this on the traditional idea that Art is the product of Genius, and Genius an unaccountable, unanalysable element (Costelloe, 'The New and the Old Art Criticism', p. 834).

112 William Kingdon Clifford, *Seeing and Thinking* (London: Macmillan, 1879), pp. 33–4.

2   'The mote within the eye'

1 Alfred Russel Wallace, *The Wonderful Century. Its Successes and its Failures* (London: Swan Sonnenschein and Co. Ltd., 1898), pp. 68–9.

2 Mary Douglas, *Purity and Danger. An Analysis of the Concepts of Pollution and Taboo* (1966; London and New York: Routledge, 1984), p. 35.

3 Peter Stallybrass and Allon White, *The Politics and Poetics of Transgression* (London: Methuen, 1986), p. 130.

4 Charles Dickens, *Great Expectations* (1861; Oxford: Clarendon Press, 1993), p. 107.

5 Ibid., p. 318.

6 For the role of dirt and cleanliness in mapping human 'progress', see Anne McClintock, *Imperial Leather. Race, Gender and Sexuality in the Colonial Contest* (London and New York: Routledge, 1995).

7 J. G. McPherson, 'Dust', *Longman's Magazine* 18 (1891), pp. 49–50.

8 John Ruskin, *Modern Painters*, v (1860), *The Complete Works of John Ruskin*, ed. E. T. Cook and Alexander Wedderburn, 39 vols. (London: George Allen, 1903–12), VII, p. 139.

9 See 'Dust and Hygiene', *All the Year Round* 3rd series 13 (1895), pp. 154–8; John Tyndall, 'On Dust and Disease', *Fraser's Magazine* ns 1 (1870), pp. 302–10.

10   Alfred Tennyson, 'Edwin Morris' (1851, written 1839), *The Poems of Tennyson*, ed. Christopher Ricks (London and Harlow: Longmans, 1969), pp. 708, 714.

11   Charles Dickens, *Our Mutual Friend* (1864–5; London: Penguin, 1971), p. 191.

12   W. E. Henley, 'Trafalgar Square', in William Nicholson, *London Types, Quatorzains by W. E. Henley* (London: William Heinemann, 1898), p. [vii]. The sonnet illustrates Nicholson's print of a sandwich-boardman advertising Seeley's *Ecce Homo*.

13   Henry Mayhew, *London Labour and the London Poor*, 4 vols. (London: Griffin, Bohn and Co., 1861–2), ii, p. 188.

14   Charles Dickens, *Bleak House* (1853; New York and London: W. W. Norton, 1977), p. 29.

15   Elizabeth Barrett Browning, *Aurora Leigh* (1856), ed. Margaret Reynolds (New York and London: W. W. Norton, 1998) p. 78 lines 179–80. For an overview of this topic, see Peter Brimblecombe, *The Big Smoke: A History of Air Pollution in London since Medieval Times* (London and New York: Methuen, 1987).

16   McPherson, 'Dust', p. 58.

17   John Ruskin, *The Storm-Cloud of the Nineteenth Century*, Lecture i (1884), *Works*, xxxiv, p. 38. See also Michael Wheeler, ed., *Ruskin and Environment: The Storm Cloud of the Nineteenth Century* (Manchester University Press, 1995); Anthony S. Wohl, *Endangered Lives. Public Health in Victorian Britain* (London: Methuen, 1983), ch. 8, ' "The Black Canopy of Smoke": Atmospheric Pollution'.

18   Wallace, *The Wonderful Century*, p. 102.

19   Sir Robert Grant, 'Psalm civ', *Sacred Poems* (London: Saunders and Otley, 1839), p. 35 – subsequently set to music as hymn, 'O worship the King'.

20   'Fallen from the Clouds', *All the Year Round* 8 (22 November 1862), p. 256.

21   Robert Brudenell Carter, 'Lighting', in *Our Homes, and How to Make Them Healthy* (London, Paris and New York: Cassell, Petter, Galpin and Co., 1883–5), pp. 397–8.

22   H. P. Malet, *Incidents in the Biography of Dust* (London: Trübner and Co., 1877), p. 34.

23   Carter, 'Lighting', p. 398.

24   Mrs Isabella Beeton, *The Book of Household Management* (London: S. O. Beeton, 1861), p. 1001.

25 'Dust and Hygiene', p. 157.

26 Ibid., p. 154. For histories of housework, which allow one to place concerns about dust in broader contexts about hygiene and labour, see Caroline Davidson, *A Woman's Work is Never Done: A History of Housework in the British Isles 1650–1950* (London: Chatto and Windus, 1982); Margaret Horsfield, *Biting the Dust: The Joys of Housework* (London: Fourth Estate, 1997); Suellen Hoy, *Chasing Dirt: The American Pursuit of Cleanliness* (New York and Oxford: Oxford University Press, 1995).

27 Florence Nightingale, *Notes on Nursing for the Labouring Classes* (London: Harrison, 1868), p. 73.

28 Ann Thwaite, *Emily Tennyson: The Poet's Wife* (London: Faber and Faber, 1996), p. 350.

29 F. Oppert, *On Melanosis of the Lungs and Other Lung Diseases Arising from the Inhalation of Dust* (London: John Churchill and Sons, 1866), pp. 3–4. The work is reprinted from the *Medical Press and Circular* (1866).

30 Douglas Galton, 'Warming and Ventilation', *Our Homes*, p. 489.

31 Elizabeth Gaskell, *North and South* (1854–5; London: Penguin Books, 1970), p. 139.

32 Ibid., p. 146.

33 Emily Eden, *Up the Country* (1866; London: Virago, 1983), p. 110.

34 Ibid., p. 64.

35 Ibid., p. 71.

36 Ibid., p. 215.

37 Two Twenty Years' Residents [Flora Annie Steele and Grace Gardiner], *The Complete Indian Housekeeper and Cook* (Edinburgh: Frank Murray, 1890), p. 57.

38 Ibid., pp. 53, 174.

39 Gail Ching-Liang Low, *White Skins / Black Masks. Representation and Colonialism* (London and New York: Routledge, 1996), pp. 162–3.

40 Douglas, *Purity and Danger*, p. 35.

41 Michael Thompson, *Rubbish Theory. The Creation and Destruction of Value* (Oxford University Press, 1979), p. 11.

42 See Harvey Peter Sucksmith, 'The Dust-heaps in *Our Mutual Friend*', *Essays in Criticism* 23 (1973), pp. 206–12. Freud's speculations can be found in 'Character and Anal Eroticism' (1908), *The Standard Edition. of the Complete Psychological Works of Sigmund Freud* (London: Hogarth Press and the Institute of Psychoanalysis, 1953–74), IX p. 169, and *The Interpretation of Dreams, Works*, V, p. 403.

43 [John Capper], 'Important Rubbish', *Household Words* 11 (19 May 1855), pp. 376–9.

44 'Our Dust-bins', *Leisure Hour* 17 (1868), p. 719.

45 Ibid.

46 Mayhew, *London Labour*, 11, p. 30. This was originally published in the 'Labour and the Poor' series in the *Morning Chronicle*, 3 December 1849: Mayhew's description is of the by-products treated in the Lancashire cotton town of Oldham, though the centre of the shoddy trade was in fact around Batley, in West Yorkshire. See Samuel Jubb, *The History of the Shoddy Trade* (London: Houlston and Wright; Manchester: John Heywood; Batley: J. Fearnsides, 1860); J. C. Malin, 'The West Riding Recovered Wool Textile Industry *c.* 1813–1939', unpublished Ph.D., University of York, 1979. Jubb stresses recycling potential: 'Shoddy dust too, which is the dirt emitted from rags and shoddy in their processes, is useful as tillage', p. 23.

47 'Our Dust-bins', p. 720.

48 *Steam Power from House Dust for Electric Lighting and Other Purposes; Produced by the Patented Process of The Refuse Disposal Company, Limited* (London: Refuse Disposal Company, 1892).

49 H. A. Forde and her sisters, *Dust Ho! and Other Pictures from Troubled Lives* (London: Christian Knowledge Society, *c.* 1885), p. 13.

50 Andrew H. Miller, *Novels Behind Glass. Commodity Culture and Victorian Narrative* (Cambridge University Press, 1995), p. 125.

51 Ruskin, *Modern Painters*, v, *Works* vii, p. 207.

52 'Gamaliel' (possibly W. Edwin Page), *Diamonds from Dust; Or, The Philosopher's Dream Realized* (London: The London Female Guardian Society, 1905), p. 12.

53 Charles Reed, *Diamonds in the Dust. A New Year's Address for Sunday Scholars* (London: Sunday School Union, 1866), pp. 21–2.

54 Mabel Mackintosh, *Dust, Ho! or, Rescued from a Rubbish Heap* (London: John F. Shaw and Co., 1891).

55 Eustace R. Conder, *Dust, and Other Short Talks with Children* (Leeds: W. Brierley; London: Hodder and Stoughton, 1882), p. 1.

56 Alfred Tennyson, *Maud* (1855), *Poems*, p. 1086.

57 Conder, *Dust*, p. 3.

58 Sir Arthur Conan Doyle, *A Study in Scarlet* (1887), *The Penguin Complete Sherlock Holmes* (London: Penguin Books, 1981), p. 34.

59 Harriet Martineau, *Eastern Life, Present and Past*, 3 vols. (London: Edward Moxon, Son and Co., 1848), 1, p. 60.

60 The phrase is Augustine Birrell's, who refers to 'That great dust-heap called "history"', 'Carlyle', *Collected Essays*, 2 vols. (London: Elliot Stock, 1902), I, p. 5.

61 Ouida, 'Street Dust', *Street Dust and Other Stories* (London: F. V. White and Co., 1901), pp. 50, 56.

62 Tennyson, 'The Lotos-Eaters' (1832), *Poems*, p. 434.

63 Tennyson, 'Aylmer's Field' (1864), *Poems*, p. 1160.

64 Tennyson, *In Memoriam A. H. H.* (1850), *Poems*, p. 886.

65 Ibid., p. 893.

66 Ibid., p. 893.

67 Ibid., p. 907.

68 Ibid., p. 912.

69 Ibid., p. 862.

70 Ibid., p. 967.

71 Ibid., p. 981. The reference is to Isaiah 34:4.

72 Edward Bulwer Lytton, *The Last Days of Pompeii*, 3 vols. (London: Richard Bentley, 1834) III, pp. 309–10.

73 Gerard Manley Hopkins, 'The Sea and the Skylark' (probably 1877; definitely completed by 1882), *The Poetical Works of Gerard Manley Hopkins*, ed. Norman H. Mackenzie (Oxford: Clarendon Press, 1990), p. 143.

74 Susan Buck-Morss, *The Dialectics of Seeing. Walter Benjamin and the Arcades Project* (Cambridge, Mass., and London: MIT Press, 1989), pp. 95–6.

75 Tennyson, 'Mariana' (1830), lines 78–9.

76 See Gillian Beer, 'Helmholtz, Tyndall, Gerard Manley Hopkins: Leaps of the Prepared Imagination', in *Open Fields: Science in Cultural Encounter* (Oxford: Clarendon Press, 1996), pp. 242–72, and, more generally, 'Wave Theory and the Rise of Literary Modernism', in Beer, *Open Fields*, pp. 295–318.

77 John Tyndall, *Essays on the Use and Limit of the Imagination in Science* (London: Longman, Green and Co., 1870), p. 26.

78 Ibid., p. 36.

79 Ibid., p. 51.

80 A. W. Moore, ed., *Infinity* (Aldershot: Dartmouth Publishing Co., 1993), p. xi.

81 Tyndall, 'Scientific Use of the Imagination', *Essays*, p. 51.

82 Oliver Lodge, 'Ruskin's Attitude to Science', *St George* 8 (1905), p. 290, quoted in Ruskin, *Works*, XXXVII, p. 525. Lodge continues:

'Such rebellion of the artistic instinct is never in my judgment altogether to be despised, and in the present instance it has been to a great extent justified by the mathematical discovery of Lord Rayleigh that the discontinuity of *air itself*, due to its atomic structure, is sufficient to cause a very perceptible reflexion of the small waves of light, so that the active particles which are effective in causing the blue of the sky are probably chiefly the atoms of oxygen and nitrogen themselves, without the need for any admixture of even the finest terrestrial dust carried upwards by winds and the like.' In fact, Ruskin first encountered Tyndall's theories in 1869: he records in the Preface to *The Queen of the Air* that he is reading Tyndall's 'On Chemical Rays, and the Light of the Sky', *Notices of Proceedings of the Royal Institution* 5 (1869), 429–50 (Ruskin, *Works*, XIX, p. 292).

83 Wallace, *The Wonderful Century*, p. 71.

84 Ibid., pp. 73–4.

85 Hopkins, 'The remarkable sunsets', *Nature* 29 (3 January 1884), pp. 222–3; reprinted in *The Correspondence of Gerard Manley Hopkins and Richard Watson Dixon*, ed. Claude Colleer Abbott (London: Oxford University Press, 1935), pp. 161–6.

86 Robert Bridges, *Eros and Psyche* (London: George Bell, 1885), pp. 10–11. See further Richard D. Altick, 'Four Victorian Poets and an Exploding Island', *Victorian Studies* 3 (1960), pp. 249–60; Thomas A. Zaniello, 'The Spectacular English Sunsets of the 1880s', in Jim Paradis and Tom Postlewait, eds., *Victorian Science and Victorian Values: Literary Perspectives*, Annals of the New York Academy of Sciences 360 (1981), pp. 247–67. As Altick notes, Hopkins wrote to Bridges on 1 January 1885, as soon as he read the poem: ' "The description . . . so closely agrees with an account I wrote in *Nature*, even to details which were local only, that it is very extraordinary: you did not see my letter, did you?" Hopkins' suspicion is decently veiled, but it is unmistakable, and, one feels, not without basis' (Altick, 'Four Victorian Poets', p. 256).

87 Richard le Gallienne, 'Sunset in the City', *English Poems* (London: Elkin Mathews and John Lane at the Bodley Head, 1892), p. 101.

88 Wallace, *The Wonderful Century*, p. 76.

89 Ibid., p. 77. Aitken's scientific essays are collected in John Aitken, *Collected Scientific Papers of John Aitken*, ed. Cargill G. Knott (Cambridge University Press, 1923). A succinct summary of his

ideas about dust and rainfall can be found in Aitken's article 'Dust' for the eleventh edition of the *Encyclopaedia Britannica* (1910–11).

90 Cited in Leonard Archbutt, *Dust. A Paper Read Before the Nomadic Club, Derby. March 20th, 1891* (London and Derby: Bemrose and Sons, 1891), p. 14.

91 Wallace, *The Wonderful Century*, p. 83.

92 G. H. Lewes, *Problems of Life and Mind. Third Series, The Physical Basis of Mind*, 2 vols. (London: Trübner and Co., 1879), II, p. 192.

93 Ibid., p. 200.

94 George Eliot, *Middlemarch* (1871–2; Oxford: Clarendon Press, 1986), p. 409.

95 Philip Henry Gosse, *Evenings at the Microscope; Or, Researches Among the Minuter Organs and Forms of Animal Life* (London: Society for Promoting Christian Knowledge, 1859), p. iii. For the history of the microscope, see Stella Butler, R. H. Nuttall and Olivia Brown, *The Social History of the Microscope* (Cambridge: Whipple Museum, 1986); Brian J. Ford, *The Revealing Lens: Mankind and the Microscope* (London: Harrap, 1973), and *Single Lens: The Story of the Simple Microscope* (London: Heinemann, 1985); Catherine Wilson, 'Visual Surface and Visual Symbol: The Microscope and the Occult in Early Modern Science', *Journal of the History of Ideas* 49 (1988), pp. 85–108.

96 The Hon. Mrs W. [Mary Ward], *A World of Wonders Revealed by the Microscope* (London: Groombridge and Sons, 1858), p. 8.

97 Revd. J. G. Wood, *Common Objects of the Microscope* (London: Routledge, Warne and Routledge, 1861), p. 3.

98 [Ward], *A World of Wonders*, p. 24.

99 Wood, *Common Objects*, p. 98.

100 William B. Carpenter, *The Microscope: And its Revelations* (London: John Churchill, 1856), p. 36.

101 Thomas Hardy, *Two on a Tower* (1882; Oxford University Press, 1993), p. 64.

102 Tennyson, 'Vastness' (1885), *Poems*, p. 1346. For the treatment of astronomy in nineteenth-century poetry, see Jacob Korg, 'Astronomical Imagery in Victorian Poetry', Paradis and Postlewait, *Victorian Science and Victorian Values*, pp. 137–58; and, more particularly on Tennyson, Francis Golffing, 'Tennyson's Last Phase: The Poet as Seer', *Southern Review* 2 (1966), pp. 264–85. In relation to astronomy and the sense of smallness which it could induce, precisely the same theological points were made as in relation to the

use of the microscope. For example, Christina Rossetti, in *Time Flies* (London: Society for Promoting Christian Knowledge, 1885), asks, rhetorically: 'If certain stars which present mere dimness and obstruction to our eyes are notwithstanding genuine celestial bodies fulfilling their proper revolution in their legitimate orbit, may not some human fellow creatures who to us exhibit no sign of grace, yet be numbered among the children of God, and have their lot among the saints?' (p. 208).

103 John Tyndall, *Natural Philosophy in Easy Lessons* (London: Cassell, Petter and Galpin, 1869), p. 6.

104 Wallace, *The Wonderful Century*, p. 68.

105 Tyndall, 'Scientific Use of the Imagination', *Essays*, p. 41.

3 Blindness and insight

1 John M. Hull, *Touching the Rock. An Experience of Blindness* (London: Society for the Promotion of Christian Knowledge, 1990), p. 153. Drusilla Modjeska draws on this book in a moving section of her novel *The Orchard* (Sydney: Pan Macmillan, 1994), in which the central character fears that she is losing her sight.

2 Gerard Manley Hopkins, 'Binsey Poplars' (1879), *The Poetical Works of Gerard Manley Hopkins*, ed. Norman H. Mackenzie (Oxford: Clarendon Press, 1990), p, 157.

3 For a full description of the history of this painting, see Malcolm Warner's entry in *The Pre-Raphaelites* (London: The Tate Gallery / Penguin Books, 1984), pp. 134–6. See also Allen Staley, *The Pre-Raphaelite Landscape* (Oxford: Clarendon Press, 1973), pp. 53–5.

4 William Moon, *Consequences and Ameliorations of Blindness* (London: Longmans, 1873), p. 1.

5 Karl Kroeber, *British Romantic Art* (Berkeley, Los Angeles and London: University of California Press, 1986), p. 35.

6 Jacques Derrida, *Memoirs of the Blind. The Self-Portrait and Other Ruins*, tr. Pascale-Anne Brault and Michael Naas (Chicago and London: University of Chicago Press, 1993), p. 2.

7 *Spectator*, 17 May 1856, p. 571.

8 'Fine-Art Gossip', *Athenaeum* 1488 (3 May 1856), pp. 590–1. The reviewer's scorn of typological symbolism is most succinctly exemplified in the summary of Holman Hunt's *The Scapegoat*: 'the goat is but a goat, and we have no right to consider it an allegorical

animal, of which it can bear no external marks. Of course the salt may be sin, and the sea sorrow, and the clouds eternal rebukings of pride, and so on, – but we might spin these fancies from anything – from an old wall, a centaur's beard, or a green duck pool.'

9   Quoted in Tate Gallery, *The Pre-Raphaelites*, p. 134.

10   W. Hanks Levy, *Blindness and the Blind* (London: Chapman and Hall, 1872), p. 4.

11   Revd. B. G. Johns, *Blind People: Their Works and Ways* (London: John Murray, 1867), p. 71.

12   Sacheverell Sitwell, writing in 1937, confidently added to the range of explanations for the girl's blindness, his interpretation consciously resting on cultural currency drawn from the later nineteenth century. The painting, he claims, 'has its moral message conveyed in sentimental form. All the beauties of nature surround the blind girl, but she is barred from them, since it is possible for the knowledge of a later generation to add to the point of the story, by an affliction which is inherited from sin. The fault of her parents has deprived her of sight. Millais, then, had created a dramatic or pathetic situation of which only half the meaning was apparent to him. But it was a discovery in dramatics, no less than a remarkable and beautiful picture. The unconscious touch of Ibsen in its theme gives it, indeed, a dramatic restraint which is the more telling' (*Narrative Pictures. A Survey of English Genre and its Painters* (London: B. T. Batsford, 1937), p. 9).

13   J. H. Fyfe, 'The Ways and Works of the Blind', *Good Words* 2 (1861), p. 313.

14   *Punch* 25 (19 November 1853), p. 217.

15   For a full description of all the institutions and charities assisting the blind in mid-Victorian London, see Edmund C. Johnson, *The Blind of London* (London: John Mitchell, 1860).

16   *Spectator*, 17 May 1856, p. 571. In fact, the blind girl is not actually fingering the harebells, but a very distinctly painted clover-leaf: a signification of Irishness, or maybe a token of the Trinity?

17   John Kitto, *The Lost Senses. Series II. – Blindness* (London: Charles Knight and Co., 1845), p. 86.

18   'The Blind', *National Review* 10 (1860), p.102.

19   Johns, *Blind People*, p. 88.

20   Of course, having made her point, Gaskell rescues Margaret from a disabled life in the final paragraph of the book, where the regaining

of her sight is one of the elements which goes to make up an up-beat ending.

21 Christina Walkley, *The Ghost in the Looking Glass: The Victorian Seamstress* (London: P. Owen, 1981); Teri J. Edelstein, 'They sang "The Song of the Shirt": The Visual Ideology of the Seamstress', *Victorian Studies* 23 (1980), pp. 183–210.

22 Henry Mayhew, *London Labour and the London Poor*, 4 vols. (London: Griffin, Bohn and Co., 1861–2), I, pp. 342–3.

23 Thomas Hood, 'The Song of the Shirt' (1843), *The Complete Poetical Works of Thomas Hood*, ed. Walter Jerrold (London: Henry Froude, 1906), pp. 625–6.

24 'The Needlewomen's Farewell', *Punch* 18 (1850), p. 14.

25 Robert Aitken, *The Teaching of the Types. Tracts for the Clergy and the Earnest Minded* (Oxford: T. and G. Shrimpton, 1854), pp. 3–4.

26 For an extended examination of the place of the rainbow in litera-ture and in painting, see George Landow, *Images of Crisis: Literary Iconology, 1750 to the Present* (London: Routledge and Kegan Paul, 1982), pp. 156–79. John Tyndall discusses the phenomenon of the double bow, and makes other scientific observations on the princi-ples of refraction, in 'The Rainbow and its Congeners', *New Fragments* (London: Longman, Green and Co., 1892), pp. 199–223.

27 John Ruskin, *Modern Painters*, III (1856), *The Complete Works of John Ruskin*, ed. E. T. Cook and Alexander Wedderburn, 39 vols. (London: George Allen, 1903–12), V, p. 387. Millais famously repainted this double rainbow after a correspondent to the *Art Journal* (August 1856, p. 236) complained of his 'glaring want of attention to natural phenomena' despite all the 'boasted attention' of the Pre-Raphaelite 'school to the truth of Nature': he originally painted both bows with their colours in the same order, rather than realising that they should be reversed in the complementary bow.

28 Thomas Bull, *The Sense Denied and Lost* (London: Longman Green, Longman and Roberts, 1859), pp. 65–6.

29 William Holman Hunt, *Pre-Raphaelitism and the Pre-Raphaelite Brotherhood* 2 vols. (London: Macmillan and Co., 1905) I, p. 351.

30 John Ruskin, '"The Light of the World"', letter first published in *The Times*, 5 May 1854, *Works*, XII, pp. 329–30. For further discussion of Hunt's painting, see Jeremy Maas, *Holman Hunt and 'The Light of the World'* (Aldershot: Wildwood House, 1987).

31   Revd Richard Glover, *The "Light of the Word" [sic] or Holman Hunt's Great Allegorical Picture Translated into Words* (London: Wertherm, Macintosh and Hunt, 1862), pp. 11–12.

32   Edwin Sherratt, *A Popular Treatise on the Origin, Nature, and Properties of Light: Shewing the Wisdom, Goodness, and Great Designing Hand of the Beneficent Creator* (London: Simpkin, Marshall and Co., 1856), p. 11.

33   Lieut. R. W. H. Hardy, *Incidental Remarks on some Properties of Light; Being Part V. of An Essay on Vision* (London: Bell and Daldry, 1856), p. 3.

34   Charlotte Brontë, *Jane Eyre* (1847; New York and London: W. W. Norton and Company, 1987), p. 397.

35   *Morning Chronicle* (5 May 1856), p. 7.

36   *Art Journal* ns 2 (1856), p. 166. For an illuminating discussion of this painting, see Michael Hancher, '"Urgent private affairs": Millais's "Peace concluded, 1856"', *Burlington Magazine* 133 (1991), pp. 499–506.

37   Martin Jay, *Downcast Eyes. The Denigration of Vision in Twentieth-Century French Thought* (Berkeley: University of California Press, 1993), p. 51.

38   For an important discussion of the relationship between blindness and the sacred, see William R. Paulson, *Enlightenment, Romanticism, and the Blind in France* (Princeton University Press, 1987), pp. 5–9.

39   See William J. Bouwsma, 'Calvin and the Renaissance Crisis of Knowing', *Calvin Theological Journal* 17 (1982), p. 204.

40   'The Blind', *National Review* 10 (1860), p. 96.

41   [Dinah Mulock Craik], 'Blind', *The Unkind Word and Other Stories*, 2 vols. (London: Hurst and Blackett, 1870), p. 7.

42   John Milton, *Paradise Lost* (1674) III, *The Poems of John Milton*, ed John Carey and Alastair Fowler (London and Harlow: Longmans, 1968), pp. 563–6.

43   Andrew Marvell, 'On Milton's Paradise Lost' (1674), *The Poems and Letters of Andrew Marvell*, ed. H. M. Margoliouth; 3rd edn, vol. 1, *Poems*, revised by Pierre Legouis with the collaboration of E. E. Duncan-Jones (Oxford: Clarendon Press, 1971), p. 139.

44   William E. Aytoun, 'Blind Old Milton', *Blackwood's Edinburgh Magazine* 5 (1841), pp. 811–13.

45   Elizabeth Barrett Browning, *Essays on the Greek Christian Poets and the English Poets* (New York: James Miller, 1863), p. 197.

46   Elizabeth Barrett Barrett to Robert Browning, 20 March 1845, in
     Elvan Kintner, ed., *The Letters of Robert Browning and Elizabeth
     Barrett Barrett 1845–1846*, 2 vols. (Cambridge, Mass.: The Belknap
     Press of Harvard University Press, 1969) I, p. 41.

47   Stephen Phillips, 'To Milton, – Blind', *Poems* (London and New
     York: John Lane, The Bodley Head, 1898), p. 43.

48   W. Hanks Levy, *Blindness and the Blind: Or, a Treatise on the Science of
     Typology* (London: Chapman and Hall, 1872), p. 241. For a full study
     of Milton's blindness, see Eleanor Gertrude Brown, *Milton's
     Blindness* (New York: Columbia University Press, 1934).

49   Brontë, *Jane Eyre*, p. 573.

50   James Smith, *All Things Preaching Christ; Or, A Profitable Walk*
     (Cheltenham: Willey, *c.* 1840), p. 16.

51   Revd. H. J. Lewis, *Human Blindness and Divine Guidance* (Brigg:
     William Cressey, 1874), p. 4.

52   John Hamilton Thom, *Spiritual Blindness and Social Disruption*
     (London: John Chapman, 1849), p. 3.

53   Ibid., p. 24.

54   Christopher Wordsworth, *On Spiritual Blindness* (Oxford and
     London: John Henry and James Parker, 1857), p. 4.

55   Revd E. B. Pusey, *Sinful Blindness Amidst Imagined Light* (Oxford and
     London: Parker; London, Oxford and Cambridge: Rivingtons,
     1873), pp. 4–5.

56   Richard Proctor, *The Expanse of Heaven. A Series of Essays on the Won-
     ders of the Firmament* (London: Henry S. King and Co., 1873), p. 219.

57   John Guille Millais, *The Life and Letters of Sir John Everett Millais*, 2
     vols. (London: Methuen and Co., 1899), I, pp. 238–9.

58   Alfred Tennyson, quoted in Hallam Tennyson, *Alfred Lord Tennyson:
     A Memoir*, 2 vols. (London: Macmillan, 1897), I, p. 380.

59   See Malcolm Warner, 'John Everett Millais's *Autumn Leaves*: "a
     picture full of beauty and without subject"', in Leslie Parris, ed.,
     Pre-Raphaelite Papers (London: The Tate Gallery / Allen Lane, 1984),
     pp. 126–42.

60   Warner, *Pre-Raphaelite Papers*, p. 131.

61   *The Times*, 3 May 1856, p. 10.

62   'The Royal Academy', *Saturday Review*, 10 May 1856, p. 32. The
     reviewer identified the flower being held by the girl with an apple as
     a gentian, which was conventionally associated with bitterness.

63   *Art Journal* ns 2 (1856), p. 171.

64   *Athenaeum*, 3 May 1856, p. 590.

65   *Daily News*, 8 May 1856, p. 2.

66   *The Times*, 12 May 1856, p. 12.

67   George P. Landow, *William Holman Hunt and Typological Symbolism* (New Haven and London: Yale University Press, 1979), p. 111.

68   P. T. Forsyth, *Religion in Recent Art: Expository Lectures on Rossetti, Burne-Jones, Watts, Holman Hunt and Wagner* (1889; London: Hodder and Stoughton, 1901), p. 198.

69   Paul de Man, *Blindness and Insight. Essays in the Rhetoric of Contemporary Criticism* (2nd edn, revised; London: Methuen, 1983), pp. 111, 106.

70   'The Royal Academy. Exhibition the Eighty-Eighth: 1856', *Art Journal* 18 (1856), p. 171.

71   Elizabeth Barrett Browning to Sarianna Browning, November 1856, *The Letters of Elizabeth Barrett Browning*, ed. Frederic G. Kenyon, 2 vols. (London: Smith Elder, 1897) II, p. 242.

72   Elizabeth Barrett Browning, *Aurora Leigh* (1856), ed. Margaret Reynolds (New York and London: W. W. Norton, 1996), p. 308.

73   Ibid., p. 6.

74   Ibid., p. 9.

75   Ibid., p. 22.

76   Ibid., p. 230.

77   Ibid., p. 15.

78   Ibid., p. 58.

79   Ibid., p. 62. This simile, conveying the vulnerability of making one's feelings transparent, is curiously like the phrase Anthony Trollope used in his obituary of William Thackeray: 'He carried his heart-strings in a crystal case, and when they were wrung or when they were soothed all their workings were seen by friend and foe' (Anthony Trollope, 'W. M. Thackeray', *Cornhill Magazine* 9 (1864), p. 135).

80   Barrett Browning, *Aurora Leigh*, p. 209.

81   Ibid., pp. 52, 53.

82   Ibid., p. 150.

83   Ibid., p. 148.

84   Robert Browning, 'Introductory Essay' to the *Letters of Percy Bysshe Shelley* (1852), reprinted Robert Browning, *The Poems, Volume I*, ed. John Pettigrew (London: Penguin, 1981), p. 1001.

85   Ibid., p. 1002.

86   Barrett Browning, *Aurora Leigh*, p. 237.

87 Elizabeth Barrett Browning to John Kenyon, March 1855, Houghton Library, Harvard University. Quoted in Reynolds, *Aurora Leigh*, p. 331.

88 Barrett Browning, *Aurora Leigh* p. 98.

89 Although Barrett Browning repudiated the idea that she had been influenced by Brontë's novel, contemporaries were quick to draw a parallel – George Eliot, for example, saying that 'we are especially sorry that Mrs Browning has added one more to the imitations of the catastrophe in "Jane Eyre", by smiting her hero with blindness before he is made happy in the life of Aurora' ('Belles Lettres', *Westminster Review* ns 11 (1857), p. 306).

90 Barrett Browning, *Aurora Leigh*, p. 286.

91 John Tyndall, *Essays on the Use and Limit of the Imagination in Science* (London: Longman, Green and Co., 1870), p. 54.

92 Barrett Browning, *Aurora Leigh*, p. 239.

93 Walter Pater, *The Renaissance* (1873; London: Macmillan, 1900), p. 37.

94 Paulson, *Enlightenment, Romanticism, and the Blind*, p. 13.

4 Lifting the veil

1 Quoted Leon Edel, *Henry James: A Life* (New York: Harper and Row, 1985), p. 467. James was in fact referring to his mode of narrating *The Turn of the Screw*.

2 *Mirror*, ns 5 (1844), p. 231, quoted by Richard D. Altick, *The Shows of London* (Cambridge, Mass., and London: The Belknap Press of Harvard University Press, 1978), p. 340. For discussion of these anatomical models, see Altick, *The Shows of London*, pp. 55–6, 338–42; Ludmilla Jordanova, *Sexual Visions. Images of Gender in Science and Medicine Between the Eighteenth and Twentieth Centuries* (Hemel Hempstead: Harvester Wheatsheaf, 1989), pp. 43–65; Alison Smith, *The Victorian Nude. Sexuality, Morality and Art* (Manchester and New York: Manchester University Press, 1996), pp. 50–1.

3 Barbara Maria Stafford, *Body Criticism. Imaging the Unseen in Enlightenment Art and Medicine* (Cambridge, Mass.: The MIT Press, 1991), p. 17.

4 Michel Foucault, *The Birth of the Clinic. An Archaeology of Medical Perception* (1963; trans. A. M. Sheridan Smith, London: Tavistock Publications, 1973), p. 120.

5 Quoted in G. J. Barker-Benfield, *The Horrors of the Half-Known Life: Male Attitudes Towards Woman and Sexuality in Nineteenth-Century America* (New York: Harper and Row, 1976), p. 95.

6 Edith Simcox, quoted in *The George Eliot Letters*, ed. Gordon S. Haight, 9 vols. (New Haven and London: Yale University Press, 1954–78), IX, p. 220.

7 See Carroll Viera, '"The Lifted Veil" and George Eliot's Early Aesthetic', *Studies in English Literature 1500–1900* 24 (1984), pp. 749–767; and Sandra M. Gilbert and Susan Gubar, *The Madwoman in the Attic: The Woman Writer and the Nineteenth-Century Literary Imagination* (New Haven and London: Yale University Press, 1979), pp. 443–77.

8 For a full discussion of the implication of veil imagery in relation to *The Lifted Veil*, see Gilbert and Gubar, *The Madwoman in the Attic*, pp. 443–73. See also Eve Kosofsky Sedgwick, 'The Character in the Veil: Imagery of the Surface in the Gothic Novel', *PMLA* 96 (1981), pp. 255–70, and, on 'the veiling/unveiling of women's bodies as vehicles for thinking about knowledge, especially of a scientific or medical kind', Jordanova, *Sexual Visions*, pp. 87–110.

9 [Probably David T. Ansted], 'Giants and Dwarfs', *Temple Bar* 1 (1861), p. 543.

10 Unsigned article, 'Mr Darwin's Recent Inductions', *Eclectic Review* 14 (1868), p. 350.

11 George Eliot, *The Lifted Veil* (1859; London: Virago, 1985), p. 26.

12 Ibid., p. 4. See Gillian Beer, 'Myth and the Single Consciousness: *Middlemarch* and "The Lifted Veil"', in Ian Adam, ed., *This Particular Web: Essays on Middlemarch* (University of Toronto Press, 1975), pp. 91–115, and Terry Eagleton, 'Power and Knowledge in *The Lifted Veil*', *Literature and History* 9 (1983), pp. 52–61.

13 See Robert M. Young, *Mind, Brain, and Adaptation in the Nineteenth Century: Cerebral Localization and its Biological Context from Gall to Ferrier* (New York and Oxford: Oxford University Press, 1970, repr. 1990).

14 *George Eliot Letters*, IX, p. 220.

15 Rhoda Broughton and Elizabeth Bisland, *A Widower Indeed* (London: James R. Osgood, McIlvaine and Co., 1892), p. 276.

16 This story is found in Wilkie Collins, *The Queen of Hearts*, 3 vols. (London: Hurst and Blackett, 1859). See, further, Catherine Crowe on prophetic dreams in *The Night Side of Nature: or, Ghosts and Ghost Seers*, 2 vols. (London: T. C. Newby, 1848), I, pp. 107–64.

17 George Eliot, *Daniel Deronda* (1876; Oxford: Clarendon Press, 1984), p. 460.

18 Ibid., p. 461.

19 G. H. Lewes, *The Biographical History of Philosophy*, 4 vols. (London: Charles Knight, 1845–6), IV, p. 256.

20 Eliot, *Lifted Veil*, p. 20.

21 Ibid., p. 26.

22 Ibid., p. 36.

23 Ibid., p. 26.

24 Ibid., p. 47.

25 Ibid., p. 41.

26 Ibid., p. 52.

27 Lawrence Rothfield, *Vital Signs. Medical Realism in Nineteenth-Century Fiction* (Princeton University Press, 1992), p. 106.

28 Eliot, *Lifted Veil*, p. 44.

29 B. M. Gray, 'Pseudo-science and George Eliot's *The Lifted Veil*', *Nineteenth-Century Fiction* 36 (1982), pp. 407–23. It is worth noting Alison Winter's important point, that 'Mesmerism was an ocular practice in a more dynamic sense than phrenology and physiognomy. It provided both a display and an account of the way displays affected audiences, an account of the power of looking as well as a powerful sight for Victorians to see. It often achieved its displays through the use of the eye, since one of the primary means of establishing the trance was through sustained eye contact. The power of looking and the relations of influence operating between the person looking and the thing being looked at were at the heart of experiments' (Alison Winter, *Mesmerized. Powers of Mind in Victorian Britain* (Chicago and London: University of Chicago Press, 1998), pp. 30–1).

30 George Eliot to George Combe, 22 April 1852, *George Eliot Letters*, VIII, p. 45.

31 Eliot, *Lifted Veil*, p. 6.

32 William Gregory, *Letters to a Candid Inquirer on Animal Magnetism* (London: Taylor, Walton and Maberly, 1851), p. 427.

33 A notable exception is Malcolm Bull who, in 'Mastery and Slavery in *The Lifted Veil*', *Essays in Criticism* 48 (1998), links my own physiological emphasis with those other quasi-scientific forms in which Eliot had been interested when he writes that 'What has not been noted is the close parallel between this experiment and the theory of magnetism. Meunier's experiment involved the transfer of a bodily fluid from one individual to another, so allowing the dead person to regain the consciousness lost a few moments earlier. According to Gregory, magnetism worked in a similar way in that it, too, involved

the transfer of fluid. When someone was magnetized, it was "by the action of the operator, who, whether by passes, gazing, or contact, throws some of his odyle into the system of the patient". Other writers on magnetism put it more explicitly, describing magnetism as the "transfusion of the sensitive principle between living bodies."' (p. 257). Bull's references are to Gregory, *Letters*, p. 298, and J. C. Colquhoun, *Isis Revelata: An Enquiry into the Origin, Progress, and Present State of Animal Magnetism* 2 vols. (Edinburgh and London: Maclachan and Stewart, 1836), II, p. 52.

34   Eagleton, 'Power and Knowledge', p. 61. This is, of course, no more than an application of the meditation on Latimer's part which Eliot inserts into the text: 'So absolute is our soul's need of something hidden and uncertain for the maintenance of that doubt and hope and effort which are the breath of its life, that if the whole future were laid bare to us beyond to-day, the interest of all mankind would be bent on the hours that lie between; we should pant after the uncertainties of our one morning and our one afternoon; we should rush fiercely to the Exchange for our last possibility of speculation, of success, of disappointment: we should have a glut of political prophets foretelling a crisis or a no-crisis within the only twenty-four hours left open to prophecy. Conceive the condition of the human mind if all propositions whatsoever were self-evident except one, which was to become self-evident at the close of a summer's day, but in the meantime might be the subject of question, of hypothesis, of debate. Art and philosophy, literature and science, would fasten like bees on that one proposition which had the honey of probability in it, and be the more eager because their enjoyment would end with sunset' (*Lifted Veil*, pp. 43–4).

35   Judith Wilt, *Ghosts of the Gothic. Austen, Eliot, and Lawrence* (Princeton University Press, 1980), p. 185.

36   Mary Jacobus, *Reading Woman. Essays in Feminist Criticism* (London: Methuen, 1986), p. 269.

37   Beryl Gray, 'Afterword', *Lifted Veil*, p. 87.

38   Gray, 'Pseudo-science', p. 420.

39   Jennifer Uglow, *George Eliot* (London: Virago, 1987), p. 118.

40   U. C. Knoepflmacher, *George Eliot's Early Novels. The Limits of Realism* (Berkeley and Los Angeles: University of California Press, 1968), p. 148.

41   Eliot, *Lifted Veil*, p. 9.

42 For biographical details, see J. M. Olmsted, *Charles-Edouard Brown-Séquard: A Nineteenth-Century Neurologist and Endocrinologist* (Baltimore: The Johns Hopkins Press, 1946).

43 Olmsted, *Brown-Séquard*, p. 42.

44 E. Brown-Séquard, 'Recherches sur la possibilité de rappeler temporairement la vie des individus mourant de maladie', *Journal de la Physiologie de l'homme et des animaux* 1 (1858), p. 672. This and other translations from the French are my own.

45 Eliot, who had been told of this work by Emilia Pattison, commented in a letter to William Blackwood of 12 June 1879: 'I call this amusing – I ought rather to have said typical of the relation my books generally have with the French mind' *George Eliot Letters*, VII, p. 163.

46 A. Vulpian, *Leçons sur la Physiologie générale et comparée du système nerveux faite au muséum d'histoire naturelle* (Paris: G. Baillière, 1866), p. 460.

47 [Weir Mitchell], 'Was He Dead?' *Atlantic Monthly* 25 (1870), pp. 86–102. I am grateful to Lucy Bending for drawing this story to my attention.

48 John Blackwood to George Eliot, 18 May 1859, *George Eliot Letters*, III, p. 67.

49 George Henry Lewes, *The Physiology of Common Life*, 2 vols. (Edinburgh and London: William Blackwood, 1859) II., p. 254.

50 Ibid., p. 239

51 Eliot, *Lifted Veil*, p. 32.

52 Lewes, *Physiology*, I., p. 271.

53 Ibid., p. 241.

54 Eliot, *Lifted Veil*, p. 31.

55 Lewes, *Physiology*, I, p. 239.

56 Julia Kristeva, *Powers of Horror: An Essay in Abjection* (1980, trans. L. Roudiez; New York: Columbia University Press, 1982), p. 71.

57 Ibid., p. 4.

58 See Charles Egerton Jennings, *Transfusion: Its History, Indications, and Modes of Application* (London: Baillière, Tindall and Cox, 1883), pp. 3, 22, 35.

59 Bram Stoker, *Dracula* (1897; Oxford University Press, 1983), p. 128.

60 Ibid., p. 149.

61 Ernest Jones, *On the Nightmare* (London: The Hogarth Press and the Institute of Psycho-analysis, 1931), p. 110.

62 Elisabeth Bronfen, *Over Her Dead Body. Death, Femininity and the Aesthetic* (Manchester University Press, 1992), p. 317.

63 Jacobus, *Reading Woman*, p. 269.

64 Alice Meynell, *The Colour of Life and other Essays on Things Seen and Heard* (London: John Lane, 1896), pp. 1, 6.

65 Eliot, *Lifted Veil*, pp. 19–20.

66 Ibid., p. 21.

67 Lewes, *Physiology*, II, pp. 3–4.

68 George Eliot, *Middlemarch* (1871–2; Oxford: Clarendon Press, 1986), p. 10.

69 George Eliot to Barbara Leigh Smith Bodichon, 5 December 1859, George Eliot *Letters*, III, p. 227.

70 George Eliot to Sara Hennell, 8 February 1861, *George Eliot Letters*, III, p. 376.

71 This phrase is in fact Lewes's, from an essay of 1865, demonstrating still further the two-way circulation of ideas in this personal and intellectual partnership: George Lewes, *The Principles of Success in Literature*, ed. T. Shaper Knowlson (London: Walter Scott, 1898), p. 55.

72 George Eliot, *Adam Bede* (1859; London: Penguin Books, 1980), pp. 115–16.

73 Eliot, *Middlemarch*, p. 316.

74 Ibid., pp. 161–2.

75 [G. H. Lewes], 'Seeing is Believing', *Blackwood's Edinburgh Magazine* 88 (1860), p. 381.

76 For a revision of his position, see George Henry Lewes, 'Spiritualism and Materialism (Part I)', *Fortnightly Review* 25 (1876), pp. 479–93, and 'Spiritualism and Materialism (Part II)', *Fortnightly Review* 25 (1876), pp. 707–19.

77 Lewes, *Principles*, p. 30. For a clear and concise contemporary account of the relation between vision, perception and consciousness, which implicitly demonstrates how Lewes's views at this stage of his career build on the conclusions first of Descartes and then of Kant, see Thomas H. Huxley, 'On Descartes' "Discourse Touching the Method of Using one's Reason Rightly and of Seeking Scientific Truth"' [1870], *Methods and Results. Essays by Thomas H. Huxley* (London: Macmillan, 1893), pp. 172–90.

78 Lewes, *Principles*, p. 30.

79 John Tyndall, 'From a Lecture addressed to Teachers at the South Kensington Museum, April 30, 1861', *Essays on the Use and Limit of the*

Imagination in Science (London: Longman, Green and Co., 1870), pp. 3–4.

80 J. Tyndall, 'Atoms, Molecules, and Ether Waves', *Longman's Magazine* 1 (1882), p. 29.

81 Tyndall, *Essays*, p. 41.

82 Lewes, *Principles*, pp. 32–3.

83 Ibid., p. 50.

84 Ibid., p. 54. Even when dealing with the most extreme flights of fancy, though, Lewes is careful to impress that 'Imagination can only recall what Sense has previously impressed . . . Objects as fictitious as mermaids and hippogriffs are made up from the gatherings of Sense' (p. 56).

85 Ibid., p. 55.

86 Ibid., p. 63.

87 Ibid., p. 22.

88 Ibid., p. 48.

89 Ibid., p. 50.

90 Eliot, *Daniel Deronda*, p. 477.

91 Tyndall, 'Atoms, Molecules, and Ether Waves', p. 29.

92 Ibid., p. 51.

93 Ibid., p. 57.

5 Under the ice

1 George Joachim Goschen, 'The Use of Imagination in Study and in Life', address delivered at Edinburgh University, 19 November 1891, *The Cultivation and Use of Imagination* (London: Edward Arnold, 1893), p. 52.

2 Ibid., p. 54.

3 Ibid., p. 84.

4 John Tyndall, 'On the Scientific Use of the Imagination', *Essays on the Use and Limit of the Imagination in Science* (London: Longman, Green and Co., 1870), p. 16.

5 For popular scientific demonstrations, see Richard Altick, *The Shows of London*, (Cambridge, Mass.: The Belknap Press of Harvard University Press, 1978), pp. 363–89; David Gooding, '"In Nature's School": Faraday as an Experimentalist', in David Gooding and Frank A. J. L. James, eds., *Faraday Rediscovered. Essays on the Life and Work of Michael Faraday, 1791–1867* (Basingstoke: Macmillan, 1985), pp. 105–35. For Tyndall and demonstrations, see D. Thompson,

'John Tyndall and the Royal Institution', *Annals of Science* 13 (1957), pp. 9–21.

6 Tyndall, 'Scientific Use of the Imagination', pp. 15–16.

7 Ibid., p. 18.

8 Ibid., pp. 21–2.

9 *Lancet* (24 September 1870), quoted by Tyndall in *Essays*, p. 7.

10 Ibid., p. 15.

11 Dorothy Wordsworth, 'Journal of a Tour on the Continent 1820', *Journals of Dorothy Wordsworth*, ed. E. de Selincourt (London: Macmillan, 1941), p. 286. In the previous century, this 'standing paradox', as the traveller and glaciologist James Forbes called it in 1862, could be explained away by reference to a divine scheme. Thus Grouner, in Kéralio's translation of his *Histoire naturelle des glacières de Suisse* (1770), concluded his work on this point, seeing transcendental significance in the juxtaposition of ice and meadow: 'Par-tout le bien & le mal sont unis par la Sagesse éternelle, and concourent également l'ordre universel: partout on peut reconnoître cette grande vérité, que l'ordre est la grande loi du ciel.' But by the mid nineteenth century, very different types of explanation were being sought for such paradoxical juxtapositions.

12 John Ruskin, *Modern Painters,* v (1860), *The Complete Works of John Ruskin*, ed. E. T. Cook and Alexander Wedderburn, 39 vols. (London: George Allen, 1903–12), VII, p. 105. See vol. XXVI pp. xxxiii–xli for a discussion of Ruskin's involvement in nineteenth-century glaciation controversy, and Letter 34 of *Fors Clavigera*, *Works*, XXVII, pp. 635–43.

13 Lord Byron, 'Manfred', *The Complete Poetical Works*, ed. J. McGann, 7 vols. (Oxford: Clarendon Press, 1980–93) IV (1986), p. 55.

14 *Pall Mall Gazette*, 10 December 1887, quoted Ruskin, *Works*, XXXIV, p. 726.

15 W. D. Niven, ed., *The Scientific Papers of James Clerk Maxwell,* 2 vols. (Cambridge University Press, 1890) I, p. 156. See, further, Robert H. Kargon, 'Model and Analogy in Victorian Science: Maxwell and the French Physicists', *Journal of the History of Ideas* 30 (1969), pp. 423–36; Joseph Turner, 'Maxwell and the Method of Physical Analogy', *British Journal for Philosophy of Science* 6 (1955), pp. 226–38. The literature of metaphor's role within science is vast, but, for this aspect of metaphoricity, see W. M. Leatherdale, *The Role of Analogy, Model and Metaphor in Science* (Amsterdam: North-Holland, 1974), and, more broadly, Marcel Danesi, 'Thinking is Seeing: Visual Metaphors and

the Nature of Abstract Thought', *Semiotica* 80 (1990), pp. 221–37, and Stephen Tyler, 'The Vision Quest in the West, or What the Mind's Eye Sees', *Journal of Anthropological Research* 40 (1984), pp. 23–40.

16 Professor Clark-Maxwell, 'Molecules', lecture delivered before the British Association at Bradford, *Nature* 8 (25 September 1873), p. 438.

17 Charles Kingsley, quoted in J. C. Shairp, *Life and Letters of J. D. Forbes* (London: Macmillan, 1873), p. 162.

18 John Tyndall, *The Glaciers of the Alps. Being a Narrative of Excursions and Ascents, An Account of the Origin and Phenomenon of Glaciers, and An Exposition of the Physical Principles to which they are Related* (London: John Murray, 1860), p. [v].

19 Percy Bysshe Shelley, 'Mont Blanc', *The Complete Poetical Works of Percy Bysshe Shelley*, ed. N. Rogers, 4 vols. (Oxford University Press, 1975), II, pp. 78–9.

20 Mary Shelley, *The Journals of Mary Shelley 1814–1844*, ed. P. R. Feldman and D. Scott-Kilvert, 2 vols. (Oxford University Press, 1987), I, p. 119.

21 Percy Bysshe Shelley, *The Letters of Percy Bysshe Shelley*, ed. F. L. Jones 2 vols. (Oxford University Press, 1964), I, pp. 499–500.

22 Ibid., p. 499.

23 Leslie Stephen, *The Playground of Europe* (London: Longmans, Green and Co., 1871), pp. 30–1.

24 Helen Maria Williams, *A Tour in Switzerland; Or, A View of the Present State of the Governments and Manners of those Cantons: With Comparative Sketches of the Present State of Paris*, 2 vols. (Dublin: P. Wogan, 1798), II, p. 19.

25 William Coxe, in Williams, *Tour in Switzerland*, II, pp. 292–5.

26 'Eliza', from 'A Tour to the Glaciers of Savoy', *Eighteenth-Century Women Poets. An Oxford Anthology*, ed. Roger Lonsdale (Oxford University Press, 1989), p. 498.

27 Edward Gibbon, *Autobiography*, ed. M. M. Reese (London: Routledge and Kegan Paul, 1971), pp. 50–1, 113.

28 Stephen, *Playground of Europe*, pp. 28–9.

29 Tyndall, *Glaciers of the Alps*, p. 13.

30 For the history of nineteenth-century glaciology, see M. T. Greene, *Geology in the Nineteenth Century* (Ithaca: Cornell University Press, 1982); A. Hallam, *Great Geological Controversies* 2nd edn (Oxford University Press, 1989); B. Hansen, 'The Early History of Glacial Theory in British Geology', *Journal of Glaciology* 9 (1970), pp. 135–41.

31 William Wordsworth, 'Resolution and Independence' (1802), *'Poems, in Two Volumes' and Other Poems, 1800–1807*, ed. J. Curtis (Ithaca: Cornell University Press, 1983), p. 126.

32 See, further, chapter 3 of Kenneth Bendiner, *An Introduction to Victorian Painting* (New Haven and London: Yale University Press, 1985), pp. 47–63.

33 Wordsworth, *Poems*, p. 126.

34 Adam Sedgwick, *Annals of Philosophy* 9 (1825), p. 241, quoted in Hallam, *Great Geological Controversies*, p. 87.

35 Charles Lyell, *Principles of Geology, Being an Attempt to Explain the Former Changes of the Earth's Surface, by Reference to Causes Now in Operation*, 3 vols. (London: John Murray, 1830–3).

36 See Hallam, *Great Geological Controversies*, p. 91.

37 Mary Shelley, *Frankenstein or the Modern Prometheus*, ed. M. K. Joseph (1818; London: Oxford University Press, 1969), p. 96.

38 Alfred Wills, *Wanderings Among the High Alps*, 2nd edn, revised (London: Richard Bentley, 1858), p. 354.

39 Ibid., p. 355.

40 John Tyndall, *Hours of Exercise in the Alps* (London: Longmans, Green and Co., 1871) p. 75.

41 James D. Forbes, *Travels through the Alps of Savoy and Other Parts of the Pennine Chain*, 2nd edn (1843; Edinburgh: Adam and Charles Black, 1845), p. 22.

42 Wills, *Wanderings*, p. 366.

43 Ruskin, *Fors Clavigera* (1873), *Works*, XXVII, p. 642.

44 Forbes, *Travels*, p. 387.

45 G. Burnet, *Bishop Burnet's Travels through France, Italy, Germany, and Switzerland* (printed as *Dr Burnet's travels, or Letters containing an account of what seemed most remarkable in Switzerland, Italy, France, and German, &c.* (1687; Edinburgh: Thomas Glas, 1752)), p. 11.

46 Part of a letter from William Burnet, Esq., FRS, to Dr Hans Sloane, concerning the icy mountains of Switzerland, Geneva, 12 October 1708, *Philosophical Transactions of the Royal Society* 320 (March and April 1709), pp. 316–17.

47 Louis Agassiz, *A Journey to Switzerland and Pedestrian Tours in that Country* (London: Smith, Elder and Co., 1833), p. 241.

48 Forbes, *Travels*, p. 59.

49 Stephen, *Playground of Europe*, p. 50.

50 Percy Shelley, *Letters*, I, p. 499.

51 Forbes, *Travels*, p. 192.

52 [J.R. Leifchild], 'Glaciers', *British Quarterly Review* 32 (1860), p. 347.

53 Percy Bysshe Shelley, 'Prometheus Unbound', *Complete Poetical Works of Percy Bysshe Shelley*, ed. T. Hutchinson (1905; London: Oxford University Press, repr.1952), p. 208.

54 Stephen, *Playground of Europe*, pp. 15–18.

55 Ruskin, according to the *Pall Mall Gazette* (10 December 1887), quoted *Works*, XXXIV, pp. 725–6.

56 'Alpine Notes: Exorcising the Glaciers', *Alpine Journal* 9 (1880), p. 495.

57 Henry Wadsworth Longfellow, *Hyperion: A Romance* (1839; London: George Routledge and Sons, 1886), p. 152.

58 James D. Forbes, 'On Glaciers', *Good Words* 3 (1862), p. 342.

59 Tyndall, *Glaciers of the Alps*, p. 20.

60 Gerard Manley Hopkins, journal entry for 20 July 1868, *The Journals and Papers of Gerard Manley Hopkins*, ed. Humphry House; completed by G. Storey (London: Oxford University Press, 1959), p. 178.

61 Wordsworth, 'Illustration. The Jung-Frau and the Fall of the Rhine near Schaffhausen'(1820), *The Poetical Works of William Wordsworth*, ed. E. de Selincourt and H. Darbishire (London: Clarendon Press, 1959), III, pp. 382–3.

62 Longfellow, *Hyperion*, p. 149.

63 Tyndall, *Glaciers of the Alps*, p. 106.

64 Ruskin, *Deucalion* (1875), *Works*, XXVI, p. 133.

65 Ruskin to Effie Gray, 15 December 1847, in *The Order of Release. The Story of John Ruskin, Effie Gray and John Everett Millais Told for the First Time in their Unpublished Letters*, ed. Admiral Sir W. James (London: John Murray, 1948), p. 68.

66 Unsigned article [J. H. Burton], 'At the Alps Again. Part II', *Blackwood's Edinburgh Magazine* 102 (1867), p. 551.

67 Ruskin, *Modern Painters*, III, *Works*, V, p. 320.

68 Ruskin, *Fors Clavigera* (1873), *Works*, XXVII, p. 635.

69 Anthony Trollope, *Can You Forgive Her?* (1864–5; Oxford University Press, 1982), p. 44.

70 [E. J. Davis], *Pyrna: A Commune; or, Under the Ice*, (London: Bickers and Son, 1875), p. 58.

71 Davis, *Pyrna*, p. 143.

72 George Meredith, *The Egoist* (1879; Harmondsworth: Penguin, 1968), p. 100.

73 Unsigned article, 'Glaciers', *North British Review* 31 (1859), p. 91.

74   John Tyndall, 'On the Scientific Use of the Imagination' (1870), in *Scientific Use of the Imagination and other Essays*, 3rd edn (London: Longmans, Green and Co., 1872), p. 33.

75   Ibid., p. 6.

6   **The buried city**

1   Sigmund Freud, *Civilization and its Discontents* (1930), *The Standard Edition of the Complete Psychological Works of Sigmund Freud*, ed. James Strachey, 24 vols. (London: Hogarth Press and the Institute of Psycho-Analysis, 1953–74), vol. XXI (1960), p. 70. 'Archaeology', as Malcolm Bowie has reminded us, 'was for Freud the supreme combination of art and science and exerted a special fascination upon him throughout his career': a career which 'spanned a golden age of archaeological discovery'. Freud was 'an avid reader of archaeological memoirs and a spendthrift collector of antiquities'; archaeological references are strewn and embedded throughout his works. See Malcolm Bowie, *Freud, Proust and Lacan: Theory as Fiction* (Cambridge University Press, 1987), p. 18.

2   Freud, 'A Note Upon the "Mystic Writing Pad"', *Standard Edition*, vol. XIX, p. 227.

3   Freud, *Civilization*, pp. 70–1.

4   Rosalind Williams, *Notes on the Underground. An Essay on Technology, Society, and the Imagination* (Cambridge, Mass., and London: MIT Press, 1990), p. 48.

5   Thomas De Quincey, 'Suspiria de Profundis', *Blackwood's Edinburgh Magazine* 57 (1845), pp. 269–85, 489–502, reprinted in Grevel Lindop, ed., *Confessions of an English Opium-Eater and Other Writings* (Oxford University Press, 1985), p. 140. Josephine McDonagh, 'Writings on the Mind: Thomas De Quincey and the Importance of the Palimpsest in Nineteenth-Century Thought', *Prose Studies* 10 (1987), pp. 207–24, does an excellent job of putting De Quincey's ideas about the palimpsest into a full nineteenth-century context. She relates his use of the trope to G. H. Lewes's, and I am indebted to her work in what follows, particularly in my conclusion. It would seem that Freud had not read De Quincey on the palimpsest: see Charles L. Proudfit, 'Thomas De Quincey and Sigmund Freud: Sons, Fathers, Dreamers – Precursors of Psychoanalytic Developmental Psychology', in Robert Lance Snyder, ed., *Thomas*

De Quincey. Bicentenary Studies (Norman and London: University of Oklahoma Press, 1985), pp. 94–5.

6   De Quincey, 'Suspiria de Profundis', p. 145.

7   Ibid., p. 145.

8   Forbes Benignus Winslow, *On Obscure Diseases of the Brain and Disorders of the Mind* (1860; 4th edn, London: John Churchill, 1868), p. 291.

9   De Quincey, 'Suspiria de Profundis', p. 145.

10 James Forbes, *Travels through the Alps of Savoy and Other Parts of the Pennine Chain* (1843; 2nd edn Edinburgh: Adam and Charles Black, 1845), p. 22.

11 For a useful brief recent discussion about the location of the memory, see Mortimer Mishkin and Tim Appenzeller, 'The Anatomy of Memory', *Scientific American* 256 (1987), pp. 62–71.

12 F.W. Edridge-Green, *Memory. Its Logical Relations and Cultivation* (London: Baillière, Tindall and Cox, 1888), p. 3.

13 G. H. Lewes, *Problems of Life and Mind*, 3rd series, 2 vols. (London: Trübner and Co., 1879), II, p. 113.

14 Sir James Paget, *Lectures on Surgical Pathology delivered at the Royal College of Surgeons of England*, ed. William Turner, 2nd edn (London: Longmans, Green, 1853), p. 40

15 Lewes, *Problems of Life and Mind*, II, p. 119.

16 Ibid., p. 121.

17 Christina Rossetti, 'Memory' (1857), *Poems and Prose*, ed. Jan Marsh (London: J. M. Dent, 1994), p. 60.

18 Thomas Richards, *The Imperial Archive. Knowledge and the Fantasy of Empire* (London and New York: Verso, 1993), p. 11.

19 Frances Power Cobbe, 'Unconscious Cerebration', *Darwinism in Morals, and Other Essays* (London and Edinburgh: Williams and Norgate, 1872), p. 308. The article was first published in *Macmillan's Magazine* 23 (1870), pp. 24–37, as 'Unconscious Cerebration: A Psychological Study'.

20 *The Confessions of Saint Augustine*, trans. E. B. Pusey (London: Dent, 1907), p. 213.

21 E. S. Dallas, *The Gay Science*, 2 vols. (London: Chapman and Hall, 1866), I, pp. 209–10.

22 Ibid., p. 213.

23 Cobbe, 'Unconscious Cerebration', p. 323.

24 William B. Carpenter, *Principles of Mental Physiology, with Their*

Applications to the Training and Discipline of the Mind, and the Study of its Morbid Conditions, 2nd edition (London: Henry S. King and Co., 1875), p. 436.

25   William Stokes, *Memory,* 7th and enlarged edn (London: Houlston and Sons, 1876), p. 83. Many of the late Victorian popular writings about improving the memory relied heavily on classical and medieval ideas: for these, see Frances Yates, *The Art of Memory* (London: Routledge and Kegan Paul, 1966).

26   John Samson, *Inventions and their Commercial Development: A Practical Handbook for Inventors and Investors Showing How to Invent, What to Invent, How to Patent, How to Make Money by Inventions* (London: Messrs Simpkin, Marshall, Hamilton, Kent and Co., 1896), p. 2. I am indebted to Clare Pettitt for this reference.

27   George Eliot, *Middlemarch* (1872; New York and London: W. W. Norton, 1977), pp. 134–5.

28   Charles Dickens, *Pictures from Italy* (1846; London: Penguin Books, 1998), p. 118.

29   Ibid., p. 118.

30   Walter Benjamin, *Charles Baudelaire: A Lyric Poet in the Age of High Capitalism* (trans. Harry Zohn, London: New Left Books, 1973), p. 35.

31   Dickens, *Pictures from Italy,* p. 93.

32   Ibid., p. 93.

33   Ibid., p. 77.

34   Richard Altick, *The Shows of London* (Cambridge, Mass., and London: Harvard University Press, 1978), p. 220.

35   Charles Dickens to John Forster, 30 August 1846, *The Letters of Charles Dickens. Volume Four, 1844–46,* ed. Kathleen Tillotson (Oxford: Clarendon Press, 1977), p. 612.

36   Dickens, *Pictures from Italy,* pp. 73–4.

37   Ibid., p. 182.

38   Ibid., p. 83.

39   Ibid., p. 137.

40   Ibid., p. 171.

41   Ibid., p. 187.

42   Sir Edward Bulwer-Lytton, *The Last Days of Pompeii* (1834; London: J. M. Dent, Everyman edn, 1906), p. 356.

43   Ibid., p. 357.

44   W. H. Davenport Adams, *Beneath the Surface; Or, the Wonders of the Underground World* (London: T. Nelson and Sons, 1876), p. 11.

45   Ibid., pp. 324–5.

46   Edmund Spenser, *The Faerie Queene* (1596), Book I, Canto VII, ix, *The Poetical Works of Edmund Spenser*, (ed. J. C. Smith, Oxford: Clarendon Press), 3 vols., 1909, p. 97.

47   Mary Douglas, *Purity and Danger: An Analysis of the Concepts of Pollution and Taboo* (London: Routledge and Kegan Paul, 1966), p. 121.

48   Charles Dickens, *Bleak House* (1853; New York and London: W. W. Norton, 1977), p. 403.

49   Charlotte Brontë to W. S. Williams, 29 March 1848, in T. J. Wise and J. A. Symington, *The Brontës: Their Lives, Friendships and Correspondence*, 4 vols. (Oxford: Basil Blackwell, 1933), II, p. 201. Michael Warnke, *Political Landscape. The Art History of Nature* (1992; trans. David McLintock, London: Reaktion Books, 1994), p. 95, notes that the imagery of the volcano was in fact co-opted, at the time of the French Revolution, *to* the radical cause. He reproduces (p. 98) A. Desperet's engraving *The Third Eruption of the Volcano of 1789*, showing the word 'Liberté' being precipitated from a volcano along with rocks and ash and lava.

50   Charlotte Brontë, *Jane Eyre* (1848; New York and London: W. W. Norton, 1987), p. 190.

51   Charlotte Brontë, *Villette* (1853; Oxford: Clarendon Press, 1984), p. 51.

52   William Hale White, *Mark Rutherford's Deliverance. Being the Second Part of his Autobiography* (1885; London: Oxford University Press and Humphrey Mitford, 1936), p. 68.

53   Peter Stallybrass and Allon White, *The Politics and Poetics of Transgression* (London: Methuen, 1986), pp. 134–5.

54   Friedrich Engels, *The Condition of the Working Class in England in 1844* (1845; trans. 1886; London: Penguin, 1987), p. 86. See further Steven Marcus, *Engels, Manchester, and the Working Class* (London: Weidenfeld and Nicolson, 1974).

55   Engels, *Condition of the Working Class*, p. 87.

56   Thomas Miller, *Picturesque Sketches of London, Past and Present* (London: Office of the National Illustrated Library, 1852), pp. 206–7.

57   John Hollingshead, *Underground London* (London: Groombridge and Sons, 1862), pp. 2–3.

58   John Parker, 'On the Literature of the Working Classes', in Viscount Ingestre, ed., *Meliora: Or Better Times to Come. Being the Contributions of Many Men Touching the Present State and Prospects of Society*, 2 vols. (London: John W. Parker and Son, 1852–3), II, p. 193.

59   Alexander Thomson, 'Our Treatment of the Lower and Lowest Classes of Society', in Ingestre, *Meliora*, I, p. 18.

60   See Kathryn Hume, 'Eat or Be Eaten: H. G. Wells's *Time Machine*', *Philological Quarterly* 69 (1990), pp. 233–51.

61   Patrick Brantlinger, *Rule of Darkness. British Literature and Imperialism, 1830–1914* (Ithaca and London: Cornell University Press, 1988), pp. 246–7.

62   General Booth, *In Darkest England and The Way Out* (London: International Headquarters of the Salvation Army, 1890), pp. 12–13.

63   Hollingshead, *Underground London*, p. 60.

64   Ibid., p. 2.

65   Ibid., p. 1.

66   Ibid., p. 130.

67   Ibid., p. 55.

68   Henry Mayhew, quoted in Michael Harrison, *London Beneath the Pavement* (London: Peter Davies, 1961), p. 97.

69   Hollingshead, *Underground London*, pp. 70–1, 79.

70   Henry Mayhew, '"Home is Home, Be It Never So Homely"', in Ingestre, *Meliora*, I, p. 276.

71   Charles Kingsley, *Alton Locke* (1850; London: Macmillan, 1908), p. 262.

72   Sidney Godolphin Osborne, 'Immortal Sewerage', in Ingestre, *Meliora*, II, p. 7.

73   Hollingshead, *Underground London*, p. 11.

74   Victor Hugo, *Les Misérables* (translated N. Denny, Harmondsworth: Penguin, 1980, 2 vols.), II, p. 369; quoted in Stallybrass and White, *Politics and Poetics of Transgression*, pp. 140–1.

75   *The Wild Boys of London; Or, The Children of the Night*, I (London: Newsagents' Publishing Co., 1863), p. 294. I am very grateful to Sally Powell for finding this reference.

76   Constance Classen, David Howes and Anthony Synnott, *Aroma. The Cultural History of Smell* (London and New York: Routledge, 1994), p. 89. Their reference is to Charles Darwin, *The Descent of Man and Selection in Relation to Sex* (1871; 2nd revised edn, New York: D. Appleton, 1898), pp. 17–18. The authors extend their observation about the hierarchisation of the senses in the nineteenth century to questions of gender: sight, they argue, 'increasingly became associated with men, who – as explorers, scientists, politicians or industrialists – were perceived as discovering and dominating the world

through their keen gaze. Smell, in turn, was now considered the sense of intuition and sentiment, of home-making and seduction, all of which were associated with women' (p. 84).

77   For the pitfall of privileging the visual above other senses, see Constance Classen, *Worlds of Sense. Exploring the Senses in History and Across Cultures* (London and New York: Routledge, 1993).

78   Walter J. Ong, *The Presence of the Word: Some Prolegomena for Cultural and Religious History* (New Haven: Yale University Press, 1967), p. 128.

79   Ibid., pp. 129–30.

80   For a comprehensive account of the London sewage system, see David Owen, *The Government of Victorian London, 1855–1889. The Metropolitan Board of Works, the Vestries, and the City Corporation*, ed. R. Macleod (Cambridge, Mass.: The Belknap Press of Harvard University Press, 1982), pp. 47–73. Chapter 4 of Anthony S. Wohl, *Endangered Lives. Public Health in Victorian Britain* (London: J. M. Dent and Sons, 1983), pp. 80–116, gives a good general account of sewage conditions and reform throughout Victorian England.

81   William Feaver, *The Art of John Martin* (Oxford: Clarendon Press, 1975), p. 125. The quotation is from Byron's *Sardanapalus* (1821), Act v, sc. i, lines 195–7.

82   Hollingshead, *Underground London*, p. 99.

83   Ibid., p. 208.

84   Ibid., p. 201.

85   For these and other developments, see F. L. Stevens, *Under London. A Chronicle of London's Life-Lines and Relics* (London: J. M. Dent, 1939), and Harrison, *London Beneath the Pavement*.

86   Charles Dickens, *Hard Times* (1854; London: Penguin, 1995), p. 210. For the early history of the telegraph in England, see Iwan Rhys Morus, 'The Electric Ariel: Telegraphy and Commercial Culture in Early Victorian England', *Victorian Studies* 39 (1996), pp. 339–78. Some very stimulating discussion concerning telecommunications and communication in a wider sense within Victorian England can be found in Trev Lynn Broughton, *Men of Letters, Writing Lives. Masculinity and Literary Auto/Biography in the Late Victorian Period* (London and New York: Routledge, 1999), pp. 41–59.

87   See John Glover, *London's Underground. An Illustrated History of the World's Premier Underground System* (1951; 8th edn, Shepperton: Ian Allen, 1996).

88   Dion Boucicault, *After Dark* (1868), reprinted in J. O. Bailey, ed.,
      British Plays of the Nineteenth Century (New York: Odyssey Press,
      1966), p. 300. Although the playbill and original printed version
      announce that the play was the authorised adaptation of Mmes
      Grange and Dennery's *Les oiseaux de proie*, Bailey suggests that this
      particular scene was probably based on Augustin Daly's *Under the
      Gaslight*, which had been playing at the Whitechapel Pavilion in July
      1868, before *After Dark* opened at the Princess's Theatre on 12
      August: in *Under the Gaslight*, however, the train runs in the open air,
      and a modern *frisson* is created by shifting the setting to the
      Metropolitan Railway (p. 281).

89   Hollingshead, *Underground London*, p. 130.

90   Ibid., p. 23.

91   Williams, *Notes on the Underground*, p. 54.

92   Carpenter, *Principles of Mental Physiology*, p. 429.

93   Michel de Certeau, *The Practice of Everyday Life* (1984; trans. Steven
      Randall, Berkeley, Los Angeles and London: University of
      California Press, 1988), p. 92.

94   Ibid., p. 93.

95   M. Merleau-Ponty, *Phenomenology of Perception* (trans. Colin Smith,
      1962; London and New York: Routledge, 1995), p. 255.

96   Thomas Carlyle, 'On History' (1830), *Critical and Miscellaneous
      Essays*, 5 vols. (London: Macmillan, 1899), II, pp. 89–90.

97   See further Laura Otis, *Organic Memory: History and the Body in the
      Late Nineteenth and Early Twentieth Centuries* (Lincoln and London:
      University of Nebraska Press, 1994).

98   G. H. Lewes, *Problems of Life and Mind. First Series, Psychological
      Principles* (London: Trübner and Co., 1874), p. 120.

99   Jacques Derrida, *Writing and Difference* (trans. Alan Bass, London
      and Henley: Routledge and Kegan Paul, 1978), pp. 226–7.

7   The rôle of the art critic

1   John Ruskin, *Academy Notes, 1859. Society of British Artists*, *The
     Complete Works of John Ruskin*, 39 vols., ed. E. T. Cook and Alexander
     Wedderburn (London: George Allen, 1903–12), XIV, pp. 256–7.

2   James McNeill Whistler, *The Gentle Art of Making Enemies*, 2nd and
     enlarged edn (London: Heinemann, 1892), p. 30.

3   Ibid., p. 30.

4 For a full account of this trial, see Linda Merrill, *A Pot of Paint: Aesthetics on Trial in Whistler v. Ruskin* (Washington and London: Smithsonian Institution Press, 1992).

5 Whistler, *Gentle Art*, p. 29.

6 Ibid., p. 26.

7 Merrill, *A Pot of Paint*, p. 259.

8 'The Action', Whistler, *Gentle Art*, p. 5.

9 Albrecht Dürer, *The Writings of Albrecht Dürer*, trans. and ed. W. M. Conway (first published as *Literary Remains of Albrecht Dürer*, Cambridge University Press, 1889; reprinted London: Peter Owen, 1958), p. 177.

10 Sir Joshua Reynolds, *The Works of Sir Joshua Reynolds*, ed. Edmund Malone, 3 vols. (4th edn, corrected, London: T. Cadell, Jun., and W. Davies, 1801) II, p. 186.

11 Unsigned article, 'A Few Words about the Cartoons', *New Monthly Magazine* 69 (1843), p. 261.

12 Frederick Wedmore, 'Mr Whistler's Theories and Mr Whistler's Art', *Nineteenth-Century* (1879), p. 334.

13 Whistler, *Gentle Art* p. 25.

14 Ibid., p. 31.

15 The lecture was repeated in Cambridge, Oxford, and four more times in London: on the last of these occasions, its notoriety was used to launch the discussion-oriented Chelsea Arts Club in 1891.

16 Whistler, *Gentle Art*, p. 149.

17 Ibid., p. 146.

18 Ibid., p. 139.

19 Ibid., p. 152.

20 Ibid., pp. 148–9. Joseph Archer Crowe and Giovanni Battista Cavalcaselle published their methodologically pioneering *A New History of Painting in Italy from the Second to the Sixteenth Century*, 3 vols. (London: John Murray, 1864–6) in 1864, followed by other joint works.

21 Whistler, *Gentle Art*, p. 152.

22 Francis Turner Palgrave, *Essays on Art* (London and Cambridge: Macmillan, 1866), p. vi.

23 J. B. Atkinson, 'Decline of Art: Royal Academy and Grosvenor Gallery', *Blackwoods* 138 (1885), p. 4. Atkinson sustained a campaign in *Blackwoods* against democracy in the arts for almost three decades. See George P. Landow, 'There Began to Be a Great Talking

about the Fine Arts', in Josef L. Altholz, ed., *The Mind and Art of Victorian England* (Minneapolis: University of Minnesota Press, 1976), p. 128.

24   Frederic Harrison, 'A Few Words about Picture Exhibitions', *Nineteenth-Century* 24 (1888), p. 32.

25   Ibid., p. 146.

26   Oscar Wilde, 'Mr Whistler's Ten O'Clock', *Pall Mall Gazette*, 21 February 1885, p. 14.

27   Sheridan Ford, introduction to Whistler, *The Gentle Art of Making Enemies* (New York: F. Stokes and Bro., 1890), p. 29.

28   Henry James, 'On Art-Criticism and Whistler', *Nation*, 13 February 1879, p. 199.

29   Henry James, 'On Some Pictures Lately Exhibited', *Galaxy* 20 (1875), p. 89.

30   For the emergence of a class of professional art critics in the 1860s, see Elizabeth Prettejohn, 'Aesthetic Value and the Professionalization of Victorian Art Criticism 1837–78', *Journal of Victorian Culture* 2 (1997), pp. 71–94. She traces not only the avenues for art criticism within the press, and the values which critics sought to promote, but notes that these men (as they almost ubiquitously were) 'were soon able to offer articles on art theory, foreign art, and the art of the past, as well as exhibition reviews, to a variety of periodicals. Indeed, the professionals began to assert autonomy from the periodical press remarkably quickly: from the mid-1860s, they began to publish books in all of the new areas of their expertise, as well as republishing their anonymous reviews in signed collections' (p. 78).

31   Ruskin, *The Laws of Fésole* (1877–8), *Works*, XV, p. 378.

32   Ruskin, *Modern Painters*, III, *Works*, V, p. 333.

33   George L. Hersey claims that Ruskin is 'the first great negative critic in the history of art. Before him art critics, in so far as they may be said to have existed as a separate species, principally concerned themselves with what they considered to be good art. Ruskin concerned himself equally with the good and with what he felt, perhaps even more passionately, to be bad' ('Ruskin as an Optical Thinker', in John Dixon Hunt and Faith M. Holland, eds., *The Ruskin Polygon. Essays on the Imagination of John Ruskin* (Manchester University Press, 1982), p. 57. The literature on Ruskin and aesthetics is very extensive: of particular relevance are Raymond E. Fitch, *The Poison Sky. Myth and Apocalypse in Ruskin* (Athens and London: Ohio

University Press, 1982); Elizabeth K. Helsinger, *Ruskin and the Art of the Beholder* (Cambridge, Mass., and London: Harvard University Press, 1982); and George Landow, *The Aesthetic and Critical Theories of John Ruskin* (Princeton University Press, 1971).

34   Ruskin, *The Eagle's Nest* (1872), *Works*, XXII, pp. 194–5.

35   Ibid., p. 200.

36   Ruskin, 'Morning Thoughts at Geneva' (1876), *Works,* XXIX, pp. 575–6.

37   Ruskin, *Modern Painters,* I (1843), *Works*, III, pp. 141–2.

38   Ruskin, *Modern Painters,* IV (1856), *Works*, VI, p. 368.

39   Ruskin, *Modern Painters,* I, *Works*, III, pp. 142–3.

40   Ruskin, *The Stones of Venice* (1853), *Works*, XI, pp. 202–3.

41   Ruskin, *The Cestus of Aglaia* (1866), *Works*, XIX, p. 150. For Ruskin's views on photography, see further Michael Harvey, 'Ruskin and Photography', *Oxford Art Journal* 7 (1984), pp. 25–33.

42   Walter Benjamin, 'The Work of Art in the Age of Mechanical Reproduction' (1936; trans. Harry Zohn, in *Illuminations*, ed. Hannah Arendt, (New York: Harcourt, Brace and World, 1968), p. 222.

43   See Jeremy Maas, *Gambart: Prince of the Victorian Art World* (London: Barrie and Jenkins, 1975), and Dianne Sachko Macleod, *Art and the Victorian Middle Class: Money and the Making of Cultural Identity* (New York: Cambridge University Press, 1996).

44   Pierre Bourdieu, *Distinction. A Social Critique of the Judgement of Taste* (1979; trans. Richard Nice, London: Routledge and Kegan Paul, 1984), p. 77, and see Paul DiMaggio and Michael Unseem, 'Social Class and Arts Consumption', *Theory and Society* 5 (1978), p. 152.

45   Pierre Bourdieu, 'Cultural Reproduction and Social Reproduction', *Knowledge, Education and Cultural Change*, ed. Richard Brown (London: Tavistock, 1973), p. 73.

46   Unsigned review, 'An English Critic of French Painting, 1868', *North American Review* (1868), reprinted in John L. Sweeney, ed., *The Painter's Eye. Notes and Essays on the Pictorial Arts by Henry James* (1956; Madison: University of Wisconsin Press, 1989), p. 33.

47   Philip G. Hamerton, 'Art Criticism', *Cornhill Magazine* 8 (1863), p. 334. Hamerton (1834–94) studied painting in Paris in the 1850s, and French criticism – 'the most discriminating and the most accurate in the world', he called it (Philip Gilbert Hamerton, *Philip Gilbert Hamerton: An Autobiography 1834–1858, and a Memoir by his Wife*, (E.

Hamerton), *1858–1894* (London: Seeley and Co., 1897), p. 201) – formed the model for his own writing on art. Invitations to write for the press followed the publication of *A Painter's Camp in the Highlands*, 2 vols. (Cambridge and London: Macmillan and Co., 1862). He contributed to the *Fine Arts Quarterly Review*, the *Cornhill*, *Macmillan's*, and around 1865 succeeded Francis Palgrave as regular art correspondent to the *Saturday Review*. He resigned this position in 1868, although continuing to write for the *Saturday* as well as the *Globe* and the *Pall Mall Gazette*, in order to concentrate on the launching and editorship of the high-quality artistic monthly, the *Portfolio*.

48 Hamerton, 'Art Criticism', p. 337.

49 Ibid., p. 338.

50 Ibid., p. 335.

51 Ibid.

52 Ibid., p. 337.

53 Ibid.

54 Ibid., p. 339.

55 Ibid., p. 340.

56 John Ruskin, *Notes on Some of the Principal Pictures Exhibited in the Rooms of the Royal Academy* (1855), *Works*, XIV, p. 5.

57 Frances P. Verney, 'Where are We in Art?' *Contemporary Review* 36 (1879), p. 597.

58 J. Dawson, *Practical Journalism: How to Enter Thereon and Succeed* (London: L. Upcott Gill, 1885), p. 56.

59 Hamerton, 'Art Criticism', p. 335.

60 Ibid., p. 341.

61 Ibid., p. 340.

62 Unsigned article, 'Art Criticism', *Saturday Review* 55 (19 May 1883), p. 624. The condescending terms extend, of course, to the implied critic, since having recourse to John Lemprière's *Classical Dictionary* constitutes reliance on secondary, summarising sources, rather than the possession of an education which has provided a grounding in classical writers.

63 Unsigned review, 'The Royal Academy (First Notice)', *Athenaeum* no. 3158 (5 May 1888), pp. 572–3.

64 *Art Journal* ns 2 (1856), p. 164.

65 Philip Gilbert Hamerton, 'Liber Memorialis: On the Artistic Observation of Nature', *Art Journal* 28 (1866), p. 1.

66 Ibid., p. 1.

67 George Henry Lewes, *The Physiology of Common Life*, 2 vols. (Edinburgh and London: William Blackwood, 1859) II, p. 68.

68 Robert Louis Stevenson, *Across the Plains, With Other Memories and Essays* (1879; London: Chatto and Windus, 1892), p. 66.

69 George Henry Lewes, *Problems of Life and Mind. Third Series*, 2 vols. (London: Trübner and Co., 1879), p. 141.

70 Hamerton, 'Liber Memorialis', p. 2.

71 Ibid., p. 2.

72 Harry Quilter, *Opinions on Men, Women and Things* (London: Swann Sonnenschein and Co., 1909), p. 287.

73 Quilter, *Opinions*, p. 234. He conveniently ignores the legal wrangles of his arch-enemy Whistler.

74 Ibid., p. 245.

75 Unsigned article (W. H. Leeds), 'Strictures on Art and Exhibitions', *Fraser's Magazine* 2 (1830), p. 96.

76 Unsigned review, 'The Royal Academy Exhibition II', *Saturday Review* 3 (23 May 1857), p. 475.

77 Unsigned review, 'The Suffolk-Street and Portland Galleries', *Saturday Review* 11 (4 May 1861), p. 447.

78 Unsigned review, 'The British Institution and the "Female Artists" Exhibitions', *Saturday Review* 13 (8 March 1862), p. 271.

79 Mrs Russell Barrington, 'Is a Great School of Art Possible in the Present Day?', *Nineteenth Century* 5 (1879), p. 720.

80 Archibald Henderson, *George Bernard Shaw: Man of the Century*, 2 vols. (London: Hurst and Blackett, 1911), I, p. 171.

81 Ella Hepworth Dixon, *The Story of a Modern Woman* (1894; London: Merlin Press, 1990), p. 142.

82 Ibid., pp. 143–4.

83 Helene E. Roberts, 'Exhibition and Review: The Periodical Press and the Victorian Art Exhibition System', in Joanne Shattock and Michael Wolff, eds., *The Victorian Periodical Press: Samplings and Soundings* (Leicester University Press, 1982), p. 87.

84 Norman MacColl to F. G. Stephens, 10 May 1871, Bod. ms. don.d.116 f. 42–3. The Matthew Arnold essay to which he refers is 'The Literary Influence of Academies' (1864), *The Complete Prose Works of Matthew Arnold*, ed. R. H. Super, 11 vols., vol. III, *Lectures and Essays in Criticism* (University of Michigan Press, 1962), pp. 253–4.

85 Defendant's Brief for *Whistler v. Ruskin* 1878, ms. in the Pennell Collections, National Library of Congress, Washington.

86   Verney, 'Where are We in Art?', p. 597.

87   E. P. Davies, *The Reporter's Handbook* (London: F. Pitman, 1884), p. 38.

88   Ibid., p. 40.

89   A. A. Reade, *Literary Success; Being a Guide to Practical Journalism* (London: Wyman and Sons, 1885), p. 90.

90   Percy Russell, *The Author's Manual* (London: Digby and Long, 1891), p. 59.

91   Harry Quilter, *Preferences in Art, Life and Literature* (London: Swann Sonnenschein and Co., 1892), p. vii.

92   Unsigned article, 'Art Criticism', *Saturday Review* 55 (19 May 1883), p. 25.

93   Henry Morley, 'Pictures at the Royal Academy', *Fortnightly Review* 17 (1872), p. 695.

94   Francis Turner Palgrave, *Handbook to the Fine Art Collections in the International Exhibition of 1862* (London and Cambridge: Macmillan, 1862).

95   Henry Blackburn, *Pictorial Notes in the National Gallery. The British School* (London: Chatto and Windus, 1877), p. 60.

96   Harry Furniss, 'A Growl at the RA', *Daily News* (7 May 1887), p. 5. He was supported in the same paper by an editorial on 10 May, 'The RA and the Critics', which asserted that 'probably the younger and less known men suffer most from the taste of critical views as managed at present' (p. 5); an editorial in the *Saturday Review* 53 (14 May 1887), p. 678, however, condemned Furniss's letter, saying that although his accusations were just, reform was not to be accomplished through 'bad jests, and might as well as not be treated in decent English'.

97   Pamela Gerrish Nunn, 'Critically Speaking', *Women in the Victorian Art World*, ed. Clarissa Campbell Orr (Manchester and New York: Manchester University Press, 1995), p. 105.

98   See Clare Richter Sherman with Adèle M. Holcomb, eds., *Women as Interpreters of the Visual Arts, 1820–1979* (Westport, Conn., and London: Greenwood Press, 1981).

99   Nunn, 'Critically Speaking', p. 118. Hilary Fraser has argued that the emphasis placed by Vernon Lee on the involvement of subjectivity in acts of spectatorship clears a potential space for a distinctively woman's viewpoint: 'Women and the Ends of Art History: Vision and Corporeality in Nineteenth-Century Critical Discourse', *Victorian Studies* 42 (1998–9), pp. 77–100.

100 John Ruskin, 'Arrows of the Chace', *Works*, xxxiv, p. 576, reprinted from the *Pall Mall Gazette* (21 October 1884), which in its turn was quoting from a series of papers on journalism being contributed by Arthur Reade to the *Printing Times*.

101 The Picture Gallery Boy, 'At Whistler's', *Bat* 2 (4 May 1886), p. 123.

102 The Picture Gallery Boy, 'At McLean's-Tooth's-The French Gallery', *Bat* 2 (30 March 1886), p. 12.

103 D. S. M., 'The Royal Academy – I', *Spectator* 68 (7 May 1892), p. 642. For MacColl's career as an art critic, see D. S. MacColl, *Confessions of a Keeper, and Other Papers* (London: A. Maclehose, 1931).

8   Criticism, language and narrative

1 William Michael Rossetti, *Fine Art, Chiefly Contemporary* (London: Macmillan, 1867), p. 157.

2 Ibid., pp. viii–ix.

3 James McNeill Whistler, quoted in 'Celebrities at Home: Mr James Whistler at Cheyne Walk', *World* 203 (22 May 1878), pp. 4–5.

4 James McNeill Whistler, *The Gentle Art of Making Enemies*, 2nd enlarged edition (London: William Heinemann, 1892), p. 146.

5 For discussion of the moral vocabulary of art criticism during the period, see Kate Flint, 'Moral Judgement and the Language of English Art Criticism 1870–1910', *Oxford Art Journal* 6 (1983), pp. 59–66.

6 See, for a brief outline of developments, Elizabeth Prettejohn, 'Aesthetic Value and the Professionalization of English Art Criticism', *Journal of Victorian Culture* 2 (1977), pp. 74–80 and 83–8, and for an extensive discussion of the way in which this vocabulary was used, particularly by D. S. MacColl and R. A. M. Stevenson, to introduce the principles of Impressionist art to the British public, Kate Flint, *Impressionists in England. The Critical Reception* (London: Routledge and Kegan Paul, 1984), pp. 15–21.

7 For discussion of Victorian narrative painting, see: Lindsay Errington, *Social and Religious Themes in English Art 1840–1860* (New York and London: Garland Publishing, 1984); Martin Meisel, *Realizations. Narrative, Pictorial, and Theatrical Arts in Nineteenth-Century England* (Princeton University Press, 1983).

8 Mrs Russell Barrington, 'Is a Great School of Art Possible in the Present Day?' *Nineteenth Century* 5 (1879), p. 120.

9   'Introduction', *Magazine of Art* 1 (1878), pp. 2, 4. Despite the elevated tone of its editorial material, the *Magazine* nevertheless took a more populist approach when it came to its choice of articles.

10   'Mr Whistler's Exhibition', *Saturday Review* 55 (24 February 1883), p. 242.

11   Walter Crane, *Line and Form* (London: George Bell and Sons, 1900), p. 4.

12   Ibid., p. 22.

13   John Ruskin, *Modern Painters* III, *The Complete Works of John Ruskin*, 39 vols., ed. E. T. Cook and Alexander Wedderburn (London: George Allen, 1903–12), V, pp. 126–7.

14   Unsigned article [J. B. Atkinson], 'The Royal Academy and Other Exhibitions', *Blackwood's Edinburgh Magazine* 8 (1860), p. 82. The painting under discussion is Holman Hunt's *The Finding of Christ in the Temple*.

15   Mary Stodart, *Female Writers: Thoughts on their Proper Sphere and on their Powers of Usefulness* (London: R. B. Seeley and W. Burnside, 1842), p. 83.

16   [Atkinson], 'Royal Academy', p. 68.

17   Matthew Arnold, 'On the Modern Element in Literature' (1857; first published 1869), *The Complete Works of Matthew Arnold*, ed. R. H. Super, 11 vols., vol. 1 (1961), p. 22.

18   F. T. Palgrave, 'Poetry and Prose in Art', *Essays on Art* (London and Cambridge: Macmillan, 1866), p. 205. With his *Golden Treasury of English Poetry* (1861), Palgrave was highly influential in establishing a popular canon within the English poetic tradition.

19   Mrs Ellis, *The Beautiful in Nature and Art* (London: Hurst and Blackett, 1866), p. 10.

20   'The New Criticism', *Artist* 14 (1893), p. 296.

21   W. P. Bayley, 'Visits to the Paradise of Artists III', *Art Journal* 28 (1866), p. 105.

22   The literature on whether photography could, or could not, be considered an art form was copious, and, despite its relevance to my theme, I have not space to engage in a full discussion of it here. Joseph Pennell's essay, 'Is Photography among the Fine Arts?' *Contemporary Review* 72 (1897), pp. 824–36, provides a good place from which to enter Victorian debates on the topic.

23   Francis Turner Palgrave, *Handbook to the Fine Art Collections in the International Exhibition* (London and Cambridge: Macmillan, 1862), p. 56.

24   Bayley, 'Paradise of Artists', p. 105.

25   Ibid., pp. 105–6.

26   Whistler, 'Whistler v. Ruskin', *Gentle Art*, p. 9.

27   Editorial, *Fine Art Journal* (Christmas 1872), p. iv. Despite its title, this was a publication aimed at a general audience, combining high-quality artistic reproductions with short stories and a survey of the coming year.

      The point of view which maintained that a work of art should require no further explanation beyond its own existence had parallels in some nineteenth-century literary circles. W. G. B. Murdoch quotes John Davidson's maxim to the effect that 'literary criticism is always attempting a very absurd thing – the explanation of passionate utterance by utterance that is unimpassioned: it is like trying to paint a sunset in lamp-black' (quoted by W. G. B. Murdoch, 'The Art of Criticism', *Memoirs of Swinburne: with Other Essays* (Edinburgh: J. and J. Gray, 1910), p. 125). A specific analogy with visual practices could be employed in order to emphasise the principle. Thus Charlotte Brontë, for example, writing to her publishing friend and adviser W. S. Williams, explains aspects of Lucy Snowe's character to him, adding that if the full expression of these aspects is not to be found in the novel, there must be a great fault somewhere. 'I might explain away a few other points', she adds, 'but it would be too much like drawing a picture and then writing underneath the name of the object intended to be represented. We know what sort of pencil that is which needs an ally in the pen' (quoted by Elizabeth Gaskell, *The Life of Charlotte Brontë,* 2 vols. (London: Smith, Elder and Co.,1857), II, p. 268).

28   W. J. T. Mitchell, *Picture Theory* (Chicago and London: University of Chicago Press, 1994), p. 96.

29   Walter Pater, 'The School of Giorgione', *The Renaissance: Studies in Art and Poetry* (1873; 2nd edn, revised, London: Macmillan and Co., 1877), p. 135.

30   Ibid., p. 137.

31   Ibid., p. 138.

32   Ibid., p. 140.

33   Even before Pater uttered his description of 'all the arts in common aspiring towards the principle of music' (*The Renaissance*, p. 140), it was by analogy with music that the possibility of abstract art was aired. In 1871, H. R. Haweis drew a clear distinction between painting and musical composition as currently practised: the painter

finds his material on the surface of the world, in the landscape through which he walks, but the composer finds only the rough material of sound around him in everyday life, which has to be subjected to rigorous organisation, 'refined and made luminous by deliberate arrangement' (H. R. Haweis, *Music and Morals* (London: Strahan and Co., 1871), p. 8). He saw that colour could provide a rival to sound as a vehicle for pure emotion, but 'no method has yet been discovered of arranging colour by itself for the eye, as the musician's art arranges sound for the ear. We have no colour pictures depending solely on colour as we have symphonies depending solely upon sound . . . I will express my conviction that a Colour-art exactly analogous to the Sound-art of music is possible, and is amongst the arts which have to be traversed in the future' (p. 32).

34   See Flint, Introduction to *Impressionists in England*, pp. 1–30.

35   Ruskin, *The Stones of Venice* (1851), *Works*, XI, p. 428.

36   The following figures indicate the number of works, in all categories, exhibited at the Royal Academy Summer Exhibitions during the latter half of the century which were based on a literary theme, or identified in the catalogue by means of a quotation:

1855	147 of 1,558	(9.43%)
1865	122 of 1,077	(11.33%)
1875	132 of 1,408	(9.37%)
1885	129 of 2,134	(6.04%)
1895	105 of 1,713	(6.12%)

See further Richard D. Altick, *Paintings from Books. Art and Literature in Britain, 1760–1900* (Columbus: Ohio State University Press, 1985), especially chapter 12 (pp. 234–51) on Victorian responses to literary painting.

37   For a discussion of how paintings may be read as offering a reading of literary texts in a way which allows the latter to be brought into an ideological dialogue with visual materials, see Lynne Pearce, *Woman/Image/Text. Readings in Pre-Raphaelite Art and Literature* (Hemel Hempstead: Harvester Wheatsheaf, 1991).

38   F. T. P., 'The British School of Painting', *International Exhibition 1862: Official Catalogue of the Fine Art Department* (London: Truscott, Son and Simmons, 1862), pp. 3, 5.

39   H. A. Taine, *History of English Literature,* 2 vols. (1863; trans. H. Van Laun, Edinburgh: Edmonston and Douglas, 1871), II, p. 190.

40 Robert L. Patten, *George Cruikshank's Life, Times, and Art. Volume 2: 1835–1878* (Cambridge: The Lutterworth Press, 1966), p. 259.

41 Charles Lamb, 'On the Character and Genius of Hogarth' (1810), *Poems Plays and Miscellaneous Essays of Charles Lamb*, ed. Alfred Ainger (London: Macmillan, 1914), p. 273.

42 Theophile Gautier, 'English Art from a French Point of View', *Temple Bar* 5 (1862), p. 322.

43 Ruskin, *Modern Painters* III, *Works*, v, p. 126.

44 Ibid., p. 126.

45 Unsigned article, 'Mr Holman Hunt', *Saturday Review* 61 (20 March 1886), p. 405.

46 Ruskin, *Works*, XII, p. 334.

47 As pointed out by Judith Bronkhurst, pointing to Hunt's own identification of the engraving in his 1865 pamphlet on *The Light of the World*, in her valuable entry on this painting in The Tate Gallery, *The Pre-Raphaelites* (London: Tate Gallery / Penguin Books, 1984), p. 121.

48 For a fuller discussion of Ruskin's reading of *The Awakening Conscience*, and the differing contexts in which it might be interpreted, see Kate Flint, 'Reading the Awakening Conscience Rightly', in Marcia Pointon, ed., *Pre-Raphaelites Re-viewed* (Manchester and New York: Manchester University Press, 1989), pp. 45–65.

49 Unsigned review, 'The Royal Academy', *Art Journal* 28 (1866), p. 166.

50 Karl Marx, 'Private Property and Communism' (1844), quoted by Jean-Christophe Agnew, 'The Consuming Vision of Henry James', in Richard Wightman Fox and T. J. Jackson Lears eds., *The Culture of Consumption. Critical Essays in American History, 1880–1980* (New York: Pantheon Books, 1983), p. 75.

51 Henry James, *The Golden Bowl* (1905; 1909 edn, 2 vols., New York: Charles Scribner's Sons) I, p. 31.

52 Agnew, 'Consuming Vision, p. 73: Agnew quotes Jean Baudrillard, *For a Critique of the Political Economy of the Sign*, trans. Charles Levin (1972; St Louis: Telos Press, 1981), p. 92.

53 Ronald Paulson, *Emblem and Expression: Meaning in English Art of the Eighteenth Century* (London: Thames and Hudson, 1975), p. 8.

54 Palgrave, *Handbook to the Fine Art Collections in the International Exhibition*, p. 61.

55 Pierre Bourdieu, *Distinction. A Social Critique of the Judgement of Taste* (1979; trans. Richard Nice (London: Routledge and Kegan Paul, 1984)), pp. 76–7.

56 Susan P. Casteras puts this painting alongside a number of others which exploit the emotive theme of the disrupted home, troping around the ideal of hearthside domesticity. See 'The Unsettled Hearth: P. H. Calderon's *"Lord! Thy Will be Done"* and the Problematics of Women in Victorian Interiors', in Ellen Harding, ed., *Re-framing the Pre-Raphaelites: Historical and Theoretical Essays* (Aldershot: Scolar Press, 1996), pp. 149–72.

57 For this last detail, and for general discussion concerning the painting, I am greatly indebted to Penelope Gurland.

58 Stefan Morawski, *Inquiries into the Fundamentals of Aesthetics* (Cambridge: MIT Press, 1974), p. 359.

59 Tom Taylor, *The Railway Station* (London: n.p., 1862). For an extended contextualisation of *The Railway Station*, see Mary C. Dowling, *The Artist as Anthropologist. The Representation of Type and Character in Victorian Art* (Cambridge University Press, 1989), ch. 6, pp. 232–316. For Taylor's relationship to Frith, see Shearer West, 'Tom Taylor, William Powell Frith, and the British School of Art', *Victorian Studies* 33 (1990), pp. 307–26.

60 Taylor, *The Railway Station*, p. 10.

61 Ibid., p. 10.

62 Ibid.

63 Ibid.

64 John Berger, *Ways of Seeing* (Harmondsworth: Penguin, 1972), p. 16; Norman Bryson, *Vision and Painting. The Logic of the Gaze* (Basingstoke and London: Macmillan, 1983); Martin Jay, *Downcast Eyes. The Denigration of Vision in Twentieth-Century French Thought* (Berkeley and Los Angeles and London: University of California Press, 1993), pp. 54–5.

65 The phrase is Charles Baudelaire's, mediated through Walter Benjamin's *Charles Baudelaire: A Lyric Poet in the Age of High Capitalism* (trans. Harry Zohn, London: New Left Books, 1973).

66 For a discussion of the way this principle could be adopted in travel writing, see my introduction to Charles Dickens's *Pictures from Italy* (London: Penguin, 1998).

67 Gillian Beer, 'The Reader's Wager: Lots, Sorts, and Futures' (1990), *Open Fields* (Oxford: Clarendon Press, 1996), p. 277.

68 For readings of this painting, see Sander Gilman, 'I'm Down on Whores: Race and Gender in Victorian London', *Anatomy of Racism*, ed. David T. Goldberg (Minneapolis: University of Minnesota Press, 1990), pp. 146–50; Lynda Nead, 'Seduction,

Prostitution, Suicide: *On the Brink* by Alfred Elmore', *Art History* 5 (1982), pp. 310–22.

69   Percy Fitzgerald, *Fatal Zero. A Diary Kept at Homburg*, 2 vols. (London: Tinsley Brothers, 1869) II, pp. 6–7.

70   Revd E. Newton Jones, *The Love of Money the Root of all Evil, or The Sin of Gambling: A Sermon* (London: Whittaker and Co; Barnard Castle: Atkinsons, 1856), p. 13.

71   Ibid., p. 6.

72   Revd C. H. Spurgeon, 'The Serpent in Paradise; or, Gambling at Monte Carlo', *The Sword and the Trowel* 15 (1879), p. 260.

73   William Powell Frith, *My Autobiography and Reminiscences*, 2 vols. (London: Richard Bentley, 1887), II, p. 121.

74   Frith, *My Autobiography*, II, p. 144.

75   Andrew Steinmetz, *The Gaming Table: Its Votaries and its Victims, In All Times and Countries, Especially in England and in France*, 2 vols. (London: Tinsley, 1870), I, p. viii. See also H. M., *On the Analogy Between the Stock Exchange and the Turf* (London: Effingham Wilson, 1885), reprinted from the *City Quarterly Magazine* (1885).

76   C. H. Spurgeon, *Gambling – A Common Snare* (London: Passmore and Alabaster, 1887), p. 2. His distinction, between legitimate and illegitimate forms of speculation, was a commonly held one: see, for example, Venerable Archdeacon Diggle, *Speculation and Gambling* (London: SPCK, 1899). Other commentators heaped on the reasons for why gambling is wrong: it wastes intellect, position, time, energy and enthusiasm, and cited Ruskin as an authority on the subject: 'betting is one of the ways of wasting time of all the vilest, because it wastes not time only, but the interests and energy of your minds', *The Crown of Wild Olive* (1866), *Works*, XVIII, p. 488. See, in particular, Arthur T. Barnett, *Why are Betting and Gambling Wrong?* (London: SPCK, 1897).

77   Ibid., p. 4.

78   Tom Taylor, *The Race for Wealth. A Series of Five Pictures by W. P. Frith, RA Now Exhibiting at the King Street Galleries* (London: n.p., 1880), p. 19.

79   The original quotation, 'subjects I consider'd as writers do my picture was my stage and men and women my actors who were by mean[s] of certain actions and express[ions] to exhibit a dumb shew', is from William Hogarth, *'The Analysis of Beauty' with the Rejected Passages from the Manuscript Drafts and 'Autobiographical Notes'*, ed. Joseph Burke (Oxford University Press, 1955), pp. 216 and 209.

80   Taylor, *The Race for Wealth*, p. 2.

81   In addition to his career as an art critic, Taylor was a popular and successful playwright, which made him particularly alert to the potential for dramatic – as opposed to fictional – analogies between painting and literary forms. See Winton Tolles, *Tom Taylor and the Victorian Drama* (New York: Columbia University Press, 1940).

82   Taylor, *The Race for Wealth*, p. 9.

83   Ibid., p. 7.

84   Ibid., p. 10.

85   A notable exception is recorded by Frith: 'In the comic paper called *Fun*, the admirable artist of that journal, Mr Sullivan, laid hold of my puppets, and made them play a different game. He represented the clergyman as ruined, it is true; but he declined to punish the swindler, who rolls along a street in his carriage accompanied by his vulgar wife, without the least display of sympathy for the poor parson, who is reduced to sweeping a crossing over which the carriage has just passed. I will not dispute the probability of the truth of my friend Sullivan's version, for I know instances of it; but, naturally, I prefer my own' (Frith, *My Autobiography* II, p. 144).

86   'Picture Exhibition', *Saturday Review* 49 (27 March 1880), p. 412.

87   H. Taine, *Notes on England* (trans. W. F. Rae, London: Strahan and Co., 1872), p. 331.

88   Tom Wolfe, *The Painted Word* (New York: Farrar, Straus and Giroux, 1975), p. 42.

89   Charles Taylor, *Sources of the Self. The Making of the Modern Identity* (Cambridge, Mass.: Harvard University Press, 1989), p. 47.

9   Surface and depth

1   Susan Stanford Friedman, 'Women's Autobiographical Selves: Theory and Practice', in Shari Benstock, ed., *The Private Self. Theory and Practice of Women's Autobiographical Writings* (London: Routledge, 1988), p. 38. She is drawing on Sheila Rowbotham, *Woman's Consciousness, Man's World* (London: Penguin, 1973).

2   Lynda Nead, *The Female Nude. Art, Obscenity and Sexuality* (London and New York: Routledge, 1992), p. 11.

3   Henry James, 'The Picture Season in London', *Galaxy* (1877): reprinted in John L. Sweeney, ed., *The Painter's Eye. Notes and Essays on the Pictorial Arts* (1956; Madison: University of Wisconsin Press, 1989), p. 144. See also an earlier version of this review, 'The

Grosvenor Gallery and the Royal Academy', *Nation* 24 (31 May 1877), pp. 320–1. For a discussion of Burne-Jones's aesthetics in relation to contemporary ideas about the female body, see J. B. Bullen, *The Pre-Raphaelite Body. Fear and Desire in Painting, Poetry, and Criticism* (Oxford: Clarendon Press, 1998), pp. 149–216.

4   Charles Harrison, 'On the Surface of Painting', *Critical Inquiry* 15 (1989), p. 296.

5   Oscar Wilde, 'The Grosvenor Gallery', *Dublin University Magazine* (1877), p. 118.

6   *Daily Telegraph* (1 May 1877), p. 5.

7   *Morning Post* (1 May 1877), p. 6. Burne-Jones himself was anxious about the red wall coverings, sending a note to his friend Hallé, the exhibition's Secretary, protesting that 'It sucks all the colour out of pictures, and only those painted in grey will stand it. Merlin doesn't hurt because it's black and white, but the Mirror is gone I don't know where.' G. B-J. [Georgiana Burne-Jones], *Memorials of Edward Burne-Jones*, 2 vols. (London: Macmillan, 1904), II, p. 77.

8   [Georgiana Burne-Jones], *Memorials*, II, p. 75.

9   *Globe* (1 May 1877), p. 3.

10 *Pall Mall Gazette* (2 May 1877), p. 11. Comyns Carr was involved with the founding of the Grosvenor Gallery: Lindsay had seen a series of articles written by Carr in the *Pall Mall Gazette* advocating the reform of the Royal Academy – see J. Comyns Carr, *Some Eminent Victorians: Personal Recollections in the World of Art and Letters* (London: Duckworth and Co.), 1908.

11 *Morning Post* (1 May 1877), p. 6.

12 *Illustrated London News* (12 May 1877), p. 450.

13 *Spectator* (19 May 1877), p. 632.

14 *Globe* (16 May 1877), p. 6.

15 H. Heathcote Statham, 'The Grosvenor Gallery', *Macmillan's Magazine* 36 (1877), p. 113.

16 Ibid., p. 117.

17 Ibid., p. 113.

18 *Morning Post* (1 May 1877), p. 6.

19 See, in particular, the responses to *Laus Veneris*: Frederick Wedmore, in the *Temple Bar*, described the figure of Venus as 'so wan and death-like, so stricken with disease of the soul, so eaten up and gnawed away with disappointment and desire' (Frederick Wedmore, 'Some Tendencies in Recent Painting', *Temple Bar* 53 (1878), p. 339); Henry James, in the *Nation* (23 May 1878) wrote that

she had 'the aspect of a person who has had what the French call an "intimate" acquaintance with life' (*The Painter's Eye*, p. 162).

20   Sidney Colvin, 'The Grosvenor Gallery', *Fortnightly Review* 27 (1877), p. 828.

21   *Athenaeum* no. 2584 (5 May 1877), p. 583.

22   *Standard* (3 May 1877), p. 6.

23   *Globe* (16 May 1877), p. 6.

24   Ibid.

25   *Morning Post* (1 May 1877), p. 6.

26   *Daily News* (2 May 1877), p. 6.

27   James Sully, *Sensation and Intuition: Studies in Psychology and Aesthetics* (London: Henry S. King, 1874), p. 340.

28   Ibid., p. 344.

29   Ibid., p. 358.

30   James Sully, *My Life and Friends* (London: T. Fisher Unwin, 1918), pp. 139–42.

31   Ibid., p. 182.

32   [James Sully], 'The Undefinable in Art', *Cornhill Magazine* 38 (1878), p. 559.

33   Ibid.

34   Ibid., p. 360.

35   See Robert Schumann, *Music and Musicians. Essays and Criticisms*, trans., ed. and annotated by Fanny Raymond Ritter, 2 vols. (London: William Reeves, 1877).

36   [Sully], 'The Undefinable in Art', p. 561.

37   Ibid., p. 562.

38   Ibid., pp. 564–5.

39   Ibid., p. 565.

40   Ibid., p. 571.

41   Ibid., pp. 561–2. Sully's evaluative terms here are remarkably similar to those put forward by George Eliot in her unpublished 'Notes on Form in Art', written in 1868, in which she writes on how an increasingly broad and discriminating development of knowledge 'arrives at the conception of wholes composed of parts more and more multiplied and highly differed, yet more and more absolutely bound together by various conditions of common likeness or mutual dependence. And the fullest example of such a whole is the highest example of Form: in other words, the relation of multiplex interdependent parts to a whole which is itself in the most varied and therefore the fullest relation to other wholes' (George Eliot,

Selected Essays, Poems and Other Writings, ed. A. S. Byatt and Nicholas Warren (London: Penguin, 1990), p. 232).

42 James Sully, 'Art and Psychology', *Mind* 1 (1876), p. 467.

43 Ibid., p. 471.

44 Herbert Spencer, *The Principles of Sociology* (1876; 3rd edn revised and enlarged, 2 vols., London: Williams and Northgate, 1885), 1, p. 116. The first edition of this work was reviewed in the first number of *Mind* by Alexander Bain, who paid particular attention to Spencer's notion of '*duality*, or double existence – in sight and out of sight' (*Mind* 1 (1876), p. 131).

45 Spencer, *Principles*, p. 118.

46 Wilde, 'The Grosvenor Gallery', p. 123.

47 Sully, *My Life and Friends*, p. 57.

48 George Eliot, *Daniel Deronda* (1876; Oxford: Clarendon Press, 1984), p. 3.

49 Ibid., p. 9.

50 Ibid., p. 3.

51 Jacqueline Rose, 'George Eliot and the Spectacle of the Woman', *Sexuality in the Field of Vision* (London: Verso, 1989), p. 118.

52 Eliot, *Daniel Deronda*, p. 7.

53 Ibid., p. 638.

54 Ibid., p. 64.

51 Ibid., p. 12.

56 Ibid., p. 96.

57 Ibid., p. 140.

58 Ibid.

59 For Eliot's attitudes towards race and empire in *Daniel Deronda*, see Katherine Bailey Linehan, 'Mixed Politics: The Critique of Imperialism in *Daniel Deronda*', *Texas Studies in Literature and Language* 34 (1992), pp. 323–46; Susan Meyer, *Imperialism at Home: Race and Victorian Women's Fiction* (Ithaca and London: Cornell University Press, 1996), pp. 157–94.

60 Eliot, *Daniel Deronda*, p. 275.

61 Ibid., p. 169.

62 Ibid., p. 171.

63 Ibid.

64 Ibid., p. 173.

65 Ibid., p. 442. It is tempting to see the influence of Whistler's painting in the terms in which Eliot envisages this scene, especially since she employs a musical as well as a visual register in describing its effects.

66   George Henry Lewes, *Problems of Life and Mind. First Series. The Foundations of a Creed,* 2 vols. (London: Trübner and Co., 1874), I, p. 132.

67   M. H. Pirenne, *Optics, Painting & Photography* (Cambridge University Press, 1970), p. 9.

68   In terms of following Lewes's intellectual development in its European context, Peter Allan Dale, *In Pursuit of a Scientific Culture* (Madison: University of Wisconsin Press, 1989), is exceptionally helpful, particularly pp. 60–136. The standard biographies of Lewes (Rosemary Ashton, *G. H. Lewes: A Life* (Oxford and New York: Oxford University Press, 1991); David Williams, *Mr George Eliot: A Biography of George Henry Lewes* (London: Hodder and Stoughton, 1983)) are very disappointing on this aspect of his career.

69   Hermann von Helmholtz, *Treatise on Physiological Optics* (1867; revised and enlarged 1909–11; ed. and trans. James P. C. Southall, 3 vols., Rochester, N. Y.: The Optical Society of America, 1924–5), III, p. 1.

70   Lewes, *Problems,* I, p. 156.

71   Ibid., p. 124.

72   Eliot, *Daniel Deronda,* p. 439.

10   Hallucination and vision

1   Unsigned review, 'The Royal Academy First Notice', *The Times* (2 May 1903), p. 13. Collier himself, however, observed that his so-called 'problem pictures . . . are nothing of the kind. The ones that have been so termed merely depict little tragedies of modern life, and I have always endeavoured to make their meanings perfectly plain.' Quoted in his obituary, 'John Collier', *The Times* (12 April 1934), p. 17.

2   Hilda Orchardson Gray, *The Life of Sir William Quiller Orchardson, RA* (London: Hutchinson, 1930), p. 276.

3   Claude Phillips, 'The Royal Academy. II', *Academy,* 25 May 1895, p. 449.

4   M. H. Spielmann, 'The Royal Academy Exhibition. – I', *Magazine of Art* 18 (1895), p. 244.

5   M. H. Spielmann, *Millais and his Works* (Edinburgh and London: William Blackwood and Sons, 1898), p. 119.

6   Joseph Kestner, in *Masculinities in Victorian Painting,* builds on the diversity of contemporary readings of *A Reverie:* 'is this a study of

male narcissism? male double standard? male assessment of the dichotomous nature of woman (mistress/wife)? male regret at marriage? male propensity to deny the existence of women's physicality? male negotiation of castration by repudiating the castrated/lacking female body? male regret at seducing a woman (the wraith's hair is unbound)? male objectification of women? Dicksee constructs the canvas to activate these and other readings'. All readings, for Kestner, lead towards a demonstration of the fact that by the end of the century, 'the male's role in the family and his interaction with women was becoming problematized and conflicted in a period of transitional negotiation of masculinity' (Aldershot: Scolar Press, 1995, p. 172).

7   Odilon Redon, *A Soi-même: Journal (1867–1915)*, quoted Martin Jay, *Downcast Eyes. The Denigration of Vision in Twentieth-Century French Thought* (Berkeley, Los Angeles and London: University of California Press, 1993), p. 157.

8   Edmund Parish, *Hallucinations and Illusions. A Study of the Fallacies of Perception* (London: Walter Scott, 1897), pp. 3–5.

9   For the history of responses to hallucinations, see T. R. Sarbin and J. B. Juhasz, 'The Historical Background of the Concept of Hallucination', *Journal of the History of the Behavioural Sciences* 5 (1967), pp. 339–58, and the introductory chapter to Peter D. Slade and Richard P. Bentall, *Sensory Deception. A Scientific Analysis of Hallucination* (London and Sydney: Croom Helm, 1988). For changing attitudes towards madness, see Roy Porter, *Mind-forg'd Manacles: A History of Madness in England from the Restoration to the Regency* (London: Athlone, 1987); Andrew T. Scull, *Museums of Madness: The Social Organization of Insanity in Nineteenth-Century England* (London: Allen Lane, 1979); and Vieda Skultans, *English Madness: Ideas on Insanity, 1590–1890* (London: Routledge and Kegan Paul, 1979).

10   J. E. D. Esquirol, 'Sur les Illusions de Sens chez les Aliénés', *Archives Générales de Médecine* 2 (1832), pp. 5–23, quoted Slade and Bentall, *Sensory Deception*, p. 8.

11   William W. Ireland, *The Blot upon the Brain: Studies in History and Psychology* (London: Bell and Bradfute, 1885), pp. 2–3.

12   Allon White, *The Uses of Obscurity. The Fiction of Early Modernism* (London, Boston and Henley: Routledge and Kegan Paul, 1981), p. 48.

13   Eliza Lynn Linton, 'Our Illusions', *Fortnightly Review* 55 (1891), pp. 595–6. Linton herself passed from sectarian Christianity to agnosticism. Her faith was challenged, among other factors, by the fact that scientific achievements unknown to Christ had done so much good for humanity: in particular, her own poor eyesight led her to concentrate on the example of how religion failed to aid vision in a practical sense, by eradicating ophthalmia. See Nancy Fix Anderson, *Woman Against Women in Victorian England. A Life of Eliza Lynn Linton* (Bloomington and Indianapolis: Indiana University Press, 1987), p. 142.

14   J. H. Blount, 'On the Terms Delusion, Illusion, and Hallucination', *Asylum Journal of Mental Science* 2 (1856), p. 499.

15   Slade and Bentall, *Sensory Deception*, p. 9.

16   James Sully, *Illusions. A Psychological Study* (London: C. Kegan Paul, 1881), pp. 2–3.

17   Ibid., p. 21.

18   Ibid., p. 23.

19   Francis Galton, *Inquiries into Human Faculty and its Development* (London: Macmillan and Co., 1883), p. 378.

20   Ibid., p. 379.

21   Ibid., p. 85.

22   Ibid., p. 88. Galton was not the first scientist to observe that people differ in their ability to call up sensory experiences from memory: this was noted by Gustav Theodor Fechner in his *Elemente der Psychophysik* (1860). Stephen Kosslyn notes that a 1965 survey concerning visual imagery, with a broadly similar base to Galton's, produced radically different results, 97 per cent of respondents claiming to be able to visualise things in their mind's eye. He suggests that in the intervening period, imagery has become more widely accepted as a component within scientific inquiry, and that it is possible that the development of movies and television has encouraged people to become more visual in their thinking. See Stephen M. Kosslyn, *Ghosts in the Mind's Machine. Creating and Using Images in the Brain* (New York and London: W. W. Norton and Co., 1983), pp. 195–6. See further by Kosslyn, *Image and Mind* (Cambridge, Mass. and London: Harvard University Press, 1980), and *Image and Brain. The Resolution of the Imagery Debate* (Cambridge, Mass., and London: MIT Press, 1994). For mental imaging in relation to reading literature, see Elaine Scarry, 'On

Vivacity: The Difference between Daydreaming and Imagining-Under-Authorial-Instruction', *Representations* 52 (1995), pp. 1–26.

23 Galton, *Inquiries into Human Faculty*, p. 113.

24 Ibid., p. 99.

25 Ibid., p. 167.

26 Ibid., p. 163.

27 Sir John Herschel, 'On Sensorial Vision', lecture delivered before the Leeds Philosophical and Literary Society, 1858, *Familiar Lectures on Scientific Subjects* (London: Alexander Strahan, 1867), p. 404.

28 Ibid., p. 404.

29 A. Gauld, *The Founders of Psychical Research* (London: Routledge and Kegan Paul, 1968), pp. 208–9. See also Janet Oppenheim, *The Other World. Spiritualism and Psychical Research in England, 1850–1914* (Cambridge University Press, 1985), and Alex Owen, *The Darkened Room. Women, Power and Spiritualism in Late Victorian England* (London: Virago, 1989).

30 *Proceedings of the Society of Psychical Research* 10 (1892), p. 33.

31 See R. C. Finucane, *Appearances of the Dead. A Cultural History of Ghosts* (London: Junction Books, 1982), pp. 194–211; also Brian Inglis, *Natural and Supernatural: A History of the Paranormal from Earliest Times to 1914* (London: Hodder and Stoughton, 1977).

32 Mrs Henry Wood, 'Reality or Delusion?', in Richard Dalby, ed., *The Virago Book of Victorian Ghost Stories* (London: Virago, 1988), p. 103.

33 Sheridan Le Fanu to George Bentley, quoted by Julia Briggs, *Night Visitors. The Rise and Fall of the English Ghost Story* (London: Faber, 1977), p. 49. As Briggs says, this in fact 'does not seem a very apt comment' on this particular story.

34 Margaret Oliphant, 'The Open Door' (1881), in Dalby, *Ghost Stories*, pp. 160–1.

35 Ireland, *The Blot upon the Brain*, p. 3.

36 Oliphant, 'The Open Door', p. 158.

37 Ibid., p. 165.

38 Ibid., p. 170.

39 Ibid., p. 172.

40 Ibid., p. 183.

41 Ibid., pp. 183–4.

42 Ibid., p. 152.

43   Rudyard Kipling, 'The Phantom 'Rickshaw' (1885), *Wee Willie Winkie. Under the Deodars. The Phantom 'Rickshaw, and Other Stories* (London: Macmillan, 1951), p. 126.

44   Ibid., p. 127.

45   Ibid., p. 154.

46   Ibid., p. 156.

47   Ibid., p. 157.

48   This interpretation is broadly in line with that offered by Sandra Kemp in *Kipling's Hidden Narratives* (Oxford: Basil Blackwell, 1988), pp. 54–6. Kemp illuminatingly explores, although not in relation to this story, Kipling's interest in theosophy and the occult (pp. 29–50).

49   Zohreh T. Sullivan, *Narratives of Empire. The Fictions of Rudyard Kipling* (Cambridge University Press, 1993), p. 61.

50   Ibid., p. 63.

51   Kipling, 'The Phantom 'Rickshaw', p. 125.

52   Ibid., p. 143.

53   Ibid., p. 145.

54   Kipling's interest in vision, both literal and metaphorical, is explored in relation to *The Light That Failed* and *Kim* by Mark Kinkead-Weekes, 'Vision in Kipling's Novels', in Andrew Rutherford, ed., *Kipling's Mind and Art* (Edinburgh and London: Oliver and Boyd, 1964), pp. 197–234.

55   Edward Said, *Orientalism* (1978; London: Penguin, 1995), p. 190. For the degree to which Said's analysis is based upon masculinist conceptions of the Orient, and on masculinist versions of the gaze (and has proved extremely influential in further studies based on similar methodological assumptions), see the revisionist study by Reina Lewis, *Gendering Orientalism. Race, Femininity and Representation* (London and New York: Routledge, 1996).

56   Andrew Lang, 'Magic Mirrors and Crystal Gazing', *Monthly Review* 5 (1901), pp. 117–18.

57   Edward William Lane, *An Account of the Manners and Customs of the Modern Egyptians*, 3 vols. (London: Charles Knight, 1846), II, pp. 93–9. Lane came to believe that the scrying he had witnessed could in fact be ascribed to his interpreter, Osman Effendi (in reality a renegade Scotsman). See Sophia Poole, *The Englishwoman in Egypt* (London: Charles Knight and Co., 1844) II, pp. 162ff. It is worth noting, however, that a very similar narrative involving the solving of a robbery by an Arab scryer in the Malay peninsula is offered by Walter W. Skeat, *Malay Magic* (London: Macmillan, 1900), p. 538.

58   George Eliot, *Adam Bede* (1859; London: Penguin, 1985), p. 49.

59   See Theodore Besterman, *Crystal-Gazing: A Study in the History, Distribution, Theory and Practice of Scrying* (London: William Rider and Son, 1924), p. 89.

60   See Northcote W. Thomas, *Crystal Gazing. Its History and Practice, with a Discussion of the Evidence for Telepathic Scrying* (London: Alexander Moring, 1905), p. 43.

61   Ling Roth, *Natives of Sarawak*, 2 vols. (London: Truslove and Hanson, 1896) I, p. 273.

62   Thomas Livingstone Mitchell, *Three Expeditions into the Interior of Eastern Australia, with Descriptions of the Recently Explored Region of Australia Felix, and of the Present Colony of New South Wales*, 2nd edn, 2 vols. (London: T. and W. Boone, 1839), II, p. 344.

63   D. G. Brinton, *Essays of an Americanist* (Philadelphia: Porter and Coates, 1890), p. 97.

64   J.G. Bourke, *The Medicine-Men of the Apache,* Ninth Annual Report of the Bureau of Ethnology (Washington: Bureau of Ethnology, 1892), p. 461.

65   V. M. Mikhailovskii, 'Shamanism in Siberia and European Russia', *Journal of the Anthropological Institute of Great Britain and Ireland* 24 (1895), p. 155.

66   H. Callaway, *The Religious System of the Amazulu* (Natal, 1870: reissued, London: The Folk-Lore Society, 1884), pp. 340–7.

67   Paul B. du Chaillu, *A Journey to Ashango-Land: And Further Penetration into Equatorial Africa* (London: J. Murray, 1867), pp. 173–4.

68   H. G. Wells, 'The Crystal Egg', *The Complete Short Stories of H. G. Wells* (New York: St Martin's Press, 1971), p. 633.

69   Ibid. p. 634.

70   Ibid., p. 638.

71   Ibid., p. 643.

72   Sophia de Morgan, *From Matter to Spirit. The Result of Ten Years' Experience in Spirit Manifestations* (London: Longman, Green, Longman, Roberts, and Green, 1863), p. 110.

73   Ibid., p. 53.

74   Andrew Lang, *Cock Lane and Common-Sense* (London: Longmans, Green and Co.,1894), p. 222. Lang, it should be noted, continued to be fascinated by the practice of crystal gazing, both from an anthropological point of view (see chapter 5, 'Crystal Visions, Savage and Civilised' in *The Making of Religion* (London: Longmans, Green and Co., 1898), pp. 90–112) and as it was practised in modern English

society. He became increasingly credulous of the idea that it 'yielded apparent traces of the existence of unexplored regions of human faculty', whilst 'many psychologists, at least in France, now admit the reality of the faculty of crystal gazing. But that the pictures can convey intelligence as to what is, unknown to the gazer, in another person's mind, or is actually occurring at a distance, *that* science will not believe in our time: will not even consider the question. It is my humble aspiration to collect evidence copious and strong enough to induce official professors to give it consideration' ('Magic Mirrors and Crystal Gazing', p. 128).

75   Lang, *Cock Lane*, pp. 213–14. As most commentators on hallucination noted, these *illusions hypnagogigues* were first named and described by Louis Maury in 'Des hallucinations hypnagogigues de système nerveux', *Annales Medico-Psychologiques* 11 (1848), p. 26.

76   Ibid., pp. 217–18. Lang's reference does not appear to be accurate, but there is mention in this number of the *Proceedings of the Society for Psychical Research* of Miss X(A. Goodrich-Freer)'s *Essays in Psychical Research* (London: George Redway, 1899), which includes an essay 'On the Faculty of Crystal Gazing'.

77   Edmund Parish, *Hallucinations and Illusions. A Study of the Fallacies of Perception* (London: Walter Scott, 1897), p. 66.

78   H. G. Wells, 'The Time Machine', *Complete Short Stories*, p. 11.

79   See Harry M. Geduld, ed., *The Definitive 'Time Machine'* (Bloomington and Indianapolis: Indiana University Press, 1987), pp. 93–4.

80   Charles H. Hinton, 'What is the Fourth Dimension?' (1884), reprinted in Rudolf v. B. Rucker, ed., *Speculations on the Fourth Dimension. Selected Writings of Charles H. Hinton* (New York: Dover, 1980), pp. 17–18.

81   Galton, *Inquiries into Human Faculty*, p. 98.

82   H. G. Wells, 'The Remarkable Case of Davidson's Eyes', *Complete Short Stories*, p. 281.

83   Ibid., p. 282.

84   Ibid., p. 283.

85   Such an explanation could have been provided by contemporary readers familiar with theories of 'crisis apparitions' and spontaneous telepathy, as comprehensively investigated in Edmund Gurney, Frederic Myers and Frank Podmore, *Phantasms of the Living*, 2 vols. (London: Trubner and Co., 1886).

86 Eliot, *Daniel Deronda* (1876; Oxford: Clarendon Press, 1984), p. 478.

87 Daniel Cottom has gone so far as to argue that 'art came to be the legitimate supernatural in that it was understood to be the proper medium for the exercise of the powers traditionally attributed to the supernatural. In art one could manipulate human destinies, make people appear and disappear, see into the minds of others, hear the voices of the dead, levitate above this earth, do practically any godlike thing, and yet proceed under the assumption that the results represented ordinary nature' (*Abyss of Reason: Cultural Movements, Revelations, and Betrayals* (New York: Oxford University Press, 1991), p. 94).

88 For the growth of psychology as a discipline during the nineteenth century, see Henri F. Ellenberger, *The Discovery of the Unconscious: The History and Evolution of Dynamic Psychology* (London: Allen Lane,1970), and, within Britain in particular, Sally Shuttleworth and Jenny Bourne Taylor, eds., *Embodied Selves: An Anthology of Psychological Texts* (Oxford University Press, 1998), and Taylor, *In the Secret Theatre of Home: Wilkie Collins, Sensation Narrative and Nineteenth-Century Psychology* (London: Routledge, 1988).

Conclusion. The Victorian horizon

1 [F. G. Stephens], *Notes on a Collection of Pictures by Mr John Everett Millais, RA, Exhibited at the Fine Art Society's Rooms, 148 New Bond Street 1881* (London: Fine Art Society Ltd, 1881), pp. 24–5.

2 Henri Lefebvre, *The Production of Space* (1974; trans. Donald Nicholson-Smith, 1991; Oxford and Malden: Blackwell, 1998), p. 97.

3 Cornelius A. Van Peursen, 'The Horizon', in Frederick A. Elliston and Peter McCormick, *Husserl. Expositions and Appraisals* (Notre Dame and London: University of Notre Dame Press, 1977), p. 182. I am greatly indebted to this stimulating piece for the ideas it suggests about the nature and properties of the horizon.

4 Alfred Tennyson, 'Ulysses' (1842), *The Poems of Tennyson*, ed. Christopher Ricks (London and Harlow: Longmans, 1969), p. 563.

5 James Harlaw, *The Charm of Millais* (London and Edinburgh: T. C. and E. C. Jack, 1913), p. 39.

6 James Anthony Froude, *English Seamen in the Sixteenth Century. Lectures delivered at Oxford, Easter Terms 1893–4* (1895; London: Longmans, Green and Co., 1919), p. 2.

7   J. R. Seeley, *The Expansion of England* (1883; ed. John Gross, Chicago and London: University of Chicago Press, 1971), p. 140.

8   Harlaw, *The Charm of Millais*, p. 38.

9   J. W. Burrow claims that Raleigh was the epitome of Victorian imperial enthusiasm for Elizabethan expansionism. See *A Liberal Descent. Victorian Historians and the English Past* (Cambridge University Press, 1981), pp. 231–3. For a general discussion of Millais and imperialism, see Joseph A. Kestner, 'The Pre-Raphaelites and Imperialism: John Everett Millais's *Pizarro, The Boyhood of Raleigh* and *The North-West Passage*', *Journal of Pre-Raphaelite Studies* ns 4 (1995), pp. 51–66.

10   David Garrick, 'Heart of Oak' (1759), lines 4–8.

11   William Shakespeare, *King John* II. i. 26–8.

12   Edith Nesbit, 'Under Convoy', *Leaves of Life* (London: Longmans, Green and Co., 1889), pp. 46–7.

13   Matthew Arnold, 'Dover Beach' (1851?, pub. 1867), *The Poems of Matthew Arnold*, ed. Kenneth Allott; 2nd edn, ed. Miram Allott (London and New York: Longman, 1979), p. 256.

14   Alfred Tennyson, 'Locksley Hall' (1842), lines 15–16.

15   George Eliot, *Middlemarch* (1871–2; Oxford: Clarendon Press, 1986), p. 777.

16   Charles Darwin, *The Voyage of the Beagle* (1845, 1860; London: J. M. Dent, 1906), p. 484.

17   John Ruskin, *Modern Painters,* II, (1846), *The Complete Works of John Ruskin,* 39 vols., ed. E. T. Cook and Alexander Wedderburn (London: George Allen, 1903–12), IV, pp. 79–81.

18   John Milton, *Paradise Lost,* (1674), *The Poems of John Milton*, ed. John Carey and Alastair Fowler (London and Harlow: Longmans, 1968), pp. 1054–5.

19   A. W. Moore, *Infinity* (Aldershot: Dartmouth Publishing Co., 1993), p. xi.

20   Alfred Tennyson, 'Tithonus' (1860), *Poems*, p. 1114.

21   Louisa Clifton, *Journal 1841*, typescript copy MS 2801, National Library of Australia, reproduced in Michael Ackland, ed., *The Penguin Book of 19th Century Australian Literature* (Ringwood, Victoria: Penguin, 1993), p. 3.

22   Robert Louis Stevenson, *Across the Plains, With Other Memories and Essays* (London: Chatto and Windus, 1892), pp. 40, 43.

23   W. H. Breton, *Excursions in New South Wales, Western Australia and Van Diemen's Land* (London: Richard Bentley, 1833), p. 103.

24 Paul Carter, *The Road to Botany Bay. An Essay in Spatial History* (London and Boston: Faber and Faber, 1987), pp. 286–91.

25 Joanna Baillie, 'London' (1840; reprinted in Isobel Armstrong and Joseph Bristow, *Nineteeth-Century Women Poets. An Oxford Anthology*, Oxford: Clarendon Press, 1996), pp. 65–6; lines 3, 17–18, 35.

26 'Australie' (Emily Manning), 'The Weatherboard Fall', *The Balance of Pain and Other Poems* (London: George Bell and Son, 1877), pp. 87–8.

27 Rosalind Krauss, *The Optical Unconscious* (Cambridge, Mass., and London: MIT Press, 1993), p. 2.

28 Joseph Conrad, *Lord Jim* (1900; London: J. M. Dent, 1923), p. 92.

29 Ibid., p. 17.

30 Ibid., p. 19.

31 Ibid., pp. 101–2.

32 Ibid., p. 197.

33 Ibid., p. 215.

34 Karl Kroeber, *British Romantic Art* (Berkeley, and Los Angeles and London: University of California Press, 1986), p. 195.

35 As argued by John Gage, *Color in Turner* (New York: Praeger, 1969), p. 126.

36 Julia Kristeva, *Desire in Language*, ed. Leon S. Roudiez, trans. Thomas Gora, Alice Jardine and Leon S. Roudiez (New York: Columbia University Press, 1980), p. 225. See also Rudolph Arnheim, *Art and Visual Perception: The New Version* (Berkeley: University of California Press, 1974).

37 In invoking 'the aesthetics of the sublime', I am deliberately leaving open the possibility of understanding responses to Turner's works according to a Burkean version of sublimity, which would locate the essence of the sublime within the natural forces, or the Kantian version, which conversely acknowledges sublimity to be a characteristic of the perceiving mind. Whilst there is, of course, a considerable gulf between these two positions, the generalisations involved in the conceptualisation and terminology of each allow little space for the personal, individualised subjectivity which, I argue, is a feature of the response that Whistler's works invite.

38 Ruskin, *The Elements of Drawing* (1857), *Works*, xv, p. 27.

39 Krauss, *The Optical Unconscious*, p. 11.

40 Thomas Hardy, *Far from the Madding Crowd* (1874; London: Macmillan, 1912), p. 16. For Hardy's informed interest not just in painting, but in the theory of sight, see J. B. Bullen, *The Expressive*

Eye. Fiction and Perception in the Work of Thomas Hardy (Oxford University Press, 1986).

41   Van Peursen, 'The Horizon', p. 184.

42   R. H. Horne, *The Poor Artist; Or, Seven Eye-sights and One Object* 2nd edn, with a preliminary essay on 'Varieties of Vision in Man', (London: John van Voorst, 1871), pp. xlvi–xlvii.

43   Ibid., pp. xlviii–xlvix.

44   Edmund Husserl, *Cartesian Meditations* (1931; The Hague: M. Nijhoff, 1960), #19, p. 44.

45   Ibid., p. 45. I am indebted in this section of my argument to David Woodruff Smith and Donald McIntyre for their chapter, 'Husserl's Notion of Horizon', *Husserl and Intentionality. A Study of Mind, Meaning, and Language* (Dordrecht, Boston and London: D. Reidel, 1982), pp. 227–65.

46   Hubert Damisch, *The Origins of Perspective* (1987; trans. John Goodman, Cambridge, Mass and London: MIT Press, 1994), p. 82.

47   [Sir David Brewster], 'The Sight and How to See', *North British Review* 26 (1856), p. 145.

48   G. H. Lewes, *The Problems of Life and Mind. First Series. The Foundations of a Creed* (London: Trübner and Co., 1874), pp. 315–17.

49   Eliot, *Middlemarch*, p. 628.

50   Lewes, *Problems of Life and Mind*, p. 14. Lewes's objections are not just against those who search after theological answers (and in his repudiation of these he was in complete contrast to Tyndall's underlying, if unassertive, Christian beliefs), and to spiritualism, but also to Hegelians. For his anti-Hegelianism in matters of perception, see Peter Allan Dale, *In Pursuit of a Scientific Culture. Science, Art, and Society in the Victorian Age* (Madison: University of Wisconsin Press, 1989), pp. 66ff.

51   Millais, *Life*, II, p. 48.

52   Algernon Swinburne, 'The Death of Sir John Franklin', *The Complete Works of Algernon Charles Swinburne*, ed. Sir Edmund Gosse and Thomas James Wise, 19 vols. (New York: Russell and Russell, 1925), I, p. 3.

53   Millais, *Life*, II, p. 55.

54   Francis Spufford notes that this picture 'also performs its evocation of the English exploring spirit without needing to make any reference whatsoever to those tens of thousands of other "natives", as remote as any Hottentot from the national community primed to

interpret it, who have a rather closer connection with the Arctic: the indigenous inhabitants of the ice. It seems that *The North-West Passage* is complete without Inuit either. No harpoon or fur or vanishingly tiny tacked-up drawing of a kayak represents them, though they appear in almost every account of almost every journey. What makes Millais' omission particularly telling is that in this he appears to go against the grain of Victorian fascination with the polar peoples. They were far from being generally ignored' (*I May be Some Time* (London: Faber and Faber, 1996), p. 187).

55 Although she does not specifically explore the notion of the horizon, the discussion of ethnography and distance in Mary Helms, *Ulysses' Sail: An Ethnographic Odyssey of Power, Knowledge, and Geographical Distance* (Princeton University Press, 1988), is of particular relevance here.

56 George Eliot, *Daniel Deronda* (1876; Oxford: Clarendon Press, 1984), p. 119.

57 Ανοδο (M. E. Coleridge), 'Eyes' (1896), in Isobel Armstrong and Joseph Bristow, eds., *Nineteenth-Century Women Poets* (Oxford: Clarendon Press, 1996), p. 757.

Bibliography

Primary sources

Adams, W. H. Davenport, *Beneath the Surface; or, the Wonders of the Underground World* (London: T. Nelson & Sons, 1876).

Agassiz, Louis, *A Journey to Switzerland and Pedestrian Tours in that Country* (London: Smith, Elder & Co., 1833).

Aitken, John, *Collected Scientific Papers of John Aitken*, ed. Cargill G. Knott (Cambridge University Press, 1923).

Aitken, Robert, *The Teaching of the Types. Tracts for the Clergy and the Earnest Minded* (Oxford: T. and G. Shrimpton, 1854).

Akenside, Mark, *The Poetical Works of Mark Akenside* (1845; reprinted New York: AMS Press, 1969), pp. 175–6.

[Ansted, David T.], 'Giants and Dwarfs', *Temple Bar* 1 (1861), pp. 533–43.

Archbutt, Leonard, *Dust. A Paper Read Before the Nomadic Club, Derby. March 20th, 1891* (London and Derby: Bemrose and Sons, 1891).

Arnold, Matthew, *The Complete Prose Works of Matthew Arnold*, ed. R. H. Super, 11 vols. (Ann Arbor: University of Michigan Press, 1960–77).

[Atkinson, J. Beavington], 'The Royal Academy and Other Exhibitions', *Blackwood's Edinburgh Magazine* 88 (1860), pp. 65–84.

Atkinson, J. Beavington, 'The Decline of Art: Royal Academy and Grosvenor Gallery', *Blackwood's Edinburgh Magazine* 138 (1885), pp. 1–25.

Augustine, Saint, *The Confessions of Saint Augustine*, trans. E. B. Pusey (London: Dent, 1907).

'Australie' (Emily Manning), *The Balance of Pain and Other Poems* (London: George Bell & Son, 1877).

Aytoun, William, 'Blind Old Milton', *Blackwood's Edinburgh Magazine* 5 (1841), pp. 811–13.

Barnett, Arthur T., *Why are Betting and Gambling Wrong* (London: SPCK, 1897).

Barrett, Elizabeth Barrett, and Robert Browning, *The Letters of Robert Browning and Elizabeth Barrett Barrett 1845–1846*, ed. Elvan Kintner, 2 vols. (Cambridge, Mass.: The Belknap Press of Harvard University Press, 1969).

Barrington, Emilie I., 'Is a Great School of Art Possible in the Present Day?' *Nineteenth Century* 5 (1879), pp. 714–32.

Baudelaire, Charles, *Mon Coeur mis à nu* (c. 1861), *Oeuvres Complètes*, ed. Claude Pichois, 2 vols. (Paris: Gallimard, 1975).

Beeton, Isabella, *The Book of Household Management* (London: S. O. Beeton, 1861).

Birrell, Augustine, *Collected Essays*, 2 vols. (London: Elliot Stock, 1902).

Blackburn, Henry, *Pictorial Notes in the National Gallery. The British School* (London: Chatto & Windus, 1877).

Booth, General, *In Darkest England and The Way Out* (London: International Headquarters of the Salvation Army, 1890).

Boucicault, Dion, *After Dark* (1868), reprinted in J. O. Bailey, ed., *British Plays of the Nineteenth Century* (New York: Odyssey Press, 1966).

Bourke, J. G., *The Medicine-Men of the Apache* (Ninth Annual Report of the Bureau of Ethnology, U.S.A.: Washington, 1892).

Breton, W. H., *Excursions in New South Wales, Western Australia and Van Diemen's Land* (London: Richard Bentley, 1833).

[Brewster, Sir D.], 'The Sight and How to See', *North British Review* 26 (1856), pp. 145–84.

Bridges, Robert, *Eros and Psyche* (London: George Bell, 1885).

Brinton, D. G., *Essays of an Americanist* (Philadelphia: Porter and Coates, 1890).

Brontë, Charlotte, *Jane Eyre* (1847; New York and London: W. W. Norton & Company, 1987).

    Villette (1853; Oxford: Clarendon Press, 1984).

Broughton, Rhoda, and Elizabeth Bisland, *A Widower Indeed* (London: James R. Osgood, McIlvaine & Co., 1892).

Browning, Elizabeth Barrett, *Aurora Leigh* (1856), ed. Margaret Reynolds (London and New York: W. W. Norton & Co., 1996).

    The Letters of Elizabeth Barrett Browning, ed. Frederic G. Kenyon, 2 vols. (London: Smith Elder, 1897).

    Essays on the Greek Christian Poets and the English Poets (New York: James Miller, 1863).

Browning, Robert, *The Poems, Volume I*, ed. John Pettigrew (London: Penguin, 1981).

Bull, Thomas, *The Sense Denied and Lost* (London: Longman, Green, Longman, and Roberts, 1859).

B.-J., G. [Burne-Jones, Georgiana], *Memorials of Edward Burne-Jones*, 2 vols. (London: Macmillan, 1904).

Burnet, G., *Bishop Burnet's Travels through France, Italy, Germany, and Switzerland* (printed as *Dr. Burnet's travels, or Letters containing an account of what seemed most remarkable in Switzerland, Italy, France, and Germany, &c.*, 1687 (Edinburgh: Thomas Glas, 1752).

[Burton, J. H.], 'At the Alps Again. Part II', *Blackwood's Edinburgh Magazine* 102 (1867), pp. 540–54.

Byron, Lord, *The Complete Poetical Works*, ed. J. McGann, 7 vols., 1980–93 (Oxford: Clarendon Press, 1986).

Callaway, H., *The Religious System of the Amazulu* (Natal, 1870; reissued London: The Folk-Lore Society, 1884).

Carlyle, Thomas, *Sartor Resartus* (1831; London: Chapman and Hall, 1896).

Critical and Miscellaneous Essays, 5 vols. (London: Macmillan, 1899).

Carpenter, William B., *The Microscope: and its Revelations* (London: John Churchill, 1856).

Principles of Mental Physiology, with Their Applications to the Training and Discipline of the Mind, and the Study of its Morbid Conditions (2nd edn; London: Henry S. King & Co., 1875).

Carr, J. Comyns, *Some Eminent Victorians: Personal Recollections in the World of Art and Letters* (London: Duckworth & Co., 1908).

Carter, Robert Brudenell, *Our Homes, and How to Make Them Healthy* (London, Paris and New York: Cassell, Petter, Galpin and Co., 1883–5).

'Medicine and Surgery', in Thomas Humphry Ward, ed., *The Reign of Queen Victoria*, 2 vols. (London: Smith, Elder & Co.: 1887), II, pp. 388–444.

Clifford, William Kingdon, *Seeing and Thinking* (London: Macmillan, 1879).

Cobbe, Frances Power, *Darwinism in Morals, and Other Essays* (London and Edinburgh: Williams and Norgate, 1872).

Collins, Wilkie, *The Queen of Hearts*, 3 vols. (London: Hurst & Blackett, 1859).

Colvin, Sidney, 'The Grosvenor Gallery', *Fortnightly Review* 27 (1877), pp. 820–33.

Conder, Eustace R., *Dust, and Other Short Talks with Children* (Leeds: W. Brierley, and London: Hodder and Stoughton, 1882).

Conrad, Joseph, *Lord Jim* (1900; London: J. M. Dent, 1923).

Costelloe, Mary Whitall, 'The New and the Old Art Criticism', *Nineteenth Century* 35 (1894), pp. 828–37.

Craik, Dinah Mulock, *The Unkind Word and Other Stories*, 2 vols. (London: Hurst and Blackett, 1870).

Crane, Walter, *Line and Form* (London: George Bell & Sons, 1900).

Crowe, Catherine, *The Night Side of Nature: or, Ghosts and Ghost Seers*, 2 vols. (London: T. C. Newby, 1848).

Dallas, E. S., *The Gay Science*, 2 vols. (London: Chapman and Hall, 1866).

Darwin, Charles, *The Voyage of the Beagle* (1845; 1860; London: J. M. Dent, 1906).

   The Descent of Man and Selection in Relation to Sex (1871; 2nd revised edn, New York: D. Appleton, 1898).

Davies, E. P., *The Reporter's Handbook* (London: F. Pitman, 1884).

[Davis, E. J.], *Pyrna: A Commune; or, Under the Ice* (London: Bickers & Sons, 1875).

Dawson, J., *Practical Journalism: How to Enter Thereon and Succeed* (London: L. Upcott Gill, 1885).

de Morgan, Sophia, *From Matter to Spirit. The Result of Ten Years' Experience in Spirit Manifestations* (London: Longman, Green, Longman, Roberts & Green, 1863).

De Quincey, Thomas, *Confessions of an English Opium-Eater and Other Writings*, ed. Grevel Lindop (Oxford University Press, 1985).

Dickens, Charles, *Pictures from Italy* (1846; London: Penguin, 1998).

   Dombey and Son (1848; Oxford: Clarendon Press, 1974).

   Bleak House (1853; New York and London: W. W. Norton, 1977).

   Hard Times (1854; London: Penguin Books, 1995).

   Our Mutual Friend (1864–5; London: Penguin, 1971).

   The Letters of Charles Dickens. Volume Four, 1844–46, ed. Kathleen Tillotson (Oxford: Clarendon Press, 1977).

Diggle, Venerable Archdeacon, *Speculation and Gambling* (London: SPCK, 1899).

Dixon, Ella Hepworth, *The Story of a Modern Woman* (1894; London: Merlin Press, 1990).

Doyle, Sir Arthur Conan, *The Penguin Complete Sherlock Holmes* (London: Penguin Books, 1981).

du Chaillu, Paul B., *A Journey to Ashango-Land: and Further Penetration into Equatorial Africa* (London: J. Murray, 1867).

Eden, Emily, *Up the Country* (1866; London: Virago, 1983).

Edrige-Green, F. W., *Memory. Its Logical Relations and Cultivation* (London: Baillière, Tindall and Cox, 1888).

[Eliot, George], 'Belles Lettres', *Westminster Review* n.s.11 (1857), pp. 306–26.

Eliot, George, *Adam Bede* (1859; London: Penguin Books, 1980).

   The Lifted Veil (1859; London: Virago, 1985).

Middlemarch (1871–2; Oxford: Clarendon Press, 1986).

Daniel Deronda (1876; Oxford: Clarendon Press, 1984).

The Impressions of Theophrastus Such (1879; London: J. M. Dent, 1995).

The George Eliot Letters, ed. Gordon S. Haight, 9 vols. (New Haven and London: Yale University Press, 1954–78).

Selected Essays, Poems and Other Writings, ed. A. S. Byatt and Nicholas Warren (London: Penguin, 1990).

Ellis, Mrs, *The Beautiful in Nature and Art* (London: Hurst and Blackett, 1866).

Engels, Friedrich, *The Condition of the Working Class in England in 1844* (1845; trans. 1886; London: Penguin, 1987).

Fitzgerald, Percy, *Fatal Zero. A Diary Kept at Homburg*, 2 vols. (London: Tinsley Brothers, 1869).

Forbes, James, *Travels through the Alps of Savoy and Other Parts of the Pennine Chain* (1843; 2nd edn, Edinburgh: Adam and Charles Black, 1845).

Forde, H. A., and her sisters, *Dust Ho! and Other Pictures from Troubled Lives* (London: Christian Knowledge Society, c. 1885).

Forsyth, P. T., *Religion in Recent Art: Expository Lectures on Rossetti, Burne-Jones, Watts, Holman Hunt and Wagner* (1889; London: Hodder and Stoughton, 1901).

Frith, William Powell, *My Autobiography and Reminiscences*, 2 vols. (London: Richard Bentley, 1887).

Froude, James Anthony, *English Seamen in the Sixteenth Century. Lectures delivered at Oxford, Easter Terms 1893–4* (1895; London: Longmans, Green and Co., 1919).

Furniss, Harry, 'A Growl at the R.A.', *Daily News* (7 May 1887), p. 5.

Galton, Francis, *Inquiries into Human Faculty and its Development* (London: Macmillan & Co., 1883).

'Gamaliel' (possibly W. Edwin Page), *Diamonds from Dust; or, The Philosopher's Dream Realized* (London: The London Female Guardian Society, 1905).

Gaskell, Elizabeth, *North and South* (1854–5; London: Penguin Books, 1970).

The Life of Charlotte Brontë, 2 vols. (London: Smith, Elder & Co., 1857).

Gautier, Theophile, 'English Art from a French Point of View', *Temple Bar* 5 (1862), pp. 320–26.

Gibbon, Edward, *Autobiography*, ed. M. M. Reese (London: Routledge & Kegan Paul, 1971).

Glover, Revd Richard, *The 'Light of the Word' [sic] or Holman Hunt's*

Great Allegorical Picture Translated into Words (London: Wertherm, Macintosh, and Hunt, 1862).

[Goodrich-Freer, A.], Miss X, *Essays in Psychical Research* (London: George Redway, 1899).

Goschen, George Joachin, *The Cultivation and Use of Imagination* (London: Edward Arnold, 1893).

Goose, Philip Henry, *Evenings at the Microscope; or, Researches Among the Minuter Organs and Forms of Animal Life* (London: Society for Promoting Christian Knowledge, 1859).

Grant, Sir Robert, *Sacred Poems* (London: Saunders and Otley, 1839).

Greene, M. T., *Geology in the Nineteenth Century* (Ithaca: Cornell University Press, 1982).

Gregory, William, *Letters to a Candid Inquirer on Animal Magnetism* (London: Taylor, Walton and Maberly, 1851).

Gurney, Edmund, Frederic Myers and Frank Podmore, *Phantasms of the Living*, 2 vols. (London: Trubner and Co., 1886).

Hamerton, Philip G., 'Art Criticism', *Cornhill Magazine* 8 (1863), pp. 334–43.

'Liber Memorialis: On the Artistic Observation of Nature', *Art Journal* 28 (1866), p. 1.

Philip Gilbert Hamerton: An Autobiography 1834–1858, and a Memoir by his Wife, (E. Hamerton), 1858–1894 (London: Seeley & Co., 1897).

Hardy, Lieut. R. W. H., *Incidental Remarks on some Properties of Light; Being Part V. of An Essay on Vision* (London: Bell and Daldry, 1856).

Hardy, Thomas, *Far from the Madding Crowd* (1874; London: Macmillan, 1912).

Harlaw, James, *The Charm of Millais* (London and Edinburgh: T. C. and E. C. Jack, 1913).

Harrison, Frederic, 'A Few Words about Picture Exhibitions', *Nineteenth Century* 24 (1888), pp. 30–44.

Haweis, H. R., *Music and Morals* (London: Strahan & Co., 1871).

Herschel, Sir John, 'On Sensorial Vision', lecture delivered before the Leeds Philosophical and Literary Society, 1858, *Familiar Lectures on Scientific Subjects* (London: Alexander Strahan, 1867).

Hinton, Charles H., 'What is the Fourth Dimension?' (1884), reprinted in Rudolf v. B. Rucker, ed., *Speculations on the Fourth Dimension. Selected Writings of Charles H. Hinton* (New York: Dover, 1980).

H. M., *On the Analogy Between the Stock Exchange and the Turf* (London: Effingham Wilson, 1885).

Hogarth, William, *'The Analysis of Beauty' with the Rejected Passages from the Manuscript Drafts and 'Autobiographical Notes'*, ed. Joseph Burke (Oxford University Press, 1955).

Hollingshead, John, *Underground London* (London: Groombridge and Sons, 1862).

Holman Hunt, William, *Pre-Raphaelitism and the Pre-Raphaelite Brotherhood*, 2 vols. (London: Macmillan & Co., 1905).

Hood, Thomas, *The Complete Poetical Works of Thomas Hood*, ed. Walter Jerrold (London: Henry Froude, 1906).

Hopkins, Gerard Manley, *The Poetical Works of Gerard Manley Hopkins*, ed. Norman H. Mackenzie (Oxford: Clarendon Press, 1990).

The Correspondence of Gerard Manley Hopkins and Richard Watson Dixon, ed. Claude Colleer Abbott (London: Oxford University Press, 1935).

The Journals and Papers of Gerard Manley Hopkins, ed. Humphry House; completed by G. Storey (London: Oxford University Press, 1959).

Horne, R. H., *The Poor Artist; or, Seven Eye-sights and One Object* (2nd edn, with a preliminary essay on 'Varieties of Vision in Man' London: John van Voorst, 1871).

Howitt, Anna Mary, *An Art-Student in Munich*, 2 vols. (London: Longman, Brown, Green and Longmans, 1853).

Huxley, Thomas, *Collected Essays*, 9 vols. (London: Macmillan, 1893–4).

The Works of Thomas Henry Huxley, 6 vols. (New York: D. Appleton and Co., 1897).

Ingestre, Viscount, ed., *Meliora: or Better Times to Come. Being the Contributions of Many Men Touching the Present State and Prospects of Society*, 2 vols. (London: John W. Parker & Son, 1852, 1853).

Ireland, William W., *The Blot upon the Brain: Studies in History and Psychology* (London: Bell & Bradfute, 1885).

James, Henry, *The Portrait of a Lady* (1881; revised edn, New York: Charles Scribner's Sons, 1908).

The Golden Bowl (1905; 1909 edn, London: Macmillan, 1923).

James, Admiral Sir W., ed., *The Order of Release. The Story of John Ruskin, Effie Gray and John Everett Millais told for the first time in their unpublished letters* (London: John Murray, 1948).

Jennings, Charles Egerton, *Transfusion: Its History, Indications, and Modes of Application* (London: Baillière, Tindall and Cox, 1883).

Johns, Revd B. G., *Blind People: Their Works and Ways* (London: John Murray, 1867).

Johnson, Edmund C., *The Blind of London* (London: John Mitchell, 1860).

Jones, Revd E. Newton, *The Love of Money the Root of all Evil, or The Sin of Gambling: A Sermon* (London: Whittaker & Co; Barnard Castle: Atkinsons, 1856).

Jubb, Samuel, *The History of the Shoddy Trade* (London: Houlston and Wright; Manchester: John Heywood; Batley: J. Fearnsides, 1860).

Kingsley, Charles, *Alton Locke* (1850; London: Macmillan, 1908).

Kipling, Rudyard, *Wee Willie Winkie. Under the Deodars. The Phantom 'Rickshaw, and Other Stories* (London: Macmillan, 1951).

Kitto, John, *The Lost Senses. Series II. – Blindness* (London: Charles Knight & Co., 1845).

Lamb, Charles, 'On the Character and Genius of Hogarth' (1810), ed. Alfred Ainger, *Poems Plays and Miscellaneous Essays of Charles Lamb* (London: Macmillan, 1914).

Lane, Edward William, *An Account of the Manners and Customs of the Modern Egyptians*, 3 vols. (London: Charles Knight, 1846).

Lang, Andrew, *Cock Lane and Common-Sense* (London: Longmans, Green & Co., 1894).

    The Making of Religion (London: Longmans, Green & Co., 1898).

    Adventures in Books (London: Longmans, Green & Co., 1905).

Lavater, Johann Casper, *Essays on Physiognomy, Designed to Promote the Knowledge and the Love of Mankind* (1774–8; trans. Thomas Holcroft 1789–98; 9th edn, 1855).

[Leeds, W. H.], 'Strictures on Art and Exhibitions', *Fraser's Magazine* 2 (1830), pp. 93–110.

Le Gallienne, Richard, *English Poems* (London: Elkin Mathews and John Lane at the Bodley Head, 1892).

[Leifchild, J. R.], 'Glaciers', *British Quarterly Review* 32 (1860), pp. 341–66.

Levy, W. Hanks, *Blindness and the Blind: or, a Treatise on the Science of Typology* (London: Chapman and Hall, 1872).

Lewes, G. H., *A Biographical History of Philosophy* (4 vols.; London: Charles Knight, 1845–6).

    The Physiology of Common Life, 2 vols. (Edinburgh and London: William Blackwood, 1859).

[Lewes, G. H.], 'Seeing is Believing', *Blackwood's Edinburgh Magzine* 88 (1860), pp. 381–95.

Lewes, George Henry, 'Spiritualism and Materialism (Part I)', *Fortnightly Review* 25 (1876), pp. 479–93, and 'Spiritualism and Materialism (Part II)', ibid., pp. 707–19.

    Problems of Life and Mind, 3rd series, 2 vols. (London: Trübner & Co., 1879).

    The Principles of Success in Literature, ed. T. Shaper Knowlson (London: Walter Scott, 1898).

Lewis, Revd H. J., *Human Blindness and Divine Guidance* (Brigg: William Cressey, 1874).

Linton, Eliza Lynn, 'Our Illusions', *Fortnightly Review* o.s. 55 (1891), pp. 584–97.

Longfellow, Henry Wadsworth, *Hyperion: A Romance* (1839; London: George Routledge and Sons, 1886).

Low, Charles, *Four National Exhibitions in London and their Organisers* (London: T. Fisher Unwin, 1892).

Lytton, Edward Bulwer, *The Last Days of Pompeii*, 3 vols. (London: Richard Bentley, 1834).

MacColl, D. S., *Confessions of a Keeper, and other Papers* (London: A. Maclehose, 1931).

Mackintosh, Mabel, *Dust, Ho! or, Rescued from a Rubbish Heap* (London: John F. Shaw & Co., 1891).

McPherson, J. G., 'Dust', *Longman's Magazine* 18 (1891), pp. 49–59.

Malet, H. P., *Incidents in the Biography of Dust* (London: Trübner and Co., 1877).

Martineau, Harriet, *Eastern Life, Present and Past*, 3 vols. (London: Edward Moxon, Son & Co., 1848).

Marvell, Andrew, *The Poems and Letters of Andrew Marvell*, ed. H. M. Margoliouth, 3rd edn, vol. I, *Poems*, revised by Pierre Legouis with the collaboration of E. E. Duncan-Jones (Oxford: Clarendon Press, 1971).

Maxwell, James Clerk, *The Scientific Papers of James Clerk Maxwell*, ed. W. D. Niven, 2 vols. (Cambridge University Press, 1890).

Mayhew, Henry, *London Labour and the London Poor*, 4 vols. (London: Griffin, Bohn & Co., 1861–2).

Mayhew, Henry and John Binny, *The Criminal Prisons of London and Scenes of Prison Life* (London: Griffin, Bohn and Company, 1862).

Meredith, George, *The Egoist* (1879; Harmondsworth: Penguin, 1968).

Meynell, Alice, *The Colour of Life and other Essays on Things Seen and Heard* (London: John Lane, 1896).

Millais, John Guille, *The Life and Letters of Sir John Everett Millais*, 2 vols. (London: Methuen & Co., 1899).

Miller, Thomas, *Picturesque Sketches of London, Past and Present* (London: Office of the National Illustrated Library, 1852).

Milton, John, *The Poems of John Milton*, ed. John Carey and Alastair Fowler (London and Harlow: Longmans, 1968).

Mitchell, Thomas Livingstone, *Three Expeditions into the Interior of Eastern Australia, with Descriptions of the Recently Explored Region of Australia Felix, and of the Present Colony of New South Wales*, 2 vols. (2nd edn, London: T. and W. Boone, 1839).

[Mitchell, Weir], 'Was He Dead?' *Atlantic Monthly* 25 (1870), pp. 86–102.

Moon, William, *Consequences and Ameliorations of Blindness* (London: Longmans, 1873).

Morley, Henry, 'Pictures at the Royal Academy', *Fortnightly Review* 17 (1872), pp. 692–704.

Murdoch, W. G. B., 'The Art of Criticism', *Memoirs of Swinburne: with Other Essays* (Edinburgh: J. and J. Gray, 1910).

Nesbit, Edith, *Leaves of Life* (London: Longmans, Green & Co., 1889).

Nicolson, William, *London Types, Quatorzains by W. E. Henley* (London: William Heinemann, 1898).

Nightingale, Florence, *Notes on Nursing for the Labouring Classes* (London: Harrison, 1868).

Oppert, F., *On Melanosis of the Lungs and Other Lung Diseases Arising from the Inhalation of Dust* (London: John Churchill and Sons, 1866).

Ouida, *Street Dust and Other Stories* (London: F. V. White & Co., 1901).

Paget, Sir James, *Lectures on Surgical Pathology delivered at the Royal College of Surgeons of England*, ed. William Turner, 2nd edn (London: Longmans, Green, 1853).

Palgrave, Francis Turner, *Handbook to the Fine Art Collections in the International Exhibition of 1862* (London and Cambridge: Macmillan, 1862).

F. T. P., 'The British School of Painting', *International Exhibition 1862: Official Catalogue of the Fine Art Department* (London: Truscott, Son & Simmons, 1862).

Essays on Art (London and Cambridge: Macmillan, 1866).

Parish, Edmund, *Hallucinations and Illusions. A Study of the Fallacies of Perception* (London: Walter Scott, 1897).

Pater, Walter, *The Renaissance* (1873; London: Macmillan, 1900).

Pennell, Joseph, 'Is Photography among the Fine Arts?' *Contemporary Review* 72 (1897), 824–36.

Poole, Sophia, *The Englishwoman in Egypt* (London: Charles Knight & Co., 1844).

Proctor, Richard, *The Expanse of Heaven. A Series of Essays on the Wonders of the Firmament* (London: Henry S. King & Co., 1873).

'The Photographic Eyes of Science', *Longman's Magazine* 1 (1883), pp. 439–62.

Pusey, Revd E. B., *Sinful Blindness Amidst Imagined Light* (Oxford and London: Parker; and London, Oxford and Cambridge: Rivingtons, 1873).

Quilter, Harry, *Preferences in Art, Life and Literature* (London: Swann Sonnenschein & Co., 1892).

Opinions on Men, Women and Things (London: Swann Sonnenschein & Co., 1909).

Reade, A. A., *Literary Success; Being a Guide to Practical Journalism* (London: Wyman & Sons, 1885).

Reed, Charles, *Diamonds in the Dust. A New Year's Address for Sunday Scholars* (London: Sunday School Union, 1866).

Reynolds, Sir Joshua, *The Works of Sir Joshua Reynolds*, ed. Edmund Malone, 3 vols. (4th edn, corrected, London: T. Cadell, Jun., & W. Davies, 1801).

Rossetti, Christina, *Time Flies* (London: SPCK, 1885).

    Poems and Prose, ed. Jan Marsh (London: J. M. Dent, 1994).

Rossetti, Dante Gabriel, *The Collected Works of Dante Gabriel Rossetti*, ed. William Michael Rossetti, 2 vols. (London: Ellis and Elvey, 1888).

Rossetti, William Michael, *Fine Art, Chiefly Contemporary* (London: Macmillan, 1867).

Roth, Ling, *Natives of Sarawak*, 2 vols. (London: Truslove and Hanson, 1896).

Russell, Percy, *The Author's Manual* (London: Digby & Long, 1891).

Samson, John, *Inventions and their Commercial Development: A Practical Handbook for Inventors and Investors Showing How to Invent, What to Invent, How to Patent, How to Make Money by Inventions* (London: Messrs Simpkin, Marshall, Hamilton, Kent & Co., 1896).

Schumann, Robert, *Music and Musicians. Essays and Criticisms*, trans., ed. and annotated by Fanny Raymond Ritter, 2 vols. (London: William Reeves, 1877).

Seeley, J. R., *The Expansion of England* (1883; ed. John Gross, Chicago and London: University of Chicago Press, 1971).

Shairp, C., *Life and Letters of J. D. Forbes* (London: MacMillan, 1873).

Shelley, Mary, *Frankenstein or the Modern Prometheus*, ed. M. K. Joseph (1818; London: Oxford University Press, 1969).

    The Journals of Mary Shelley 1814–1844, ed. P. R. Feldman and D. Scott-Kilvert, 2 vols. (Oxford University Press, 1987).

Shelley, Percy Bysshe, *The Letters of Percy Bysshe Shelley*, ed. F. L. Jones, 2 vols. (Oxford University Press, 1964).

    The Complete Poetical Works of Percy Bysshe Shelley, ed. N. Rogers, 4 vols. (Oxford University Press, 1975).

    Complete Poetical Works of Percy Bysshe Shelley, ed. T. Hutchinson (1905; reprinted London: Oxford University Press, 1952).

Sherratt, Edwin, *A Popular Treatise on the Origin, Nature, and Properties of Light: Shewing the Wisdom, Goodness, and Great Designing Hand of the Beneficent Creator* (London: Simpkin, Marshall and Co., 1856).

Simmel, Georg, 'The Metropolis and Mental Life' (1903), in David Frisby and Mike Featherstone, eds., *Simmel on Culture* (London: Sage Publications, 1997), pp. 174–85.

Skeat, Walter W., *Malay Magic* (London: Macmillan, 1900).

Smith, James, *All Things Preaching Christ; or, A Profitable Walk* (Cheltenham: Willey, *c.* 1840).

Spencer, Herbert, *The Principles of Sociology* (1876; 3rd edn, revised and enlarged, 2 vols., London: Williams and Northgate, 1885).

Spenser, Edmund, *The Poetical Works of Edmund Spenser*, ed. J. C. Smith, 3 vols. (London: Oxford at the Clarendon Press, 1909).

Spielmann, M. H., *Millais and his Works* (Edinburgh and London: William Blackwood and Sons, 1898).

Spurgeon, C. H., *Gambling – A Common Snare* (London: Passmore and Alabaster, 1887).

Statham, H. Heathcote, 'The Grosvenor Gallery', *Macmillan's Magazine* 36 (1877), pp. 112–18.

Steam Power from House Dust for Electric Lighting and Other Purposes; Produced by the Patented Process of The Refuse Disposal Company, Limited (London: Refuse Disposal Company, 1892).

Steinmetz, Andrew, *The Gaming Table: Its Votaries and its Victims, In All Times and Countries, Especially in England and in France*, 2 vols. (London: Tinsley, 1870).

Stephen, Leslie, *The Playground of Europe* (London: Longmans, Green & Co., 1871).

[Stephens, F. G.], *Notes on a Collection of Pictures by Mr. John Everett Millais, R. A., Exhibited at the Fine Art Society's Rooms, 148 New Bond Street 1881* (London: Fine Art Society Ltd, 1881).

Stevenson, Robert Louis, *Across the Plains, With Other Memories and Essays* (1879; London: Chatto and Windus, 1892).

   The Esssays of Robert Louis Stevenson, ed. Malcolm Elwin (London: MacDonald, 1950).

Stodart, Mary, *Female Writers: Thoughts on their Proper Sphere and on their Powers of Usefulness* (London: R. B. Seeley and W. Burnside, 1842).

Stoker, Bram, *Dracula* (1897; Oxford University Press, 1983).

Stokes, William, *Memory* (7th and enlarged edn, London: Houlston & Sons, 1876).

Sully, James, *Sensation and Intuition: Studies in Psychology and Aesthetics* (London: Henry S. King, 1874).

   'Art and Psychology', *Mind* 1 (1876), pp. 467–78.

[Sully, James], 'The Undefinable in Art', *Cornhill Magazine* 38 (1878), pp. 559–72.

Sully, James, *Illusions. A Psychological Study* (London: C. Kegan Paul, 1881).

    My Life and Friends (London: T. Fisher Unwin, 1918).

Swinburne, Algernon, *The Complete Works of Algernon Charles Swinburne*, ed. Sir Edmund Gosse and Thomas James Wise 19 vols. (New York: Russell and Russell, 1925).

Taine, H. A., *History of English Literature*, 2 vols. (1863; trans. H. Van Laun, Edinburgh: Edmonston & Douglas, 1871).

    Notes on England (trans. W. F. Rae, London: Strahan & Co., 1872).

Taylor, Tom, *The Railway Station* (London: no publisher, 1862).

    The Race for Wealth. A series of Five Pictures by W. P. Frith, R. A. Now Exhibiting at the King Street Galleries (London: no publisher, 1880).

Tennyson, Alfred, *The Poems of Tennyson* (London & Harlow: Longmans, 1969).

Tennyson, Hallam, *Alfred Lord Tennyson: A Memoir*, 2 vols. (London: Macmillan, 1897).

Thom, John Hamilton, *Spiritual Blindness and Social Disruption* (London: John Chapman, 1849).

Thomas, Northcote W., *Crystal Gazing. Its History and Practice, with a Discussion of the Evidence for Telepathic Scrying* (London: Alexander Moring, 1905).

Thomas, W. L., 'The Making of "The Graphic"', *Universal Review* 2 (1888), pp. 80–93.

Trollope, Anthony, *Can You Forgive Her?* (1864–5; Oxford University Press, 1982).

    'W. M. Thackeray', *Cornhill Magazine* 9 (1864).

Turnley, Joseph, *The Language of the Eye: The Importance and Dignity of the Eye as Indicative of General Character, Female Beauty, and Manly Genius* (London: Partridge & Co., 1856).

Turnor, Hatton, *Astra Castra* (London: Chapman and Hall, 1860).

Two Twenty Years' Residents [Flora Annie Steele and Grace Gardiner], *The Complete Indian Housekeeper and Cook* (Edinburgh: Frank Murray, 1890).

Tyndall, John, *The Glaciers of the Alps. Being a Narrative of Excursions and Ascents, An Account of the Origin and Phenomenon of Glaciers, and An Exposition of the Physical Principles to which they are related* (London: John Murray, 1860).

    Natural Philosophy in Easy Lessons (London: Cassell, Petter and Galpin, 1869).

    'On Dust and Disease', *Fraser's Magazine* n.s. 1 (1870). pp. 302–10.

Essays on the Use and Limit of the Imagination in Science (London: Longman, Green & Co., 1870).

Hours of Exercise in the Alps (Longman: Longmans, Green, & Co., 1871).

Six Lectures on Light. Delivered in America in 1872–1873 (London: Longmans, Green and Co., 1873).

'Atoms, Molecules, and Ether Waves', *Longman's Magazine* 1 (1882), pp. 29–40.

New Fragments (London: Longman, Green & Co., 1892).

Unsigned article, 'A Few Words about the Cartoons', *New Monthly Magazine* 69 (1843), pp. 260–5.

'London from Aloft', *Strand* (July 1891), pp. 492–8.

'Dust and Hygiene', *All the Year Round* 3rd series 13 (1895), pp. 154–8.

Verney, Frances P., 'Where are We in Art?' *Contemporary Review* 36 (1879), pp. 588–600.

von Helmholtz, Hermann, *Popular Lectures on Scientific Subjects* (trans. E. Atkinson, London: Longmans, Green and Co., 1873).

Vulpian, A., *Leçons sur la Physiologie générale et comparée du système nerveux faite au muséum d'histoire naturelle* (Paris: G. Baillière, 1866).

Wallace, Alfred Russel, *The Wonderful Century. Its Successes and its Failures* (London: Swan Sonnenschein & Co., Ltd, 1898).

W., The Hon. Mrs [Ward, Mary], *A World of Wonders Revealed by the Microscope* (London: Groombridge & Sons, 1858).

Wedmore, Frederick, 'Some Tendencies in Recent Painting', *Temple Bar* 53 (1878), pp. 334–48.

'Mr. Whistler's Theories and Mr. Whistler's Art', *Nineteenth Century* 6 (1879), pp. 334–43.

Wells, H. G., *The Complete Short Stories of H. G. Wells* (New York: St Martin's Press, 1971).

Whistler, James McNeill, *The Gentle Art of Making Enemies* (2nd and enlarged edn, London: Heinemann, 1892).

White, William Hale, *Mark Rutherford's Deliverance. Being the Second Part of his Autobiography* (1885; London: Oxford University Press and Humphrey Mitford, 1936).

The Wild Boys of London; or, The Children of the Night, 1 (London: Newsagents' Publishing Co., 1863).

Wilde, Oscar, 'The Grosvenor Gallery', *Dublin University Magazine* (1877), pp. 118–26.

'Mr. Whistler's Ten O'Clock', *Pall Mall Gazette* (21 February 1885), p. 14.

Williams, Helen Maria, *A Tour in Switzerland; or, A View of the Present*

State of the Governments and Manners of those Cantons: with comparative sketches of the Present State of Paris, 2 vols. (Dublin: P. Wogan, 1798).

Wills, Alfred, *Wanderings Among the High Alps*, 2nd edn, revised (London: Richard Bentley, 1858).

Winslow, Forbes Benignus, *On Obscure Diseases of the Brain and Disorders of the Mind* (1860; 4th edn, London: John Churchill, 1868).

Wood, Revd J. G., *Common Objects of the Microscope* (London: Routledge, Warne and Routledge, 1861).

Wood, Joseph, 'Sight and Insight', *Modern Review* 1 (1880), pp. 224–34.

Wordsworth, Dorothy, *Journals of Dorothy Wordsworth*, ed. E. de Selincourt (London: Macmillan, 1941).

Wordsworth, Christopher, *On Spiritual Blindness* (Oxford and London: John Henry and James Parker, 1857).

Wordsworth, William, *The Poetical Works of William Wordsworth*, ed. E. de Selincourt and H. Darbishire (London: Clarendon Press, 1959).

Secondary sources

Ackland, Michael, ed., *The Penguin Book of 19th Century Australian Literature* (Ringwood, Victoria: Penguin, 1993).

Agnew, Jean-Christophe, 'The Consuming Vision of Henry James', in Richard Wightman Fox and T. J. Jackson Lears, eds., *The Culture of Consumption. Critical Esssays in American History, 1880–1980* (New York: Pantheon Books, 1983), pp. 97–100.

Altick, Richard D., 'Four Victorian Poets and an Exploding Island', *Victorian Studies* 3 (1960), pp. 249–60.

The Shows of London (Cambridge, Mass., and London: The Belknap Press of Harvard University Press, 1978).

Paintings from Books. Art and Literature in Britain, 1760–1900 (Columbus: Ohio State University Press, 1985).

Anderson, Nancy Fix, *Woman Against Women in Victorian England. A Life of Eliza Lynn Linton* (Bloomington and Indianapolis: Indiana University Press, 1987).

Anderson, Patricia, *The Printed Image and the Transformation of Popular Culture 1790–1860* (Oxford University Press, 1991).

Arac, Jonathan, *Commissioned Spirits: The Shaping of Social Motion in Dickens, Carlyle, Melville, and Hawthorne* (New Brunswick: Rutgers University Press, 1979).

Armstrong, Isobel, 'Transparency: Towards a Poetics of Glass in the

Nineteenth Century', in Francis Spufford and Jenny Uglow, eds., *Cultural Babbage. Technology, Time and Invention* (London and Boston: Faber and Faber, 1996), pp. 123–48.

Armstrong, Isobel, and Joseph Bristow, eds., *Nineteenth-Century Women Poets. An Oxford Anthology* (Oxford: Clarendon Press, 1996).

Arnheim, Rudolph, *Art and Visual Perception: The New Version* (Berkeley: University of California Press, 1974).

Ashton, Rosemary, *The German Idea. Four English Writers and the Reception of German Thought, 1800–1860* (1980; London: Libris, 1994).

G. H. Lewes: A Life (Oxford and New York: Oxford University Press, 1991).

Barker-Benfield, G. J., *The Horrors of the Half-Known Life: Male Attitudes Towards Woman and Sexuality in Nineteenth-Century America* (New York: Harper and Row, 1976).

Baudrillard, Jean, *For a Critique of the Political Economy of the Sign*, trans. Charles Levin (1972; St Louis: Telos Press, 1981).

Beer, Gillian, 'Myth and the Single Consciousness: *Middlemarch* and "The Lifted Veil"', in Ian Adam, ed., *This Particular Web: Essays on Middlemarch* (University of Toronto Press, 1975), pp. 91–115.

Darwin's Plots (London: Routledge and Kegan Paul, 1983).

'"Authentic Tidings of Invisible Things": Vision and the Invisible in the Later Nineteenth Century', in Teresa Brennan and Martin Jay, eds., *Vision in Context. Historical and Contemporary Perspectives on Sight* (New York and London: Routledge, 1996), pp. 85–98.

Open Fields: Science in Cultural Encounter (Oxford: Clarendon Press, 1996).

Bendiner, Kenneth, *An Introduction to Victorian Painting* (New Haven and London: Yale University Press, 1985).

Benjamin, Walter, 'The Work of Art in the Age of Mechanical Reproduction' (1936); trans. Harry Zohn, in *Illuminations*, ed. Hannah Arendt (New York: Harcourt, Brace and World, 1968).

Charles Baudelaire: A Lyric Poet in the Age of High Capitalism (trans. Harry Zohn; London: New Left Books, 1973).

Berger, John, *Ways of Seeing* (Harmondsworth: Penguin, 1972).

Besterman, Theodore, *Crystal-Gazing: A Study in the History, Distribution, Theory and Practice of Scrying* (London: William Rider & Son, 1924).

Boone, Joseph, A., 'Depolicing *Villette*: Surveillance, Invisibility, and the Female Erotics of "Heretic Narrative"', *Novel* 26 (1992), pp. 20–42.

Borzello, Frances, *Civilising Caliban. The Misuse of Art 1875–1980* (London and New York: Routledge and Kegan Paul, 1987).

Bourdieu, Pierre, *Distinction. A Social Critique of the Judgement of Taste* (1979; trans. Richard Nice, London: Routledge & Kegan Paul, 1984).

Bowie, Malcolm, *Freud, Proust and Lacan: Theory as Fiction* (Cambridge University Press, 1987).

Bowlby, Rachel, *Just Looking. Consumer Culture in Dreiser, Gissing and Zola* (New York and London: Methuen, 1985).

Brantlinger, Patrick, *Rule of Darkness. British Literature and Imperialism, 1830–1914* (Ithaca and London: Cornell University Press, 1988).

Briggs, Julia, *Night Visitors. The Rise and Fall of the English Ghost Story* (London: Faber, 1977).

Brimblecombe, Peter, *The Big Smoke: a History of Air Pollution in London since Medieval Times* (London and New York: Methuen, 1987).

Bronfen, Elisabeth, *Over Her Dead Body. Death, Femininity and the Aesthetic* (Manchester University Press, 1992).

Brooks, Peter, *Body Work. Objects of Desire in Modern Narrative* (Cambridge, Mass., and London: Harvard University Press, 1993).

Broughton, Trev Lynn, *Men of Letters, Writing Lives. Masculinity and Literary Auto/Biography in the Late Victorian Period* (London and New York: Routledge, 1999).

Brown, Eleanor Gertrude, *Milton's Blindness* (New York: Columbia University Press, 1934).

Brown, Richard, ed., *Knowledge, Education and Cultural Change: Papers in the Sociology of Education* (London: Tavistock, 1973).

Bryson, Norman, *Vision and Painting. The Logic of the Gaze* (Basingstoke and London: Macmillan, 1983).

Buck-Morss, Susan, *The Dialectics of Seeing. Walter Benjamin and the Arcades Project* (Cambridge, Mass., and London: MIT Press, 1989).

Bull, Malcolm, 'Mastery and Slavery in *The Lifted Veil*', *Essays in Criticism* 48 (1998), pp. 244–61.

Bullen, J. B., *The Expressive Eye. Fiction and Perception in the Work of Thomas Hardy* (Oxford University Press, 1986).

   The Pre-Raphaelite Body. Fear and Desire in Painting, Poetry and Criticism (Oxford: Clarendon Press, 1998).

Burrow, J. W., *A Liberal Descent. Victorian Historians and the English Past* (Cambridge University Press, 1981).

Butler, Stella, R. H. Nuttall and Olivia Brown, *The Social History of the Microscope* (Cambridge: Whipple Museum, 1986).

Cahan, David, ed., *Hermann von Helmholtz and the Foundations of 19th-Century Science* (Berkeley: University of California Press, 1993).

Carter, Paul, *The Road to Botany Bay. An Essay in Spatial History* (London and Boston: Faber and Faber, 1987).

Cartwright, Lisa, *Screening the Body: Tracing Medicine's Visual Culture* (Minneapolis: University of Minnesota Press, 1995).

Casteras, Susan, P., 'The Unsettled Hearth: P. H. Calderon's *"Lord! Thy Will be Done"* and the Problematics of Women in Victorian Interiors', in Ellen Harding, ed., *Re-framing the Pre-Raphaelites: Historical and Theoretical Essays* (Aldershot: Scolar Press, 1996), pp. 149–72.

Casteras, Susan, P., and Colleen Denney, eds., *The Grosvenor Gallery. A Palace of Art in Victorian England* (New Haven and London: Yale University Press, 1996).

Christ, Carol T., *The Finer Optic. The Aesthetic of Particularity in Victorian Poetry* (New Haven and London: Yale University Press, 1975).

Classen, Constance, *Worlds of Sense. Exploring the Senses in History and Across Cultures* (London and New York: Routledge, 1993).

Classen, Constance, David Howes and Anthony Synnott, *Aroma. The Cultural History of Smell* (London and New York: Routledge, 1994).

Cosslett, Tess, *The 'Scientific Movement' and Victorian Literature* (Brighton: The Harvester Press, 1982).

Cottom, Daniel, *Abyss of Reason: Cultural Movements, Revelations, and Betrayals* (New York: Oxford University Press, 1991).

Cowling, Mary, *The Artist as Anthropologist. The Representation of Type and Character in Victorian Art* (Cambridge University Press, 1989).

Crary, Jonathan, *Techniques of the Observer. On Vision and Modernity in the Nineteenth Century* (Cambridge, Mass., and London: MIT Press, 1990).

Dalby, Richard, ed., *The Virago Book of Victorian Ghost Stories* (London: Virago, 1988).

Dale, Peter Allan, *In Pursuit of a Scientific Culture. Science, Art, and Society in the Victorian Age* (Madison: University of Wisconsin Press, 1989).

Damisch, Hubert, *The Origins of Perspective* (1987; trans. John Goodman, Cambridge, Mass., and London: MIT Press, 1994).

Danesi, Marcel, 'Thinking is Seeing: Visual Metaphors and the Nature of Abstract Thought', *Semiotica* 80 (1990), pp. 221–37.

Davidson, Caroline, *A Woman's Work is Never Done: A History of Housework in the British Isles 1650–1950* (London: Chatto and Windus, 1982).

de Certeau, Michel, *The Practice of Everyday Life* (1984; trans. Steven Randall, Berkeley, Los Angeles, London: University of California Press, 1988).

de Lauretis, Teresa, and Stephen Heath, eds., *The Cinematic Apparatus* (London and Basingstoke: Macmillan, 1980).

de Man, Paul, *Blindness and Insight. Essays in the Rhetoric of Contemporary Criticism* (2nd edn, revised, London: Methuen, 1983).

Derrida, Jacques, *Writing and Difference* (trans. Alan Bass, London and Henley: Routledge and Kegan Paul, 1978).

   Memoirs of the Blind. The Self-Portrait and Other Ruins (trans. Pascale-Anne Brault and Michael Naas, Chicago and London: University of Chicago Press, 1993).

DiMaggio, Paul, and Michael Unseem, 'Social Class and Arts Consumption', *Theory and Society* 5 (1978), pp. 141–61.

Douglas, Mary, *Purity and Danger. An Analysis of the Concepts of Pollution and Taboo* (1966; London and New York: Routledge, 1984).

Eagleton, Terry, 'Power and Knowledge in *The Lifted Veil*', *Literature and History* 9 (1983), pp. 52–61.

Edel, Leon, *Henry James: A Life* (New York: Harper and Row, 1985).

Edelstein, Teri J., 'They sang "The Song of the Shirt": The Visual Ideology of the Seamstress', *Victorian Studies* 23 (1980), pp. 183–210.

   'Augustus Egg's Triptych: A Narrative of Victorian Adultery', *Burlington Magazine* 125 (1983), pp. 202–10.

Edwards, Elizabeth, ed., *Anthropology and Photography 1860–1920* (New Haven and London: Yale University Press, 1992).

Ellenberger, Henri F., *The Discovery of the Unconscious: The History and Evolution of Dynamic Psychology* (London: Allen Lane, 1970).

Errington, Lindsay, *Social and Religious Themes in English Art 1840–1860* (New York and London: Garland Publishing, 1984).

Eve, A. S., and C. H. Creasey, *Life and Work of John Tyndall* (London: Macmillan, 1945).

Fahnestock, Jeanne, 'The Heroine of Irregular Features', *Victorian Studies* 24 (1981), pp. 325–50.

Farwell, Beatrice, *The Cult of Images: Baudelaire and the C19th Media Explosion* (University College of Santa Barbara Art Museum, 1977).

Feaver, William, *The Art of John Martin* (Oxford: Clarendon Press, 1975).

Finucane, R. C., *Appearances of the Dead. A Cultural History of Ghosts* (London: Junction Books, 1982).

Fisher, Judith, L., 'Image versus Text in the Illustrated Novels of William Makepeace Thackeray', in Christ and Jordan, *Victorian Literature and the Victorian Visual Imagination*, pp. 60–87.

Fitch, Raymond E., *The Poison Sky. Myth and Apocalypse in Ruskin* (Athens and London: Ohio University Press, 1982).

Flint, Kate, 'Moral Judgement and the Language of English Art Criticism', *Oxford Art Journal* 6 (1983), pp. 59–66.

   Impressionists in England. The Critical Reception (London: Routledge and Kegan Paul, 1984).

   'Reading *The Awakening Conscience* Rightly', in Marcia Pointon, ed., *Pre-Raphaelites Re-viewed* (Manchester and New York: Manchester University Press, 1989), pp. 45–65.

Ford, Brian J., *The Revealing Lens: Mankind and the Microscope* (London: Harrap, 1973).

   Single Lens: The Story of the Simple Microscope (London: Heinemann, 1985).

Forster, John, *Life of Dickens* [1872–4], ed. J. W. Ley (London: Cecil Palmer, 1928).

Foucault, Michel, *The Birth of the Clinic. An Archaeology of Medical Perception* (*Naissance de la Clinique*, 1963; trans. A. M. Sheridan Smith, London: Tavistock Publication, 1973).

   Discipline and Punish. The Birth of the Prison (*Surveiller et Punir: Naissance de la Prison*, 1975; trans. Alan Sheridan, London: Allen Lee, 1977).

Fox, Celina, 'The Development of Social Reportage in English Periodical Illustration during the 1840s and early 1850s', *Past and Present* 74 (1977), pp. 90–111.

Freud, Sigmund, *The Standard Edition of the Complete Psychological Works of Sigmund Freud* (London: Hogarth Press and the Institute of Psychoanalysis, 1953–74).

Friedman, Susan Stanford, 'Women's Autobiographical Selves: Theory and Practice', in Shari Benstock, ed., *The Private Self. Theory and Practice of Women's Autobiographical Writings* (London: Routledge, 1988), pp. 34–62.

Furst, *Realism*, ed. Lilian R. (London and New York: Longman, 1992).

Gage, John, *Color in Turner* (New York: Praeger, 1969).

Gallagher, Catherine, *The Industrial Reformation of English Fiction. Social Discourse and Narrative Form 1832–1867* (Chicago and London: University of Chicago Press, 1985).

Galperin, William H., *The Return of the Visible in British Romanticism* (Baltimore and London: Johns Hopkins University Press, 1993).

Gauld, A., *The Founders of Psychical Research* (London: Routledge and Kegan Paul, 1968).

Geduld, Harry M., ed., *The Definitive 'Time Machine'* (Bloomington and Indianapolis: Indiana University Press, 1987).

Gernsheim, Helmut, *The Origins of Photography* (New York: Thames and Hudson, 1982).

Gernsheim, Helmut, and Alison Gernsheim, *The History of Photography: From the Earliest Use of the Camera Obscura up to 1914* (London: Oxford University Press, 1955).

Gilbert, Sandra M., and Susan Gubar, *The Madwoman in the Attic: The Woman Writer and the Nineteenth-Century Literary Imagination* (New Haven and London: Yale University Press, 1979).

Glover, John, *London's Underground. An Illustrated History of the World's Premier Underground System* (Shepperton: Ian Allen, 1951; 8th edn, 1996).

Goldberg, David T., ed., *Anatomy of Racism* (Minneapolis: University of Minnesota Press, 1990).

Golffing, Francis, 'Tennyson's Last Phase: the Poet as Seer', *Southern Review* 2 (1966), pp. 264–85.

Gooding, David, '"In Nature's School": Faraday as an Experimentalist', in David Gooding and Frank A. J. L. James, eds., *Faraday Rediscovered. Essays on the Life and Work of Michael Faraday, 1791–1867* (Basingstoke: Macmillan, 1985), pp. 105–35.

Gould, Stephen J., *The Mismeasure of Man* (1982; Harmondsworth: Penguin, 1984).

Gray, B. M., 'Pseudo-science and George Eliot's *The Lifted Veil*', *Nineteenth-Century Fiction* 36 (1982), pp. 407–23.

Gray, Hilda Orchardson, *The Life of Sir William Quiller Orchardson, R. A.* (London: Hutchinson, 1930).

Green-Lewis, Jennifer, *Framing the Victorians. Photography and the Culture of Realism* (Ithaca and London: Cornell University Press, 1996).

Greenhalgh, Paul, *Ephemeral Vistas. The Expositions Universelles, Great Exhibitions and World's Fairs, 1851–1939* (Manchester University Press, 1988).

Hallam, A., *Great Geological Controversies* (2nd edn, Oxford University Press, 1989).

Hancher, Michael, '"Urgent private affairs": Millais's "Peace concluded, 1856"', *Burlington Magazine* 133 (1991), pp. 499–506.

Hansen, B., 'The Early History of Glacial Theory in British Geology', *Journal of Glaciology* 9 (1970), pp. 135–41.

Harrison, Charles, 'On the Surface of Painting', *Critical Inquiry* 15 (1989), pp. 292–336.

Harrison, Michael, *London Beneath the Pavement* (London: Peter Davies, 1961).

Harvey, J. R., *Victorian Novelists and Their Illustrators* (New York University Press, 1971).

Harvey, Michael, 'Ruskin and Photography', *Oxford Art Journal* 7 (1984), pp. 25–33.

Helms, Mary, *Ulysses' Sail: An Ethnographic Odyssey of Power, Knowledge, and Geographical Distance* (Princeton University Press, 1988).

Helsinger, Elizabeth K., *Ruskin and the Art of the Beholder* (Cambridge, Mass., and London: Harvard University Press, 1982).

Henderson, Archibald, *George Bernard Shaw: Man of the Century*, 2 vols. (London: Hurst and Blackett, 1911).

Hersey, George L., 'Ruskin as an Optical Thinker', in John Dixon Hunt and Faith M. Holland, eds., *The Ruskin Polygon. Esssays on the Imagination of John Ruskin* (Manchester University Press, 1982), pp. 44–64.

Horsfield, Margaret, *Biting the Dust: The Joys of Housework* (London: Fourth Estate, 1997).

Horton, Susan R., 'Were They Having Fun Yet? Victorian Optical Gadgetry, Modernist Selves', in Christ and Jordan, *Victorian Literature and the Victorian Visual Imagination*, pp. 1–26.

Hoy, Suellen, *Chasing Dirt: The American Pursuit of Cleanliness* (New York and Oxford: Oxford University Press, 1995).

Hull, John M., *Touching the Rock. An Experience of Blindness* (London: SPCK, 1990).

Hume, Kathryn, 'Eat or Be Eaten: H. G. Wells's *Time Machine*', *Philological Quarterly* 69 (1990), pp. 233–51.

Husserl, Edmund, *Cartesian Meditations* (1931; The Hague: M. Nijhoff, 1960).

Hyde, Ralph, *Panoramania* (London: Trefoil Publications and the Barbican Art Gallery, 1988).

Inglis, Brian, *Natural and Supernatural: A History of the Paranormal from Earliest Times to 1914* (London: Hodder and Stoughton, 1977).

Ivins, William, *Prints and Visual Communication* (London: Routledge and Kegan Paul, 1953).

Jacobus, Mary, *Reading Woman. Essays in Feminist Criticism* (London: Methuen, 1986).

Jay, Martin, *Downcast Eyes. The Denigration of Vision in Twentieth-Century French Thought* (Berkeley: University of California Press, 1993).

Jones, Ernest, *On the Nightmare* (London: The Hogarth Press and the Institute of Psycho-analysis, 1931).

Jordanova, Ludmilla, *Sexual Visions. Images of Gender in Science and Medicine Between the Eighteenth and Twentieth Centuries* (Hemel Hempstead: Harvester Wheatsheaf, 1989).

Kargon, Robert H., 'Model and Analogy in Victorian Science: Maxwell and the French Physicists', *Journal of the History of Ideas* 30 (1969), pp. 423–36.

Kearns, Katherine, *Nineteenth-Century Literary Realism. Through the Looking-Glass* (Cambridge University Press, 1996).

Kestner, Joseph, *Masculinities in Victorian Painting* (Aldershot: Scolar Press, 1995).

'The Pre-Raphaelites and Imperialism: John Everett Millais's *Pizarro, The Boyhood of Raleigh* and *The North-West Passage*', *Journal of Pre-Raphaelite Studies* n.s. 4 (1995).

Kinkead-Weekes, Mark, 'Vision in Kipling's Novels', in Andrew Rutherford, ed., *Kipling's Mind and Art* (Edinburgh and London: Oliver and Boyd, 1964), pp. 197–234.

Knoepflmacher, U. C., *George Eliot's Early Novels. The Limits of Realism* (Berkeley and Los Angeles: University of California Press, 1968).

Korg, Jacob, 'Astronomical Imagery in Victorian Poetry', in Paradis and Postlewait, *Victorian Science and Victorian Values*, pp. 137–58.

Kosslyn, Stephen M., *Image and Mind* (Cambridge, Mass., and London: Harvard University Press, 1980).

Ghosts in the Mind's Machine. Creating and Using Images in the Brain (W. W. Norton and Co.: New York and London, 1983).

Image and Brain. The Resolution of the Imagery Debate (Cambridge, Mass., and London: MIT Press, 1994).

Krasner, James, *The Entangled Eye. Visual Perception and the Representation of Nature in Post-Darwinian Narrative* (New York and Oxford: Oxford University Press, 1992).

Krauss, Rosalind, *The Optical Unconscious* (Cambridge, Mass., and London: MIT Press, 1993).

Kristeva, Julia, *Desire in Language*, ed. Leon S. Roudiez, trans. Thomas Gora, Alice Jardine, and Leon S. Roudiez (New York: Columbia University Press, 1980).

Powers of Horror: An Essay in Abjection (1980, trans. L. Roudiez; New York: Columbia University Press, 1982).

Kroeber, Karl, *British Romantic Art* (Berkeley, Los Angeles, and London: University of California Press, 1986).

Landow, George, *The Aesthetic and Critical Theories of John Ruskin* (Princeton University Press, 1971).

'There Began to Be a Great Talking about the Fine Arts', in Josef L. Altholz, ed., *The Mind and Art of Victorian England* (Minneapolis: University of Minnesota Press, 1976), pp. 124–45.

Victorian Types, Victorian Shadows (London: Routledge and Kegan Paul, 1980).

Images of Crisis: Literary Iconology, 1750 to the Present (London: Routledge and Kegan Paul, 1982).

Langbauer, Laurie, *Women and Romance. The Consolations of Gender in the English Novel* (Ithaca and London: Cornell University Press, 1990).

Leatherdale, W. M., *The Role of Analogy, Model and Metaphor in Science* (Amsterdam: North-Holland, 1974).

Lefebvre, Henri, *The Production of Space* (1974; trans. Donald Nicholson-Smith, 1991; Oxford and Malden: Blackwell, 1998).

Levine, George, *The Realistic Imagination. English Fiction from Frankenstein to Lady Chatterley* (Chicago and London: University of Chicago Press, 1981).

Darwin and the Novelists. Patterns of Science in Victorian Fiction (Cambridge, Mass., and London: Harvard University Press, 1988).

Lewis, Reina, *Gendering Orientalism. Race, Femininity and Representation* (London and New York: Routledge, 1996).

Linehan, Katherine Bailey, 'Mixed Politics: the Critique of Imperialism in *Daniel Deronda', Texas Studies in Literature and Language* 34 (1992), pp. 323–46.

Loeb, Lori Anne, *Consuming Angels. Advertising and Victorian Women* (New York and Oxford: Oxford University Press, 1994).

Lonsdale, Roger, ed., *Eighteenth-Century Women Poets. An Oxford Anthology* (Oxford University Press, 1989).

Low, Gail, *White Skins/Black Masks. Representation and Colonialism* (London: Routledge, 1996).

Maas, Jeremy, *Gambart: Prince of the Victorian Art World* (London: Barrie and Jenkins, 1975).

Holman Hunt and The Light of the World (Aldershot: Wildwood House, 1987).

McClintock, Anne, *Imperial Leather. Race, Gender and Sexuality in the Colonial Contest* (New York and London: Routledge, 1995).

McDonagh, Josephine, 'Writings on the Mind: Thomas De Quincey and the Importance of the Palimpsest in Nineteenth-Century Thought', *Prose Studies* 10 (1987), pp. 207–24.

McGann, Jerome J., *Towards a Literature of Knowledge* (Oxford: Clarendon Press, 1989).

Macleod, Dianne Sachko, *Art and the Victorian Middle Class: Money and the Making of Cultural Identity* (New York: Cambridge University Press, 1996).

Marcus, Steven, *Engels, Manchester, and the Working Class* (London: Weidenfeld and Nicolson, 1974).

Marvin, Carolyn, *When Old Technologies Were New. Thinking About Electric Communication in the Late Nineteenth Century* (New York and Oxford: Oxford University Press, 1988).

Meisel, Martin, *Realizations. Narrative, Pictorial, and Theatrical Arts in Nineteenth-Century England* (Princeton University Press, 1983).

Merleau-Ponty, M., *Phenomenology of Perception* (trans. Colin Smith, 1962; London and New York: Routledge, 1995).

Merrill, Linda, *A Pot of Paint: Aesthetics on Trial in Whistler v. Ruskin* (Washington and London: Smithsonian Institution Press, 1992).

Meyer, Susan, *Imperialism at Home: Race and Victorian Women's Fiction* (Ithaca and London: Cornell University Press, 1996).

Miller, Andrew H., *Novels Behind Glass. Commodity Culture and Victorian Narrative* (Cambridge University Press, 1995).

Miller, D. A., *The Novel and the Police* (Berkeley, Los Angeles, and London: University of California Press, 1988).

Miller, J. Hillis, 'Optic and Semiotic in *Middlemarch*', in Jerome H. Buckley, ed., *The Worlds of Victorian Fiction* (Cambridge, Mass.: Harvard University Press, 1975), pp. 125–45.

Mishkin, Mortimer, and Tim Appenzeller, 'The Anatomy of Memory', *Scientific American* 256 (1987), pp. 62–71.

Mitchell, W. J. T., *Picture Theory. Essays on Verbal and Visual Representation* (Chicago and London: University of Chicago Press, 1994).

Moore, A. W., ed., *Infinity* (Aldershot: Dartmouth Publishing Co., 1993).

Morawaski, Stefan, *Inquiries into the Fundamentals of Aesthetics* (Cambridge, Mass.: MIT Press, 1974).

Morus, Iwan Rhys, 'The Electric Ariel: Telegraphy and Commercial Culture in Early Victorian England', *Victorian Studies* 39 (1996), pp. 339–78.

Nead, Lynda, 'Seduction, Prostitution, Suicide: *On the Brink* by Alfred Elmore', *Art History* 5 (1982), pp. 310–22.

    Myths of Sexuality. Representations of Women in Victorian Britain (Oxford and New York: Basil Blackwell, 1988).

The Female Nude. Art, Obscenity and Sexuality (London and New York: Routledge, 1992).

Newall, Christopher, *The Grosvenor Gallery Exhibitions: Change and Continuity in the Victorian Art World* (Cambridge University Press, 1995).

Nunn, Pamela Gerrish, 'Critically Speaking', *Women in the Victorian Art World*, ed. Clarissa Campbell Orr (Manchester and New York: Manchester University Press, 1995), pp. 107–24.

Oettermann, Stephan, *The Panorama. History of a Mass Medium* (1980; trans. Deborah Lucas Schneider, New York: Zone Books, 1997).

Olmsted, J. M., *Charles-Edouard Brown-Séquard: A Nineteenth Century Neurologist and Endocrinologist* (Baltimore: The Johns Hopkins Press, 1946).

Ong, Walter J., *The Presence of the Word: Some Prolegomena for Cultural and Religious History* (New Haven: Yale University Press, 1967).

Oppenheim, Janet, *The Other World. Spiritualism and Psychical Research in England, 1850–1914* (Cambridge University Press, 1985).

Otis, Laura, *Organic Memory: History and the Body in the Late Nineteenth and Early Twentieth Centuries* (Lincoln and London: University of Nebraska Press, 1994).

Owen, Alex, *The Darkened Room. Women, Power and Spiritualism in Late Victorian England* (London: Virago, 1989).

Owen, David, *The Government of Victorian London, 1855–1889. The Metropolitan Board of Works, the Vestries, and the City Corporation*, ed. R. Macleod (Cambridge, Mass.: The Belknap Press of Harvard University Press, 1982).

Paradis, Jim and Tom Postlewait, eds., *Victorian Science and Victorian Values: Literary Perspectives, Annals of the New York Academy of Sciences* 360 (1981), pp. 247–67.

Patten, Robert L., *George Cruikshank's Life, Times, and Art. Volume 2: 1835–1878* (Cambridge: The Lutterworth Press, 1966).

Paulson, William R. *Enlightenment, Romanticism, and the Blind in France* (Princeton University Press, 1987).

Pearce, Lynne, *Woman/Image/Text. Readings in Pre-Raphaelite Art and Literature* (Hemel Hempstead: Harvester Wheatsheaf, 1991).

Phelan, Peggy, *Unmarked. The Politics of Performance* (London and New York: Routledge, 1993).

Pick, Daniel, *Faces of Degeneration. A European Disorder, c. 1848 – c. 1918* (Cambridge University Press, 1989).

'Stories of the Eye', in Roy Porter, ed., *Rewriting the Self. Histories from the Renaissance to the Present* (London and New York: Routledge, 1997), pp. 186–99.

Pirenne, M. H., *Optics, Painting and Photography* (Cambridge University Press, 1970).

Porter, Roy, *Mind-forg'd Manacles: a History of Madness in England from the Restoration to the Regency* (London: Athlone, 1987).

Prettejohn, Elizabeth, 'Aesthetic Value and the Professionalization of Victorian Art Criticism 1837–78', *Journal of Victorian Culture* 2 (1997), pp. 71–94.

Reiser, Stanley Joel, *Medicine and the Reign of Technology* (Cambridge University Press, 1978).

Richards, Thomas, *The Commodity Culture of Victorian England. Advertising and Spectacle, 1851–1914* (1990; London and New York: Verso, 1991).

   The Imperial Archive. Knowledge and the Fantasy of Empire (London: Verso, 1993).

Roberts, Helene E., 'Exhibition and Review: The Periodical Press and the Victorian Art Exhibition System', in Joanne Shattock and Michael Wolff, eds., *The Victorian Periodical Press: Samplings and Soundings* (Leicester University Press, 1982), pp. 79–107.

Roly, L. T. C., *The Aeronauts. A History of Ballooning 1783–1903* (Gloucester: Alan Sutton, 1985).

Rose, Jacqueline, *Sexuality in the Field of Vision* (London: Verso, 1989).

Rothfield, Lawrence, *Vital Signs. Medical Realism in Nineteenth-Century Fiction* (Princeton University Press, 1992).

Ryan, James R., *Picturing Empire. Photography and the Visualization of the British Empire* (London: Reaktion Books, 1977).

Sarbin, T. R., and J. B. Juhasz, 'The Historical Background of the Concept of Hallucination', *Journal of the History of the Behavioural Sciences* 5 (1967), pp. 339–58.

Scarry, Elaine, *Resisting Representation* (New York and Oxford: Oxford University Press, 1994).

   'On Vivacity: The Difference between Daydreaming and Imagining-Under-Authorial-Instruction', *Representations* 52 (1995), pp. 1–26.

Schivelbusch, W., *The Railway Journey: the Industrialization of Space and Time* (Leamington Spa: Basil Blackwell, 1986).

   Disenchanted Night. The Industrialisation of Light in the Nineteenth Century (1983; trans. Angela Davies, Oxford, New York, and Hamburg: Berg, 1988).

Scull, Andrew T., *Museums of Madness: The Social Organization of Insanity in Nineteenth-Century England* (London: Allen Lane, 1979).

Sedgwick, Eve Kosofsky, 'The Character in the Veil: Imagery of the Surface in the Gothic Novel', *PMLA* 96 (1981), pp. 255–70.

Seltzer, Mark, *Henry James and the Art of Power* (Ithaca: Cornell University Press, 1984).

   Bodies and Machines (New York and London: Routledge, 1992).

Shaw, W. David, 'The Optical Metaphor: Victorian Poetics and the Theory of Knowledge', *Victorian Studies* 23 (1980), pp. 293–324.

Sherman, Clare Richter, ed., with Adèle M. Holcomb, *Women as Interpreters of the Visual Arts, 1820–1979* (Westport and London: Greenwood Press, 1981).

Shuttleworth, Sally, *Charlotte Brontë and Victorian Psychology* (Cambridge University Press, 1996).

Shuttleworth, Sally, and Jenny Bourne Taylor, eds., *Embodied Selves: An Anthology of Psychological Texts* (Oxford University Press, 1998).

Sitwell, Sacheverell, *Narrative Pictures. A Survey of English Genre and its Painters* (London: B. T. Batsford, 1937).

Skultans, Vieda, *English Madness: Ideas on Insanity, 1590–1890* (London: Routledge and Kegan Paul, 1979).

Slade, Peter D., and Richard P. Bentall, *Sensory Deception. A Scientific Analysis of Hallucination* (London and Sydney: Croom Helm, 1988).

Smith, Alison, *The Victorian Nude. Sexuality, Morality and Art* (Manchester and New York: Manchester University Press, 1996).

Smith, David Woodruff, and Donald McIntyre, *Husserl and Intentionality. A Study of Mind, Meaning, and Language* (Dordrecht, Boston, and London: D. Reidel, 1982).

Smith, Lindsay, *Victorian Photography, Painting and Poetry: the Enigma of Visibility in Ruskin, Morris and the Pre-Raphaelites* (Cambridge University Press, 1995).

   The Politics of Focus: Women, Children and Nineteenth-century Photography (Manchester University Press, 1998).

Spielmann, M. H., *The History of Punch* (London: Cassell and Co., 1895).

Spufford, Francis, *I May be Some Time* (London: Faber and Faber, 1996).

Spurr, David, *The Rhetoric of Empire. Colonial Discourse in Journalism, Travel Writing, and Imperial Administration* (Durham, N.C., and London: Duke University Press, 1993).

Stafford, Barbara Maria, *Body Criticism. Imaging the Unseen in Enlightenment Art and Medicine* (Cambridge, Mass.: MIT Press, 1991).

Staley, Allen, *The Pre-Raphaelite Landscape* (Oxford: Clarendon Press, 1973).

Stallybrass, Peter, and Allon White, *The Politics and Poetics of Transgression* (London: Methuen, 1986).

Stevens, F. L., *Under London. A Chronicle of London's Life-Lines and Relics* (London: J. M. Dent, 1939).

Stevens, Joan, 'Thackeray's *Vanity Fair*', *Review of English Literature* 6 (1965), pp. 19–38.

'Thackeray's Pictorial Capitals', *Costerus: Essays in English and American Language and Literature*, 2 (1974), pp. 113–40.

Sucksmith, Harvey Peter, 'The Dust-heaps in *Our Mutual Friend*', *Essays in Criticism* 23 (1973), pp. 206–12.

Sullivan, Zohreh T., *Narratives of Empire. The Fictions of Rudyard Kipling* (Cambridge University Press, 1993).

Sussman, Herbert L., *Fact into Figure* (Columbus: Ohio State University Press, 1979).

Sweeney, John L., ed., *The Painter's Eye. Notes and Essays on the Pictorial Arts by Henry James* (1956; Madison: University of Wisconsin Press, 1989).

Sweeney, Patricia, 'Thackeray's Best Illustrator', *Costerus: Essays in English and American Language and Literature*, 2 (1974), pp. 83–112.

Tagg, John, *The Burden of Representation: Essays on Photographies and Histories* (London: Macmillan, 1988).

Tambling, Jeremy, '*Middlemarch*, Realism and the Birth of the Clinic', *English Literary History* 57 (1990), pp. 939–60.

Tate Gallery, *The Pre-Raphaelites* (London: The Tate Gallery / Penguin Books, 1984).

Taylor, Charles, *Sources of the Self. The Making of the Modern Identity* (Cambridge, Mass.: Harvard University Press, 1989).

Taylor, Jenny Bourne, *In the Secret Theatre of Home: Wilkie Collins, Sensation Narrative and Nineteenth-Century Psychology* (London: Routledge, 1988).

Thompson, D., 'John Tyndall and the Royal Institution', *Annals of Science* 13 (1957), pp. 9–21.

Thompson, Michael, *Rubbish Theory. The Creation and Destruction of Value* (Oxford University Press, 1979).

Thwaite, Ann, *Emily Tennyson: The Poet's Wife* (London: Faber and Faber, 1996).

Tolles, Winton, *Tom Taylor and the Victorian Drama* (New York: Columbia University Press, 1940).

Trodd, Anthea, *Domestic Crime in the Victorian Novel* (London: Macmillan, 1989).

Turner, Frank M., 'Victorian Scientific Naturalism and Thomas Carlyle', *Victorian Studies* 28 (1975), pp. 325–43.

Turner, Joseph, 'Maxwell and the Method of Physical Analogy', *British Journal for Philosophy of Science* 6 (1955), pp. 226–38.

Tyler, Stephen, 'The Vision Quest in the West, or What the Mind's Eye Sees', *Journal of Anthropological Research* 40 (1984), pp. 23–40.

Tytler, Graeme, *Physiognomy in the European Novel: Faces and Fortunes* (Princeton University Press, 1982).

Uglow, Jennifer, *George Eliot* (London: Virago, 1987).

Urry, John, *The Tourist Gaze. Leisure and Travel in Contemporary Societies* (London: Sage Publications, 1990).

Van Peursen, Cornelius A., 'The Horizon', in Frederick A. Elliston and Peter McCormick, *Husserl. Expositions and Appraisals* (Notre Dame and London: University of Notre Dame Press, 1977), pp. 182–201.

Viera, Carroll, ' "The Lifted Veil" and George Eliot's Early Aesthetic', *Studies in English Literature 1500–1900* 24 (1984), pp. 749–67.

Walkley, Christina, *The Ghost in the Looking Glass: The Victorian Seamstress* (London: P. Owen, 1981).

Warner, Malcolm, 'John Everett Millais's *Autumn Leaves*: "a picture full of beauty and without subject" ', in Leslie Parris, ed., *Pre-Raphaelite Papers* (London: The Tate Gallery / Allen Lane, 1984), pp. 126–42.

Warnke, Michael, *Political Landscape. The Art History of Nature* (1992; trans. David McLintock, London: Reaktion Books, 1994).

Warnock, Mary, *Memory* (London and Boston: Faber and Faber, 1987).

Waterfield, Giles, ed., *Palaces of Art: Art Galleries in Britain, 1790–1990* (London: Dulwich Picture Gallery and the National Gallery of Scotland, 1991).

West, Shearer, 'Tom Taylor, William Powell Frith, and the British School of Art', *Victorian Studies* 33 (1990), pp. 307–26.

Wheeler, Michael, ed., *Ruskin and Environment: The Storm Cloud of the Nineteenth Century* (Manchester University Press, 1995).

White, Allon, *The Uses of Obscurity. The Fiction of Early Modernism* (London, Boston and Henley: Routledge and Kegan Paul, 1981).

Williams, David, *Mr. George Eliot: a Biography of George Henry Lewes* (London: Hodder and Stoughton, 1983).

Williams, Raymond, *The English Novel from Dickens to Lawrence* (London: Chatto and Windus, 1970).

Williams, Rosalind, *Notes on the Underground. An Essay on Technology, Society, and the Imagination* (Cambridge, Mass., and London: MIT Press, 1990).

Williamson, C. N., 'Illustrated Journalism in England: Its Development', *Magazone of Art* 13 (1890), pp. 297–301, 334–40, 391–6.

Wilson, Catherine, 'Visual Surface and Visual Symbol: The

Microscope and the Occult in Early Modern Science', *Journal of the History of Ideas* 49 (1988), pp. 85–108.

Wilt, Judith, *Ghosts of the Gothic. Austen, Eliot and Lawrence* (Princeton University Press, 1980).

Winter, Alison, *Mesmerized. Powers of Mind in Victorian Britain* (Chicago and London: University of Chicago Press, 1998).

Wise, T. J., and J. A. Symington, *The Brontës: Their Lives, Friendships and Correspondence*, 4 vols. (Oxford: Basil Blackwell, 1933).

Wohl, Anthony S., *Endangered Lives. Public Health in Victorian Britain* (London: Methuen, 1983).

Wolfe, Tom, *The Painted Word* (New York: Farrar, Straus, and Giroux, 1975).

Wormald, Mark, 'Microscopy and Semiotic in *Middlemarch*', *Nineteenth-Century Literature* 50 (1996), pp. 501–24.

Yates, Frances, *The Art of Memory* (London: Routledge and Kegan Paul, 1966).

Young, Robert M., *Mind, Brain, and Adaptation in the Nineteenth Century: Cerebral Localization and its Biological Context from Gall to Ferrier* (New York and Oxford: Oxford University Press, 1970; repr. 1990).

Zaniello, Thomas, A., 'The Spectacular English Sunsets of the 1880s', in Paradis and Postlewait, *Victorian Science and Victorian Values*, pp. 247–67.

Periodicals

Academy
Alpine Journal
Art Journal
Artist
Asylum Journal of Mental Science
Athenaeum
Bat
Daily News
Daily Telegraph
Eclectic Review
Globe
Good Words
Graphic
Household Words
Illustrated London News
Journal de la Physiologie de l'homme et des animaux

Lancet
Leisure Hour
Mind
Morning Chronicle
Morning Post
Nation
National Review
Notices of Proceedings of the Royal Institution
Pall Mall Gazette
Philosophical Transactions of the Royal Society
Punch
Saturday Review
Spectator
The Times
World

Unpublished material

Defendant's Brief for *Whistler* v. *Ruskin* 1878, ms. in the Pennell
    Collections, National Library of Congress, Washington.
Flint, Kate, 'The English Critical Reaction to Contemporary Paint-
    ing 1878–1910', D.Phil. Oxford University, 1985 (Bodleian
    Ms.D.Phil.c.5579).
MacColl, Norman, to F. G. Stephens, 10 May 1871 (Bod. ms. don.d.116
    f. 42–3).

Index